Auguste Gratry

Guide to the Knowledge of God

A study of the chief theodicies

Auguste Gratry

Guide to the Knowledge of God
A study of the chief theodicies

ISBN/EAN: 9783337219239

Printed in Europe, USA, Canada, Australia, Japan

Cover: Foto ©Lupo / pixelio.de

More available books at **www.hansebooks.com**

GUIDE

TO

THE KNOWLEDGE OF GOD

A

Study of the Chief Theodicies

By A. GRATRY

PROFESSOR OF MORAL THEOLOGY AT THE SORBONNE

TRANSLATED BY

ABBY LANGDON ALGER

WITH AN INTRODUCTION BY

WILLIAM ROUNSEVILLE ALGER

(*This Work was Crowned by the French Academy*)

BOSTON
ROBERTS BROTHERS
1892

TABLE OF CONTENTS.

Part First.

CHAPTER I.

EXPLANATORY.

CHAPTER II.

PLATO'S THEODICY.

CHAPTER III.

ARISTOTLE'S THEODICY.

CHAPTER IV.

SAINT AUGUSTINE'S THEODICY.

CHAPTER V.

SAINT ANSELM'S THEODICY.

CHAPTER VI.

SAINT THOMAS AQUINAS' THEODICY.

CHAPTER VII.

THEODICY OF THE SEVENTEENTH CENTURY.

Philosophic character of the seventeenth century: unity of mind of its great men; unity of process.

DESCARTES.

BOSSUET.

LEIBNITZ.

CHAPTER VIII.

ON THE ATTRIBUTES OF GOD.

CHAPTER IX.

INFINITESIMAL PROCESS.

Part Second.

CHAPTER I.

THE TWO DEGREES OF THE DIVINE INTELLIGIBLE.

CHAPTER II.

RELATIONS BETWEEN REASON AND FAITH.

CHAPTER III.

RELATIONS BETWEEN REASON AND FAITH (*Continued*).

CHAPTER IV.

CHAPTER V.

CHAPTER VI.

SUMMARY AND CONCLUSION.

INTRODUCTION TO THE TRANSLATION.

By William Rounseville Alger.

IN its original language the work here translated has passed through many editions, and has attained the rank of an authoritative classic. It is characterized by such comprehensiveness of scope, such force and beauty of style, such amplitude of learning, such ripeness and precision of thought, such depth of experience, and such catholicity of spirit that no one can fitly read it without being instructed, stimulated, and edified. The author sweeps with the ease of a consummate mastery through the wisdom of twenty-five centuries, gathers up the chief treasures deposited there by the kings of insight, and presents them constructed into one harmonious whole. The question with which he grapples as strenuously as any one ever has done, is whether the human mind is able to attain to a real knowledge of God. To the examination of this sublime theme he brings both an intense earnestness and an unfailing sobriety; while adding to these high qualities all that historic erudition and training can yield from without, or personal acumen and consecration furnish from within. The result, as embodied in the present volume, is one with which, in point of attractiveness and solid value, no work on the same subject within the entire compass of English literature can for a moment stand a comparison.

Gratry answers the question, Can man know God? in the most effective way possible, by setting forth, in systematic outline and with appropriate detail, the experimental and critical conclusions at which a large number of the most illustrious thinkers of our race, from Plato and Aristotle to Fénelon and Leibnitz, have actually arrived on that subject. He lays bare the methods they employed, the difficulties they encountered, the arguments they constructed, the aids they received, the results they conquered, and their fundamental agreement through all. He does this with an incisiveness of thought, a summarizing skill, a patience, an impartiality, and a lucidity most admirable and most delightful. It is true that as we pass on from name to name there seems to be a good deal of repetition. But there is ever a variety in the sameness, a progressive growth in the exposition, a cumulative gain through the repeatals, which fully reward the reader. As he goes over, in theodicy after theodicy, what appear to be quite identical statements, he will more and more find doubts dissolved, objections answered, obscurities illuminated, peace bestowed, assurance and satisfaction breaking in. There are very few, even among professional students of philosophy, who will not find themselves abundantly repaid for a patient perusal of all the repetitions in these freighted pages, — so momentous are the themes treated, and so masterly is the treatment.

One of the central traits of this work is the appeal the author makes for the action of human nature in its integrity as regulated by the sovereign unity of the rational principle. He protests against the division of the soul into a collection of abstracting faculties which operate separately and breed all sorts of error, fiction, and confusion. He quotes approvingly the bold remark of Fénelon, "Reason is even more wanting on earth than religion." Having also cited the great saying of Saint Thomas, "In the moral order, crimes against nature are worse than sacrilege," he adds, "So in the intellectual order that crime against nature which attacks reason is worse than the sacrilege which attacks faith; for to ruin reason is to prostrate the religious edifice by undermining the ground."

The vindication of the powers and rights of reason, so nobly illustrated in the whole body of the work, has been formally stated by Gratry in the following eloquent passage, which is no less timely than it is just and weighty:

"What is the common and natural state of the reason among men? We see it all about us. God is still unknown to the majority of men, and almost all are profoundly ignorant of their destiny, their nature, and their duty. The majority still reject the unmistakable light thrown upon human questions by universal reason, aided by God, and they are unable to pass this first and natural initiatory step, and far from attaining to the higher initiation which God has prepared for all. Very few men even succeed in gaining complete mastery of their body; nearly all live a fortuitous and turbulent life, conducive to premature old age and untimely death.

"How few reasonable beings there are who cultivate in themselves the sacred gift of reason! The greater number cultivate the earth; others cultivate nothing. Throughout humanity, with but rare exceptions, reason, that sacred talent intrusted by God to every man on his entrance into this world, remains sterile or buried.

"Bossuet, speaking of reason hidden in the flesh, says: 'What efforts must we not make to distinguish our soul from our body! How many of us there are who never attain to the knowledge or slightest perception of this distinction!' 'How many are there who rise somewhat above this mass of flesh, and clear their soul from it?'

"Yes, there are but very few men in whom reason is distinct from the mass of instincts, sensations, and wants, constituting a free force and an independent power. With almost all it is a sorely oppressed force, a power subordinated, not only to the imagination, the senses, interests, and desires, but also to the current of the blood and the disposition, the influence of the matter which feeds our body, and the forces of physical nature. Reason, the logical varnish of a purely animal life, the blind and trivial bond of our passions, desires, humors, and sensations,—reason, blended with the whole, and carried away by the general movement, obeys slavishly, instead of ruling.

"There are, among God's creatures, animals belonging to the lower grades of life. Their body is but a uniform mass, without distinct organs. Each point represents as well as any other the essential centres of life, and exercises all its functions vapidly and indifferently. There is no distinct heart or brain; all is confounded in the sum total of the mass. Well, just such is the intellectual organization of the multitude at the present day. Reason is in the germ, but not developed; it is spread throughout the mass, but is destitute of distinct central organ. It does not form, let me repeat, a free force and an independent power. The minds of such men may be compared to those inferior organizations in the animal scale which have no distinct brain.

"And with those who have developed the germ of reason to some slight degree, how is the development accomplished? 'We seldom encounter anywhere other than warped intellects,' said Arnaud in the seventeenth century. What would he say now?

"What is a warped intellect? Bacon defines it very happily: 'It is a mirror without symmetry, irregular, in the beams of the sun.' Joubert uses the same figure in regard to one of our more excessive thinkers: 'Thomas has a concave head; it exaggerates and enlarges everything which it reflects.' Now, just as crooked mirrors deform every image, so a warped intellect distorts the data which might raise it to the heights of truth. This one-sided intelligence falsifies the truth which strikes it; it is addressed in words of truth, it hears falsehood; beauty and sublimity are held up before it, it sees only deformity. This may be accounted for. Just as unsymmetrical surfaces are fantastic and distorted mirrors which falsify by their unevenly developed dimensions, so a warped intellect is a disproportionately developed intellect. For is not our weak understanding usually employed in the exclusive direction of one ruling passion, one fixed idea or supreme prejudice? Who is there whose intellectual mirror is a regular surface in every direction, spherical as the vault of heaven, or smooth as the mirror of the waters?

"Certainly the majority of minds are strange and distorted reflectors.

"Being thus formed, they can derive only error from the spectacle of visible things and of the inner actions of the soul, and from that of human events. They gaze, and fancy that they see everything; they do see everything but the sum total and the proportions. It is thus that we observe the world, that we write history, and that we describe mankind. It is thus that, day by day, we retrace present facts visible to every eye; and the tale is false. We do not deliberately lie, but we give everything factitious dimensions, conformed to the desired effect. We enlarge what pleases us, and render imperceptible whatever offends. We are false, and we see things as we ourselves are.

"There is another natural infirmity of the reason, which is very apparent at the present time. Even those who think somewhat correctly, think but little and almost fruitlessly, because they are isolated, because each mind sees by itself alone; union and association of intellectual forces are yet to come. The confusion of tongues, the antagonism of sects, the subdivision of intellectual persons, and above all, the secret question at the bottom of every heart, 'God or no god,' the question which divides mankind into two camps, — is anything more than this needed to keep apart those who think? The sphere of the intellectual world is still inhabited on the exterior, not at the centre, where all rays meet, but only on the surface, where all are divided: so that there are, in the world of science and of thought, regions divided by space, subject to different heavens, speaking different languages, and much more foreign to one another than the various races of the earth. Each science is surrounded by a high wall, and so is every intellect. The unity of the human mind is less attained than that of the globe.

"If we would save religion, society, and civilization, the first work to undertake is the restoration of public reason. We must re-establish in the minds of men a knowledge of and respect for reason and its laws, and the practice of these laws, logic. It must be known, for it has been forgotten, that there are both error and truth in the world, and that the one may be distinguished from the other; that there is a true method of human thinking, — that is to say, there are fixed principles and legitimate processes; that these principles and processes have been practised in all ages instinctively by many persons, and might have been so in a certain sense by all; that they were practised with some conscientiousness and with admirable results by philosophical minds in every century; but that they were ignored and violated by the blind criticism and lawless practice of sophists in all ages; that the true philosophical method, without being yet very completely defined, has nevertheless, in the course of ages, been determined and developed by the success of its applications and the even clearer sense of those great intellects who made use of it; but that there exists a false method and a sophistical process, which has never ceased to impede the advance of philosophy by its perturbing action, and that this power of contradiction, ever increasing, seems to borrow strength from the very progress of truth.

"This being thoroughly perceived, we must proceed to separate these shadows and this light; that is, we must at last learn to make a scientific distinction between sophistry and philosophy. We must give their true names, in history, to philosophers and sophists. Moving in a direction contrary to contemporary eclecticism, philosophy must at last proceed to the necessary excommunication of its domestic foes, instead of greeting and embracing them. The erroneous method, and that which leads to truth, must be exactly defined; we must recognize, what is manifest enough, that the sophistical process is nothing but the philosophical method *inverted*.

"The division once accomplished, and the sophists set apart, we must restore the legitimate rule of reason and philosophy among us by the study of genuine philosophers, by the practice and knowledge of their method, as well as by a study of the sophists, considered as a counter proof and demonstration through the absurd.

"Philosophy, a universal science, must come forth from its isolation and look face to face at the special branches of science which regard philosophy with contempt. Philosophy, as a wise writer expresses it, must cross the boundary-line, enter the domain of science, and take possession of it. It is right that all these branches of science which philosophy created should be subject to it ; or rather, it is right that the human mind should cease to be divided into regions unknown each to the other, and that the various sciences should resume their natural relations in the unity of philosophy.

"Still more must be done, if we are to re-establish the serious education of reason among us.

"It is not enough that science should exist, — it must become a part of human intelligence; and reason must be actually developed in every man, or at least in the majority of those who desire to think, and believe that they do so.

"Now, so long as we blindly refuse to recognize that the solid and healthy growth of thought proceeds from the growth of the entire soul and will, there can be no mental change. There can be no advance of reason without a corresponding advance in moral strength and freedom. Intellect and will, reason and freedom, are the two wings of the soul, upon which it rises to its only object, which is goodness, and at the same time truth.

"Farther yet, — and this is the supreme question in the life of the human mind and its history, a vital question for the human intellect, — is our reason conjoined to that of God, or is it wholly separate? Is reason destined to become holy, or to sink into degradation? At which extreme is it to stop? For it will not remain at this sterile and changeable intermediate, which is the end of nothing; it must either fall or rise.

"Reason is a force that seeks for its beginning and end. Now, the truth is, that the beginning and the end of reason is God. The human heart seeks God no more unceasingly than reason does. Only in this pursuit the mind, as well as the heart, is subject to change. When the human heart changes, we have moral perversion. When the human mind changes, we have intellectual perversion, — the vice of sophists. 'Truth,' says Saint Augustine, 'lies in placing in God these three things, — the cause of the world, the supreme good, the fulcrum of reason.' Nothing more profound could be said. Very certainly the whole history of philosophy and sophistry is contained in that sentence. Only Saint Augustine makes no mention here of the final abyss into which the sophist plunges when, setting God apart from reason, he undermines the latter to discover its origin.

"But what happens when, far from dividing it from God, we conjoin the two, and reason follows its research to the end? 'Reason,' says Saint Augustine, — 'reason, attaining its end, becomes virtue.' But what virtue? Let us see.

"There is a height, according to Saint Augustine, where reason stops. This is its end. This is plain to every true philosopher. 'The science of the human mind,' said Royer-Collard, 'will have been carried to the highest degree of perfection which it can attain when it can derive ignorance from its primary source.'

"There is, therefore, let us say with Saint Augustine, a height where reason stops : this is its end. But there it goes on in something which is not itself; as one river flows into another, or is borne to the ocean. This is the point where the mind of man is continued in the mind of God himself, and is subject to it. This subjection, or rather this high degree of elevation of the human reason, subject to the mind of God, is faith. Faith, — that is the virtue to which reason soars when it attains its end. 'Faith is indeed,' says Pascal, 'the last step of reason.' Only we must of course agree as to this capital truth whose admission or rejection decides the destinies of the world and the human mind.

"We affirm that this subjection of the human mind to the Spirit of God is not the destruction of reason, but its final perfection. Reason, said Saint Thomas Aquinas, the most exact of philosophers as well as the greatest of theologians, — reason is capable of a two-fold perfection ; namely, its proper and natural perfection, resulting from its own principles and its own powers, and the perfection which it borrows from its union and subjection to the Spirit of God himself, — a principle higher and greater than it. This is its final and supernatural perfection ; it is the human mind engrafted upon the Divine mind, if we may so express it. Reason then bears fruits which it could not bear ; and as the poet says, repeating the words of Nature herself, —

"'Admires those fruits which are not hers.'

"These fruits are those of the Spirit of God become the directly fertilizing principle of human reason, which none the less retains its individual principles.

"Far from diminishing reason, the introduction of the higher principle lifts it to incomparable greatness, vivifies its powers, and increases the fruitfulness of its natural principle.

"This alliance, in one sense, may be compared to the divine alliance, to which Saint Thomas Aquinas alludes when he says, 'Divine knowledge in the soul of Christ did not kill human knowledge, but made it more luminous.'

"It is of this alliance that a holily far-sighted spirit said, early in the seventeenth century: 'There are three kinds of knowledge, — purely divine knowledge, the purely human knowledge, and *knowledge at once human and divine, which is indeed the true knowledge of Christians.*'

" It was this alliance which the genius of the seventeenth century, the parent of knowledge, actually sought. Instituted by those great men who were all at once theologians, philosophers, and scientists, from Kepler down to Leibnitz, — passing by Pascal, Descartes, Malebranche, Bossuet, and Fénelon, — this sacred alliance of all departments of intellect one with the other, and of the human mind with the divine mind, was the cause of the greatness and creative fertility of that period, the most luminous in history. But since this tie was severed, we have only dimmed that matchless light, and most of us can no longer even see it.

" So that when human reason is conjoined to God through faith, — history shows it, — besides the new and sublime data which result, its natural powers are increased, its individual principles bear their rarest natural fruits, mingled with divine fruits. When, on the contrary, reason breaks the alliance always offered to every mind, in every age, this refusal, this reversion to its unaided self, this isolation and sacrilegious negation, weaken its natural powers, and lead it, from negation to negation, to deny itself, — an intellectual suicide whose name is sophistry.

" Consider the great and wonderful symbolism, too little understood and too little heeded, which the eighteenth century affords us in that final scene when man strove to reject God and to worship himself and his own reason only !

" What did man do when he attempted to place human reason on the altar, to adore that alone ?

" Let history speak. He placed a naked prostitute upon the altar. That is, he put upon the altar reason smeared with mud, reason smothered in flesh and blood.

" And what was cast down from that altar to make way for this infamous goddess ? Heed the answer well ! Human reason was cast down, but human reason allied with God.

" Men did not know, they do not yet know, that human reason can find place upon a Catholic altar.

" What is there, then, on the Catholic altar if it be not Jesus Christ ? And what is Jesus Christ, if he be not God allied to man ? ' The Divine Word,' says our dogma, ' took on, in its incarnation, a human soul, *a human soul gifted with reason.*'

" I give the exact statement, in the language of the Church : ' Verbum divinum animam humanam, *eamque rationis participem,* assumpsit.'

"Thus, according to our dogma, human reason, in actual presence, was upon the Catholic altar; it was there conjoined with God. It was driven thence, to be replaced by human reason degraded and dragged through the mud. The holy altar was stripped of the supreme reason, the reason of Jesus, the reason of the Man-God, and replaced by the feeble reason of a lewd crew. Men were given their choice of alliance, — reason allied to filth, or reason conjoined to God. They made their choice.

"We will not rest satisfied with this choice. We will reject what we took, and take back what we rejected. Soon, I hope, the majority of us will understand what was so happily and finely expressed in a now famous address : 'The great question, the supreme question, which now absorbs all minds, is the question put by those who recognize and those who do not recognize a *supernatural, sure, and supreme order of things.* . . . For our present and future safety alike, faith in the supernatural order, submission to the natural order, must re-enter the world, and the human soul must be born again in great minds as well as in simple ones, in the highest as well as in the humblest regions.'

"Yes, our present and future safety demand faith in the supernatural order.

"At this price reason may resume its sway over us; the mind may be lifted up and rescued. At this price we may yet see something of Leibnitz's great prediction accomplished : 'Let us hope that a time may come when men will devote themselves to reason more than they have hitherto done.' Upheld by God, and living by faith, far more men will succeed in some degree in freeing their soul and reason from this weight of flesh, and in living, throughout an entire lifetime, by the love of justice and truth alone ; more men will take up, conscientiously and vigorously, literature, science, and philosophy, as sacred instruments to be used for the good of humanity, for the increase of light, wisdom, and dignity among men, for the progress of the world towards God."

Few works can compare with this one by Professor Gratry as an exhibition of the compass of human reason and of what Saint Thomas Aquinas calls "the much-misappreciated power of reasoning." He clearly shows the truth of the assertion

of Descartes and Leibnitz, repeated by Cardinal Gerdil, that
the existence of God and his infinite perfections may be as
rigorously proved as the solution of any mathematical problem. He shows this with the most brilliant originality, by
proving that *the demonstration of the existence of God is the
supreme achievement of a general process of the reason, of
which the infinitesimal methods of geometry are but a special
application.* The attention of the reader is particularly in-
vited to the exposition of this assertion where it occurs in
the following pages. It is no less fruitful and illuminating
in its consequences than it is startlingly original in itself.

The character and life of the illustrious author of this
work were in full keeping with his attainments and fame.
He was not merely a scholar and a philosopher, but likewise
a philanthropist and a saint, who thoroughly lived the doctrine he taught. In his spiritual will were found, after his
death, these touching words : " I leave to every human being
whom I have ever greeted or blessed, or to whom I have
ever spoken any word of esteem or affection, the assurance
that I love and bless him twice and thrice as much as I said.
I entreat all such to pray for me, that I may attain to the
kingdom of love, whither I will draw him too through the
infinite goodness of our Father."

In order to bring the two volumes of the original within
the compass of a single larger volume in the translation, the
superfluous appendices and some of the foot-notes containing the texts rendered by the author in the body of his work,
have been omitted. The prefaces to the first three editions,
abounding with personal and local references, as well as a
long and polemical Introduction, have likewise been left out.

The editor of this translation deems it his duty, in bringing the work before the public in its English dress, to add a
word of protest against the view which Gratry gives of the
German school of philosophy as presented in the culminating

exposition of Hegel. Ecclesiastical prejudice, national bias, differences in points of view and in nomenclature, have prevented many Catholic thinkers of the highest ability, including even Rosmini, from seeing the real depth and the solid result of the speculative movement begun by Kant, advanced by Fichte, and carried through by Hegel. Because the dialectic of the transcendental school is that of a negative unity, its foes charge it with being exclusively negative, and ending in nihilism. But Aristotle says, in the first chapter of the last book of his Metaphysics, "All contraries inseparably belong to a subject." Hegel was the first thinker systematically to develop this statement through all its implications. He showed, as Fichte had partly done before, that every lower set of contraries is reconciled in a higher category, whose unity contains and mediates them, the highest category being *free self-consciousness.* The negative dialectic presupposes the affirmative, as the affirmative dialectic presupposes the negative; because both presuppose the absolute dialectic, without which neither of these could be. Thus the negative phase of the dialectic, when completed, is found to carry also the opposite phase, and to coincide with the whole sphere of a self-determining unity. Hegelianism ends neither with atheism nor pantheism nor nihilism, but with a solidly grounded vision of God, freedom, and immortality.

This does not affect the value of the present work in its positive exposition, which unveils a mine of matchless wealth, hidden, for the most part, from the Protestant world by ignorance and prejudice. The central part of the divine wisdom of the Catholic Church, the speculative insight cumulatively developed in a broadening and brightening river of tradition by its peerless thinkers and saints through so many centuries, is here freely offered to all who are able to understand it and willing to receive it.

GUIDE TO THE KNOWLEDGE OF GOD.

Part First.

CHAPTER I.

EXPLANATORY.

"WISDOM," says Bossuet, "consists in knowing God and knowing one's self." These words are, in brief, a true definition of philosophy.

They mean, at the outset, that philosophy is the search for wisdom; that is, the search, both theoretical and practical, for goodness and truth. They declare that philosophy is not that abstract and purely speculative knowledge of which Bossuet also says elsewhere, "Woe to that barren knowledge which never turns to love, and is false to itself!"

These words, moreover, limit the object of philosophy. That object is God and man; it is man seeking through the intellect and the will to find goodness and truth, which are God.

On the other hand, this definition does not divide those things which are incapable of division, and does not exclude from philosophy a knowledge of bodies and of the visible world. "For," says Bossuet, "to know man, we must know that he is made up of two parts, which are the body and the soul." Hence we see that philosophy also treats of visible and material nature, especially in its relation to the soul and to God.

So that the various divisions of philosophy are —

I. THE KNOWLEDGE OF GOD (Theodicy).

II. THE KNOWLEDGE OF THE SOUL, considered in its relations to God and the body (Psychology).

III. LOGIC, which is a further development of psychology, and which studies the soul through its *intelligence,* and the laws of that intelligence.

IV. MORALS, which is another outgrowth of psychology, and which studies the soul through its *will,* and the laws of that will.

We shall explain these different divisions of philosophy, each in turn, beginning with the theodicy.

This order is that of Descartes, Fénelon, Malebranche, and Saint Thomas Aquinas. Bossuet followed the inverse order. But we prefer to begin with the theodicy, because in our view it implies the whole of philosophy. It shows it to us as a unity, a totality; it contains all its roots. Everything proceeds from it; it is therefore the starting-point.

Moreover, the theodicy, which is the loftiest, most profound department of philosophy, is also the simplest. Ideas of infinity and perfection, as Descartes, Bossuet, and the majority of philosophers remark, are the first which awakening reason reveals to us, — which proves that reason first impels us towards God. It is the cause of nature, at the same time that it is the absolute order of truths taken in themselves.

But by theodicy must not be understood only the knowledge of God; it also means most particularly the knowledge of the human mind aspiring towards God.

The theodicy is the knowledge of that wonderful process of the reason which soars towards God and aspires to know and prove his existence, nature, and attributes.

From this point of view we shall realize later how the theodicy sums up all philosophy in a single question,

namely, the proof of the existence of 'God and his attributes, — a question which the readers of this book will, I
hope, find neither barren nor commonplace, and upon which
we must at once enter.

I.

Is it possible to prove the existence of God? Is it essential? Is not the truth of the existence of God self-evident
and indemonstrable as an axiom? Can there be atheists?

It seems at first that this proposition, *God is*, is identical
with the similar proposition, *Being is*. And so it really is
to all who know the meaning of the word God, since that
word means "Him who is." This statement, therefore, is
one of those which are evident as soon as their terms are
known. Its terms imply its truth, for the subject and attribute are identical; and it bears its certainty on its face, as
does this, — The whole is greater than a part.

But all men do not know the meaning of the word God,
all not understanding that God is none other than He who
is. The truth of God's existence is not clear to all, and it
requires to be proved from a basis of universal ideas. The
proposition which asserts it is identical, but its identity is
not apparent to all eyes.

And in fact there are atheists. Atheism, both theoretical
and practical, is a profound vice, — or rather, the radical vice
of the heart and human mind. No age has been free from
it. Our own is more fully infected by it than we think.
Practical atheism is visible to every eye, and philosophical
atheism is revealed under the form of pantheism. More yet,
express, exact, avowed, and declared atheism has a school of
its own; and this school of new atheism, more scientific
than the old atheism, is built upon a foundation which it
calls *Modern Science*.

It is not difficult, in truth, to do justice to this would-be modern science. We shall prove, in the proper place, that it is nothing else than the radical vice of the human heart and mind disguised as doctrine, and that its scientific semblance comes from the fact that it applies, though in inverse order, the true method and fundamental process of reason.

But first let us assert that the existence of God can be strictly proved, and that no geometrical theorem is more certain. This is, moreover, the opinion of Descartes, as well as of Leibnitz; the learned Cardinal Gerdil said the same.

We shall treat this point, which implies all metaphysics, all morals, all logic, and all the theory of the method, with the fulness which is deserved by this prime question of philosophy, whose basis and summary it is.

II.

In the first place, if there are true proofs of the existence of God, these proofs must be within the reach of all men; for the light of God shines, and should shine, upon every man in this world.

Therefore, to find useful proofs of the existence of God, we should seek his origin and reality in some ordinary and daily act of the human mind; and this sublime and simple act being found, it will suffice to describe it, and translate it into philosophical language. We shall then prove its scientific value.

Now, this ordinary daily act of the human soul, mind, and heart, intellect and will, is no other than the universal fact of *prayer;* and I mean, philosophically speaking, by prayer what Descartes defines when he says, "I feel that I am a finite being, unceasingly striving for and aspiring to something better and greater than I am." Prayer is the movement of the soul from the finite towards the infinite.

Scorn of present reality, so natural to man ; expectation of an ideal future, so habitual to the soul ; instinctive sense of the marvellous, and presentiment of infinity, — are the source of this sublime and simple act, which proves God.

Who does not know it? The soul of man, especially when it is pure and lofty, in its vigor and youth, conceives and desires without bounds all the beauties and virtues of which it sees any trace. All boundaries, all limits, all imperfections, are destroyed. Being is conceived in all its plenitude ; the mind conceives of eternal love, happiness without change, truth without shadow, a will stronger than any obstacle, strength and energy that play with time and space, and of wonders, sudden creations realized by a word, a gesture, or a wish. All these premonitions of the heart of man, all these golden dreams of childhood, all these intoxications of ideal nectar, imply a true and strictly scientific method. Analyzed by reason, this poetry, this faith, contain the strict proof of the existence of God and his attributes.

In fact, this is the poetic and ordinary process which, with the help of education and tradition, lifts the majority of men to the knowledge of God. The spectacle of the world, the sense of life, the sight of finished beings and created beauties, when the heart and imagination grasp them to enlarge and urge them to infinity, by effacing evil, bounds, and limits, that impulse of the soul towards infinity from the finite, — this it is that gives men an idea of God, a natural knowledge and love of him.

And this intellectual and moral impulse, of which every human soul is capable, is the act and the fundamental process of the life of reason and the moral life. We say that the act and fundamental process of a life of reason and a moral life consist, as Bossuet expresses it, in passing without any circuit of reasoning, although by a very justifiable impulse

2

of the reason, from the finite to the infinite, — from the genuine finite being which we are, which we see, which we can actually touch, to the infinite Being, really and actually existing, which the existence of the finite implies and supposes.

And while the simple, the ignorant, the humble, and the young, by a wholly instinctive and poetic method, perform this chief and necessary act of reason, this natural act of the soul is the foundation of the most scientific of methods, and all the demonstrations of the existence of God, given us by true philosophers of all times, summed up and exactly defined by the seventeenth century, are but the philosophical translation of the ordinary process which all men employ.

This we shall show by enumerating and analyzing these various demonstrations, the entire substance of which we will afterwards sum up, and will prove their unerring exactness.

III.

But before entering into details and studying these proofs one by one, referring each to its author, we will set forth, without going into particulars, the nature and conditions of the complete essential proof, to which all others lead back more or less directly, according as they are more or less explicit, solid, and luminous. What we now simply state will be developed and demonstrated later on.

We must know that there are two processes of reasoning, the one as exact as the other, — *syllogism* and *induction*. Syllogism is tolerably familiar. But induction is not the vague process which it is supposed to be, — it is a precise process; it is the chief process of reasoning, and has been practised in all ages by all great minds as well as by the humblest, but it has never yet been sufficiently analyzed by any one. We will attempt this analysis by means of logic.

These two processes may also be called the *syllogistic* process and the *dialectic* process. They correspond to what Leibnitz called the *logic of deduction* and the *logic of invention*, or the *analytical part* and the *inventive part* of logic. They correspond to the two kinds of minds which we find among men, and which we may represent by Aristotle and Plato. Aristotle called them *syllogism* and *induction ;* Plato calls them *syllogism* and *dialectic.* The seventeenth century deserves the credit for establishing the truly mathematical precision of the second process, by *bringing it into practical use,* as Leibnitz says ; which was done by the works of Descartes, Malebranche, and Fénelon, and by the great discovery of Leibnitz, the invention of the infinitesimal calculus, — a wonderful invention, which consists of actually introducing into mathematics this chief process of reasoning.

This process, which in geometry is carried to mathematical infinity, is also carried, in metaphysics, to the infinite Being, which is God. Exact as geometry, it is also much the simpler and quicker of the two processes of reasoning. Its very simplicity and rapidity have hitherto prevented any complete analysis of it.

It consists, any degree of entity, beauty, or perfection being given, — which we always have so soon as we are, see, or think, — it consists, we say, in instantly destroying in thought the limits of the finite being and the imperfect qualities which we possess, or which we see, in order that we may affirm without other intermediary the infinite existence of the one Being and his perfections, corresponding to those we see.

Assuredly the process is a simple one ; any one may use it, and the smallest minds, on certain points, employ it as quickly as others : but it is precise. This is now proved by the works of the seventeenth century, analyzed and compared.

This process is not only applicable to the proof of the

existence of God, but it leads up in everything to principles and ideas; and as several philosophers, who will be quoted in due time, declare, it is a universal process of invention.

Absolutely distinct from syllogism, it is quite as exact; it alone gives the majors used by syllogism.

This process, like syllogism, may rest either upon an abstraction or a fact, an idea or a reality, upon a conception which is *a priori* true or false, or upon an experience.

If the syllogism depend upon a simple possibility, which does not exist, upon a chimera, or even on a contradiction, which cannot be true, its deductions will be of the nature of the primary cause: a series of non-existent possibilities, or even a series of chimeras or a series of contradictions is deduced, sooner or later ending in downright absurdity, — that is to say, in a conspicuous contradiction. But if it rest upon a real postulate, derived from the nature of things, — as, for instance, Newton's law, — all the deductions drawn from it will be true, genuine, and existent in the nature of things.

Now, it is precisely the same with the other process. Whether we take for our starting-point a pure possibility which does not exist, or a contradictory statement, or even, as Descartes says, a *conception proceeding from nothing*, which does not and cannot exist, the assertion obtained by the dialectic process will be a simple possibility, a chimera, or a contradiction. But if it be based upon an experimental postulate, a reality, or some actual and positive quality existing in things, then its results will be as real as the point of departure, — as real as those of the syllogism. If, for instance, it depended, as in certain German theories, upon the *idea of non-being*, it would affirm, as the Germans do, an *absolute non-being*, and all the resultant absurdities; it would thus plainly obtain only a chimera and a monster. But if it rest upon some conception of being, — a conception which is clearly possible, — it asserts the possibility of an infinite Being; if, moreover, it add to this the experience of any real being whatsoever, actually existing, it concludes in the infinite Being, no longer as merely possible, but as really and actually existing.

And these assertions, which proceed from finite reality to infinite reality, are always true; since in metaphysics, as in geometry, every positive finite has its corresponding infinite. We can always go on asserting to infinity the existence of any real and positive quality, finite though it be, which we see. The assertion is always true, in God. This is because in metaphysics, as in geometry, as Leibnitz observes, "Finite laws always hold good of infinity, and *vice versa.*"

But if the process *de facto* be true, *de facto* again, all do not always carry it out. Just as every mind does not always infer the consequences of principles with which it is familiar, so, too, every mind does not always move from every finite to the corresponding infinite, or from every phenomenon to ideas, or from every creature to God. Just as there are minds without any *syllogistic* impulse, so too there are minds destitute of *dialectic* force. There are intellects which possess neither the one nor the other, — neither deduction nor invention. All are necessarily deductive when they are driven to it. There is a logical constraint which can force any man to see a consequence in a principle; but all, as a matter of course, are not necessarily inventive; all do not possess the dialectic impulse, — there is no intellectual constraint possible upon this point. The intellect may lose or recover its strength of impulse towards the infinite. That depends upon the energy, the elasticity, of the soul and moral freedom, this impulse being alike and indissolubly intellectual and moral; and it cannot be other than a movement of the human soul as a unity. The intellectual movement towards infinity is always true, always possible, since

man is endowed with reason; but as a fact, it cannot take
place in the soul without the corresponding moral movement. This is why diseased souls can never perform it,
even when the words of others assert it and execute it in
their presence. A deduction presented from without is not
always understood by a mind but slightly developed; but a
moment more, a moment of careful attention, will make it
clear. The dialectic passage from the finite to the infinite
is still oftener overlooked by weak or diseased minds; a
moment of more active attention is not enough, — a cure
and moral change are requisite.

This fact, but too little noted, is most important. It touches
on the bond and relation between logic and morals, intellect
and will, reason and liberty. There is a bond between reason and liberty, — this is unquestionable; there are opinions
which are entirely free. Some schools of philosophy admit
that all opinions are free and unbiassed: this is evidently a
mistake; for how can deduction be free? A syllogistic conclusion is inevitable when the primary causes are given.
But still it is false to say that every true opinion is inevitable. Dialectic advance from the finite to the infinite, and
the opinion which results, is both true and free, yet although
always true, is never obtained save under conditions which
depend upon freedom. The first moral condition of the existence of these dialectic decisions which proceed from every
finite to the infinite, is what may be called the *sense of infinity*, — that divine sense which is always given, which is
the omnipresent charm of the Sovereign Good for every soul.
Then, according to the free reciprocal adaptation of each
soul to this attraction of infinity, it pronounces, or does
not pronounce, the true opinion which leads from every
finite to infinity. It may even — as the whole history of
philosophy, especially modern German philosophy, proves
— pronounce that false opinion which leads from every
finite, in an opposite direction from infinity, to nothing.

The proof of the existence of God therefore results from one of the two processes essential to reason, but, as a fact, is worked out freely, morally as well as rationally.

This, I admit, is quite contrary to our wretched logical habits, which presuppose an absolute separation of logic and morals. But this gratuitous supposition might even be called strange, since it admits that intellect and will, two faculties of a single soul, have no common root where they touch; this supposition, I say, is as false as it is strange. It has been, it still is, one of the stumbling-blocks of philosophy. It is unquestionable that, as a certain intellectual condition, and not only a condition but an act, a voluntary act, attention, is requisite to execute one of the movements of reason, to form or to comprehend a syllogism; so too we also require a certain moral state, — which we may call *a right sense,* — and a voluntary and moral act, to understand and execute the other movement of reason. A *right sense* — which is moreover the same thing as the *divine sense* — is that hidden reason to which Pascal refers when he says, "The heart has its reasons which the reason does not know." It is this hidden reason which the fool lacks when he says in his heart, "There is no God."

Such, then, is the nature, such are the conditions, of the true proof of the existence of God.

In brief, the true proof of the existence of God is nothing else but the use of one of the two processes of reasoning, — the chief one, that which gives the majors, and which constitutes *the logic of invention.*

Every application of this process involves the proof of the existence of God.

Let us repeat: this process consists, starting from every finite being and every finite quality, in affirming, by the suppression of finite limits, the infinite Being, or the infinite perfections corresponding to the finite that we see.

And this assertion is always true, according to the principle laid down by Leibnitz, that *finite laws hold good of infinity, and vice versa;* in other words, that the finite is an image of the infinite, — which results, as Leibnitz also remarks, from the fact that everything is governed by God, who governs all in conformity to himself.

This process is as sure as geometry, to which, moreover, it is applied. This application is known as the infinitesimal calculus.

On the other hand, this process is never *de facto* literally carried out, and only reaches God by a simultaneous act of intellect and will, reason and liberty. Its power in the mind is the *divine sense*, the sense of infinity, or, if you will, the inevitable attraction of the Sovereign Good for every soul. But this power, given to all, acts or ceases to act, or even changes its course, according to the moral state of the soul.

We believe that we have proved all this in the totality of the present work in such a manner that it will henceforth be regarded as among the truths acquired by philosophy.

We may be opposed at first; but as all opposition will be vain, we hope our adversaries will soon have recourse to declaring that these things have been known in every age, particularly in the seventeenth century, and that there is nothing new in what we say. We shall hasten to agree to this, merely reserving to ourselves the honor of having thrown more vivid light upon this central point of philosophy, where all rays meet.

This settled, let us turn to details, and proceed to the historic study of the proofs of the existence of God.

We shall enter most minutely into this question, studying in turn the theodicy of Plato, Aristotle, Saint Augustine, Saint Anselm, and Saint Thomas Aquinas; then take up the theodicy of the seventeenth century, treating of Descartes,

Pascal, Malebranche, Fénelon, Bossuet, Leibnitz, and the authors of two Latin Theodicies, unknown even to the trained public, which are the two finest and most complete ever written in any age.

We shall linger the more willingly upon this point, because it will at the same time afford us a study of the history of philosophy.

The history of the above-named philosophers is very nearly the whole history of philosophy. Now, we know a philosopher by his theodicy. The theodicy of a writer contains his method, implies his logic and his ethics, is his system of metaphysics and his theory of ideas also, therefore his psychology. In this sense all philosophy may be found in the theodicy.

In treating, therefore, of the theodicy of all the great minds, each in its turn, we give at the same time a summary, and a brief history, of philosophy.

CHAPTER II.

PLATO comes first in chronological order; this is fortunate. Of all men who discussed the subject of God previous to the Christian era, he is the greatest. He has been called the divine; Bossuet so styles him, and this is his distinguishing name among philosophers. Moreover, Plato is the especial representative of one of the two processes of human reason, — the chief one, that which leads up to God.[1] If Aristotle was the immortal and perfect lawgiver for the other process, Plato, without actually establishing the laws of that which forms his glory, — laws which could not be defined exactly until the seventeenth century, — Plato at least indicated them, and gave us, besides, the finest example of their use which human reason in the antique world produced.

The glory reverted to the school of Socrates. And why? Because the impulse of reason towards genuine infinity — an impulse which constitutes that chief process to which we refer, and which gives us the proof of the existence of God — can only be carried out *de facto*, in consequence of a moral state, under the impelling force of that "*power*," as Bossuet says, which is the "*divine sense;*" or, if you prefer, the "*attraction of the desirable and intelligible*," as Aristotle expresses it.

Now, the Socratic and Platonic school is of all ancient schools the most moral, and the one which best knew, under-

---

[1] Janet's admirable thesis on the "Dialectic of Plato" should be read on this subject. This brilliant work, but too little known, should be one of the first things read by all who desire to study Plato.

stood, and described the real attraction of Supreme Goodness for the soul of man.

Socrates is, in fact, as modern sophists very aptly complain, the founder of moral philosophy. His doctrine, as has been well said, is little more than a theory of virtue; "and its only aim, according to the best judges," says Thomassin, "is to purify our affections by means of morality."[1] Plato therefore claimed — and this was the root of his system — to rely wholly upon that love of goodness and that moral state without which reason does not apply the dialectic process leading up to God. To him, the beginning of all things was Goodness; he knew that Goodness is the father of light, that the action of the mind which rises to God depends upon the forces of love, that this process, which he so happily calls the "*movement of the soul's wings*," implies a moral state, an outburst of love towards God, and that the soul can only put out wings by dint of virtue.

This is why Plato knew and practised more than any other man in antiquity the chief process of reasoning. This is why he knew and proved the existence of the true God.

Plato knew that there are two processes of reasoning, and not merely one. He knew that the most potent of these two processes, quite as exact as the other, is the scientific truth of which poetry is merely the image. For this very reason he was a poet in thought as well as by nature, like all philosophers who have made especial use of the chief process of reason. He understood that very beautiful metaphors are true, because they imply the truth of the dialectic method, and that this chief form of philosophical thought is, in its spirit, like poetry itself, simple, easy, and popular. Plato knew above all — he repeats it incessantly — that sensuality and passion are the obstacle to light in the soul,

[1] Thomassin, Dogm. Theol., vol. ii. chap. x. p. 11.

and that this obstacle must be overcome before we can rise
to truth through reason.   He knew that there are two
courses open to the soul and its love, one of which leads the
mind to illusion and error, the other to truth ; that philosophy is indivisibly a work of reason and freedom, of intellect
and will, — far more, a work of sacrifice and virtue.   It · is
for this reason that he so constantly expounds the wonderful
Socratic saying : " To philosophize is to learn how to die."

And lastly, Plato knew that there are three soul-spheres,
three lives, in man ; and he states this as clearly as Pascal.
He describes the highest of the three as the contact of God
with the roots of the soul ; and this *divinity* [1] in the soul,
when the obstacle of vice is removed, is the power that lifts
the reason to eternal truths.   We must acknowlege that true
philosophy is not, in Plato, unmixed with error, — that is
only given to Christians ; but he possessed all philosophy,
all its essential features, all its fundamental elements.

Plato has all the characteristics of true philosophic genius ; he is the most brilliant instance in antiquity of
those perfect minds which, as has been well said, use alike
their reason and their heart, their learning and their poetry,
their feet and their wings, to attain to truth.   It therefore
belonged to him to give in the ancient world the great proof
of the existence of God.   Let us see if he succeeded.

II.

Let us first recall the nature of the process that gives the
true proof of the existence of God and his attributes.

Those visible things being given which beget one another,
which are born and die, which change and which pass away,
which might not exist, which are limited and imperfect, —
the mind should exceed these finite and visible beings, and

-----
[1] Τὸ θεῖον.

rise through their images to the eternal, invisible, immutable ideas which correspond to the images. We should rise
from every finite object to the corresponding infinite. We
shall see later, through the aid of geometry itself, that this
is no vague mental action, but an exact process. This
process destroys in thought the limits of finite being, and
the imperfections of the qualities revealed to it by things,
and asserts that the idea formed in our mind by this suppression of limits and defects, this idea of infinite being and
infinite perfection, corresponds to a reality truer, more actual, than the very object which we touch, and whence
dialectic reasoning starts. It asserts that all these supreme
realities are in God, and are God. Such is, at least, the duty
of the mind in the light of reason ; and, in fact, the mind
fulfils this duty whenever the moral obstacle that impedes
its progress is removed.

Did Plato fully understand this process ? Did he state literally, did he know that the sum total of immutable, eternal,
infinite ideas is in God,—is the Word of God, which is God ?
Some deny this; we believe that we should affirm it, with
Saint Augustine, Bossuet, Leibnitz, and Fénelon.

In any case, whether Plato himself knew or did not know
it,—and I believe that he knew it,—his dialectic process
actually ends in God, in the infinite. This is the nature and
the law of the process. Plato really made that supreme use
of reason which consists in passing by a simple impulse,
which is at the same time scholarly and systematic, from
everything to God ; from the finite, the variable, and the
uncertain to the infinite, immutable, and inevitable.

My readers may judge of this by the brief statement
which follows, and which will be verified later by quotations
from the text.

There is first in the soul a gift of God, which results from
contact with God, and which is that voice, that inner tute-

lary spirit given by God to every soul. This divine element, this sense of immortality and divinity, is the prime and essential element, the principle and very root of the soul, in its triple life. This is the power which proceeds from God and leads us up to God. Now, man does not rise to God by the mind alone, by the reason taken in that abstract sense in which sophists understand it; man rises to the knowledge of God only *through his whole soul;* first by his will, by doing good, which directs the eye where it should look, then purifies it, makes it capable' of seeing. Knowledge of God implies a free moral element. The part of the will consists in conquering those moral obstacles which prevent us from developing the divine sense within us, or which destroy it. This divine sense is the condition, founded on experience, of a knowledge of God. Such is the moral part of the process that leads us up to God.

The intellectual and logical part is properly the *dialectic.* Dialectic is the process which advances, starting from this visible world, to the idea of Being itself, Goodness itself, — absolute Being and Goodness. Thus dialectic, whose motive-power, principle, and force lie in the divine sense set free and made active by virtue, also relies in its action upon the data of the visible world, which *stimulate* the mind, both by likeness and contrast, to *recall* the supreme object, wholly different from these as it is, of which they are but the images. Dialectic progress consists in never pausing until Being itself, the Supreme Good which is, is attained. Reason starts from sensible things, as a conditional and essential point of departure; but it goes beyond and aside from these sensible postulates, which stimulate it to recall intelligible things, seeing their unlikeness to the intelligible. From these postulates it passes to the essential ideas which our reason implies, such as geometric truths, which are, as Plato frequently repeats with a depth of meaning which is but too seldom understood, shadows of the light of God. From these shadows it learns to infer the existence of the sun.

Let us show all this by quotations.

III.

In the first place, the most important of philosophical facts — that central spring of the moral and rational life which we call *the divine sense*, and which is the real source of the proof of God's existence — was so familiar to Socrates and Plato, and was taught by them with such full conviction, in so concrete a form, that it was this very thing which produced the misunderstanding relative to the *dœmon* of Socrates. Plato explains the meaning of this word in the most philosophic manner when he shows that this *dœmon* was only the voice of conscience, the innate love of God.

In the Apology, Plato puts these words into the mouth of Socrates: "The cause of all is merely what you have often heard me say, 'There is a divine will which speaks to me' ... (θεῖόν τι καὶ δαιμόνιον). 'I have heard this voice from my youth up. ...'" This voice is that "of God, which orders me to live by seeking wisdom and a knowledge of myself. ... I ought then rather to obey God than you, O Athenians!" It is clear that by *dœmon* (δαιμόνιον) Socrates here understands the voice of God.

Cicero understands it in the same way when he asserts that "Socrates' dœmon is that *something divine* which checked him, and which he always obeyed."

The dying Socrates said: "Let us go whither God leads;" and he obeyed that divine voice even in death. Which suggests to a learned author the following thoughts: "That God was the voice which rang in his innermost soul, that light which illumined his intellect and declared to him what he was to do. It is what is commonly known as Socrates' dæmon. . . . Socrates frequently refers to it as to a sort of spiritual director, sometimes calling it dæmon, and sometimes God. He always seems to take it seriously, especially here, where he relies upon it both for life and death. According to some, Socrates understood by this the true God. Others are of a different opinion." Saint Justin has no doubt about it; Saint Augustine hesitates.

Plato, moreover, in his Timæus, explains it in a way which, as it seems to us, leaves no room for contradiction. We will go into the details of this explanation, because it leads us away from the incidental question of Socrates' dæmon, and shows us what may be called the heart of dialectic, the centre of Plato's philosophy, theology, and morals, the true power upon which Platonism depends to prove the existence of God, that motive power which we have called the *divine sense.*

In his fine close to Timæus, Plato expresses himself as follows: —

"We have already said that the soul possesses a triple life, each part of which has its place and its distinct action. . . . Now, you must know touching the chief of these three lives, that it is the *dæmon* which God has given to every man. That part of the soul is that which occupies, as they say, the highest realm within us, and which, through its celestial parentage, lifts us from the earth and makes her the fruit of heaven rather than of earth,— which is profoundly true ; for at that point which is the *very origin of our soul,* there the *divine* holds linked to it our *root,* our life principle, and uplifts the whole man." [1]

Nothing can be plainer; the word *dæmon* (δαίμων) means precisely the divine sense in the soul, that point at which God touches us, the point which is our root, our origin, our source (πρώτη φύσις, ῥίζα); that point, as Plato admirably expresses it, whereby God holds us linked to him (τὸ θεῖον τὴν κεφαλὴν καὶ ῥίζαν ἡμῶν ἀνακρεμαννύν).

[1] Timæus, 89, 90.

It clearly results from these quotations that, according to Plato, there are in man not three souls, as he is sometimes made to say, but there are in the soul three regions, three parts, three lives, — what matters the word, — the highest of which is at the very root of the soul; that contact with God which links us to him and lifts us to heaven, and that it is the same thing which Socrates called his divine voice and his dæmon.[1]

This triple life pointed out by Plato in the soul, corresponds to the three worlds mentioned by Pascal, — the material world, the spiritual world, and the divine world, which is God; a triple life, which brings us into relation with nature through sensation, with the soul through the inner sense, with God through the divine sense; the triple life known and described by Christian mystics when they say, "Let us turn from the outward inward, and from the inward let us

---

[1] The misunderstanding in regard to the three souls must be made clear by these quotations. We read in the passage quoted from Timæus, τρία ψυχῆς εἴδη, and not τρία ψυχῶν εἴδη. Further on we read τοὺς τρεῖς τόπους τῆς ψυχῆς, *the three regions of the soul.* Elsewhere Plato speaks of the parts of the soul, two of which, particularly, are distinct, the one rational, λογιστικὸν νοῦς, which he also calls elsewhere, ἀρχὴν ψυχῆς ἀθάνατον (Timæus); the other the irrational, or fleshly, ἀλογιστικὸν, or ἐπιθυμητικόν, which are united by the θυμός or θυμοειδές (De Rep. IV.). This distinction doubtless refers to that one of the three faculties, *knowledge, will,* and *feeling,* which he establishes in the same book of the Republic. Plato had no more faith in three souls than Saint Thomas, who nevertheless makes a distinction between the rational soul, the sensitive soul, and the vegetative soul.

Moreover, in Plato, εἶδος is often used as a synonym for μέρος; we often find εἶδος καὶ μέρος — εἴδη καὶ μέρη.

Cicero did not believe that Plato spoke of several souls, but of several spheres of the soul: *Partes animi, secundum Platonem.*

As for Aristotle, in his "Book of the Virtues and Vices," in the beginning, he says (Bekker's edition, page 1249): Τριμεροῦς δὲ τῆς ψυχῆς λαμβανομένης κατὰ Πλάτωνα, τοῦ μὲν λογιστικοῦ ἀρετή ἐστιν ἡ φρόνησις, τοῦ δὲ θυμοειδοῦς ἥ τε πρᾳότης καὶ ἡ ἀνδρεία, τοῦ δὲ ἐπιθυμητικοῦ ἥ τε σωφροσύνη καὶ ἡ ἐγκράτεια, ὅλης δὲ τῆς ψυχῆς ἥ τε δικαιοσύνη. Aristotle therefore admits here, with Plato, that there are these three parts of the soul, and names them as he does, and in his book on the Soul he none the less maintains the unity of the soul (p. 411).

mount to higher things;" the triple life which one of the
deepest thinkers of this century, Maine de Biran, rediscovered
in the soul by his persistent analysis, in spite of the prejudi-
ces of his starting-point, which admitted of but one.

And when Plato speaks of the highest of the three (κυριώ-
τατον ψυχῆς εἶδος), that which he calls *divine* (τὸ θεῖον), and
elsewhere the *immortal principle of the soul* (ἀρχὴν ψυχῆς
ἀθάνατον), when he assigns it an especial place and habita-
tion, at the very root (ῥίζα) where God holds us linked to
himself (τὸ θεῖον ἀνακρεμαννύν), whence the first genesis of
the soul proceeds (ἐκεῖθεν ὅθεν ἡ πρώτη τῆς ψυχῆς γένεσις
ἔφυ), Plato then speaks like Bossuet, who, pointing out
this particular region of the soul, this inner sanctuary, exclaims, "Hearken in thy innermost soul; hearken *in that
place where the truth makes itself heard,* where pure and
simple ideas are found." And elsewhere, after saying, "The
soul therefore is made for God, *it is to him that it should
ever be conjoined and as it were linked,* through its knowledge and affection," Bossuet speaks of "a spot in the soul so
deep and so retired that the senses do not suspect its existence, it is so remote from their domain!"

Light is also thrown upon all this in the first Alcibiades,
when he is advised by the philosopher, if he would know his
soul, to look into that *place in the soul* where especially
resides the virtue of the soul, wisdom, that is to say, the
divine element of the soul; then to consider the object itself,
of which this part of the soul is the image, in God.[1] For we
can never know ourselves if we look into that part of the
soul which is all shadow, and where God is not[2] (εἰς τὸ ἄθεον
καὶ σκοτεινόν). We must look into the divine part; and
that part of the soul is to the soul what the pupil is to the
eye, — the very centre, the primary sense, the channel itself
of vision.[3] And it is by looking into this place in the soul,

---

[1] Alcibiades, I. 133 C.   [2] Ibid., 134 E.   [3] Ibid., 133 B, 134 D.

where light and divinity dwell (εἰς τὸ θεῖον καὶ λαμ-
πρὸν); that the soul unfolds *winged love* within itself (ἔρωτα
ὑπόπτερον).[1]

Thus, finally, it is clear that, according to Plato, there is a
region in the soul, a central point of the soul, which he calls
its root, its primary cause, its origin, and that this point is
divine; that is to say, it contains a gift which God has bestowed on every man, by touching him at that point, and
linking him to himself.

Whether we call this divine attribute *divine spirit*, or
divine sense, or the *voice of conscience*, or the *attraction of
supreme goodness, attraction of the desirable and intelligible,
innate love of beatitude, innate idea of justice and injustice,
natural law written on the heart*, whatever name we give to
this first, chief fact of all philosophy, which results from the
fact that the soul only is and exists because God is and touches
it, — it will always be true that this divine attribute, peculiar
to all men, is the principle and power which give its impulse to the mind as well as to the whole soul, in all its
aspirations towards God.

This Plato establishes in every possible way.

Let us now proceed to state the use which should be, in
his opinion, made of this attribute.

IV.

This divine attribute is the first cause of every movement
of the mind towards God. The secondary cause is man's
attempt to purify his soul, and thus remove the obstacle
which interferes with the action of that force which God
has given us.

"Knowledge," says Plato, "is not what some imagine when
they declare that they will give it to a mind which has it not,

[1] Alcibiades, I. 135 E.

which would be like giving sight to a blind man. This is a great mistake. There is within us a force, there is in every mind an organ, by means of which every man may acquire knowledge. We must treat this organ as we should the eye, were it impossible to turn it away from darkness to the light, save by employing our whole body, — *we must turn away our reason with our whole soul;* we must *turn it away* from the things which pass, to the One Being, and lift our spiritual vision to that radiant centre of Being which we call Goodness.[1] Instruction can only teach us how to direct the mind, and to turn its attention easily and effectually towards the light; education does not give us sight, it merely strives to direct in the right way the sight which already exists, but which is turned in the wrong direction, and does not look where it should look.

"There are, in the soul, qualities which may be acquired by exercise and habit, as the body acquires certain powers and certain habits. But reason shows its divine origin, and proves that it comes from something higher than ourselves, in that it never loses its power, but becomes useful or injurious, *according to the way in which we use it.*[2] Have you never noticed how quickly and clearly the small soul of the wicked grasps the things upon which it is bent, and what power it acquires in so doing? It sees very plainly, only it chooses to direct its vision to evil things. But take those same souls in infancy, *cut away* and *prune* all the growth of passions akin to the flesh; set them free from those heavy clods which cling to the pleasures of the table and similar delights; take away that weight which drags the mental vision down to everything which is low. Instantly, in that same soul, the eye, set free, turns towards realities, and sees them as clearly as it now sees those things which absorb it."[3]

We must therefore purify the whole soul, if we wish our life and its attention to be turned and lifted towards its highest region, where the divine sense dwells. Those who do not purify themselves, remain in the lowest of the three regions of the soul, rise from there towards the middle realm, again sink back into the lowest, and thus spend their lives in this

1 De Rep., 518 C.   2 Ibid., 518 E.   3 Ibid., 519 B.

oscillation between the carnal and the passional, without ever rising to that portion of the soul which God inhabits.

"The man without wisdom and without virtue,[1] constantly a prey to and identified with all his fleshly appetites, necessarily falls into the lower region, rises from that to the middle portion, to wander thus his whole life long between the two; but to pass through both these realms, to rise, indeed, whether by the eye alone or by his life, towards that which is truly high, is a thing which he cannot do."

To attain, therefore, by the eye or by the life to that part of the soul where the divine sense dwells, the source of our knowledge of God, when we carry it out in our life and pierce it with our eye, we must first overcome the moral obstacle.

"He who surrenders himself to the double slavery of the world and the flesh (ἐπιθυμίας ἤ φιλονεικίας, the carnal and the passional), can never have other than mortal thoughts (δόγματα θνήτα)."[2]

We must therefore overcome the moral obstacle by dint of virtue, and yield to the action of the divine power which directs our thoughts towards immortality and divinity.

Let us quote the whole of that magnificent passage in which Plato teaches man how to cultivate in himself the divine sense, that he may rise to immortality and God, alike in thought and in life, — things which Socrates and Plato do not separate: —

"He who, for love of the truth, strives to develop within him a sense of the immortal and divine (γεγυμνασμένῳ φρονεῖν μὲν ἀθάνατα καὶ θεῖα), that man must needs attain immortality, in so far as human nature is capable thereof; and since he has cultivated naught save the divine (τὸ θεῖον) within him, and has fed the Divine Spirit in his soul (δαίμονα), which dwells there, he must reach supreme felicity.

---

[1] De Rep., 586.   [2] Timæus, 90.

"Now, every life is nourished by its own proper food, and by the movement which is adapted to it. But universal thoughts and movements are the natural movements of the divine within us. They are the thoughts and actions to which every man should conform; all should labor to correct, by contemplation of the harmony and the actions of the whole, those particular and irregular acts which the flesh inspires in the centre of our soul, to the end that the beholder, becoming like the object beheld, resumes his original nature, becomes fit to possess at last the perfect life which God offers to man both now and forever."[1]

Thus Plato asserts that there is in every man's soul a divine contact at that point where our soul is linked to God. This point is the root, the primary cause, the origin of our soul. Of the three lives which exist in our soul, that which God himself maintains in this part of the soul is plainly the chief, and should direct and lift the entire man towards divinity, towards immortality, towards God, in both life and thought.

But, moreover, Plato here establishes the fact, which, apparent though it be, psychology, with us, so often refuses to note, the fact of the native lawlessness to which we are born. That is to say, that there is really an obstacle to the action of that divine power which labors to lift us to God.

This obstacle is the double vice, which Plato calls *the lust of the flesh* and *anger*, which is to say, *pride* and *sensuality*, — a double form of selfishness.

The condition upon which we may rise to God, in life or in thought, is that we conquer this obstacle.

The obstacle conquered, it at once follows that man develops within him the sense of immortality and divinity, and attains to truth.

Truth leads him to immortality and happiness.

We reach this end by struggling against the innate lawlessness of our own thoughts and actions, by allying ourselves

[1] Timæus, 90.

to universal thought and action, by contemplating that universal which is God, by becoming like unto God, who gives
us immortality.

Thus, so far we clearly perceive the Platonic procedure;
we have, first, a divine attribute within us, the primary cause
and motive spring of every impulse towards God. We have,
next, on the part of man, moral strength, which breaks, by
dint of virtue and sacrifice, the shackles that hinder that
impulse. This is the moral side of the dialectic process.
Let us now turn to its logical side.

V.

The mind has a starting-point for every inquiry. This
starting-point is not always a principle of deduction, far
from it.· Where is the human mind first placed? Consequently, whence does it ordinarily start? The spectacle of
nature. It sees changes, birth and death. Assuredly it is
not from this starting-point, taken as a principle of deduction, that it will derive by syllogism the knowledge of God.
But by reason of these things it will think of God; it emerges,
on the contrary, from these things to find God.[1] It certainly
starts from the spectacle of visible things. " It is with the
senses, not elsewhere, that we begin; it is with sight, touch,
or some other sense; it cannot be otherwise."[2] But how can
all these transitory things lift us to God? Certainly not by
their identity with God. Is it by their likeness to God? Yes,
but it is quite as much by their difference and their contrast
with his eternal nature. " We see all these things striving to
resemble him, yet remaining ever remote from him."[3] And
these likenesses and contrasts alike remind us of him. You
behold one thing, *and in it you comprehend another*. Whether
this be due to likeness or to contrast, it is the object seen

---

[1] Rep., vii. 525. [2] Phædo, 75. [3] Ibid., 75.

that calls up the memory.[1]   If we see, if we hear, if we perceive any object through any sense, and if, at the same time,
besides seeing that object, we conceive another, the idea of
which is not the same, but wholly different, should we not
say that the second object, to the idea of which we have attained, is a memory suggested by the first?[2]   A man and a
lyre are not the same thing.   And yet those who love, recall
the loved object if they see the lyre which he has touched.
Such is reminiscence.[3]

"There is an element in sense, impressions of which in no way
stimulate the intellect, because it stops at the senses which are
capable of judging it; and there is another element which does,
on the contrary, stimulate the intellect, the senses being unable
to deal with it."[4]

· "The sensations which stimulate the intellect are those which
imply both likeness and contrast;[5] as, for instance, when the
sight of a certain number of objects awakens in us the idea of
unity and that of infinite quantity."[6]

"It is upon these attributes — those which stimulate the intel-
lect — that the process rests ($\mu\acute{a}\theta\eta\mu a$) which lifts us to the one
Being, and *which almost no one uses properly.*"[7]

VI.

Plato gives a full account of this process in the closing
pages of the sixth book of the Republic, which, I think, has
never been fully understood.

In this statement of logic as he understands it, Plato
defines exactly the two processes of reasoning, one of which
takes its starting-point ($\acute{v}\pi\acute{o}\theta\epsilon\sigma\iota\varsigma$)[8] as its primary source
($\acute{a}\rho\chi\acute{\eta}$), and deduces consequences from it; the other ad-
vances from its point of departure to a universal principle

---

[1] Phædo, 74.   [4] De Rep., 523 B.   [7] Ibid., 522, 523.
[2] Ibid., 73 C.   [5] Ibid., 523.   [8] Ibid., 510 *et seq.*
[3] Ibid., 73 D.   [6] Ibid., 525.

which is not contained in it (ἐπ' ἀρχὴν ἀνυπόθετον ἐξ ὑποθέσεως ἰοῦσα). One is clearly the law of syllogism ; he
calls the other the *dialectic process* (πορεία διαλεκτική).
The first process, he says, is that of geometry ; the second is
that of true philosophy.[1]

Geometricians take their definitions as their starting-point
(ποιησάμενοι ὑποθεσεῖς αὐτά). These points of departure
they take as principles, — principles of deduction from which
they derive all the rest by means of inference and manifest
identity (ἐκ τούτων δ' ἀρχόμενοι τὰ λοιπὰ ἤδη διεξίοντες
τελευτῶσιν ὁμολογούμενος).

Yet again, this process, syllogistic deduction, does not go
back to the origin of things (οὐκ ἐπ' ἀρχὴν ἰοῦσαν) ; evidently it can never rise above its starting-point, since it
deduces by means of identity (ὡς οὐ δυναμένην τῶν ὑπο-
θέσεων ἀνωτέρω ἐκβαίνειν).

The other, on the contrary, rises above its starting-point
(ἐπ' ἀρχὴν ἀνυπόθετον ἐξ ὑποθέσεως ἰοῦσα). It does not
take its starting-point as its primary source (τὰς ὑποθέσεις
ποιούμενος οὐκ ἀρχάς) ; it only takes it as a fulcrum and
to stimulate its flight (οἷον ἐπιβάσεις τε καὶ ὁρμάς). It
speeds from this to the universal principle absolutely outside and above the point of departure (μέχρι τοῦ ἀνυπο-
θέτου ἐπὶ τὴν τοῦ παντὸς ἀρχὴν ἰών).

Afterwards only, it descends through inference to all
which that principle touches and includes, once it possesses
it (ἀψάμενος αὐτῆς, πάλιν αὖ ἐχόμενος τῶν ἐκείνης ἐχομένων,
οὕτως ἐπὶ τελευτὴν καταβαίνῃ).

Such are actually the two eternal processes of reasoning,
the two divisions of logic, one of which may be called the
logic of *deduction,* the other the logic of *invention ;* or
again, the one *immanent* logic, and the other *transcendent*
logic.

---

[1] Geometry had not then been developed through the infinitesimal process.

But to what do these two processes lead, according to Plato? What are their different results?

Those who use the dialectic attain to some perception of being and of the intelligible (ὑπὸ τῆς τοῦ διαλέγεσθαι ἐπιστήμης τοῦ ὄντος τε καὶ νοητοῦ θεωρούμενον).

Those who move by induction from their starting-point (αἷς αἱ ὑποθέσεις ἀρχαί), and do not go back to the primary cause (διὰ τὸ μὴ ἐπ᾽ ἀρχὴν ἀνελθόντας), never really attain to an intelligence of their object, which is, however, intelligible if they know how to refer it to its primary cause (νοῦν οὐκ ἴσχειν περὶ αὐτά, καίτοι νοητῶν ὄντων μετὰ ἀρχῆς).

VII.

"But," says Plato, "here we have a far more difficult point. . . . I will deal with it to the best of my ability: God alone knows if it be so."

This point, in our opinion, affords Plato opportunity to settle, in an admirable manner, perhaps the most important of all philosophical questions.

The point is to distinguish the *degrees* of knowledge, and particularly of the knowledge of God.

Plato first distinguishes clearly two degrees of knowledge in general, — knowledge of *sensible* things (ὁρατόν), and knowledge of *intelligible* things (νοητόν).[1]

We shall speak of the intelligible only.

Within this degree Plato notes two others, — one of which corresponds to discursive thought (διάνοια), the other to true intellect (νόησις).

The inferior degree, that of discursive thought, corresponds to the syllogistic process which, by means of identity, catches glimpses of essential and immutable truths, but without understanding their relation to the *principle of their unity in God.*

[1] De Rep., 509.

The superior degree, that of intellect, corresponds to the dialectic process which rises to the principle of all truths.

In the superior degree, which is that of true *science* (ἐπι-στήμη),[1] superior to discursive notions (διάνοια), *the mind contemplates that which Being and truth illuminate.*[2]

But is this superior degree itself, such as it has been described, the final possibility of intellectual vision? Or at least, has it not its degrees? Is there nothing beyond the *science* that contemplates *that which Being and truth illumi-nate?* "We have," says Plato, "beyond science, Being itself and truth itself (αὐτὸ τὸ ἀληθές), which give to things truth (ἀλήθεια), and, to the mind, strength to know; and there must be, beyond science, the very remote (τελευταία), very faint vision (μόγις ὁρᾶσθαι)[3] of that selfsame Being which is supreme Goodness. For if science and truth are so fair, their source is fairer yet." "We should be mistaken," he says, "much mistaken, if we supposed that light and sight are the sun; they are images or reflections of the sun (ἡλιο-ειδῆ). So, too, we should mistake if we supposed science and truth (ἀλήθεια) to be supreme Goodness itself; they are the images or reflections of supreme Goodness (ἀγαθοειδῆ)."

So that science (ἐπιστήμη), even that acquired through the dialectic, is, according to Plato, the vision of an image (ἀγαθοειδῆ). But then can we never succeed in seeing, not merely the image (εἰκόνα), but the truth itself (αὐτὸ τὸ ἀληθές)?[4] Can we not, when we have acquired through dialectic a perception OF DIVINE PHANTOMS AND SHADOWS OF THAT WHICH IS (φαντάσματα θεῖα καὶ σκιὰς τῶν ὄντων), judge that these shadows and these images are produced by a sun which corresponds to them (σκιὰς δι' ἑτέρου τοιούτου φωτός, ὡς πρὸς ἥλιον, κρίνειν ἀποσκιαζομένας)?[5]

Yes, we can; we may attain to a vision even of the

---

[1] De Rep., 533.
[2] Ibid., 508 D.
[3] Ibid., 517.
[4] Ibid., 532.
[5] Ibid., 532.

essence of things (ἐπ' αὐτὸ ὅ ἐστιν ἕκαστον ὁρμᾶν).[1] We
may succeed in seeing the supreme Being of beings (πρὸς
τὴν τοῦ ἀρίστου ἐν τοῖς οὖσι θέαν); we may reach that highest intellectual summit (ἐπ' αὐτῷ τῷ τοῦ νοητοῦ τέλει); we
may grasp the supreme essential Being himself, through the
mind itself (αὐτὸ ὅ ἐστιν Ἀγαθὸν αὐτῇ νοήσει λάβῃ); we
may gain sight of supreme Goodness (τὴν τοῦ Ἀγαθοῦ ἰδέαν).
We see it dimly (μόγις ὁρᾶσθαι); but we may, we should,
see it.

We may do all this, says Plato, and we should do it. We
should persistently pursue this inquiry, and never pause
until we succeed in grasping, through the mind itself, the
supreme Goodness itself (καὶ μὴ ἀποστῇ πρὶν ἂν αὐτὸ ὅ
ἐστιν Ἀγαθὸν αὐτῇ νοήσει λάβῃ);[2] this is the final end of
the impulse of the mind, the term of the dialectic (τέλος
τῆς πορείας).

Thus, according to Plato, beyond even that grand knowledge
which the dialectic gives us, which is the vision of things illumined by the light of supreme Goodness, by the light of Being
and of truth itself, beyond this knowledge and this truth reflected in things, if we may so express it, we have Truth itself, Being itself; we have the idea and the sight of supreme
Goodness; we have the principle of all things; we have the
most perfect of beings and the height of the intelligible; we
have the final end and aim of the process, which is the at-
tainment of supreme Goodness itself through the mind itself,
directly and immediately. But this end, he says elsewhere,
is not attained until after death.

Plato makes these degrees of knowledge and the course
of the process clear to us, by his famous description of the
cavern, and the story of the deliverance of the captives.

First we have captivity in the cave, and then liberty
in the sunshine: which corresponds to the vision of

[1] De Rep., 532.   [2] Ibid., 532.

the two worlds, — the world of sense, and the world of intellect.

In the cave there are shadows (σκιάς) and echoes. At first they can only see by reflected rays, whether of light or of voice. Then there comes a change. They turn away from the shadows to objects and to the light (μεταστροφὴ ἀπὸ τῶν σκιῶν ἐπὶ τὰ εἴδολα καὶ τὸ φῶς).[1]

Outside the cave, in the real world, there are, Plato always affirms, many degrees of vision. At first, the captives see shadows (σκιάς); then (μετὰ τοῦτο) we have another degree, — they see the images of objects in the water (ἐν τοῖς ὕδασιν εἴδωλα); then the objects themselves, men, and animals. Then they gaze up at the sky, at first by night, to see the reflected light of the moon. "At last, after all this, they look upón the sun, — not indirectly now, apart from itself, in its image reflected in the waters, but the sun itself, by itself, in its proper place."[2]

This admirable distinction between seeing shadows, reflections, phantoms, images, and the direct sight of light in its course, — this distinction, the vast results of which we shall see later on, was afterwards even more fully established by Saint Augustine when he speaks of reason attaining to its final end (*ratio perveniens ad finem suum*); and by Saint Thomas Aquinas, when he describes the two degrees of the divine intelligible (*duplici igitur veritate divinorum intelligibilium existente*). We beg the reader to keep this point well fixed in his memory. He will understand the bearing of it later. It is the most important point in all philosophy.

For the rest, Plato seems to us to havo seen, or rather expressed, this fundamental distinction in a slightly confused way. This has given rise to discussions of his Theory of Ideas, and of the question whether to him the Word is God

---

[1] De Rep., 532.   [2] Ibid., 516 B.

or is not God. But is it surprising that a truth which escaped Malebranche, — this is the omission in his system, — and over which Bossuet hesitates, should be expressed by Plato with some ambiguity ? Moreover, to all who can see clearly the great intellectual fact in dispute, it is evident that Plato saw the truth, although he may waver in his description.

What Plato saw is, that truth as man possesses it, or finds it naturally, is only an image of God, but not the direct sight of God. Pascal says, "The truth — taken in this sense — is not God, but it is his image, and an idol which we should not adore." The essential, eternal, immutable truths of which reason gives us the certainty and the clear sight are, as Plato expresses it, but *divine phantoms* or *shadows of what is,* — a magnificent expression, of the most fruitful depth, which we cannot sufficiently admire. Even geometry, according to Plato, sees only shadows, *the dream of Being, not waking vision of Being,*[1] — another statement of deep meaning. But what man desires, and should desire, according to Plato, is to pass from shadows, reflections, echoes, and images. He desires to hurry on ; and he should do so, never pausing until he has grasped very Being, supreme Goodness itself, through his intelligence itself, — that is to say, until he has acquired direct and immediate sight of God.

Plato, therefore, sees here what Saint Augustine expresses so perfectly when he says, " God is intelligible ; these spectacles of scientific truths are so likewise. But what a difference ! [2] The earth is visible, the light of the sun is visible ; but the earth is visible only by the light of the sun. There is all the difference of earth and sky between these phantoms of assured truths and the intelligible majesty of God."[3]

---

[1] De Rep., 533 C.

[2] Soliloq., lib. i. p. 608, § 14 (vii.).

[3] Ibid., p. 686, § 11 (v.).

VIII.

Thus, we see, Plato through his dialectic was able to rise to the true God, — *to very Being, to the most perfect of beings, to the beginnings of all things, to truth itself, to supreme Goodness which is.* But did he ever really attain to the knowledge of the true God, to the genuine idea of God and his attributes? We unhesitatingly answer, Yes.

This is the opinion of Saint Augustine, Saint Thomas Aquinas, Bossuet, and also of Fénelon and Thomassin. We shall quote these decisive authorities later. Let us first show the fact.

In the tenth book of his Laws, Plato, striving to establish that there is a Providence, rises through his dialectic to the idea of God, as follows: "There are in us certain virtues: therefore God possesses fully all virtue.[1] We can do some things: God can at least do all that we can do.[2] In us there may be both good and evil: in God, not."[3]

Thus the resemblance and contrast between ourselves and God lift Plato, according to his theory, to the reminiscence of God.

These assertions, we see, are nothing but that common and natural dialectic which, in the spectacle of visible things and the sight of the human soul, effaces limits, omissions, and evil, thus elevating goodness to the infinite and affirming it to be of God. But Plato did this scientifically.

However this may be, we have already seen that Plato's God is not an abstract God. Plato's God is the absolute Being, without faults; supreme Goodness; the Being possessed of all virtue, wisdom, and providence; the sun of the intelligible world, of which the essential and universal truths which we see are the shadow. This God, the author and Father of

---

[1] Leg., 900 D.   [2] Ibid., 901 D.   [3] Ibid., 900 D.

intelligible light, is also the author and parent of the sun
and the visible world. He made the sun in his own image
to enlighten the world, as he himself enlightens the world of
intelligence.[1] He is that Goodness which we scarcely perceive, in the centre of the world of intelligence, but which,
once seen, appears as the cause of all that is good and beautiful.[2] It is towards him that the soul of the true philosopher, *which alone has wings*, strives to soar.

He who is absolutely (τῷ παντελῶς ὄντι), who is a living
absolute (τῷ παντελεῖ ζώῳ), a perfect and living intelligible
(τῷ τελεωτάτῳ καὶ νοητῷ ζώῳ), the living one who is, in
whom the ideas are (ἔνουσας ἰδέας τῷ ὃ ἔστι ζῶον), the eternal essence (ἀΐδιος οὐσία), of whom, properly speaking, we
cannot say that it has been, or will be, but only that it is
(τὸ ἔστι μόνον): it is the God who is forever (ὄντος ἀεὶ Θεοῦ).[3]
It is he who possesses motion in repose, who possesses august and sacred intelligence ; which the sophist denies. " In
God's name," exclaims Plato, "shall we be readily persuaded
that he *who is absolutely*, has neither motion, nor life, nor soul,
nor thought, that he is inert, that he is without august and
sacred intelligence ? Shall we let men tell us that he has
intelligence, but has no life ? Shall we let them tell us that
he has both, but not personality ?[4] Shall we let them tell
us that he is personal, intelligent, living, but inert? All
this would be absurd."[5]

Moreover, according to Plato, it is this God who made the
world. Everything was made by God (κατά γε Θεὸν αὐτὰ
γίγνεσθαι). The world does not proceed from a blind and
spontaneous cause producing without consciousness (ἀπό
τινος αἰτίας αὐτομάτης καὶ ἄνευ διανοίας φυούσης), but it
proceeds from a God who creates with knowledge and with

---

[1] De Rep., 508 C.   [2] Ibid., 517 C.   [8] Tim., 30 et seq.
[4] We cannot here translate otherwise the word ψύχη. This is plainly
what Plato means.
[5] Sophist.. 265 C.

divine reason (μετὰ λόγου τε καὶ ἐπιστήμης θείας, ἀπὸ Θεοῦ). The beings, which were not at first, afterwards became through the God who made them (Θεοῦ δημιουργοῦντος ὕστερον γίγνεσθαι πρότερον οὐκ ὄντα).[1]

Such is the God given by the dialectic of Plato. This God is; he is good; he is the absolute Being, Goodness itself, intelligence and providence, author and Father of the world. He is the true God.

But another decisive proof that Plato really knew the true God and his attributes, and that he constantly alludes to them, is that his entire doctrine may, be called the doctrine of ideas, and that, according to Plato, ideas exist in God, and are God.

That such is the thought of Plato, seems to us well established, in spite of all contradictions. Thomassin does not hesitate to maintain this thesis *ex professo:* " Ideas were placed in God by Plato; that is the unanimous opinion of the Fathers."[2]

When Plato says, "Ideas are in the living one who is," it seems to me that this sentence alone should suffice to settle the question.

Plato everywhere affirms that the world and all that therein is was made in the likeness of ideas. Now, in the Timæus, he asserts that things were made as they are, " to the end that the world might be as similar as possible to the intelligible and perfect living one (ἵνα τόδ᾽ ὡς ὁμοιότατον ᾖ τῷ τελεωτάτῳ καὶ νοητῷ ζώῳ)."[3]

Thus, according to Plato, ideas are actually that intelligible and perfect living one, *i. e.* God. He repeats the same thing elsewhere. "To the end," he says, "that the world may be like unto the living absolute (ἵνα τόδε . . . ὅμοιον

---

[1] Sophist., 265 C.
[2] Thom., Dog. Theol. This is the heading to chap. xii. lib. iii.
[3] Tim., 39.

4

ᾗ τῷ παντελεῖ ζώῳ)." [1] In the Timæus, Plato never ceases
to consider the *eternal exemplar of ideas* (ἀΐδιον παράδειγμα)
as being the living absolute, which includes all living intelligibles, and which is the intelligible, supreme, and perfect
beauty of all points (τὰ γὰρ δὲ νοητὰ ζῶα πάντα ἐκεῖνο ἐν
ἑαυτῷ περιλαβὸν ἔχει . . . τῷ τῶν νοουμένων καλλίστῳ καὶ
κατὰ πάντα τελέῳ)." [2] This is the assertion in exact words
that ideas, the eternal example for the world, are precisely
God.

When Plato speaks of God, who is always (ὄντος ἀεὶ Θεοῦ),[3]
who created the world by gazing at that which is always (τὸ
ὂν ἀεί), that is to say, the eternal exemplar, ideas, does not
Plato clearly state that in gazing at that which is always,
ideas, he regards only himself, who always is?

The texts in Plato which prove our thesis are superabundant. It only remains for us to show the precise cause of
the misapprehension. If there be quotations which seem to
contradict each other upon this point, it is because Plato,
like ourselves, necessarily uses the word *idea* in two different
senses, sometimes to signify the truth as it is in itself (αὐτὸ
τὸ ἀληθές), sometimes the truth as we see it in ourselves
(ἐπιστήμη καὶ ἀλήθεια). In the first case, according to
Plato, ideas are in God and are God; in the second, Being
itself, supreme Goodness, is as superior to them as the sun is
superior to the light reflected by the world, and to the vision
which we have of that light.[4] There are ideas in God and
ideas in us; and between these two meanings of the word,
there is all the difference that Saint Augustine finds between
those two lights, of which one is the *light that illumines* (*lumen illuminans*): this is God, the idea of God; and of which
the other is only the *light that is illuminated* (*lumen illuminatum*); that is, we ourselves, the idea in us, created
intelligence.

[1] Tim., 31.   [2] Ibid., 30.   [3] Ibid., 34.   [4] De Rep., 508.

All the difficulties come from this. With this key we can, I think, settle them.[1] Moreover, we should be well aware that, for some time back, Plato, as well as Aristotle, has been turned to account by Hegelian sophists, who strive to take refuge beneath his wings, and shed their darkness over his light. We will amply prove this in the proper place.

IX.

Let us now turn from the result to the process.

We see, by the fact, that Plato was familiar with the great and chief process of the reason, the only one which rises to God.

But what is very remarkable, is that he also knew, described, and combated its abuse. It seems as if he foresaw the use which the Alexandrians would make of it, and the still more absurd use which German sophists would make of it in the nineteenth century.

Plato puts the question and settles it with the utmost precision. It is strange that the importance of his solution of the point is not appreciated! Leibnitz was struck by it, and quotes it as something of great value. We have, says Plato, the philosopher and the sophist. The philosopher and the sophist are exactly opposite in mind. The first alone deals with the true dialectic, which rises to the splendors of the one Being, the object of his inquiry and his contemplation. But what is the sophist's course? What does he seek, and what does he see? Hear Plato's answer: The sophist moves towards mere nothingness. He seeks and pursues non-being, and takes refuge in its shadows.[2] That is his dwelling and the habit of his mind. Aristotle notes

---

[1] See, on this point, book iii. *de Deo*, by Thomassin, and Nourisson's thesis, "Quid Plato senserit de Idæis," — a substantial summary of a great work.

[2] Sophist., 254.

this opinion of Plato. "Plato," he says, "very fitly remarks
'that sophism rests entirely upon non-being.'"

The reader will understand later, if he does not already
see, the depth of this observation. But this is not the place
to develop it.

We merely wish to show that Plato by his process, which
is the true one, could not obtain an idol, a false god, or
the empty and abstract unity of the Alexandrines, — a
unity without being, goodness, or intelligence, — and still
less that monster of contemporary pantheism, *ontological
nonentity*. Far from this, Plato declares this tendency to
be utterly contrary to philosophy, and uses the right phrase
in regard to those who meditate upon non-existence, or,
what is the same thing, the teachers of absolute identity.
He calls their doctrine *monstrous*. "If any one call likeness unlikeness, and unlikeness likeness, it seems to me that
it would be *monstrous*." [1]   And he adds an expression
which Malebranche seems to have translated when he lays
stress upon that kind of identical proposition which strikes
him as being fundamental: *To perceive nothing, or not to
perceive anything, are one and the same thing.* "He who
says nothing, necessarily, it seems, says nothing." We need
not even admit that he says anything; he says nothing,
or rather, he does not speak, who undertakes to put into
articulate utterance that which has no existence.[2]

In the face of so plain a statement, it is not admissible to
take an unfair advantage of certain passages in the Par-
menides or any other dialogue to confound Plato with the
sophists, who do not even distinguish nothingness from
Being, and whose wholly perverted mind works the void and
produces the absurd. If obscure, vague, or even inexact
statements occasionally escape him in describing the process
which leads to the light of supreme Being and supreme

[1] Parmenid., 129.   [2] Sophist., 237 E.

Goodness; if, especially in translations, Plato seems to give a very strange idea of the infinite, — we must first carefully consider all the texts, and see whether sometimes, as certainly there are examples, we have not translated the word which should mean *undetermined*, or at most *indefinite*, as *infinite*, — which would be the exact opposite of the true meaning. Then, if we still find errors in Plato's text itself, we should not be surprised. In regard to this difficult and even yet most obscure point, no exact solution was reached until since the seventeenth century, and that solution itself is still but little known. The precise theory of the infinite, before the new era, was scarcely possible; and many Christian sages have themselves used expressions concerning this subject which have only been noted and corrected by the Catholic Church within the last two hundred years.

X.

Let us sum up all that we have said.

Plato employs the true process of reasoning which leads up to God, and he does indeed attain to the true God. He takes created things as his starting-point, not as the *principle of deduction.* He asserts that we should advance from this starting-point, taken merely as *a fulcrum for our flight,* to the *universal primary cause which is outside the starting-point;* that reason, by the true dialectic process, rises to absolute Being, which is living, intelligent, *personal,* and active, which is the cause of all beauty, all goodness, which includes all perfection, with no trace of imperfection, which is supreme Goodness itself, the Father of the world, the creator of all things, who does not produce his work spontaneously and blindly, but with knowledge and divine reason, and creates the beings which are not at first, but which become through him.

Plato shows that reason, by the other process, which is syllogistic, does not reach this end, and can never rise above its starting-point or depart from it, since it takes it as the principle of deduction by means of identity. And, in fact, it is used by the purified soul only to return to the first process, *which alone has wings* and is pre-eminently the philosophical process; intelligence does not spread its wings and turn away from darkness to the light, except with the whole soul; we must cut and prune within the soul, and, as it were, circumcise it; we must prune the natural instincts of the animal part, which turn the gaze of the soul downward; then only can it change its direction and turn to the truth. Then its gaze is bent upon that which is divine and luminous, while the wicked and the impure have nought for their eye to rest upon but the *empty shadows of God.*

This is precisely why the sophist, moving in the opposite direction from the philosopher, takes *not-being* as the end and object of his contemplation, and hides himself in the gloom of nothingness.

And these two contrary directions of thought depend upon the free use which every man makes of the gift of God; that is, of the contact of God with the root of the soul, — at that point where every soul is joined to God.

So Plato says.

It is certain that man's reason moves in this way, alike in the humblest minds and in the profoundest philosophers.

Reason, moving according to its fundamental law, should find the eternal, perfect, and infinite God, Father of men, Creator of the world. God, as Saint Paul teaches, shows himself sufficiently; he is known through visible things, and man is inexcusable if he does not recognize and glorify him: this is the duty of reason. But there is a healthy reason and a perverted reason. Healthy reason rules in the soul which enjoys moral freedom, and perverted reason in the soul which is enslaved. The one looks higher than man, the other lower.

XI.

It now remains for us to show that in our so favorable opinion of the Platonic doctrine we have gone no farther than Saint Augustine, Saint Thomas Aquinas, Bossuet, nor perhaps so far as Thomassin. We say what they say, and that is enough.

Saint Augustine sees in antiquity one true doctrine and two sects. The two sects are those of Epicurus and Zeno; the true doctrine is that of Plato.

We judge doctrine, according to Saint Augustine, by the point where it places these three things: supreme Goodness (*finem boni*), the world-cause (*causas rerum*), the fulcrum of reason (*ratiocinandi fiduciam*).

Now, Epicurus places these three things in the body and the senses: his sect is impure. Zeno places them in man himself: his sect is arrogant. Plato places them in the true God; his philosophy is the true one. So says Saint Augustine.

He asserts that the Platonists "place in the true God the creative force of all things, the light of ideas, and the good of practical life." [1] He asserts that, as Cicero abundantly proves, "they place in an immutable, eternal, in no way human, but properly divine wisdom, — the original wisdom, stimulator of the other, — these three things: supreme Goodness, the world-cause, and the fulcrum of reason." [2] Saint Paul himself, he says elsewhere, does not accuse them of ignorance of the true God. Elsewhere, again, he declares "that Platonists place God far above the nature of every created spirit. He having created not only visible nature

[1] De Civit. Dei, lib. viii. cap. ix. t. vii. p. 320.
[2] St. Aug., Epist., c. xviii. t. ii. p. 502.

but the soul itself, he enlightens every rational nature, such as the human soul is, and blesses it by admitting it to a share in his immaterial and immutable light." [1]

" Let all sects," he again says, "yield to the philosophers, who say not that man's blessedness is in his body, or in his soul, but in God alone : not as the mind enjoys the body or itself, or as men find their happiness one in the other, but indeed as the eye enjoys the light. . . . Plato places blessedness in virtue, virtue in knowledge and imitation of God ; and this itself is blessedness. He does not hesitate, he asserts that to philosophize is to love God." [2]

Such is Saint Augustine's opinion of Plato.

As for Saint Thomas Aquinas, he [3] defends Plato against Aristotle in regard to a charge which strikes him as odious. He says that it is absurd (*videtur absurdum*) to impute follies to such men as Socrates and Plato (*talibus et tantis viris*), — to men who were the most virtuous of philosophers (*qui fuerunt homines virtutibus dediti super omnes philosophos*); who established virtue as the chief good of humanity (*solas virtutes bonum hominis ponebant*), and all whose philosophy tended to virtue (*qui ad componendos mores corrigendosque totam suam philosophiam effluerunt*).

Thus, according to Saint Thomas Aquinas, Plato is not one of those philosophers whom Saint Paul stigmatizes, when he says that having known God, they have glorified him not, and on account of this have become vain in their imaginations and given themselves up to uncleanness.

If the authenticity of the book *De Regimine principum* be contested, here is another testimony, taken from the *Summa*, the last work of Saint Thomas Aquinas, the summary of all his teaching. He asserts that Plato established the idea of

---

[1] St. Aug., De Civit. Dei, lib. viii. cap. i.
[2] Ibid., cap. viii. t. vii. p. 320.
[3] De regimine principum, cap. iv. t. iv. p. 822. Paris edition.

the true God. "He established," he says, " as a being apart,
the idea of Being, the idea of the One, which he calls Being
by itself, and Unity in itself; being, unity, whence proceeds
by participation all that can be called being or unity. . . .
He also established that Being by itself, the One in itself, is
supreme Goodness; and as Goodness, Being, and Unity are
identical, he said that Goodness was God, in which all that
may be called good must share. And all this is true," says
Saint Thomas Aquinas; "it is true that there is a first Being,
which is by its very essence, which is Goodness, which is he
whom we call God. Aristotle agrees on this point with
Plato." [1]

Moreover, Saint Thomas Aquinas asserts, with Saint Justin,
that Plato knew the book of Genesis and followed it in certain points. We scarcely understand why this should be dis-
puted. Is it possible that Plato could be wholly ignorant of
Oriental traditions? Could it be that among these traditions
he knew nothing of the Jews, whose zeal and activity bring
them to the front everywhere? His utter ignorance on this
point would be very hard to explain. Plato elsewhere, like
Socrates, — and this is to be carefully noted, — everywhere
enters into tradition so far as he can. He uses with the
deepest respect, and accepts in his philosophy, all the sound
doctrines which he encounters. Plato, like every genuine
philosopher, sought after truth rather than after the mode of
finding it. He had no trace of that strange pedantry, that
barren mania known as rationalism, which consists in a desire to find the truth in a certain manner and in no other,
and of one's self alone, through unaided human reason, without
any mixture of tradition, authority, or feeling, or any especial
help from God; like a man who plays at showing his strength,
and announces that he will lift an enormous weight without
a crowbar, with a single hand, and that the left. Does not a

[1] Summæ, 1ª, q. iv. a. 4.

true workman use both hands, and all the crowbars that he can find? So, too, did Plato, who sought the truth with all his mind and with all his heart and with his whole soul, as he says we should do; who studied all traditions, and travelled far and wide to find every trace of such; who constantly invokes, as we see in his writings, the special and present help of God to know the truth, — help which, according to Thomassin, was not refused him, and through which it was given him to know the true philosophy, that of which a Father of the Church said: "The Greeks found a law of righteousness in philosophy,"[1] — a statement which Saint Thomas quotes and confirms.

To know Bossuet's opinion of Plato, we have only to quote from that chapter of his "Logic" where he treats of eternal essences,[2] and thus expresses himself: —

"These eternal truths which our ideas present are the true object of science, and therefore that we may become truly wise, Plato incessantly reminds us of those ideas which present not that which shapes itself, but that which is; not that which engenders and suffers corruption, which is seen and then passes away, which is made and destroyed, but that which eternally subsists."

"This is that intellectual world which this divine philosopher has put into the mind of God before the world was formed, and which is the model for that sublime work."

"These are the simple, eternal, immutable, imperishable, and incorruptible ideas to which he refers us if we would comprehend the truth."

"This is why he said that *our ideas, the images of divine ideas,* were also directly derived from them, and did not come through the senses, which do indeed serve, he said, to awaken them, but not to form them in our mind."

Let us now come to the testimony of Thomassin, who goes very far in regard to Plato, sometimes perhaps too far in

---

[1] Clement of Alexandria, Strom., lib. i. no. 20.
[2] Logic, liv. i. ch. xxxvii.

regard to the Platonists. Thomassin sees in the philosophy of Plato what it itself asserts, a doctrine which is both speculative and moral, a struggle against the flesh and a constant contemplation of death (*perpetua mortis meditatio et conflictatio cum corpore*) ;[1] a doctrine which unfolds, by means of reminiscence, the eternal reasons hidden in the soul (*latitantes in anima rationes per reminiscentiam excitare*); a doctrine which does not cast man upon externals, but leads him back from external things to himself, and from himself to that which is higher (*nec in externa hominem refundere, sed ab iis ad ipsum, ut ipsum summum contempletur*) ;[2] a doctrine which thus found truth, not by chance, but by its very method, as Tertullian says (*non tantum casu in verum quandoque incurrisse*)." [3]

This doctrine, adds Thomassin, strives to purify the affections, to lift our mind to God ; and the very basis of Platonism, according to Saint Augustine, is the placing of ideas in God : the Fathers agree on this point. The contrary error comes from Aristotle first, then from the Gnostics and Arians. Plato is the father of philosophy ; and he went to the verge of philosophy, having more than any other philosopher recognized and asserted the fact of the actual intervention of God, by his help and his grace, in the contemplation of immutable truths.[4] And this help was not denied him. The Platonists, again says Thomassin, are praised by Saint Augustine for attributing to divine light whatever was given them in the order of that contemplation.[5] God, in fact, aided them ; and, moreover, they found help from the Hebrews (*Dei auxilio adjuti ; deinde Hebræorum quandoque contubernio*). Thus we praise, we quote, this patrician race

---

[1] Logic, lib. vi. cap. iii. n. i., 2.   [2] Ibid., lib. i. cap. ii. n. 2.
[3] Ibid., cap. xxiv. n. 1.
[4] Dog. Theol., t. iii. lib. iv. cap. ii. n. 10.
[5] Ibid., t. ii. lib. iii. cap. v. n. 15.

of philosophers; and to make their doctrine harmonize with our dogmas is not a difficult work, still less is it a sterile task, as Saint Bernard himself proved.[1]

Finally, in the preface to his Theodicy, Thomassin thus sums up his opinion of Plato: "That which precedes will readily explain to you why, in the first part of this treatise, I have mingled in proof Plato and his disciples with the Fathers of the Church, Greek and Latin. For although for the last five hundred years our most famous teachers have gained their philosophic education in the school of Aristotle, we must remember that all the Fathers acquired theirs in the school of Plato. Baronius might truly say, ' The Academy is the antechamber to the Church;' and the admirable Saint Augustine, himself imbued with that patrician philosophy, as Cicero calls it, declares that by changing a very few words and thoughts, a Platonist becomes a Christian. To this I have clung tenaciously (*mordicus*), showing in everything the harmony of their thoughts and expressions with our Scriptures and our holy Fathers, and pointing out the differences where they exist."[2]

In the face of these amazing testimonials from the Fathers and from Catholic scholars, — testimonials paid to the Platonic philosophy, — and of this wonderful agreement between philosophy and theology, this perfect union of philosophers and theologians of the first order, we ask the meaning of that war between religion and philosophy, reason and faith, of which we have heard so much for a century past. For myself, I see but one cause for this unhealthy division of the universal light of the Word in human minds. That cause is a decay of the human mind, and a simultaneous degeneration of reason and faith. The light has grown dim in men's souls, because they are less turned towards God. Winter reigns. Faith, in those who still have it, has a lesser radiance;

---

[1] Dog. Theol., t. ii. lib. iii. cap. xxiii. n. 9.   [2] Præf., t. iii. n. 10.

shrinking and repressed in the innermost heart, it no longer sheds its divine dew upon the mind. Faith does not sufficiently seek intelligence, as Saint Augustine urges it to do. On the other hand, reason, in those who cultivate it, no longer leads to any result, and misses the object of its career, as Plato expresses it; it does not search enough to find. Those who rise highest, pause " at divine phantoms and the shadows of what is," but they do not reach "the sun which casts these shadows." Insufficiently upheld by God, whom it neither seeks nor loves, reason completes its work in but very few men. Its weak and fine-spun thoughts, its partial and broken lights, have ceased to be more than the ruins and fragments of integral philosophy. Better simple ignorance than this ignorance which ignores itself; better actual night than a gloomy twilight which deems itself broad day, and doubts not that the sun is shining.

At the present time, therefore, those souls in whom God has placed through faith the source of light, are like a clouded sky, in which the sun no longer beams; and those others, destitute of faith, but to whom God still sends a few rays from without, are like the Earth when, in the first glimmer of dawn which puts out the stars without yet giving us the sun, she no longer sees by any sign that her light cometh to her from Heaven.

CHAPTER III.

LET us understand plainly that the question of the proofs of the existence of God, which includes that of his attributes, is not a question of any particular system of philosophy, but is the question of philosophy in general. The effort of the intelligence to show that there is a God, is the search after truth, nothing less. In treating this general question, we take up the Theodicy, consequently Metaphysics; we take up Logic, because we are concerned with one of the two processes of reasoning, and that the chief one. We must evidently treat of Morals, since the condition without which nothing can be proved, the existence of God, is a moral question, a free act of our soul; then we treat of Psychology, since we are concerned with the principal acts of both the intelligence and the will: we are at the point where all branches of philosophy meet, — at the centre, the root, of philosophy. This is why we are forced first to settle this supreme question.

Let us not fear, therefore, to dwell as long as may be needful upon this central point, which includes everything, — even the history of philosophy.

I.

Aristotle arrives at the same results as Plato. For, as we shall see in the course of this work, all geniuses of the first order agree, often even when they seem or believe themselves to be in opposition. In reality, it is the sophists who contradict one another and contradict the philosophers. Cicero declares that the difference between the Academy and the Portico is only a difference of words.[1]

And yet it must be said that if, indeed, the great results are the same, there is more than a difference of words, there is a difference in the method, — at least so far as regards the statement.

There are two processes of reasoning, as we have already said. Now, we may assert and distinctly settle this point: Plato represents the one, and Aristotle the other. Plato is above all else dialectic; Aristotle is peculiarly syllogistic. It is only unconsciously that he ever handles the dialectic process, and he gives no complete analysis of it.

And yet Aristotle could not be ignorant of these two intellectual processes, and he calls them *syllogism* and *induction* (ἐπαγωγή). He says, what is true, that induction gives us primary causes; syllogism, consequences. He sees, what we have already observed, that a knowledge of primary causes considered, not as possible, but as actual and existing, presupposes experience as the point of support of induction.[2] Thus Aristotle saw the facts.

But the great difference between Plato and Aristotle is that the latter, in practice, strove to find everything, or at least to prove everything, by syllogism; and in theory he knew neither all the conditions nor all the compass of the dialectic process. He even denies, in Plato, its legitimacy; and if he himself makes use of it, it is often without knowing it, and in an implied form. For twenty years the disciple of Plato, he received the results of his work. He had in advance that supreme idea of God given us by the chief process of reason, used by Plato, and above all brought to us

---

[1] Academ., lib. i. cap. ix.
[2] Analyt. prior., lib. i. cap. xxxi. 3.

by tradition diffused throughout the world, and to which he himself alludes: Aristotle retains all these data, but he envelops them in syllogisms, so that we lose sight of the way in which the mind obtains them.

There occurs, upon this point, in the Theodicy, between Plato and Aristotle, what occurred, at the close of the seventeenth century, in the domain of geometry, between Leibnitz, the inventor of the Infinitesimal Calculus, and a famous algebraist,[1] who pretended to deny the discovery, attacked its principles as inexact and productive of error, and then tried to reproduce and demonstrate, by common algebra, the results which Leibnitz obtained by his infinitesimal method. This adversary of Leibnitz kept the Academy of Sciences in suspense for several years, twenty years after the discovery. A skilful algebraist, a bold calculator, but as a writer wrapped in obscurity, as Montucla describes him, he reached, or seemed to reach, by vast algebraic circumlocutions, and endless equations, the same results which Leibnitz found by mere play, and proved with such marvellous simplicity. Obscure and interminable equations enveloped what Leibnitz analyzed, explained, and made clear in brief and simple formulas. That which Leibnitz found by the infinitesimal method, his adversary could never have found by his algebraic method, deductive from identity to identity; but the results being given, he sometimes reproduced them by dint of hard work. Only, in his obstinate attempt to reproduce them all, there were instances where he only succeeded by the aid of false calculations and incorrect deductions, forcing a way to attain the wished-for result.

And this is what must necessarily happen, in metaphysics, to those who insist upon forcing their way by continuous reasoning, syllogism, and thus reaching from creatures to God, from finite to infinite. Sceptics stop them, and readily

[1] See Montucla, Hist. of Mathematics, ii. 360.

show them that the continuity of the deduction is only apparent, and covers up voids and gulfs which only the other process of reasoning can bridge over.

Our comparison between these philosophers and geometricians is faulty, I believe, at but one point: that is, that there was no equality between Leibnitz and his foe, while between the genius of Plato and that of Aristotle, on the contrary, there was parity. But we maintain that those who try to establish by the logic of deduction the results produced by the other process of reasoning, are like the mathematician who denied the infinitesimal calculus, would use nothing but common algebra, and used false figures in order to do without the infinitesimal method.

Did Aristotle use false trains of reasoning to establish the same results as Plato, though without succeeding at all points? We dare not affirm that he did; we submit the question to those who think themselves competent to answer it. It would be a curious study in logic. But it is certain that Plato is simple and luminous, and Aristotle is involved and obscure; that the Platonic dialectic is poetic and popular; and that the Aristotelian syllogisms, on the question of first principles, are so extremely difficult and subtle that the best-equipped intellects would find it a long and difficult task to decide whether the proofs be exact or not. Kant, we are all aware, pronounced them false; only he treats all the rest no better. But when he sets forth the type, which, in his opinion, affords the true proof, that type is nothing else, it seems, but the dialectic of Plato with its double logical and moral condition.

II.

Be this as it may, let us try to face the proofs of the existence of God as set forth by Aristotle. We will not at first refer to the original. We will take Aristotle as explained

5

by Saint Thomas Aquinas, whose genius is quite as powerful, but much more lucid than that of Aristotle. We are
fortunate to find such a guide. Saint Thomas Aquinas
takes his instances from Aristotle's collective works, he
having commented upon them all, and he sums them up
as follows in his Summa *Contra Gentes.*[1]

We quote literally : —

"Having proved that it is possible to demonstrate the existence of God, let us consider such proofs of it as have been given
to us."

"Here are those of Aristotle, who tries to prove the existence of
God in two ways, from the fact of motion."

"First proof. Everything which is in motion is moved by
something. Now, our senses show us that something moves, the
sun, for instance. Therefore it is moved by some other thing which
moves it. Moreover, either that other motor is a motion, or it is
motionless. If it be motionless, our assertion is proved, namely ;
that it is essential to establish a motionless motor, which is God.
If, on the contrary, it be in motion, it is moved by some other
motor. We must, therefore, either go on in this way forever, or
come at last to the motionless motor. But it is impossible to go
on thus forever. Accordingly, we must affirm the existence of a
primary motionless motor."

"But in this proof there are two propositions to be proved,
namely : That every moving thing in motion is moved by a
motor other than itself, and that we cannot admit of an infinite
series of motors."

"Aristotle proves the first proposition in three ways : —

"1st. If a motor be self-moving, it must contain in itself the
primary cause of its motion ; otherwise it is plain that it is moved
by some other motor. It must also be moved by a primary movement ; that is to say, by itself, and not by one of its parts, like an
animal borne along by the motion of its feet. For in this first
case the whole would not be moved by itself, but by its part, and
one part by the other.[2] This motor which moves must itself also
be divisible, have parts ; for everything that moves is divisible, as

---

[1] Lib. i. cap. iii.   [2] Physics, book vii., opening pages.

is proved in the sixth book of the Physics. This settled, the philosopher reasons thus : —

"Everything which we suppose is self-moving is moved by a primary motion. Therefore, inaction of one of its parts involves the inaction of all. For if the inaction of one part leaves the other part in motion, it ceases to be the whole itself which moves by a primary motion ; it is that part alone, since it continues to move while the other part is at rest. But nothing which stops as soon as another thing stops is self-moving ; for that object whose cessation involves the cessation of the other, is also that whose motion involves the motion of the other ; therefore that other is not self-moving. Accordingly, that which we supposed to be self-moving does not actually move of its own impulse. Accordingly, finally, all which is in motion is necessarily moved by some motor other than itself."

"We cannot destroy this reasoning by saying that what is supposed to be self-moving can have no part of it in repose ; and again, that the part can neither stop. nor move, save by accident, as Avicenna so scandalously holds (*ut Avicenna calumniatur*). In reality, the whole force of this reasoning lies in the fact that if anything be self-moving by a primary movement, and of itself, not by reason of its parts, it follows that its motion no longer depends upon an outside motor. Now, the movement of the divisible, as well as its being, depends on the being and movement of its parts ; hence it cannot move of itself by a primary motion. It is therefore not essential to the truth of the conditional proposition inferred here, that we should admit as absolutely true that the part moves in the inaction of the whole ; it is enough that the sum-total of this conditional proposition is true ; namely, That if the part be at rest, the whole will be at rest. And it may be true even if the antecedent proposition were impossible ; as in this instance : If a man were an ass, he would be an irrational animal."

"2d. Aristotle again proves the same proposition as follows : [1]

"Everything that moves by accident does not move of itself, but is moved by the movement of some other thing ; this is evident ; neither that which moves naturally, by an inward motion,

[1] Physics, text. comm., xxvii. *et infra.*

as the animal whose body is only moved by the soul; nor that which is moved by nature, by an outward motion, as heavy bodies; for everything of this kind moves only by the way of generation or else by the removal of an obstacle. Now, all that is moved is moved either by accident or by itself. If by itself, . . . etc."

Let us stop here. What will it profit us to prolong this endless chain of propositions, each more obscure and more incomprehensible than the other ? What reader would follow us ? Who now believes in this mode of reasoning ? The seventeenth century banished it under the name of Aristotelianism.

What we have just quoted is but a fourth part of the demonstration. We had yet to finish the second mode in which Aristotle proves his major : *All that is in motion is moved by something other than itself.* Then we should also be forced to give the third mode of proving that same major. After that there would still remain three other ways of proving the minor, namely : *That there is not an infinite series of motors.* Then only would the syllogism be demonstrated.

Lastly, we should have to set forth the second syllogism, which Aristotle also uses to prove, from motion, the existence of God. We shall not undertake such a task, but shall confine ourselves to a closer study of the basis of the line of reasoning which we have just shown. What we have thus far quoted includes all its postulates.

III.

Aristotle takes the position, There is motion.

And from this he concludes : Therefore there is a first motionless motor. We call this God.

Now, there are in this train of reasoning words which can in no wise be filled by the syllogisms which we have just repeated.

What! from seeing motion shall we infer the motionless, by syllogism, by means of identity?

That is to say that from the variable we infer immutability; from the imperfect, perfection; or from the finite, infinity! Let any one show us a genuine syllogism which establishes such inference from the fact of motion presented by the senses.

Where are the passage and the middle term between these two worlds? How can we derive immutability from motion by means of deduction? Clearly, it is impossible.

Most assuredly it was none of these arguments that led Aristotle to assert immobility from seeing motion.

This conclusion involves a long story in the career of the human mind. Heraclitus spent his life in saying, *Everything passes, everything slips away* (πάντα ῥέει); and amidst these passing waves he never perceived the immutable. This was the cause of his sorrow. And that sublime regret — a sense of the imperfection of this changing world, a longing for immutability — did not lead him up to the conclusion that the immutable exists. He understood motion and its strange significance, but nothing more. Plato also understood motion, and he said: All that we see slips away; everything passes, is born, and dies; and we behold nothing that does not change. But having said this, Plato did not confine himself to regret. The contrast between this changing spectacle, this perishable nature, and an innate longing for perfection, immutability, and immortality, awoke in his soul that memory of the eternal, unchanging, and perfect Being which our soul also feels; and he asserted the existence of the immovable on the occasion of that which passes. And this very point was the basis of his whole process and his whole doctrine.

Aristotle, therefore, was furnished in the advance with this result, which cannot be obtained otherwise. Aristotle possesses the truth and strives to set it forth. To explain it, he wraps it in syllogisms. This seems clear to those who are beginning to think; and Aristotle taught. These syllogisms, with which it was impossible to find the truth, were no more useful to prove it; they throw no light upon it,—they veil it. We can scarce recognize it under this disguise. We may even question whether they do not destroy it, and whether there are not gross faults of logic in this chain of reasoning. Who will prove the contrary? Who'will sift all the meanings of the words *motion, immobility, immutability,* and *inertia,* to learn whether, in one of the links in his chain, Aristotle does not confuse them?

To Aristotle, the idea of motion is identical with that of change.[1] He defines motion as *the transition from potentiality to act.*[2]

Plato made motion synonymous with life ($\kappa\iota\nu\eta\sigma\iota\nu$ $\kappa\alpha\iota$ $\zeta\omega\eta\nu$), and thence placed motion in the absolute, infinite Being ($\kappa\iota\nu\eta\sigma\iota\nu$ $\kappa\alpha\iota$ $\zeta\omega\eta\nu$ . . . $\tau\hat{\omega}$ $\pi\alpha\nu\tau\epsilon\lambda\hat{\omega}\varsigma$ $\check{o}\nu\tau\iota$). Now, Aristotle himself sometimes takes motion in the same sense as Plato, as Saint Thomas Aquinas remarks.

Nevertheless, in the proof of the existence of God through motion, it is clear that motion is understood in the sense of change, or of the transition from potentiality to act.

This established, let us put Aristotle's reasoning into exact form, and see if it be possible for us to judge from it, to admit it or to deny it.

The entire chain of reasoning may be reduced to the two following syllogisms:—

FIRST SYLLOGISM.

Major. Everything in motion is moved by a motor other than itself; in other words, nothing moves of itself.

Minor. Now, our eyes show us the fact of motion.

---

[1] Metaph., xi. 11, 12. We quote from the Berlin edition.
[2] Ibid., xi. 9.

Conclusion. Therefore, there is something else which moves that which we see in motion.

SECOND SYLLOGISM.

Major. There cannot be an infinite series of motors; in other words, there can only be a finite series of motors; in other words, there is one first motor.

Minor. Now, this motor would not be the first if it were in motion, since it would then be moved by some other thing (as results from the first major).

Conclusion. Therefore, there is one first motionless motor. We call this God.

These syllogisms are correct in form, but are they true as facts?

We see at the first glance that they are true if the majors be true. But who will prove those majors? There lie the yawning voids.

For instance, how can we prove by syllogism, starting from an obvious general proposition, *that nothing moves of itself?* Yet Aristotle tries to do so. It is in this way that he tries to establish the existence of the one first motionless motor; that is, the existence of God.

He makes the attempt; we have seen his efforts to prove the first major, namely, "*that everything in motion is moved by a motor other than itself.*" But his arguments on this point are so subtle and so doubtful that Avicenna claims that the reasoning is false; and Saint Thomas Aquinas, who considers Avicenna's objection scandalous (*ut Avicenna calumniatur*), is still forced to confess that the argument rests on a conditional proposition, whose condition may be impossible or contradictory, as in this: If man be an ass, he is an irrational animal (*Si homo est asinus, est irrationalis*).

Who shall be the judge? Is the argument good? I know not, being unable to understand all parts of it. Is it false, on account of the contradictory conditional? I dare not say so, for even in algebra we introduce and calculate with *imaginary quantities*, that is, impossibilities and contradictions. What I assert is that these syllogisms are, to say the least, not valid; they do not discover the great truth which they contain; they do not make it manifest, and if, strictly speaking, they demonstrate it, it is because they include the other process of reasoning.

Moreover, Aristotle never puts his arguments into such scholastic form as Saint Thomas has done here. But it is certain that he generally tries to deduce everything by syllogism from an evident fact or an abstract major. He seldom advances in his statement by any other than the deductive process of reasoning; and this annoying habit often deprives his reasoning — I refer to the reasoning only — of its clearness, validity, utility, sometimes perhaps its solidity.

Does it follow from this that Aristotle's Theodicy contains nothing new or valuable? Far from it; and we will now attempt to show what he accomplished.

IV.

If Aristotle be syllogistic in his statement, proceeding by abstract majors and deductions, we cannot conclude from this that in his inner mental action he retained nothing of the other process of reasoning. We have already said, and we shall show when we come to logic, that he mentions and clearly distinguishes between the two processes of reasoning, attributing to the one the invention of majors, and to the other deduction. In his profound meditations he made use — he could not but make use — of the sublime process which leads to God. But he generally managed to use it unawares, like the majority of mankind, and concealed, through a trick of style, his mode of discovery by a very different mode of statement and proof.

Be this as it may, not only did this powerful genius renew in his thought the data of tradition in regard to God, and the results of the Platonic method; but we may also say that on several points, not on all, he gave clearness and precision to Plato's theology. Had he added to the theodicy nothing but the three words, *God is pure act,* — a formula which has been marvellously commented upon and used in every way by Saint Thomas Aquinas, — he would have given the human mind an idea of capital significance.

To judge Aristotle, we should know the last chapters of the twelfth book of his Metaphysics.

We will try to give an idea of these chapters by quotations and brief commentaries. Our quotations will be given in exactly the order in which they occur in the original. We shall glean the truth from these chapters, setting aside the often inexact reasoning which he brings to bear upon it, as well as his errors in regard to the nature of the physical heavens, the imperishable nature of the stars, and the eternity of the world, — errors to correspond with which there are other metaphysical errors and inexplicable contradictions. In spite of these exceptions, these chapters are still a truly admirable summary of a theodicy.

"There are three essences, two of which are natural, and one immutable. . . . For there must necessarily be one eternal, unchanging essence."[1]

Yes, there are two natural or created essences, mind and matter; one immutable or uncreated, which is God. Saint Thomas Aquinas explains this as follows: "There are two substances which are natural, because there is motion in them; besides these two substances, there is a third which is immovable or immutable, and no longer natural." Nat-

---

[1] Metaph., xii. 6. It is a mistake to translate this: "There are three essences, two *physical*, the other immutable," for the word *physical* does not mean natural, but corporeal. Saint Thomas Aquinas translates it with perfect accuracy: *duæ quidem naturales.*

ural, mobile, subject to change, are one and the same thing, according to Aristotle; as also, on the other hand, immobile, immutable, eternal, and supernatural are terms each of which includes the other. Pascal expresses the same truth in other words: "There are three worlds, — the world of bodies, the world of mind, and the third, which is supernatural, which is God." This had been established by Genesis long before: "In the beginning *God made heaven and earth ;*" where we must understand, with the Fourth Council of the Lateran, that heaven and earth signify mind and matter, natural things, which began, which were born.

"There must," adds Aristotle, "be a first cause such that its essence is pure act."[1]

Otherwise the world could not exist, as Aristotle says. This the sophists ignore, who believe that Being began with a mere potentiality or possibility, — which is the same as saying that effects can exist without a cause.

"A being which moves without being moved is eternal, is pure essence, is pure act."[2]

The formula — God is pure essence ; God is pure act — is immensely fruitful. Saint Thomas Aquinas, who develops it by the light of his Christian genius, superior as such to that of Aristotle, extracts genuine treasures from it, discovers wonderful depths of meaning in it. We will only say here, in a few words, that when we know that God is pure essence, that is, that all is essential in God, we know that in him there is no accident, no variable or secondary qualities. His being is his essence, — that is to say, it is necessary; his knowledge is his essence, his will is his essence, his blessedness is his essence. When we know that God is pure act, — in other words, that in him everything is act, — we know that there is not in him, as in us, virtual and actual, possible and real, potentiality and act, but that with God all that is possible

---

[1] Metaph., xii. 6.   [2] Ibid., 7.

is actual; that there is nothing in him to be developed or completed; that he is already perfect; that he is not, like his creatures, capable of indefinite development, but that he is already now, if we may so express it, infinitely developed. This establishes absolutely the distinction between the finite and the infinite. To be pure essence and pure act is precisely the divine characteristic of infinity. At least, this is what Saint Thomas Aquinas asserts in these formulas, whether or no Aristotle ever perceived it.

What immediately follows in the original is both clear and profound. It is the way in which the one first motionless motor moves the other two essences.

"It moves thus. The desirable and the intelligible moves without being moved. . . . It moves as the object of love." [1]

"The supreme, desirable, and intelligible are one and the same thing (τούτων τὰ πρῶτα τὰ αὐτά)."

This essence moves as the object of love; it attracts. Here we have the universal charm or attraction of the desirable and intelligible, which, according to Aristotle, attracts everything, material and spiritual, each in its way, and which causes, without exception, all motion, — that universal attraction of which physics now knows something, and with which psychology, let us hope, will some day be familiar as the original source of all motion, all facts, the entire history of the soul. And here Aristotle makes this important remark by the way: "The object of desire is the apparition of the Beautiful; but the object of will is the Beautiful itself." [2]

Furthermore: "So soon as there is a being which moves, although motionless, and which is motionless, although in action, that being ceases to be subject to change."

"This motor, then, is a necessary being; and in so far as necessary, is the Good, and is the First Cause."

---

[1] Metaph., xii. 7.   [2] Ibid.

"Such is the First Cause, upon which hang heaven and earth." [1]

This reminds us of Plato's statement that "the divine is bound to us by the very roots of our being;" and that other Platonic doctrine, that "the First Cause is the Good itself."

Here, now, is what the First Cause actually is:—

"We taste fugitive happiness; he possesses it forever."

"His happiness is his very act; to be awake, to feel, to think, is our good; afterwards, memory and hope." [2]

But what is his act or his happiness? It is *thought in itself.*

"But thought in itself is the thought of the best in itself; and the thought above all other thought is that of the Good above all other good. Now, thought thinks itself by grasping the intelligible, and it becomes intelligible by this contact and this thinking; so that the thought and its object are one and the same thing. To grasp the intelligible, to grasp the essence, is thought: this very possession is its act. And this act, which constitutes all thought, has, it seems, a divine character; so that contemplation is certainly happiness and perfection."

"But if God continually tastes this happiness, of which man can only enjoy the fugitive taste, assuredly his bliss is wonderful; more wonderful still if this happiness is greater in him than it is in us. Now, it is so. For this very thing, this happiness itself, is his life; the intelligible in act is life; now, he is all act; so the act in itself is his life, eternal and supreme life. We call God a *perfect and eternal living being*, because continual and eternal life is in him; or rather, that life itself is God." [3]

Certainly, this is a truly profound contribution to the Theodicy, full of most fruitful and luminous points, although they are but slightly developed, and thus very remote from our habits of thought, which demand so many explanations. It is plain that we have here a powerful implicit light, and that it is not easy for human reason to go higher, or to see farther.

[1] Metaph., xii. 7.   [2] Ibid.   [3] Ibid.

In this extract we have some faint vision of deep mysteries. When Leibnitz observes the amazing phenomenon of *the reflection of minds*, which consists in the fact " that a mind is itself its own immediate object and acts upon itself, thinking of itself and of what it has done;"[1] when he recognizes "that this reduplication gives in a similar absolute substance an image of two respective substances, that which understands and that which is understood," and when, moreover, he considers that "that which is modal, accidental, imperfect, and changeable in us, is real, essential, complete, and immutable in God," Leibnitz sees in this reduplication, as it were, a trace of the plurality of divine persons in the Unity of God. It seems to us that this is exactly what Aristotle, unconsciously, no doubt, catches a glimpse of here both in the soul and in God.

He calls these three principles: 1. *Good in itself* (τὸ καθ' αὐτὸ ἄριστον). 2. *Thought in itself* (νόησις ἡ καθ' αὐτήν). 3. *Act* or *Life in itself* (ἐνέργεια δὲ ἡ καθ' αὐτὴν ἐκείνου ζωή).

But thought in itself is thought of the Good in itself (ἡ δέ νόησις ἡ καθ' αὐτὴν τοῦ καθ' αὐτὸ ἀρίστου); and thought and its object, the Good, are one and the same thing (ὥστε ταὐτὸν νοῦς καὶ νοητόν). But this mutual possession of thought and its object is its act (ἐνεργεῖ δὲ ἔχων); this act in itself is the life of God (ἐκείνου ζωή); and this excellent, eternal life is God himself (τοῦτο γὰρ ὁ Θεός). So that the Good, thought, and life, which mutually possess one another, are one and the same thing, and all this is God.

But what we should particularly note in this quotation is the method manifestly implied in it.

This method is precisely that of the Platonic dialectic : it is the only and the true method by which to lift one's self to God; it is the chief process of reasoning, a process so

---

[1] Vol. i. p. 24, complete works.

natural, simple, and direct, so native to reason, that all
men, even self-observant thinkers, employ it without knowing
it, — a process, in fine, which consists, when God is its subject, in attributing to the infinite those finite qualities which
we find in ourselves.   This is Leibnitz's remark: " God's perfections are those of our own souls, without the limits to be
found there."

" We taste a fugitive happiness," says Aristotle; " he possesses it forever."

We find fugitive happiness within ourselves; the mind
grasps this idea of happiness, destroys limitations, does away
with time, the past, the future, all change, thus makes happiness eternal, and attributes it to God.

This is not all.   What is this happiness?   To be awake,
to think, to feel, to live, in brief, this is our good.   All this
is ours partially; all this, therefore, must be God's absolutely,
infinitely.

He is forever awake, since he is all act; there is in him
nothing latent or dormant; nothing which sleeps in the possible and awaits the future; no force which rests while preparing its act: all is already act.

He thinks absolutely.   His thought is thought in itself;
it thinks the Good above all good; and moreover it is that
which it thinks.   We, when we think, try to touch and to see
the intelligible, which may be momentarily permitted to us;
he not only sees and touches the intelligible, but he is himself that intelligible.   His thought does not approach the
goal more or less closely, it is the goal.

He lives absolutely, infinitely, since his life is no other
than this act itself, this mutual penetration, and this identity of the intelligent and the intelligible, and since not
only he has this life, supreme and eternal, but what is the
crowning point, he is himself this life.   He is eternal and
perfect life.

So that plainly Aristotle rises here from what he sees in us to God, and passes from the one to the other, positing the infinite everywhere, urging everything towards the absolute, by the suppression of all limitations.

The fundamental idea of *pure* act is especially worthy of attention in this connection. We see in everything potentiality and act, possible and actual; everything that lives, becomes, grows, tends towards a superior limitation, which it is as impossible to reach as it is by adding unities to unities to reach infinity; there will always be some possibility to be developed in us, some future to be realized: this is the insuperable and necessary gulf which divides the finite and the infinite. Well! there is a Being who does not become, who is; who is absolutely, who is that superior limitation towards which everything moves and which nothing can ever reach, because we do not become infinite; we are infinite. He therefore is infinite; he is absolute development, complete and unlimited life, and the infinity of potentialities already realized. It was in this sense that Saint Thomas Aquinas said, "God is the absolute actuality of all things" (*Deus est* actualitas *omnium rerum*). This is what modern sophists fail to understand. But this is surely the sovereign idea which all reason seeks through every finite postulate; this is surely the rational process above all processes: to rise from finite to infinite, from all to God.

Furthermore: "That there is an eternal, immovable substance, distinct from sensible things, is plain from what we have just said. It is also plain that this substance has no particular size, but that it is without parts, that it is indivisible. It moves for an infinite time, and nothing finite has an infinite force."[1]

In all these statements there are exact mathematical truths. We see here the origin of the strict idea of the infi-

[1] Metaph., xii. 7.

nite.   Aristotle here catches a glimpse of that formula of prime importance which was not expressed until the seventeenth century, and even then imperfectly and not by all: that that which is infinite in one sense, is infinite in every sense; that that which is finite in a single sense is finite in every sense; that the finite and the infinite are absolutely incommunicable; but that both exist; that there are two natural, finite substances, which we see; that there is one eternal, immovable, infinite (without special size), indivisible, and absolutely continuous substance.   Aristotle understood that the infinite, the continuous, the indivisible, the eternal, and the essential are one and the same.   Elsewhere, however, he wavers, and of the two natural and movable substances he makes one, the heaven, eternal and movable during an infinite time.   This is his mistake in regard to the eternity of the world, — a mistake which contradicts his own formulas.   He ought to see that nothing eternal can be finite, or that nothing finite can be of infinite duration; as he sees that nothing finite can have infinite power.   This is the same thing.

V.

A question now remains to be solved, which we should scarcely have expected to see Aristotle consider, it seems to us so simple.

"Must this essence be regarded as unique? or are there several of them?   And if there are several, how many are there?"[1]

Now, here we find in the text an apparent contradiction of so singular a nature that the author of the finest modern work on Aristotle which we have,[2] does not fear to assert that one of the terms of the contradiction is nothing else than a thesis, which Aristotle first develops, that he may

[1] Metaph., xii. 8.   [2] M. Ravaisson.

contest it later; as, for instance, when Saint Thomas Aquinas begins his theses by positing the antitheses. But this explanation does not really agree with the text.[1] Aristotle admitted that the world was eternal: this was a source of error to him. He is obliged to admit, as it were by consequences, not only a first God, but other secondary Gods, also eternal, immovable, and indivisible. But neither the ancients nor Saint Thomas mention the smallest contradiction in this chapter. There is no contradiction, there are errors. Aristotle begins by declaring that "the primary cause of beings, the *first being*, is motionless, *whether in himself or accidentally*, and that it is he who imparts to everything the first, eternal, and simple motion.[2] But," he adds, "besides the simple, universal motion, which we say is produced by the essence of the *prime* immovable, we also see in the world other eternal motions, those of the planets,[3]

[1] Besides, Aristotle proves in his Physics, to which he refers here, that the motions of the planets are eternal, and that eternal motion can only be produced by an eternal motor, and any motion whatsoever by a motionless motor. Saint Thomas Aquinas refers us, for these proofs, to the book on Physics and the one on the Heaven.

[2] Metaph., xii. 8.

[3] Aristotle here alludes at first to the diurnal motion which seems to carry the whole celestial vault through a revolution of twenty-four hours' duration: this is what he calls the simple, primary motion; then he speaks of the various movements of the planets, each of which seems to add a motion of its own to this general and primary movement. Aristotle rests too much here upon the postulates of experience as the senses have given them to him. Plato also rested upon the experience of the senses, but he used his reason more, was freer from the illusion of the senses, less directly ready to accept it as the type of truth. In regard to the heaven and the stars, Plato probably accepted Pythagorean ideas, and distrusted appearances. But Aristotle, limiting knowledge on this point to what he saw, boldly asserts that there are seven motionless, eternal motors, because there are seven planets; and that the eighth sphere, that of the fixed stars, is moved by the immovable, eternal, and *primary* motor. Upon which Saint Thomas says (Paris edition, vol. iv. p. 453, commmentary on book xii. chap. 8 of Aristotle's Metaphysics) that in Aristotle's day astronomers had not yet observed, as they have since, the proper movement of fixed stars; but that thence Aristotle in every case, in his system, asserts the existence of too few motors.

for every spherical body is eternal, and cannot cease to be in motion: we have proved this by physics. Each of these movements, therefore, must be produced by an essence immovable in itself and eternal; for the nature of the stars is eternal in its essence. . . . It is therefore evident that there must necessarily be as many essences, eternal in their nature, immovable in themselves, and indivisible." ¹ This established, Aristotle again returns to the one first motionless motor, the first essence. He says that it alone is immaterial, because it is all act; that nothing of it is in a potential state, and that it has its end in itself, as is expressed by the Greek word *entelechy* ² (ἐν, τέλος, ἔχων), and he concludes: "The *first* motionless motor is therefore a Unity both as regards form and number." ³

But even after this he falls back into his error concerning several secondary gods, and says that the fabulous mythology of the ancients contains this basis of truth, "That the stars are gods, and that the divine surrounds all nature (ὅτι θεοί τέ εἰσιν οὗτοι καὶ περιέχει τὸ θεῖον τὴν ὅλην φύσιν);" and these secondary gods are distinguished by Aristotle from the sovereign God, in that he alone is *first*, in that he alone is immovable *both in himself and accidentally*, he alone is all act, has his end in himself, and is *entelechy*. The others are not all act, they are immovable by themselves, but movable accidentally. He alone, again, is the first desirable and the first intelligible, and the sovereign Good.

VI

God's relations with the world, according to Aristotle, are these : —

"We must now consider ⁴ how universal nature includes the Good, the sovereign Good. Is it as a separate being, existing in

¹ Metaph., xii. 8.   ² Ibid.   ³ Ibid.   ⁴ Ibid., 10.

itself, or rather as the cosmic order, or in both ways at once, as in an army? For the good of an army is its order, and it is also, its chief, — particularly its chief: order does not constitute the leader, it is the leader who gives order."

Aristotle admits both, and shows the absurdities which flow from any other system. Those, for instance, who do not accept the supreme Good as a separate principle existing by itself, those who "derive beings from non-being, or, to escape this necessity, reduce everything to absolute unity." [1]

Here Aristotle stigmatizes, as Plato does, the old absurdity of atheism which derives being from non-being, as well as the old absurdity of pantheism, which refers everything to absolute identity. He thus at once attacks the present German sophists at both ends, — those alike who admit non-being and absolute identity, and who still fancy that in Aristotle they have a powerful ally. Aristotle at the same time refutes those who admit of two opposite principles, — as these sophists also do, — and shows that they "are forced to give an opposite to supreme knowledge and wisdom, — an excess which we avoid," [2] says Aristotle. "The first principle has no opposite (οὐ γὰρ ἐστιν ἐναντίον τῷ πρώτῳ οὐθέν). The first principle is unique. Those who take for their principle number and an infinite series of essences, each essence having its principle, make the universe a collection of episodes and a host of principles (ἐπεισοδιώδη τὴν τοῦ παντὸς οὐσίαν ποιοῦσιν . . . καὶ ἀρχὰς πολλάς). But beings do not wish to be ill-governed. Homer says, "A multiplicity of leaders is of no avail. Let one alone rule : —

"Οὐκ ἀγαθὸν πολυκοιρανίη. Εἷς κοίρανος ἔστω." [3]

Thus closes, with the twelfth book of Aristotle's Metaphysics, this fine abstract of a Theodicy.

---

[1] Metaph., xii. 10. [2] Ibid. [3] Il. ii. 204.

VII.

It was doubtless to his Metaphysics that Aristotle alluded, when, on Alexander's reproaching him for having revealed the sublimities of knowledge, he replied, " I have so revealed them as not to reveal them." It is still true that these books, more than any of his others, earned for Aristotle the title of the Dark.

In his work on the World he is clearer.[1]   After developing his ideas in regard to the world, he adds, —

" It remains for us to speak briefly of the cause which contains and governs the whole.   An old tradition, circulated among all mankind by our fathers, tells us that everything comes from God and through God, that no nature suffices unto itself (οὐδεμία δὲ φύσις αὐτὴ καθ᾽ ἑαυτήν ἐστιν αὐτάρκης), and exists only by his help. . . . God is, in fact, the preserver and Father of all that is in the world, and he acts in everything that acts, not as the workman who labors and grows weary, but as an omnipotent virtue which operates. . . .[2]

" We must know of God that his might is irresistible, his beauty complete, his life immortal, his virtue supreme, and that, invisible to any mortal nature, he is visible in his works.   And surely all motions and all beings which are in the air, on the earth, or in the waters, are really the works of God, who contains the universe. . . .[3]

" God is an immutable law, a law which can be neither changed nor corrected, a law holier and better than the laws written on our tables.   Governing all by incessant activity and infallible harmony, he directs and orders the entire universe, heaven and earth, and diffuses himself throughout all beings. . . .[4]

" He is One, but he has several names, derived from his various modes of action in the world.   Does it not seem that when we call him both *Zéna* and *Dia* we mean *Him by whom we live* ? . . .[5]

---

[1] I know that the authenticity of this book is contested.   But there is a passion for disputing the authenticity of books to which we should only yield on decisive proof.

[2] De Mundo, vi. p. 397.

[3] Ibid., p. 399. .

[4] Ibid. p. 401.

[5] Ibid.

"All these names stand for God alone, as the noble Plato remarks. God therefore, according to ancient tradition, is the beginning, end, and middle of all that is, and traverses all nature in a straight line (showing to all things his direct course), ever followed by justice, the avenger of those who transgress upon this divine line, — justice which all should possess who desire to attain in the future to a state of blessedness, and all who desire to be happy in the present."[1]

VIII.

Certainly all that precedes is grand and beautiful, but we now come to a point where Aristotle's genius seems to us amazing.

Saint Thomas Aquinas[2] asserts that Aristotle first called attention to the great distinction between the two degrees of the divine intelligible, which we have already encountered in Plato.

Doubtless Aristotle is far from having seen the whole of this vast question: that was impossible in his day. But evidently he saw the truth, and grasped certain features of it with admirable precision.

In the first place, he distinguishes in man, with perfect distinctness, the two lights which Saint Augustine calls *light which illuminates* and the *light which is illuminated*, and which Fénelon describes as the *reason which borrows* and the *reason which gives*. "Everywhere in nature," says Aristotle, "we find the distinction between that which is only in the potential state, and that which, being already actual, produces the passage from potentiality to act. This distinction necessarily recurs in the soul. There is a passive intellect capable of becoming anything, and there is an active intellect capable of producing everything. The latter is like the light. Light converts into actual fact colors which only exist in potentiality. So, too, *separable* intellect (distinct from man),

---

[1] De Mundo, close of the book.   [2] Contra Gentes, cap. iii. 3.

impassive and entirely pure, is act in essence. . . . That intellect is Being itself, it alone is immortal, eternal, and without it the passive intellect can do nothing."[1]

Aristotle, therefore, perceived, in the analysis of reason, that fundamental distinction which Fénelon develops so finely, between the reason which is within us, and the reason which is God himself.

In all his works he recurs to this. He everywhere maintains that this principle, intelligent and intelligible, pure intellect, is not the same thing as the soul,[2] and that neither perception (αἰσθάνεσθαι),[3] memory, nor ordinary thought (δοξάζειν),[4] nor reasoning (λογισμός),[5] nor any discursive intellectual act (διάνοια),[6] "are the functions of contemplative intellect (νοῦς θεωρητικός),[7] but rather the functions of man, who gives life to that intellect."[8]

This intellect is radically distinct from the soul, it is a being and a substance apart which supervenes in man (ὁ δὲ νοῦς ἔοικεν ἐγγίνεσθαι οὐσία τις οὖσα);[9] which supervenes from without (θύραθεν);[10] which is divine (θεῖον εἶναι); which is separable from the soul as the eternal from the perishable (ἐνδέχεται χωρίζεσθαι, καθάπερ τὸ ἀίδιον τοῦ φθαρτοῦ);[11] which is in us as another kind of soul (ἔοικε ψυχῆς γένος ἕτερον εἶναι); as a light which not only is not given to animals, but which does not even seem to be granted to all men (ἀλλ' οὐδὲ τοῖς ἀνθρώποις πᾶσι).[12] This latter assertion would correspond with those solemn words of holy Scripture : "The sun of intelligence has not risen upon them."[13]

Aristotle, clearly, here refers to the final perfection of in-

[1] De Anima, iii. 5.   [4] Ibid.   [7] Ibid.
[2] Ibid., i. 2.   [5] Ibid., ii. 3.   [8] Ibid., i. 4.
[3] Ibid., 5.   [6] Ibid.   [9] Ibid.
[10] De Generat. Amina, ii. 3, and ii. 6.   [11] De Anima, ii. 2.
[12] "Intelligence, in the sense in which we understand it, does not seem to exist *indifferently* in all animals, or even in all men" (De Anima, i. 2).
[13] Wisdom, v. 6.

telligence, its end and last term, which Plato calls the *term
of the intellectual procedure*, and Saint Augustine, *reason
attaining its end*, — a termination which consists, according to Aristotle, in seeing the intelligible as he sees himself, in seeing him by touching him (θιγγάνων καὶ νοῶν), and
in becoming one with him (ὥστε ταὐτὸν νοῦς καὶ νοητόν);
which Saint Augustine also considers as the proper characteristic of the vision of God. But this contemplation, says
Aristotle, which is happiness, and which, in God, is continuous, is only granted to man at rare intervals.[1]

Our mind is naturally in respect to this high degree of
light as the eye of the owl in respect to the sun.[2] God
always sees this pure intelligible light, it is himself: in God
intelligence and the intelligible are identical.[3] But with regard to us, this divine light is supernatural; and the soul, in
so far as we consider it as illuminated by this light, *is not
purely natural.*[4] This light, according to Aristotle, does not
come by generation. The soul, in so far as vegetative, sensitive, rational, that is to say, in so far as including life, animality, and humanity, — the soul comes by generation, and
develops with the total germ. But this light of intelligence
alone comes to man otherwise, it only is divine.[5]

This light is the end and object of man, and the sovereign
good consists in its contemplation.

So thinks and says Aristotle. We will consider these
extracts further elsewhere. Let the reader ponder well the
beautiful words which follow: —

"If it be true that happiness is virtue in act, it is, above all, the
act of the highest virtue; it is, above all, the act of that which is
best in man. Whether this best be the intellect, or any other
principle which, by nature, should prevail in man, and which pos-

---

[1] Metaph., xii. 7.
[2] Ibid., ii. 1.
[3] Ibid., xii. 7.
[4] Part. Anim., p. 641.
[5] De Generat. Anim., ii. 2.

sesses in itself the light of the divine and the good; whether this best be the divine itself, or that which is most divine in man, in any case it is the action of that principle, acting in harmony with its own peculiar virtue, which must constitute perfect happiness. We have already said that this action is contemplation. . . . *But such a life is superior to the life of man : it is not in that he is man that he will live thus, but in that a divine principle lives within him ;* [1] and inasmuch as this principle differs from that compound which is man, just so much will its action triumph over the action of every other virtue. If the intellect be divine relatively to the man, the life according to its action will be divine relatively to human life. Man, therefore, according to the warning of the wise, must learn to rise above the mere human, to lose all sense of anything mortal, and to live immortally with the life of the higher principle which lives within him."

Let the reader take heed lest he forget these fragments from Aristotle. We shall make use of them again.

IX.

Let us close this study of Aristotle's theodicy with two remarks, one concerning the method, and the other the result.

As regards the method, it is plain that Aristotle used both processes of reasoning. This we have seen. Nothing else was possible; but Aristotle did not always realize this with sufficient distinctness.

Aristotle possessed that profound good sense peculiar to the genius which seeks truth rather than the mere means of finding it. He was particularly free from the unbearable sophistical madness which demands absolute proof of everything. " It is ridiculous" (γελοῖον), he said, " to pretend to prove that nature exists." " There are some," he says elsewhere, " who admit of no other proofs than mathematical ones; others who only need to have examples; others love to

---

[1] Moral. ad Nicom., x. 7.

lean upon the authority of the poets. There are some who demand that everything should be accurately proved, while others find such accuracy unendurable. . . . And it must be confessed that there is a certain futility beneath the pretence of accuracy. . . . We should not exact mathematical accuracy in everything, save in the case of abstract things."

Thus it was not a foregone conclusion with Aristotle to apply syllogistic deduction to every question. He knew and he maintained that majors were not to be found in this way, but rather by the other process, induction (ἐπαγωγή). At times he even calls this process Dialectic, with Plato. "This," he said, "is the bent of dialectic: it is an investigator by nature, and searches out the first principles in every branch of learning."[1] This we shall discuss more fully in logic. But we must confess that Aristotle errs in not recognizing the Platonic dialectic as one of the two processes of reasoning, — that which leads to God, that which he himself employed in his search for the first principle, for the Being all act, the eternal and perfect living one. He often unwittingly veils, disguises, and hinders this simple and powerful process, by the syllogistic form. · Hence those strange majors which are the weak side of Aristotle, the point at which modern thinkers attack him. For instance, "Every spherical body is eternal, and is eternally in motion." This is what revolted, and justly so, the sixteenth and seventeenth centuries.

But what we also affirm is that these majors were often the fruit of the profoundest thought, and the legitimate result of the process which reason possesses for the discovery of majors. Such is, for instance, one which is fundamental with Aristotle, and of which we have already spoken : "*Everything that moves is moved by some other thing*, or, rather, *Nothing is self-moving*." Who would imagine that, in another form, this major is the precise point from which Descartes starts to find God ? This we shall show.

[1] Top., i. 2.

We have only to recall that *movement*, with Aristotle, means the *path from potentiality to act.* Thus Aristotle's major means: *Everything that passes from potentiality to act, passes thus only under the action of a cause already in act.* Now, is it not clear that Descartes sees the same truth and translates Aristotle's algebra into ordinary speech, when he says: " I know that I am an imperfect, incomplete thing, dependent upon another, constantly tending and aspiring towards something better and greater than myself; but I also know, at the same time, that he upon whom I depend, possesses in himself all those great things to which I aspire, . . . *not indefinitely and only* IN POTENTIALITY, but that he enjoys them indeed ACTUALLY and INFINITELY, and so he is God." Descartes therefore saw, like Aristotle, the created being passing from potentiality to act; now, he could not thus pass into act and tend towards the best, save under the influence of a cause which is not in potentiality, but in act: and this cause which is ever in act is God. We see that this is precisely Aristotle's major. It is also exactly the process of Plato, who found the immutable in the variable, and the infinite in the finite. And, in fact, Plato says the selfsame things in the Timæus. He first asserts the absolute distinction between that which becomes and that which is absolutely; that is to say, of that which passes from potentiality to act, and that which is already all act. " Let us first distinguish the being which is always and *which has not to become,* from the being which becomes and never is entirely. Now, all that which becomes, necessarily becomes under the influence of a cause. For it is impossible for any being to become without an author." In other words, there is no effect without a cause. This is exactly Aristotle's major: *Nothing passes from potentiality to act, save through a cause already in act.* And it is in this truth that Plato, like Descartes, sees the proof of the existence of God: "*We have said that*

*all which becomes, must needs have an author who is the cause
of its becoming.* But to find and know this author and this
father of all, is a grand work."[1]

Here then, in regard to this fundamental starting-point
and in regard to the process which leads to God, we trace
Descartes back to Plato, and, what we did not expect, to
Aristotle. This is because the human mind is one, and truth
is one. By God's goodness, man stands face to face with
truth, and the light shines for every man coming into this
world. All those who see, see the same things, and all that a
man has seen is true. So Saint Thomas and Saint Augustine
alike affirm. Thus, at bottom, all geniuses of the first order
agree; and there is one human universal philosophy, which,
from this fact, has been accepted, elevated, consecrated and
crowned by Christian theology. There are none to contradict
this whole, divine and human, save the never-ending sect of
error, which, by a satanic method, succeeds in breaking away
from reason and turning away its head, that it may not see.

Our second remark in regard to Aristotle's Theodicy relates
to its result.

It is clear that this result is that of Plato, that of all wise
men, of all men subject to common-sense and followers
of reason. Aristotle — we have cited all the texts — admits of a God distinct from the world and present in the
world, all natures in which he pervades and penetrates, — a
living, omnipotent God, the first cause, efficient cause, final
cause; motionless motor, only being wholly in act, that is to
say the only being perfectly immutable, a perfect and eternal
living being; a God who is sovereign goodness and supreme
good; a God infinitely intelligent, since he is identical with
the intelligible itself, and since his act, his life, consists in
the very possession of that intelligible which is identical with
him; a God invisible in himself, visible in his works; a

[1] Timæus, p. 28.

God governing all by his action and by his Providence, as a leader governs an army; a just God, who punishes free man, the violator of his unchanging law, and rewards by happiness, now and in the future, those who cling fast to justice.

We see that this is Plato, it is tradition, it is common-sense, it is universal wisdom.

Aristotle here fully confirms Plato's saying: "All wise men have but a single voice."

It is therefore certain, — let us repeat it, and insist upon this point,— it is certain that there are universal truths in regard to which all philosophers agree, if by philosophers we mean sages, and not sophists. There is a universal philosophy, a natural and common wisdom, which is the same in all men amenable to the light of reason. All thinkers of the first rank plainly come under this head. The sophists are outside this guild. They are the heretics of reason, the sectarians of humanity. As there are in the Catholic Church articles of faith, there are in mankind articles of never-ending reason. And this universal wisdom is only denied by the false and vain minds whose pride prevents them from obeying the dictates of common-sense, and whose intellectual weakness at the same time forbids them from rising to the luminous society of great minds, — souls separated who do not live by the heart, in the fruitful warmth of the common sun, and who can no longer attain, in spirit, to the contemplation of the light which would lead back their hearts to the true source of life. These sad souls, doubly sectarian, doubly separated[1] from the universal faith and the common reason, unfortunately exist in vast numbers in this age. And the leaders of this perversion possess an audacity which the sophists never had, — they aspire to a radical change of the human conscience and the human mind and the government of the world. They undertake, and they avow it, to alter

---

[1] Eradicatæ, bis mortuæ (Epist. cath. B. Judæ, 12).

universal logic and the meaning of human language. But they will not succeed. They will, on the contrary, serve; and we intend, for our part, to use them for this purpose: they will serve clearly to separate the light from the darkness, by themselves becoming darkness, and to make the truth more apparent by proving it through their own absurdity.

If we divide into two classes the men who have thought or pretended to think ; if we call the one philosophers or sages, the others sophists, — Aristotle, as we see, has nothing in common with the sophists of any age. He is a philoso-pher properly so called, and one of the seven or eight ge-niuses of the first order. Let us again remark that he has nothing in common with that kind of mind now known as rationalists, who are the minds hesitating between sophistry and philosophy, — always much nearer to the one than to the other ; minds less keen for results than for mere proofs ; bold and prejudiced minds, which create for themselves ex-clusive methods, and reject all that does not come within the compass of these methods ; who abuse individual reason by excluding in advance all which it has not built up in each of them ; who shut it out alike from all faith and all tradi-tion and the thought of other minds, — alike from feeling, from the heart, and from knowledge of visible nature ; who, besides, mutilate reason itself, and always take its clear side and remove its warm side, the source of all light; ignoring what Seneca said: "Reason is not made up of evidence alone ; its best and greatest side is hidden and obscure."

Aristotle, through his profound good sense, the precision of his results, his respect for the thought of others and for healthy antiquity, through his great knowledge of natural facts, his intellectual universality, has nothing in common with these unfortunate and sterile eccentrics.

The foregoing is enough, we hope, to justify the admiration of the great Catholic scholars of the Middle Ages for Aristotle. Aristotle has too long been rejected by Bacon, Descartes, and above all, by Protestantism. If classical studies ever revive among us, Aristotle will resume his proper place. That vigorous genius may yet aid us to cast aside those flabby and facile habits of thought which weaken the mind, and to return to strong certainties, — to recover that strength of reason which now eludes us, and with humble and firm penetration to subject this reason to the supernatural light of divine contemplation, so that we may "rise above man and his mortal feelings to live on a higher plane than man, — the life of the superior principle which lives within us."

CHAPTER IV.

Quidquid a Platone dicitur, vivit in Augustino.

I.

WE now pass from the ancients to the moderns; from Greek philosophers to Christian sages regarded as philosophers; from Aristotle and Plato to Saint Augustine, Saint Thomas Aquinas, and others. We shall see at the first glance that Saint Augustine clings to the school of Plato, and Saint Thomas to that of Aristotle. Neither of them tries to disguise it.

I do not know why Christians are sometimes accused of abjuring philosophy, of killing reason by faith. We shall now find occasion to throw some light on this point.

Thomassin states — it is an historic fact — that Christian scholars, from the twelfth to the seventeenth century exclusively, formed themselves, as philosophers, in the school of Aristotle; whereas the Fathers of the first centuries were formed in Plato's school.

This being an undoubted fact, it follows that the Christian doctors of no century ever abjured philosophy.

And in fact, all teach that philosophy and theology, properly so called, are two not separate, but distinct things, that there is a divine knowledge and a human knowledge, which are wholly distinct, and that true Christian knowledge lies in the union of the two, without ever destroying the one by the other. Saint Thomas asserts, and faith teaches us, " that in Jesus Christ divine knowledge does not destroy human knowledge, but, on the contrary, renders it more luminous." Such is also, in our opinion, the relation between these two kinds of knowledge.

Human knowledge—that is, philosophy—from the orthodox point of view, therefore, exists, and will always exist; just as there will always be a human mind different from the mind of God.

This is why Christians, when the Gospel light illumined the world, did not have to change the elements of genuine philosophy then extant. They had merely to accept them, just as they could not otherwise than admit geometry. They received Plato and Aristotle, in the bulk of their works, as they accepted Euclid.

Certainly they developed philosophy, and will develop it still farther : they have purged it of many errors, but they have never changed its principles or its bases. We shall invent no other rules for syllogism than those given us by Aristotle; and we shall discover no other process of reasoning than the two processes represented by Aristotle and Plato. Thus there is a philosophy properly so called, distinct from revelation.

The prejudice prevailing among many men of the world, I know, is that philosophy does not exist. This is an error due to the same ignorance which leads so many others to believe that divine revelation does not exist. There is a philosophy. What is it? we are asked. We answer that it is the philosophy of Socrates, of Plato, of Aristotle, of Saint Augustine, of Saint Thomas Aquinas, of Descartes, of Bossuet, of Leibnitz, and of all geniuses of the first order, without a single exception.

I do not say that philosophy has yet attained to its fullest strength, or even that all its organs are perfectly developed; I do not say that it is yet at every point fully aware of its method; above, I do not say that it has a very great number of followers: but I say that it has existed in the human race for long centuries back, and independently of Christian revelation.

Hear Saint Augustine on this head. " As for what concerns speculative philosophy," he says, "and moral philosophy as well, there is no lack of keen and clever minds to show us that Aristotle and Plato agree, although the inattentive and incapable suppose them to be very wide apart; so that in my opinion, the struggle and strife of thought, with the help of centuries, have at last produced a genuine philosophy (*una verissimœ philosophiœ disciplina*)." Only, as Saint Augustine instantly adds, this philosophy, even begotten by human reason, could not become popular save through the incarnate Word, — which is profoundly true.

Saint Augustine believes so fully that philosophy exists in the presence of revelation that he goes on to say: "And, to tell you my entire thought, know that whatever may be this human wisdom, I do not believe I yet possess it as an entirety. I am now thirty-three years old; but that is no reason to despair of attaining it. I despise all else, — all that men deem advantages, — and I devote my life to seeking after it. . . . I have, on the one hand, Christ's authority, from which nothing shall part me; . . . but for that which the effort of my reason can attain, I am decided to possess the truth, not only through faith, but also through intelligence; and in this connection I believe I find in Plato doctrines which agree with our dogmas." So speaks the humility of genius and sanctity.

And it is well to observe that these texts, according to Thomassin, who quotes them, and according to the Benedictines, are not those to which Augustine refers in his Retractations, when he believed that he had given too much praise to Plato and the Platonists.

7

These texts, therefore, are decisive. The saint in the school of Christ reads Plato. And why? To possess, if he may, the human mind in its entirety, — all reason, all human reason, — to the end that he may bring back to God the whole man, and subject all to Jesus Christ.

II.

Let us now recall the way in which Plato distinguishes two degrees in the advance of the human mind towards intelligible light.

There are in the world of intelligence these two degrees, — vision of shadows, and vision of eternal realities; in other words, there is vision of God himself, — God, who is the sovereign Good, — and vision of divine phantoms, shadows of that which is. What are these divine phantoms, these eternal shadows of that which is eternally? They are the essential truths, the laws and axioms, the unchanging rules or definitions, of geometry, logic, and morals. This is the first degree of intellectual vision lifted above the senses; and from this vision of unchanging shadows, the soul infers the existence of a sun capable of producing these shadows. This is the work of Platonism, but nothing more. It has recognized by a legitimate process the existence of the sun; it has surmised its beauty, its benefits. Has it seen the sun itself? We say, No.

To see God! This is the business of Christianity. "No man has ever seen God," says the gospel. It is the incarnate Word that brings to man the possibility of the vision of God himself, — the direct and immediate vision. Through the incarnate Word we shall cease to guess at the sun from the shadow, we shall see the sun itself.

In our present state, our physical eye is not framed to look upon the visible sun, but only to behold the world in the light of that sun. The eye is not made for the source of light, but only for the objects which the rays from that source strike. This fact is full of deep meaning. It is the same with our soul. In the natural state of man, in that state with which we are familiar, our soul is incapable of seeing God himself; but it is made for the light which he diffuses, and which he sheds upon that soul and upon all objects. To see God himself requires a modification of human nature, a conversion, a transformation; or, rather, a new birth, which man cannot by his own efforts attain, and which God alone, who created him, can give him. After this supernatural new birth, the soul can and should see God. And its first look at God is faith, — faith, which is dim at first, like the first inkling of a great light, but which becomes clear vision in proportion to the growth of our soul. "Faith, that attempt at vision," says Bossuet; "Faith, that dawning vision," says Saint Thomas Aquinas.

This established, we can grasp the difference between Plato and Saint Augustine, and understand why we took as heading to this sketch, the words: "All that Plato says, *lives* in Augustine."

The first difference between Plato and Augustine is, that Augustine is, as it were, the type by which Plato is judged. Every one judges in this way, — theologians, philosophers, Christians, and others. We prune away in Plato, as accidental excrescences, all that does not fit this type; we praise and admire all that reminds us of it. We strive to discover, in the great philosopher, beams of that light which bathes us in the great saint. The fact is that the Theodicy of Christian philosophers, the fruit of human reason, sustained and directed in its search after God by that great and new divine postulate which is faith, is no longer, like the ancient Theodicy, a dawn mingled with shadows and illusions, seen by scarce one or two men who watch upon the mountains; it is broad day, visible to the whole world.

We have pointed out the method and results of Plato's Theodicy. Is it necessary to say that in Saint Augustine, considered solely as a philosopher, the results as to God are perfect, exact, absolute, unmixed with error, doubt, or hesitation?

Why? Because Saint Augustine did, as a moral and intellectual means of rising to God, precisely what Plato directs: he purified himself, kept himself holy, detached himself from earth, wrested from his soul those *nails* to which Plato refers, by which pleasure holds us ·fast; he despised honors, riches, sensual delights; he turned *his whole soul* to God, lived in his love and contemplation: antique and simple truths which the light of reason teaches to those who think, but between seeing and practising which there is a gulf. It is easy for me to say that I ought to keep myself holy; but it is less easy to do it, and to cross the gulf. Now, the gulf was crossed by Plato and by Augustine. When we measure the progress of "that universal man" of whom Pascal speaks, the progress of the human mind compared in these two brother geniuses, we seem to see but a single man, — first in his early and poetic youth, then in the strength of maturity. In his youth, when he was Plato, he loved virtue and truth; he said to himself, " I will be good, and I will possess knowledge; I will know the mysteries of this beautiful world; I will become acquainted with him who is its Father and author ; " and he foresaw and pursued this ideal in his rich imagination: and now, after cruel struggles, after a whole lifetime of labor and courage; after many prayers, tears, and victories; after learning by experience the source of strength ; after a new alliance with God, with God no longer dreamed of as a poetic spectacle, but possessed as the substance of life, — this man, at last triumphant, and upheld by the Father in whom he trusted, this man knows the truth; he is good, and carries in his soul, matured by the sun of

God, the forces and virtues of the fruits whereof his youth bore the flowers.

Such are Plato and Augustine, if we compare the results.

As for the theory of the method, the difference cannot be the same. Plato is particularly interested in the method, Augustine in the results. Nevertheless the general light which the saint possesses in an incomparably greater degree than the Greek philosopher, gives the saint a much clearer knowledge of the soul, and one especially more experimental; whence necessarily result new and vivid lights upon the procedure of the soul in its flight towards God.

Thus, Plato affirms that the mainspring of the dialectic or of the passage of the soul to God is love. Saint Augustine, who possesses that love in the highest degree, knows this far better than Plato, and expresses it better. Plato speaks of the divine sense, or at least of that divine part of the soul where God touches it, binds it to himself. Saint Augustine knows this sense of God by experience; in him the inner senses are all developed; he knows that inward touch of God, those inward perfumes, those savors of the soul, and those visions, those divine voices which spoke to him with far greater clearness than to Socrates, and which did not merely bid him abstain, but act, as when he heard the words, *Tolle, lege.*

Better than Plato he knew the vanity of all transitory things, of all that is born and dies, and he is still less a prey to them, whether in practice or in speculation. And yet he is never excessive: he does not, like Plato, call them *appearances which do not exist;* he calls them *the things which are less*, which, *compared to God, do not exist*, which is the most exact and precise truth. He knows their use and their relation to God better than Plato; better than Plato he knows how they proceed from God, how they belong to God, how we may see God in them.

Better than Plato, he sees the emptiness of those *eternal*

shadows, those *divine phantoms*, those cold, geometrical, logical, or other truths, which we recognize in ourselves by the
light of God. Better than he, he understands that they are
not God, but his shadow seen in the mirror of the soul;
more than he, he seeks and longs for the sun capable of
casting those shadows.

Another high advantage of Saint Augustine over Plato,
is that he clearly explains that the fulcrum of the process
which leads to God is not only the material world, but also
and more especially the inward world which is our soul; he
is intimately acquainted with the soul, and knows better than
Plato how it differs from and how it resembles God. The
ancients, Plato himself, knew their souls but slightly, through
experience. Upon this head, Christians are incomparable;
the saints and mystics are the only men who possess true
knowledge of the soul.

Lastly, it is very plain that Plato, who, according to our
views and those of most of the Fathers, does not posit ideas
elsewhere than in God, nevertheless failed to develop this
point in a thoroughly lucid way, or to assert this truth so
exactly and so often as Saint Augustine. It seems as if
Plato, too clear-sighted to posit his eternal ideas elsewhere
than in God, dared not explain that they are in God, and
how they are there. Augustine is exact and complete upon
this head.

Shall we say, on the other hand, that Saint Augustine has
borrowed much from Plato? It is certain that he did: he
never denies the fact. Only, it is with Saint Augustine in
regard to Plato as it is with Descartes in regard to Saint Augustine. Fénelon very fitly remarks that all of Descartes may
be found in Saint Augustine. Undoubtedly; but Descartes,
when meditating, studied Saint Augustine little or not at
all: he studied reason. I certainly do not say that all Saint
Augustine is contained in Plato; I say that Saint Augustine,

with greater knowledge of the past than Descartes, often saw things both in Plato and in reason.   We should merely conclude from these coincidences that these three master minds, not to mention others, saw, each for himself, the same light, and bore the same witness to it.

This settled, we will first follow, in Saint Augustine the method in action.

III.

Of all that Plato says on this subject, Saint Augustine possesses and gives us, if we may so express it, the experimental intuition.   Whatever is *said* by Plato, *lives* in Augustine.

Now, what did Plato say?   Saint Augustine himself sums it up as follows : —

"If Plato lived, and if he condescended to answer my questions; if he taught me that it is not the physical eye, but the pure mind that sees truth; that every soul, which allies itself to truth, becomes happy and perfect; that the obstacle to this good is a life subject to passions, the vision of the illusory images of the world of sense, the source of so many errors and idle opinions; that the soul must be healed before it can learn to see the unchanging form of things, and eternal beauty, always and at all points the same ; that beauty which space does not disperse, which time does not alter in its motionless unity, — beauty whose existence is unknown to men, while it exists supremely and all else is born and dies, is fluid and slips away; if he told me that all these things, in so far as they exist, are the works of the everlasting God, effected in this truth: works amidst which the rational soul can alone contemplate the eternity of God, be endowed and imbued by it, and thus merit that eternity itself; that held back by all which becomes and which passes, wounded by grief or by love, given over to sensuality and the gross habits of this life, lulled to sleep by its images and its dreams, that soul heeds not when it is told that there exists a Being visible without the physical eye, intelligible without images, and seen by the mind alone : if Plato taught me these things." [1]

This is what Saint Augustine reads in Plato.

Now, while in regard to all these questions Plato gives an outline of truth, Saint Augustine always shows it to us in action; he does not give a didactic description of his process, he relates his life. We see the living intelligence and light in his ardent soul, and we cannot but apply to him his own words when, speaking of this contemplation of the light, he says : "These things have been foretold in the proper measure by those great and matchless souls who have seen them, — who, as we believe, still see them."

Thus Plato teaches us that to attain to the sight of God, we must first heal our soul, purify it, free it from transitory things; that then it may soar to the contemplation of everlasting beauty, — that motionless unity which space does not disperse or time alter. This implies the whole theoretical and practical Theodicy. What will Saint Augustine tell us of this whole ?

In the first place, in regard to the need for purifying and healing the soul, while Plato, from this point of view, rebukes with the strongest irony the gross sensuality of men plunged in foul pleasures, Saint Augustine does more : he says little of the last degrees of the impure, — he looks into his own soul, and sees that soul, already luminous and living, still covered with wounds, almost dying, exhausted, divided, dispersed. In his actual, experimental intuition of the soul, he sounds it and penetrates it in every part; he sees in it all that prevents it from being filled with God, from knowing him, from being one with and absorbed in him ; and his words upon this point have a tone of direct experience which no art could ever imitate.

[1] De vera Relig., chap. iii. 3.

He sees in the soul what he calls the tumor of pride, — a tumor which puffs it up, which makes it empty, forces it to a lesser being, diffuses it abroad, and, as it were, causes it to cast outside itself its central life, which is God himself. "The soul," he says, "does not exist of itself, since it is changeable, and since there is in it a want of being; the soul, therefore, is nothing in itself, but all of being which it possesses is given it by God; united to God through its dependent state, the vital essence of its soul and conscience is the very presence of God. This is its secret treasure. What, then, does it mean in being puffed up with pride? It means to reach out after external things, to make the interior empty and idle, to be ever less and less. But to reach after external things is nothing else than casting forth its own entrails, — that is to say, removing God from itself, not by space, but by mind and affection." [1]

Saint Augustine sees that the soul becomes inwardly exhausted when it scatters its forces and wastes them upon externals; that it forsakes unity, stability, fulness of life; that it sinks into a state of dispersion, and into the flood of created beings which pass away and flow towards death, and which bear it away as they flow; he sees that the soul should struggle to recover, reascend, and return to life and rest: what that power is which incessantly recalls it and can heal it. Saint Augustine's vision of the soul, and its false life, compared to true life, is a translucid intuition: his description of it is most striking. No man ever described as he has done our failings and our fickleness, our longing for the immutable and our need of healing. Here is a fine example of this description: —

"God of power, comfort us, show us thy face, and save us. For, be the object what it may which turns my soul away from thee, it is riveted to some sorrow; it may cling to all beauties

[1] De Musica, lib. vi. cap. xii. 40.

outside itself, outside thee, — beauties which yet cannot exist save through thee. These beauties are born and die; they begin, they increase, they grow until they reach their highest point; that attained, they wither and fall. Everything tends downward again, and decays. When they spring up, they strive to be; and the more they labor to be, the more they hasten not to be. Such is their limitation. Thou hast given them these bounds, O Lord; they are the successive phases of things which are never complete in every part at any one time: but by their birth and death they make up that universe of which they are the parts. They are like the words of a speech, which is entire and finished when each word, having uttered all its syllables, retires, that another word may take its place.

"Let my soul therefore praise thee in these beauties, O God, Creator of all; but let it never be fastened unto these things with the glue of love and the senses of the body! For they continue to pass away, and cease to exist, and they rend my soul as they go; and as for my soul, it would fain exist, it would fain linger with that which it loves. But how can we linger with that which is not lasting, with that which is fugitive; how can we follow these things with the senses of the flesh; how can we ever grasp them as a whole when they pass away? The sense of the flesh is slow and weak, and, in its turn, it has limits. It sufficeth unto its end, but it sufficeth not to stay things running their course from their appointed starting-place to their end, to grasp at once the origin and consummation. Thy divine Word alone, which creates them, saith unto them, 'Depart and return.' Then be no longer foolish, O my soul; permit not this tumult to close the ear of thine heart. Hearken: the Word to thee also cries, Return to the place of everlasting rest, where love is not forsaken, if itself forsaketh not. Do I ever depart? saith the Word of God. Fix thy dwelling in him, O my soul! Wearied at last of illusions, restore to him what came to thee from him. Restore to Truth what Truth hath given thee, and thou shalt nevermore lose aught; what was decayed in thee shall bloom again, what languished shall be healed, what was scattered and dispersed shall be reformed and renewed. Things shall no longer bear thee away in their course, but shall stand fast with thee in the steadfast and abiding God."[1]

[1] Confess., lib. iv. cap. x. 15.

Here we have direct intuition to a degree never possessed by Plato. It is thus that Saint Augustine saw the soul, its wounds, its stigmas, its dispersedness, its illusions, its vain and painful struggle to seize and fix that which is fugitive, its mistaken and impotent sensualities, its raptures over that which vanishes; and yet in the midst, God, ever motionless and present, who recalls it, who receives it, who heals it, who restores all to it. It is thus that Saint Augustine sees and touches both the soul which would fain be purified, and the power that purifies it. We feel that all this lives within him.

And if, again, he speaks of the efforts of the purified soul to attain to the sight of God, it is still his own life that he relates : —

"I sought and I longed to know by what model we should judge the beauty of bodies, terrestrial or celestial; by what light we should judge this changing world, and say, This should be thus, but that not ; and I found, above my soul and my thoughts, themselves variable, an unchanging light and an eternal truth. I ascended from my senses to the soul which perceives through them; I went to that inward power to which the senses refer things external, that point to which the faculties of animals reach. I went still farther, and I came to reason, the judge of what the senses give us. But my reason, seeing itself, beheld itself variable, and seeing this, rose above itself and understood itself; then, leaving behind it the torpor of habit and bewildering phantasms, to find the light by which it was illumined, it cried out without hesitation that the unchangeable was superior to the changeable; and this itself was the beginning of knowledge of the unchangeable. For if it had not known it, how should it have preferred it to the changing world; how could it have left visible certainties to attain the Being one of whose rays we cannot see without trembling? Thus I understood and saw invisible things through the things which God made; but I could not fix my gaze thereon, and falling back upon my own weakness, restored to habit, I retained of this momentary intercourse only a loving memory, a regretful longing for the odors of the celestial food." [1]

[1] Confess., lib. vii. cap. xvii. 23.

When Plato says serenely, "The wise man considers the eternal light," he says well; he knows that which should be. But when Saint Augustine speaks of that ray and the darkness which followed it, and of that living memory, and of the trace of those perfumes, it is evident that he is telling us what has happened, and that he is recounting to us his own life.

Yes, this indeed is the life, the deep and actual life of a soul that seeks God and rises to God, which feels him, which has seen him.

We must repeat it: what Plato hopes and conjectures, Saint Augustine possesses and sees. What falls from the sublime lips of the philosopher, exists and lives in the soul of the saint, and bursts forth from his heart and his mouth, more divine than that of Plato, with intonations, radiance, and ardors' which the real presence of God alone can give.

IV.

We have now seen the method as a whole in action. Let us look more in detail at the theory of the method, according to Saint Augustine.

It is not to be expected that all readers will understand Saint Augustine either in what follows or what precedes. No one who does not live his life and undergo the same experiences can understand his narratives and his descriptions of life. "Give me," he says somewhere, "a man who loves, and he will understand me." So that, unless you love as he did, you cannot understand him.

Highly cultivated literary minds can but admire him; they see that his style is always vivid and full of life; they therefore see that it possesses the characteristic of beauty. But they do not sufficiently comprehend that this beauty is only the splendor of truth, and they do not perceive the strictly philosophic basis of those beauties. As almost no one knows the chief process of reason, that by which the creature mounts to God, which is at once poetic and logical, they do not see the logical thread in all this sacred poetry, or the stern reason beneath the raptures and the prayers of the saintly soul. This we must now make clear by showing that his sublime spirit was fully conscious of its acts, philosophically familiar with their nature, their range, and their absolute certainty.

The chief difficulty in this explanation and this analysis is the abundance of noble passages, among which the mind hesitates. We will select, combining and supplementing them one with the other, two or three connected passages, in which Saint Augustine states theoretically the progress of the mind towards God, as Plato tells the story of the captives in the cave, who leave false lights behind them to gain the sun of the true world.

After an ardent invocation to God, the Father of awaking and light (*pater evigilationis et illuminationis nostræ*), and before describing the process of reason which rises to God, he speaks of reason itself, and says, —

"My reason is a movement of my soul, a power which distinguishes and unites to know; it is a guide which but too few of us use to lead us to God, or even to the soul which is within us; . . . and this because, too deeply plunged in the details of sensible phenomena, it is hard for us to return into ourselves. We only apply our reason to illusory accidents; we can neither know it in itself, or in its laws."[1]

"Thus, the soul is diffused over that which is mortal: this is the fall; to reascend is to bring reason back to itself."[2] Saint Augustine then describes the same progress of reason which Plato calls dialectic, and to which he also gives that name.[3] This progress does not consist in ceasing to see

---

[1] De Ordine, lib. ii. c. xi. 30.   [2] Ibid., n. 31.   [3] Ibid., xiii. 38.

this visible world, in suppressing it in thought; we should, on the contrary, first seek the traces of reason in the world of sense.[1] We must learn to distinguish, in all that material substances show us, the visible and the intelligible, the sign and the significance.[2]

When reason can distinguish the sign from the significance in sensation, "when it has developed itself through language, it takes itself as object, and, being itself reflected, it produces the knowledge of knowledges, which we call dialectic. It is this knowledge which teaches us to teach, and which teaches us to learn; in it reason shows itself and declares what it is, what it can, and what it desires, to do. It is a knowledge which knows itself, which can and will give knowledge."[3]

"But reason desires to rise higher yet, and to pass from study of itself to contemplation of divine things! There, that it may not fall into a vacuum, *it seeks steps*, and makes itself a regular road through its previous acquisitions. It desires to see that beauty which alone, and by a mere glance, it can attain without the physical eye. But the senses hold it back. What does it do? *It half turns its gaze* towards those same sensible objects which, crying to us that they are the truth, importune us with their tumult when we would fain rise higher."[4]

Saint Augustine holds this to be an important point in the theory of the method; to him the visible world is a step, a point of support, by which to rise higher. He often recurs to this elsewhere: "I will mount higher than this very power which is in me, and will regard it as *a step* to rise to him who made me."[5] "Let us see how far reason can go *in its ascent from the visible to the invisible, from the transitory to the eternal.* I will not gaze in vain at all the beauty of the sky, the regular course of the stars. . . . I will not gaze

[1] De Ordine, lib. ii. c. xi. 33.   [2] Ibid., 34.   [3] Ibid., xiii. 38.
[4] Ibid., xiv. n. 39.   [5] Confess., lib. x. cap. viii. 12.

at them in idle curiosity, but will make use of them as *steps* to raise myself to the immutable and immortal." [1]

The way to rise to God, therefore, does not consist in destroying in one's self the images of this world, but rather in making of them steps (*gradus ad immortalia faciendus*); we should not consider them exclusively, we should consider them soberly (*in eos ipsos paululum aciem torsit*). We should consider them sufficiently to compare them, but not so much as to lose sight of the other term of the comparison. This feature of the method distinguishes healthy philosophy from the mystic sophism which destroys images.

"But in its marvellous power of discernment, reason instantly understands all the difference that lies between a sensation itself and that which it signifies." [2] It speedily recognizes that it is their laws which constitute the order, value, light, and beauty of phenomena. But what are these laws?

What are laws? Modern science knows. Saint Augustine divined: these laws are geometrical forms, — numbers. "Reason," he says, "having reached this point, understands that it is numbers that rule all the visible world." (*Intelligebat regnare numeros.*) [3]

And what are these forms and these numbers themselves? They are eternal, consequently divine, truths (*reperiebat divinos et sempiternos*); [4] they are ideas perceived by reason. Now, what reason sees always exists, and is immortal; such are numbers (*Illud quod mens videt semper est præsens et immortale approbatur; cujus generis numeri apparebant*). [5] Reason here makes an essential distinction between the numbers and the geometrical figures which the intelligence includes, and those shown to it by the eyes. Hence it

---

[1] De ver. Relig., xxix. 52.
[2] De Ordine, lib. ii. cap. xiv. 39.
[3] Ibid.
[4] Ibid., 41.
[5] Ibid., lib. iii. cap. xiv. 41.

creates geometry; it applies geometry to the forms and movements of the stars; it creates astronomy, — astronomy, that grand and potent spectacle for religious souls, that painful labor for curious minds (*magnum religiosis argumentum, tormentumque curiosis*). [1]

Thus reason sees perfectly that these forms and these geometric laws, such as it conceives them in itself, are absolutely true; but it recognizes at the same time that it perceives in things only the shadow and vestige of truth.[2]

To bear within one's self eternal ideas of which all this visible world possesses merely the shadows, — what a marvel is this! There is, then, within us something eternal; my mind, then, is immortal! Here then, at least, I am very close to what I sought. My reason, in which I perceived these divine and eternal numbers, must itself be the same as that which I see in it. Must it not itself be that primitive number which reckons the others? Whether it be so or not, it is at least certain that it possesses in itself the object of its search (*aut si id non esset, ibi tamen eum esse quo pervenire satageret*). It therefore grasps at last that Proteus who shall reveal to it the truth; it grasps him in its hands, and it holds him with all its might.[3]

It is this primitive number which counts all the rest; this single number which we must capture and never again let it escape us.[4] For we must know what unity is, and of what it is capable. Add to this the dialectic, and we shall quickly pass from the mathematic and abstract unity of sensible postulates to the sovereign unity which exists in the universe. We pass from these abstract sciences to Philosophy, and there too we find nought save unity; but a different unity, deep and divine in a far different way; and we learn at last to distinguish the two worlds, and the Father of both.

---

[1] De Ordine, lib. iii. cap. xiv. 41.
[2] Ibid. xv. 42.
[3] Ibid. 43.
[4] Ibid.

V.

Let us explain all this still further.

The soul which seeks wisdom, having reached that point, after first examining and observing itself, and having recognized that reason is itself, or is its own (*aut seipsum aut suam esse rationem*), that the numbers of reason are its beauty and its power, and that reason is itself number,— the soul goes on and says : " By this movement and this inward and secret power which is called reason, I distinguish and reunite in order to know. But why distinguish ? To judge of that which seems one, and yet is not,— or at least, that which is less of a unit than it seems. And why reunite, save to recompose unity ? Thus, whether I divide or reunite, it is unity which I love and desire. When I divide, it is that I may have pure unity ; and when I reunite, it is to have it total." [1]

Everything tends towards unity,— my reason, all nature, society, love, and friendship.[2]

What, then, is this unity ? What I seek, what I desire to know, is God. Can this logical, mathematical unity, the laws, forms, numbers, absolute, essential, eternal verities that follow from it, be God ? They give me a perfect assurance : then must not knowledge of them be knowledge of God ? [3]

Let us now refer to Plato. These truths, he says, are not God himself, nor the end of the process of reason (τέλος τῆς πορείας), but they are divine phantoms, shadows of that which is (φαντάσματα θεῖα καὶ σκιὰς τῶν ὄντων).

No, says Saint Augustine, this order of truths is neither God nor knowledge of God ; " If they were knowledge of

---

[1] De Ordine, lib. iii. cap. xv. 48.   [3] Soliloq., lib. i. cap. v. 11.
[2] Ibid.

God, in knowing them I should have the same rapture that I should have in seeing God.[1] I am forced to confess that there is all the difference of the heaven from the earth between the intelligible majesty of God and the images otherwise true and certain, which such knowledge gives us." [2]

And in fact, "God is intelligible; these logical spectacles are also intelligible: but what a difference! [3] The earth also is visible, even as light is visible; but the earth, if there were no light, could not be seen. Just as all these scientific truths, which in the eyes of those who understand them are absolutely certain, are only intelligible because they too are illumined by another sun which is theirs."

This is an important point, and it is clear. We have here the fundamental distinction between the two degrees of the intelligible world,—a distinction which many modern thinkers do not suspect, and whose absence casts them into the strangest embarrassment.

"Now," adds Saint Augustine, "reason, which cries aloud within thee, promises to show God to thy mind as the sun shows itself to thine eyes. Our mind also has eyes, and our soul has senses: and all assured truths may be compared to earthly objects upon which the sun shines and makes them visible, by shedding its light upon them: but here, the sun is God: and I, reason, am to the mind what sight itself is to the eyes." [4]

Let us stop a moment, and note that thus far the theory of the method of the progress of reason ascending to God is the same in Plato and in Saint Augustine. It is scarcely possible that there are no direct reminiscences of Plato here; and yet it is evident that Saint Augustine is profoundly original elsewhere; it is the same truth, seen and described by two minds of the first order, the second of which was

---

[1] Soliloq., lib. i. cap. v. 1.
[2] Ibid.
[3] Ibid., viii. 15.
[4] Ibid., vi. 12.

necessarily familiar with the first. But they are really two witnesses in favor of the true method.

Only, we think we may assert that Saint Augustine is more exact and more precise than Plato. Plato is sometimes vague in his description of the starting-point of dialectic reason. What he calls the starting-point (ὑπόθεσις), or the fulcrum of thought (ἐπιβάσεις καὶ ὁρμάς), by which it rises to the principle which the starting-point does not include (ἐπ' ἀρχὴν ἀνυπόθετον ἐξ ὑποθέσεως ἰοῦσα), is not always clearly the visible world to him. Neither do we see that it is the soul itself. Often, on the contrary, he seems to give us to understand, he even states, that we should solely and simply turn away from the earth to gaze only at the sun. Saint Augustine, on the contrary, is entirely explicit and exact in regard to this; he says that reason, wishing to attain to the contemplation of divine things, should, lest it fall into a void (*ne de alto caderet*), have points of support, stepping-stones (*quæsivit gradus*), an assured way through its previous acquisitions. And he declares that these points of support are given us by our sight of the world; and what no one of whom I know, but Saint Augustine, has said fitly, he asserts that we should consider them soberly, with a free and impartial eye (*aciem parce detorsit*), so that we do not linger over them, or see them only, but compare them with the world after which they are patterned: that we may grasp both their likeness and their difference in regard to the divine world, of which the visible world is the image.

It is the very uncertainty of the Platonic method upon this subject, which permits Aristotle to attack it as leading to nothing real, and proceeding only to abstractions, to the abstract unity of empty being, while *our metaphysics*, says Aristotle, that is to say, our method, *which starts from material things to raise us to that which is above*, gives us, outside and above nature, a real essence, neither abstract nor

empty. In our opinion, Aristotle errs in condemning Plato
here; but it is true that Plato was not sufficiently explicit
on this head. Saint Augustine explains it.

But this is just where Saint Augustine was incomparably
superior to Plato in analysis, precision, philosophic and scientific development. It is a question of what Plato calls *the
divine in the soul*, the familiar spirit which God gives to each
of us, and which is the mainspring of the dialectic process.

We shall understand this superiority as we go on with the
guide-book of reason given us by Saint Augustine.

VI.

Let us suppose that the reason, starting with the visible
world, has reached that degree of the intelligible world where
we find the geometric, logical, essential, absolute, eternal
truths, which are not God, but which are intelligible only
through his light. Reason understands it, understands that
these divine phantoms, these eternal shadows, are the shadow
of the divine sun : it longs to see this sun.

· Now, what, in Plato's opinion, urges reason to seek this
sun ? It is the divine within us, it is that divine spirit, that
divine part of our soul, that point and very root of the soul
($\dot{\rho}i\zeta av$), where God touches and holds us fast to him, — a sacred gift which some exercise and develop, and which leads
them to the contemplation of God, but which others stifle by
the lusts of the flesh and by pride.

Saint Augustine says the same things, but with what
wealth and with what clear-sighted precision !

To him there is God, there is the soul. God is in the soul,
the soul feels him.

Such is the pure and simple truth which explains everything.

Saint Augustine sees not only, like Plato, *the soul joined to
God by its root*, he sees a yet more intimate relation be-

tween God and the soul. God is at the centre of the heart (*intimus cordi*); he is the secret good of the soul (*hoc bonum habet intimum*);[1] God gives it life as if he were its vital essence (*ipsius Dei præsentia vegetatur*).[2] The rational soul only lives, is enlightened and happy only through the very substance of God (*animam humanam et mentem rationalem vegetari, non beatificari, non illuminari, nisi ab ipsa substantia Dei*).[3] The soul should be perpetually moulded and perfected by him, attaching itself to him (*semper ab illo fieri semperque perfici debemus inhærentes ei*).[4] For the soul to withdraw from God, is like casting forth one's very entrails (*intima projicere id est longe a se facere Deum*);[5] it is to become empty and vain, and to be less and less (*inanescere minus minusque esse*).[6]

Such is the secret and necessary contact of God with the soul. But is our soul conscious of it? Does it feel and see it? In other words, has it *the divine sense?* Yes; although withdrawn from God by the affections, it still feels the charm of the supreme Good, by some hidden remembrance (*per quamdam occultam memoriam quæ in longinqua progressam non deseruit*);[7] there is also a secret trace of the supreme unity which exists within us and disturbs us (*vestigium secretissimæ unitatis, ex qua eram, curæ habebam*).[8] Although exiled, we are not cut off from the unchangeable source (*nec tamen inde præcisi atque abrupti sumus*).[9] This is why, although in the midst of time, we do not cease to seek eternity (*ut non etiam in istis mutabilibus et temporalibus æternitatem quæreremus*).[10] Whence, unless we depended on heaven, we should not here seek these things (*unde nisi penderemus hic ea non quæreremus*).[11] All seek here below: all therefore

---

[1] De Musica, lib. vi. cap. xiii. 40.
[2] Ibid.
[3] In Joan. Tract., xxiii. 5.
[4] Ibid.
[5] De Musica, lib. vi. cap. xii. 40.
[6] Ibid.
[7] De Trinit., x. iii. 315.
[8] Confess., lib. i. cap. xx. 31.
[9] De Trinit., iv. i. 2.
[10] Ibid.
[11] Ibid.

have this sort of knowledge and of reminiscence of God (*nec amarent nisi esset aliqua notitia ejus in memoria eorum*).[1] It is a sort of idea of the Supreme God through impression (*impressa notio ipsius Boni*);[2] it is a sort of inner sense (*interior nescio quæ conscientia*).[3]

The soul exists, because God exists, has created it, preserves and sustains it. Because God touches the soul and the soul feels it, by this very thing the soul lives, it knows, and it desires, and it. is perpetually disturbed by the attraction of the sovereign Good and sovereign Truth. It bears within it absolute Being, — Truth itself, Good itself; and it necessarily feels something of this. This is what Plato calls *reminiscence*. Saint Augustine also uses this word, but understands it differently; to him this memory of God is a sort of consciousness of God, a sense of God, which comes from the presence of God. Saint Augustine thus unveils the most sublime of truths, which even Plato dared not believe, because it was as yet too great for his sublime mind.

The soul, therefore, feels God. It feels him when any object whatsoever arouses it. For, everything being an image of God, everything arouses some sense of the model. But this awakened sense instantly shows us wherein everything lacks, wherein it resembles, wherein it differs; and the soul judges of the infinite difference between the imperfect and variable image and the immutable perfection of the model. It judges created beings, "seeing in all visible beauty wherein it copies from God, and wherein it cannot copy him." [4]

At least, such is the duty and the power of the soul. Now, in reality, what does it do? Do we all see God in his creatures? Assuredly not; but why not?

"Why does not this visible beauty speak alike to all?"[5]

[1] Confess., x. 22.
[2] De Trinit., vii.
[3] Lib. de util. cred., cap. xvi.
[4] De vera Relig., xxxii. 40.
[5] Ibid., xxxiv. 64.

" Animals see it, but they cannot question it, because they have no judgment: with them reason is not the judge of the senses."[1]

" But men can question it, to the end that they may see and understand the invisible God through his visible work. Instead of that, they are made subject to this world through love of it; and having subjected themselves, they can no longer question it. The world, answers only those who judge it. It is understood only by those who compare its voice, received from without, with the truth which they bear within them." Such are the purified souls, which, never having yielded to the visible world through love, regard it with an impartial eye, master it, and judge it.

These souls, thus taking the earth as their footstool, rise higher: again becoming free, they reascend to themselves, they return towards reason (*regressus in rationem*). Restored to themselves, and free from the abuses of the outward senses, they recover the inward sense, the divine sense (*sensus animæ*); they recognize their own imperfection and variability more and more distinctly as the divine sense grows in vigor. Without yet knowing God, they fully understand that they perceive nothing, either world or soul, which can be compared to him (*qui nondum Deum nosti, unde nosti nihil te nosse Deo simile*).[2]

Repossessed of its reason, the soul is not slow to judge that the light which illumines that reason, and in which it sees all that is within it, is not itself (*spectamina illa non posse intelligi, nisi ab alio quasi suo sole illustrentur*).

The soul therefore seeks the source of that light in which it sees all these shadows. But here Plato and all philosophy stop. Those of Plato's followers who, on reaching this point, desire to go farther through philosophy, and to contemplate the source itself of light, — these, according to Saint

[1] Confess., i. 295.   [2] Soliloq., lib. i. cap. ii. 7.

Augustine, have taken the wrong road; they are following a path which looks true, but is not so.[1]

Beyond comes a wholly different order of things, — another life, another world. This is what Christianity calls the supernatural world. We cannot penetrate it by the aid of philosophy alone.[2] We can enter only through an actual new birth, — a radical cure, which allows the soul to return wholly and entirely to the source of light, and no longer exclusively attend to the objects which are revealed by that light. And this is the new birth which follows that death of which Socrates and Plato said: "To philosophize is to learn to die."

Thus Plato dimly perceived these things, and he speaks of them; but Christianity alone effects them. Saint Augustine explains this as follows.

VII.

God exists in us as force, as light, as love; we feel him. But this natural sense of the soul, given to all by the presence of God, is at first only the vague and indeterminate attraction towards the desirable and the intelligible, to which the soul has not yet responded. A few very imperfect responses to this attraction raise it to the point which we have mentioned. There must be a decisive answer, which God incessantly provokes, which is God's work in us and with us, which is the new birth, the new life. The soul which has entered this other life believes in the Being, hopes for the Truth, and desires the Good. Its three natural faculties are actually exercised under the influence of their supreme object and their supernatural life; the implicit basis of our being, which we ourselves do not know, clings to the eternal Being through faith; the intelligence clings to the light of God through hope; the will clings to the will of God

---

[1] Epist. cxx., cap. i. 6.   [2] Ibid., .4.

through love. "Without these three things, no soul can be healed in such a manner as to see God." (*Sine tribus istis anima nulla sanatur, ut possit Deum suum videre.*)[1]

Made whole, let it gaze! That gaze is still reason, but set free and made clear-sighted; that straightforward look, that perfect look, which actually follows vision, is a virtue; that look, that vision, attain to God himself. What a gaze! The gaze of "the soul is reason; but every eye that gazes does not yet see; the true and straightforward gaze, that which sees, is a virtue. Yes, true reason, upright reason, is a virtue. The gaze of the purified soul, therefore, turns towards the light, when these three things dwell within us, — faith, which believes that the object of the gaze constitutes happiness when it is seen; hope, which knows that the gaze shall see; love, which desires to see and love. Such is the gaze which follows *the vision of God himself,* and this is *the final end of the gaze;* not because the eye then rests, but because it has found the supreme object of its search. Yes, this itself is virtue, — *reason attaining to its end;* it is supreme virtue and bliss. As for vision itself, what is it but intelligence, actual and present compounded of that which understands and that which is understood, even as sight depends alike on the eye and the light?"[2]

These words are most profound and most exactly true. They touch and solve the question of the relation between Philosophy and Religion, reason and faith.

But to continue. When reason reaches its end (*ratio perveniens ad finem suum; τέλος τῆς πορείας*), then truly begins the living, real, and experimental knowledge of God, that knowledge which Saint Augustine calls indeed "*experimentalem Dei notitiam,*" — a strong expression, quoted and adopted by Saint Thomas Aquinas. Then only do the inner senses of the soul develop for God; we become

[1] Soliloq., lib. i. cap. vi. 12.   [2] Ibid., 13.

master of the other senses, because the divine sense tow-
ers above them; this sense itself develops, because we are
master of the other senses. Then, too, "by continence,
verily, is the soul bound up and brought back into One,
whence it was dissipated into many (*per continentiam
colligimur et redigimur in unum, a quo in multa defluxi-
mus*)." [1] Saint Augustine has reached this point, and entered into possession of the inner life of the soul, when
he exclaims: "My life at last shall wholly live, as wholly
full of thee (*viva erit vita mea, totaque plena te*)." [2] Then
he thus invokes the source of his life, — that life which he
possesses and touches, which he sees, whose divine savor he
tastes, whose celestial perfumes he inhales: —

"I have loved thee too late, O thou Beauty, old and yet ever
new ! I have loved thee too late ! Thou wert within me ; I was
abroad. And I sought thee abroad, and flinging myself upon
those beauties created by thee, I lost my own fair form. They
held me far from thee, those beauties, which would never exist,
did they not exist in thee. Thou hast called me ; thou hast cried
aloud ; thou hast overcome my deafness. Thou hast shone, thou
hast sparkled, and thou hast triumphed over my blindness. Thy
perfumes made themselves manifest ; I breathed, and I breathe
for thee ; I have tasted thee, I hunger and thirst after thee. I
have touched thee, and my heart has ceased to long for aught
save the abiding peace which is in thee." [8]

VIII.

We have seen the method in action, and then the theory
of the method. Let us now proceed to the results.

Let us repeat, the philosophic results acquired by Saint
Augustine in regard to the nature of God are complete,
exact, absolute, unmixed with error, equivocation, or un-

---

[1] Confess., lib. x. cap. xxix. 40.   [8] Ibid., cap. xxvii. 38.
[2] Ibid., cap. xxviii. 39.

certainty. This is the philosophy of Christians. This is
the wisdom mentioned by one of our most learned teachers, "which is," he says, "both divine and human, and
which is therefore properly true Christian wisdom." We
mean that human wisdom, illumined by divine wisdom,
whose existence Saint Thomas Aquinas makes clear to us in
these words: "The divine wisdom of Christ did not dim his
human wisdom, but increased its clarity."

In considering, therefore, merely the advance of the rational
Theodicy, the purely human and non-theological side of wisdom, we must show not only the transition of knowledge
which is almost solely speculative into knowledge which is
at the same time experimental and speculative, but also
observe greater scientific precision upon capital points,
which, moreover, all combine in a single one, — the idea
of infinity.

The ancients had no clear idea of infinity; the moderns
have that idea: the influence of Christianity has developed it.

Pythagoras so deceived himself upon this point that he
gives us the following qualities, quoted by Aristotle: on the
one hand, *the finite, perfect, good,* etc.; on the other, the
infinite, imperfect, bad, etc. To him, *finite* meant *finished,*
and *infinite* meant *indeterminate.* He had no idea of the
determinate, finished, perfect infinite; that is, in a word, of
the *infinite,* which he confounded with the *indefinite.*

Plato occasionally hesitates in regard to this matter. Still
he sees between God and his creatures such a difference
that he names as God "the One who exists absolutely" ($\tau \hat{\wp}$
$\pi a \nu \tau \epsilon \lambda \hat{\omega}_{S} \, \check{o} \nu \tau \iota$), and calls the creatures "those who always
become and never are" ($\kappa a \grave{\iota} \, \mu \grave{\eta} \, \check{o} \nu \tau a$). This implies the
idea of the infinite. But there is an equivocation here. Do
God's creatures exist, or do they not exist? Plato seems
rather to say that they do not exist; and he is forced to

this conclusion for lack of a high enough idea of the infinite. For, clearly feeling that the Being of God and the being of his creatures are incomparable, to aggrandize God and show that he is matchless, he says that his creatures do not exist.

Aristotle, by his idea of the motionless motor, and especially of the primary cause, which is *pure act*, implies the idea of infinity: however, he does not yet fully comprehend that infinite; he does not know that God is everywhere present as a whole; he knows that God is in the world, but he thinks that he occupies a central point, and that his creatures receive the life which proceeds from him, with more or less abundance, according to their physical distance from that centre. Frequently, moreover, he gives us most inexact notions of the metaphysical infinite.

But that which especially shows us how little idea of the infinite the ancients had, is their incapability of conceiving an infinite power, — in other words, a power which can create from nothing. Have we not seen that Aristotle, while saying that this world is the work of God, supposes it eternal, and that Plato also believes matter to be eternal? Neither of them knew this exact principle, most unfamiliar even in the present day: *Infinite Being is infinite in every sense; finite being is finite in every sense.* Whence it follows that finite being is finite in duration: therefore it did not always exist, for it would have already actually infinite duration. The ancients maintained that *nothing can come from nothing,* which is truth itself, if there be not an infinite power; but if there be an infinite power, the infinity in the power consists precisely in its creating, that is to say, producing that which was not, or in producing from nothing.

Now, all this has been known from the first ages of the Christian Theodicy. Saint Augustine develops it, avoiding all errors and equivocations.

Far from confounding, as Pythagoras does, the infinite with the imperfect, — two things which are exactly opposite, he says of the wisdom of God that it is infinite : "It is manifest that the measure and form of everything arise thence, and that it may be suitably called infinite, with respect not to its extension in space, but to its power, which transcends all the limits of human thought."[1] And he adds this very profound remark : "Not that this wisdom is formless and indeterminate, like a body which has no contour."[2] He declares in these words concerning that which is still discussed in our day, — that the infinite is in no wise the indeterminate.

In the same place, while stating that God is not infinite in extent, he asserts that he is everywhere and wholly present, — which is, upon this point, the exact and absolute formula :[3] "He is wholly present everywhere, like truth ; and Truth is God himself." Saint Augustine points out the two meanings of the word "infinite," — one actually signifying the infinite, while the other is very inaccurate, and signifies the indefinite, increasing size whose limit is not known, all of which is not visible. In the inaccurate sense it is applied to physical size, and in the other to the spiritual greatness of God : "In this sense it is applied to the incorporeal greatness which we call *total*, because no place can bound it, and *which may be called both total and infinite :* total, because it lacks nothing ; infinite, because it is not limited by any circumscription."[4]

As for the incomparable distance between God and his creatures, the exact and explicit idea of the infinite allows Saint Augustine to conceive of it without destroying the creatures. Why? Because infinite Being is such that finite being, although really something, is nothing when compared

---

[1] Epist., cxviii. cap. iv. 24.   [3] Ibid., 23.

[2] Ibid.   [4] Ibid.

with the infinite,—which is an exact principle now adopted
by science.   Geometricians and algebraists assert and are
justified in asserting this formula: *The addition to the infinite of any quantity, however great, adds nothing;* [1] and this
other: *However great a quantity may be, when compared to
the infinite it becomes nothing.*   This is expressed in the
Holy Scriptures by the text: "My being is as nothing before thee, O my God!" [2]   And Saint Augustine says: "Why
compare with the infinite a finite thing, however great it
may be?" [3]   And elsewhere, commenting on the phrase:
"I am He who is," he says: [4] "God exists in such manner
that, compared to him, that which has been created does not
exist. *Created beings, not compared to God, actually exist;*
for they exist through him; *but if they be compared to God,
they do not exist;* for the true Being is the immutable Being,
and he alone is immutable."

Nothing can be more exact and precise than these words.

Finally, if we seek in Saint Augustine's works for his ideas
concerning the origin of things, the creation, the relation between God and his creatures, and between the creatures and
God, here above all we must admire the precise, explicit, and
exact knowledge of the great teacher,—a truly mathematical
knowledge of the infinite, the finite, and their mutual relations.
Those absolute assertions, which the imagination does not
conceive, but which figures and geometry prove, exist already
in that powerful reason which aids the energy of faith to
surpass imagination.   Saint Augustine says boldly, leaning
upon the Catholic faith, and also because reason requires it
and the idea of the infinite proves it, *God made all from
nothing.*   It is clearly understood that Saint Augustine avoids
here the absurdity of those sophists in all ages who consider

---

[1] Algebra gives us these formulæ, which geometry confirms: $\infty + = \infty$,
and $\frac{A}{\infty} = 0$.

[2] Ps. xxxviii. 6.   [3] Enar. rat. in Psalt. xxxvi. 16.   [4] Ibid., cxxxiv. 7.

nothing as something. He goes on to explain: "The creature does not proceed from the divine nature, but from nothing.[1] To be created out of nothing is the same thing as not to be of the same nature with God.[2] When we say 'God made all from nothing,' we say no more than this: 'He had nothing outside himself with which to make his work, he made it because he willed it.'"[3] This was expressed by the Greek Fathers thus: "He made beings which were not."[4]

God made all from nothing is one of those absolute propositions implying the infinite; that is to say, incomprehensible, which the imagination does not conceive; but in metaphysics it is an exact truth, and we find very evident traces of it in mathematics. When, for instance, algebraic formulæ teach us that *finite* greatness, *however great, multiplying zero always produces zero*, it corresponds to the axiom *Ex nihilo nihil, Nothing from nothing*. But if, instead of taking a finite quantity as multiplier, we take the infinite, the statement becomes: *Zero multiplied by the infinite gives us all finite greatness.*

So, too, no finite force can create, can produce from nothing; but the omnipotent infinite can create or produce from nothing.

We shall develop in its proper place a truly wonderful theory of the creation, found in Saint Augustine at the close of his book "De Musica." This amazing intuition of the basis of things is, moreover, in perfect harmony with the answer which science is now preparing to the great question, What is matter?

We do not dwell upon the sum total of the results contained in Saint Augustine's works; these results are truth itself, as Christianity gives it to us, as human reason understands it in that light, as the modern world knows it, as we

[1] Contra Jul., lib. v. xxxi. [3] Ad Oros., iii.
[2] Ibid., xlii. [4] Τὰ ὄντα ἐποίησεν ἐκ μὴ ὄντων.

have taught it to our children ever since the first century of
the Christian era.

IX.

Let us sum up this doctrine.

How can we know God? What is the course of reason,
from the blindness and ignorance in which we are born, up
to the time when we see God?

The first step is a practical one. Few men use their reason
to rise to God. The soul must be purified. The soul is
given over to the senses. It must be brought back to reason
(*regressus in rationem*). Attached to earth, the soul is parted
from itself and from God: it knows neither God nor reason.
The soul requires a first purification, under the natural moral
law, which shall free it from animality and raise it to a rational state. Let it return to itself by a first effort to resist
the senses which divide it, and it will recover its reason, the
judge of its senses. But reason, beholding itself, sees that
it is imperfect and changeable (*quæ se quoque in me compe-
riens mutabilem*). Now, to see change and mutability, is to
regret the immutable which it conceives by contrast (*unde
nosset ipsum immutabile, quod nisi aliquo modo nosset, nullo
modo illud mutabili præponeret*). Reason therefore, judging
itself, rises above itself and understands itself (*erexit se ad intelligentiam suam*). It sees that it is not light by itself, and
seeks to know what that light is by which it is enlightened
(*ut inveniret quo lumine aspergeretur*). Thus it understands
the invisible divine by the sight of that which is created
(*tunc invisibilia tua per ea quæ facta sunt intellecta conspexi*).

But how can we conceive of the immutable by seeing that
which is mutable? How are we to seek eternity thus in
time itself (*in mutabilibus et temporalibus æternitatem quæreremus*)? It is because we cling to God and are joined to
him (*unde penderemus*); because we only exist and live in

so far as we cling to him (*semper ab illo fieri debemus inhœ-rentes ei*) ; because, thenceforth, we are conscious of him by a sort of occult memory (*per quamdam occultam memoriam*); by a luminous impression of the Sovereign Good (*impressa notio ipsius Boni*); by a sort of inner sense which urges us to seek him always (*interior nescio quœ conscientia quœren-dum Deum*).

This is the true inward principle, the power and mainspring which lift us to reason and to God, starting from the senses in which we were buried.

But it is not necessary, in order to return from the senses to reason, and from reason to God, to suppress the use of the senses. The use and acuteness of the senses is one thing; their abuse is another thing (*aliud est utilitas, vivacitas sen-tiendi; aliud libido sentiendi*). On the contrary, we must make use of them to rise and make a stepping-stone of them. It is in our sensations that we find the first vestiges of reason (*tenemus quœdam vestigia rationis in sensibus*); the mind finds these traces as soon as it discerns in the sensation the *sign* and the *significance* (*aliud* sensus ; ... *aliud* per sensum ; *pulcher motus, et pulchra motus* significatio). Reason also takes sensible things as stepping-stones (*quœsivit gradus*), stepping-stones to rise to God himself (*gradus ad immortalia faciendus*). The earth, says the Gospel, is the footstool of God. Reason contemplates sensible things that it may make use of them, but contemplates them soberly (*in eos ipsos pau-lulum aciem detorsit*), in order to seize the sensation less in itself than for what it signifies (*ratio vidit quid inter sonum, et id cujus signum esset, distaret*). This it does through its great power of abstraction (*ista potentissima secernendi*). And what does it find as the meaning of the visible symbol-ism of nature? It finds the geometric laws, forms, and num-bers which govern phenomena (*intelligebat regnare numeros*). It at once understands that these laws are eternal and divine

(*reperiebat divinos et sempiternos*).   But these forms and
numbers, these laws, in brief, are only actually found in material bodies in the state of shadows and vestiges (*in his quæ
sentiuntur umbras eorum potius atque vestigia*).   It is only
in reason itself that reason finds them absolute and true
(*quas in seipsa cogitando intuebatur verissimas*).

Here, then, I have something eternal and absolute.
Henceforth I no longer work at random to lift myself to
the divine (*non temere jam quærit illa divina*).

But is it God himself that I see when I see these true and
absolute principles, these numbers, laws, and axioms?   Far
from it, certainly.   If it were God, the sight would overwhelm me with joy (*tantum gauderem quantum Deo cognito*).   Between these truths and the holy majesty of God,
there is all the distance that there is between heaven and
earth, or the sun and the objects upon which it shines
(*quantum in suo genere a cœlo terram, tantum ab intel-
ligibili Dei majestate spectamina illa disciplina vera et
certa differre*).   These truths, such as we see them, are
not God; they are sights lit up in us by the sun of God.
There is, therefore, one world, the world of sense; another
world, the world of intelligence; and above them both,
the Father of worlds (*duos mundos, et ipsum parentem
universitatis*).

Reason advances from the world of sense to the world of
intelligence by the steps which we have just described.
But to see God himself, reason must be transformed and
become energy.   It becomes energy by becoming pure and
perfect reason (*est enim virtus vel recta vel perfecta ratio*).
It becomes energy when it attains its supreme end (*hæc est
vere perfecta virtus, ratio perveniens ad finem suum*).   What
is that end?   The very vision of God (*ipsa visio Dei quæ est
finis aspectus*).   This is supernatural, and comes through
the three virtues which God gives, — Faith, Hope, and

Charity, — three virtues without which no soul can be healed in such manner as to see God (*Fides, Spes, Caritas, . . . sine tribus istis anima nulla sanatur, ut possit Deum suum videre*). To see God, — this is the final aim of reason, in the soul united to God : this vision is the union of the soul which sees, with God himself, who is seen (*intellectus ille qui conficitur ex intelligente et eo quod intelligitur*).

But all this course is the fruit of the successive purification of the soul. It is clear that the soul which, turning away from God, should seek its own light, to the exclusion of that of God, would find only shadows (*anima si ad lucem suam attenderit tenebratur ; si ad lucem Dei, illuminatur*). The more the soul, turned away from the light of justice, struggles, the farther it is removed from light, and the deeper it is buried in the gulf of shadows (*anima avertens se a luce justitiæ, quanto magis quærit tanto plus a luce repellitur, et in tenebrosa repellitur*).

Such is, according to Saint Augustine, the course of reason towards God.

It is very plain that this course of reason implies all philosophy, — logic, morals, knowledge of the soul and of God.

Thus we desire first to exhibit philosophy, in its broad outlines, to the attentive intelligences which may consent to follow us. We try to put before them in living form the actual thought of all wise men of the first order. Their accord gives us the teachings of a human authority without a parallel. Intelligence and clear vision are requisite. I only ask you to show respect and attention to these authorities. Respectful attention to the words and testimony of these sublime geniuses or saints who, more than any others, have sought and seen the truth, will soon direct your gaze to that truth itself, which all have seen, which all describe with one accord, each aiding the other by his splendid testimony.

Little by little, their words will lead you to see for yourselves the intelligible object which they contemplated as
they spoke. Or rather, as Saint Augustine tells us, the
Master who enlightened them, the sole Master of all men,
who is in you as he was in them, will show you the
meaning of the words uttered by his most advanced disciples. You will see in the light itself the assurance, as
well as the omissions, in their teachings and in ours.

X.

We have now given a most imperfect account of Saint
Augustine's Philosophy. We have been forced to select
from his vast store of riches, and perhaps have omitted the
best. We have grasped and separated from the living
current of his thought certain features which seem chilled
by isolation. We have done what may be worse yet, —
we have repeated, out of place and out of connection, some
few of the deep accents of his soul and his love; and if
these accents fall upon the ear of one who does not love,
who does not believe or hope, they cannot be understood.
The inexperienced heart, which has never lived the life
of the most sublime and saintly love, cannot comprehend
Saint Augustine. How must it be with the empty, impure,
and perverse soul? Destitute of the divine perceptions
developed in the soul of the saint, how should I understand
that which senses I do not possess permit him to see, smell,
taste, hear, and touch of God? If he tells me of those
lights, those perfumes, and those voices, I am like a blind
man listening to an account of the sunrise: I hear the
words, I cannot see the things ; the words do not correspond
to the life I know, but to that which I do not know ; and
then how often I am tempted to say, These are words, and
nothing more !

Read Saint Augustine in the poetic period of early youth. If your soul be beautiful, you will find a certain charm; because there is nothing more complete than his genius, and the sacred inspiration of the loftiest poetry pervades his work. But you will not understand his knowledge, because you have no knowledge of your own; you will feel nothing of his love, because you have as yet no love yourself, or the love which you have is of another order. Take up Saint Augustine twenty years later, when your soul has developed, — for if the light of your soul is dimmed, you will not take up his work, — re-read him after you have lived, sought, suffered, and struggled for the truth; then you will know that mind and that soul which you did not know before; you will be amazed that you could have read without understanding, and looked without seeing. You will see the life under the words; and if you have yourself at times half seen the light, if you have possessed wisdom but for an hour, it is that wisdom and that light, all whose virtues, all whose beams, you recover here.

From this point of view only can we judge the great system of philosophy of the modern world, of which Saint Augustine is the Plato; we can understand the likeness and all the difference between these two brother geniuses, born under different skies; and in this difference we seize upon the chief feature in the history of the human mind, — a feature which, if it be understood, at last shows us what Philosophy, the true, total, useful Philosophy, is.

Christian dogma teaches us that there is the same difference between the old Mosaic law and the new law of Jesus that there is between the precept and the life, and the same difference between these two states of religion in history that there is between the image and the reality. When we are closely acquainted with Plato and Saint Augustine, and have actually practised their teachings, we see that there is in several respects, between the two systems of philosophy, the same difference as there is between the old and the new law.

Several Fathers of the Church have compared Greek philosophy to the old law; they regard it as a sort of evangelical preparation, and look upon true philosophers as prophets.[1] Now, as the Gospel tells us, when Christianity came, it came, not to destroy the law, but to fulfil it; so too it does not come to destroy the human fruit of philosophic thought, but to ripen it. It effects in the human mind and its imperishable philosophy precisely the same revolution which it causes in the eternal and universal religion of mankind.

We have seen that Plato desired, awaited, dimly foresaw this divine revelation; Saint Augustine declared it to be accomplished; and the eye which can judge sees it indeed, longed for in Plato, fulfilled in Saint Augustine.

I repeat it, the fundamental fact in the history of the human mind has been accomplished. Philosophy, properly so called (I do not refer to Theology, which is distinct from it), Philosophy, I say, has passed from infancy to manhood.

Of the two regions of the world of intelligence perceived by all who foresaw the light, the human mind occupied one, and, by a certain conjecture, regretted the other; now it occupies both.

There are two regions in the world of intelligence, let us again repeat with Plato: first that of God himself, and then that of divine phantoms, shadows of that which is, essential truths, eternal and absolute, but which are not God. Now, Plato is, of all men of the old world, the one most familiar with this distinction. Plato went as far as human reason can go in its first estate. He saw all that exists in man; he reached the very apex of the soul; he teaches, as Saint Au-

[1] Saint Clement of Alexandria, Saint Justin. See Melchio Cano, lib. x. cap. iv. and vi.

gustine observes, that the sight of the essence of God is given by a light absolutely distinct from man, absolutely divine; he knows that this light is God, that its source is the Sovereign Good; he asserts that our soul is capable of attaining to the direct and immediate vision of this source of light. And yet Saint Augustine says of Plato: He saw only the image of God; he did not find the true way to attain to the sovereign Good; he dealt with the eternal images of the True, not with the True itself; he dealt with that truth which is not God, but which is his image;[1] that is to say, Plato did not see the two regions, the difference between which he knew, he saw the lower of the two, and conjectured the other.

"It is one thing to see our peaceful fatherland from the top of a mountain and from the bosom of a wild forest, without the ability to find the road, and to seek a path of escape in vain amidst enemies who surround and pursue us, . . . it is quite another thing actually to hasten over the road which leads us home."[2]

"Platonists, therefore, know, after a certain fashion, invisible, immutable, immaterial nature; but the path that leads to this supreme beatitude, namely, Jesus Christ crucified, seems to them contemptible, they refuse to follow it, and thenceforth can never reach the sanctuary which is its resting-place and end, although the light that proceeds from it strikes their intelligence with a distant radiance."[3]

It would take too long to explain here of what use the Cross of Christ may be in philosophy. But the rest of this book will, we hope, show it in a scientific way. There will be found the deepest of philosophic truths, which was not sufficiently well known. As it has been said that there are two watersheds in history, one on this side the Cross, the other on the other side, so too it must be said that the same holds good of the human mind. These two watersheds are

[1] Confess., lib. vii. cap. ix. 14.   [3] Epist., cxx. cap. i. 4.
[2] Ibid., lib. viii. cap. xxi. 27.

just those two regions of the world of intelligence described by Plato and all other philosophers after him.

Now, at that period of history at which we write, the middle of the nineteenth century, the human mind is clearly full of trouble, confusion, and contradiction. Minds deliberate, are excited, hesitate, repel, exclude, condemn, and attack one another around a single point, — Christianity. War is waged around the Cross. Some desire to overthrow it and return to the antique world behind the Cross; others strive to uphold it and advance into the new world beyond it. Meantime, and while the battle rages, the mass of mankind dwell in an arid desert midway between the Promised Land and Egypt, — Egypt, to which they will not return, and the Promised Land, which they will surely enter. But those who refuse to go thither will die in the desert, and will drag us down with them, until a new generation shall arise, whom God may find resolved to follow him.

The sterilizers, the mortal foes of all progress of the human mind, are, in philosophy, those now called *rationalists*. I call those rationalists who rely upon pure reason in such a way as to exclude faith and all supernatural aid. We defend the rights of human reason, they say. We reply, By defending the rights of human reason as you do, do you know the depths to which you have allowed Philosophy to fall? I do not say below the seventeenth century, below the thirteenth century, below the time of the Fathers. I say below Aristotle and Plato, far below that beautiful Greek philosophy which we uphold and which you cannot uphold; you have taken it back and delivered it over to the sophists before Socrates. Gorgias and Protagoras have returned: they live, they teach, they speak and write. We hear nothing else; for as for you, you are no longer heard. You who claim to uphold Aristotle, Plato, and Descartes, and who reject the Cross of Christ as the guide of a fresh advance

in the world of intellect, what are you doing? You deny
Plato's last and highest thought. He desired to turn
towards the sun which had not yet risen; and you require
us to turn away from the sun which is actually shining. I
call that the Judaism of philosophy; and to this Judaism we
say, with Saint Paul: *Hebræi sunt, plus ego !* You are for
Aristotle and Plato, we are for them more than you; you
are for them, as the Jews were for Moses; you reject him
whom they awaited. Is this supporting Plato? It is destroying him in his totality; it is denying what Plato called
the goal of the onward march, the end of the process; it is
taking for final realities those truths, absolute no doubt,
but empty, which he called shadows of the world of intelligence and divine phantoms; it is taking Plato's dialectic in exactly the wrong way on this point; and I shall show
you that the only rationalistic philosophy, which moves and
stirs to-day, is nothing but an inversion of the Platonic
dialectic.[1]

What is to be done? We must grow and advance, as
Plato did in Saint Augustine. We must maintain the
distinction between the two regions of the world of intelligence. We must learn that the first is merely shadows and
images, and is useful only as an image and prophecy of the
second. It is the second that we must enter, with our
whole soul, as Plato expresses it, that is, with heart, life,
and mind. There must be that total change of soul which
turns us away from the shadows seen on the walls of the
cave, towards the light and the objects which cast the
shadows. We must pass from that natural vision of God,
mediately and indirectly perceived in the essential truths of
reason, to that other vision of God, the direct and immediate,
which Christianity calls supernatural; in short, we must
pass from the light of God, seen in ourselves, to the light of

[1] See the Logic, Book II.

God seen in God himself. We must advance from reason
to faith, the dim and imperfect beginning of that other light.
Does it follow from this that we forsake reason? No,
says Saint Augustine, we urge it to its last term, we make
of it a virtue, by rooting it in the faith which it preceded
and which it sought. For reason, as it is given to us, and as
it illumines us when we enter this world, teaches us to conclude the existence of the other light, which is the direct
vision of God in himself, — a direct vision which the indirect
vision of God within ourselves leads us to suspect. And
the rough outline of this vision is faith, — faith, that attempt
at vision, as Bossuet says; faith, that eye of the heart, says
Saint Augustine; faith, that incipient vision, says Saint
Thomas. Will that new vision destroy the other? Will
that divine knowledge overwhelm my human knowledge?
Will my acquaintance with God deprive me of my acquaintance with myself, and that of God which that acquaintance
implies? Saint Augustine asserts that, even in the world to
come, the soul shall see God, both in himself and in itself, —
which shows that our knowledge will remain eternally, both
human and divine, — and that that wisdom, of which philosophy is the beginning, shall endure. For if philosophy be
only God seen within us, the eternal vision is only God seen
in himself.

And when Saint Augustine says further: "There is within
my heart a depth which I do not know, and which thou
knowest, Lord! a depth which is nought but shadows until
it becomes light beneath the splendor of thy face," — Saint
Augustine, speaking thus, leads us to understand that he
perceives the two regions of the soul corresponding to the
two regions of the world of intelligence.

All philosophers have referred to this sanctuary of the
soul, where God is, and where he is necessarily, as the cause
of my being and my life. They have spoken of that point

where God touches the soul to join it to himself, by which
he makes it living by holding it in his hand. Who does
not know that this is beyond all philosophy ? The world
touches us on the surface, God at the centre, and we are
between the two, and three worlds live in us, — God, Nature,
and ourselves. Our soul is the temple, the place of contemplation. The centre, where God lives in us, is the sanctuary.
The circumference, where the world lives in us, is the outer
entrance. The intermediate enclosure is our proper abode ;
it is double, and is called intelligence and will, — will is the
more central, intelligence more external.

Plato describes a cave, in illustration of the progress and
degrees of philosophy. We may be allowed to describe a
temple.

In childhood we play about the entrance ; if we attain to
manhood of mind, we enter the enclosure. The entrance is
illumined only by the light of the material sun ; the enclosure
is illumined only by the sacred flame which shines at the
centre. The splendid images of the enclosure, the forms
which cover it, are the divine phantoms of which Plato
speaks. We gaze at them ; Christ, on entering the temple,
himself gazed at the adornments ; he saw wherein the sacred
edifice conformed to the divine model.

But there is a difference between the temple of the soul
and those temples built by the hand of man : in these latter,
the lamp which lights the sanctuary is a pale image of the
sun ; in the temple of the soul, on the contrary, the sun is
but a pale image of the lamp. Now, there are some souls
which have attained to the inner degree of the intellectual
life, which move inwardly about the temple, but do not
approach the altar. To approach the altar, one must go
past the will ; reason must become energy. Such minds are
unwilling to look at anything but these images of God, and
they become adorers of those sacred forms which are within

us, and are ourselves: as those who remain at the threshold
remain adorers of visible nature, which is less than we are.
These are the two philosopic sects which place either in
nature or in man "the sovereign Good, the cause of the
world, the fulcrum of reason."

Where does genuine philosophy begin and end?· It begins in the soul, which, having gazed at those divine phantoms illumined by the holy light proceeding from the
centre, perceives that as yet it has seen its surface only,
and not its depth; that all the light of the enclosure comes
from the centre, and that in order to gaze at the sacred
images it has never ceased to turn its back upon the source
of light, the inner sanctuary, the central place, the abode of
God in us. This is the first step of true philosophy. Its
second step is to conclude that, if the images are so fair, the
model is far more beautiful, and that the term of contemplation and the purpose of the temple is the direct contemplation of the Holy of Holies; that this Holy of Holies
is in us, but is not us; that we have seen its reflections
shining on the enclosure, on the inner surface of the soul,
and that we shall see its source in our centre. We understand that there is within us a central enclosure to which
we have never penetrated, and that we must make our way
there at last by traversing the will. Plato goes thus far, but
Saint Augustine goes farther yet: he performs what Plato
thinks; he takes his eye from those arches and all their
splendor; he ceases to move curiously about the temple;
he turns towards the sanctuary, moves towards the altar,
ascends the steps; he becomes a priest;[1] he opens the
tabernacle to touch, see, and hear God, to taste him and
live by him. He turns back: the temple is no longer empty,
— it is full of the stir of people; gone are the images and
the statues; now, the images of God are men.

[1] Gens sancta, regale sanctorum.

It seems that the soul which has tasted God, — God present in its centre, — that soul contains a thousand others: those which, being with God, are with it. Abandoning solitary and abstract reflection to seek God, it has found him; and in recovering God, has recovered mankind, its life, its common-sense, its universal communion.

When the priestly soul turns towards the altar, towards God, it sees its divine knowledge. When it turns towards the vast enclosure, which is itself, and towards the other souls, which commune with it in God, it sees its human knowledge. Both subsist in the holy sacrifice with its eternal solemnity.[1]

But there are necessary initiations before we can enter the central enclosure; there are conditions to be complied with before we can become a priest: there is one which includes them all.

This single condition consists in taking up the Cross of Jesus Christ. This is what I have called the philosophic use of the Saviour's cross. To take up the Cross of Christ is to practise the Christian sacrifice; it is to die to self in order to live again; it is to leave not only the outward life of nature which we lived upon the threshold, but also the inward life of solitary reflection, which contemplated the images in the structure of the soul. Having quitted the life of the world in us, to quit also our own life, to pass on to the life of God himself, — this is what Christianity calls "taking up your cross and dying:" and it is of such death that it is said: "If the grain of wheat die not, it remains single; if it die, it bears much fruit." Potent life, proceeding from the central point where God gives it, unfolds

---

[1] This does not mean that the soul shall have only a supernatural knowledge of God, and a natural knowledge of his creatures and itself. It will have the natural knowledge of God and his creatures, when it looks at his creatures and sees God in them; it will have supernatural knowledge of God and his creatures when it beholds God and sees his creatures in him.

all the riches of the germ which desired to die in God, and, at the tip of every twig or every ray of that life, the grain which was dead and is born again bears fruit like unto itself, — an image of the soul turned towards God, developed and become priestly, which, forasmuch as it liveth in God, makes a world of souls live within it.

There is nothing superfluous in our description of the temple. Search carefully, and you will find all this in the history of philosophy, consummated and complete.

CHAPTER V.

L IKE the two Sums of Saint Thomas, the two philosophic
works of Saint Anselm might be called "*Intelligence
Seeking for Faith*," "*Faith seeking for Intelligence.*" [1] The
latter title was at first given by Saint Anselm himself to his
second work, the *Proslogium*. As for the first, the *Monologium*, the saintly doctor tells us how he wrote the book for
his monks, who asked him for purely philosophic meditations, in which absolutely nothing should rest upon the
authority of Scripture, but everything should depend upon
the evidence of truth and the necessary conclusions of reason.[2] This is why, in the *Monologium*, he "supposes a man
seeking for truth by his unaided reason." [3] And, he says, "if
it be a question of most of the truths which we believe in
regard to God and the creation, I think that such a man,
who does not know them or does not believe them, may still,
if he be only of ordinary intellect, convince himself of them
by his unaided reason." [4]

Yet this book was at first entitled by Saint Anselm,
"Meditations on the Reason of Faith" (*Exemplum medi-
tandi de ratione Fidei*). The saintly doctor does not merely
demonstrate the existence of God and his attributes in this
work, he goes farther. He proves the necessity of Faith,
and he goes so far as to meditate on the mystery of the Holy
Trinity. He claims that, this doctrine being given and

[1] Intellectus quærens Fidem.   Fides quærens Intellectum.
[2] Monol., preface.   [3] Ibid.   [4] Ibid., chap. i.

taught by revelation, the intelligence can find profound and admirable reasons for the mystery.

Saint Anselm therefore wrote the first of his two works for the same purpose that Saint Thomas wrote the *Summa Philosophica ;* that is, to bring natural reason to bear against those who do not admit the authority of the Scriptures and of revelation.

And like Saint Thomas, after proving the existence of God, Saint Anselm too goes farther. He proves by reason the necessity of another light. From the very fact that reason on reaching a certain point fails, another light must needs intervene. Like Saint Thomas again, Saint Anselm gives his listeners a statement of that which the other light reveals to us, and compels reason to see nothing therein which is opposed to it, but, on the contrary, to discover rich stores of truth. This, moreover, is the traditional course of all Catholic schools of thought. All make a radical distinction between Faith and Reason; all maintain both; all affirm that unaided reason can accomplish certain things, that it has rights and duties: but none stops at an isolated rational doctrine; all regard healthy reason, living reason, as a power which lives and moves in the regret and desire for another power, under the attraction of a higher truth : none supposes reason apart from the superior attraction which seeks to elevate it. All consider reason as correlative to faith, and always see, either intelligence in search of faith, or else faith seeking for intelligence. And we say, with full conviction, that this point of view is not merely theological, but it is properly and rigidly philosophical. To set it aside is to desert philosophy and take up sophistry. Our future studies will show this.

II.

Now, how does Saint Anselm prove the existence of God? What is his argument? Is that argument good or bad? Is it or is it not a sound chain of reasoning? What is its place in logic? It is not for us to answer this question, lest we should seem too fully to agree with our own selves: we will rather leave it to the eminent writer who has so skilfully dis- cussed the philosophic work of Saint Anselm, and who was first, so far as we know, to understand fully the nature of his famous argument. "·I am convinced," says M. de Rému- sat, "that the foes of this argument will always have an easy victory if we persist in turning it into a syllogism. The ma- jor must always be such that it carries the decision of the question. . . . Therefore it is the major that we should con- sider. It is the fundamental idea, not mere reasoning, that we should bring to bear against our foes."[1] This is the truth in regard to Saint Anselm's argument. In our opinion we should undoubtedly bring both the fundamental idea and the force of reasoning to bear against our foes; but we must first recognize that this reasoning is not a syllogism. What then is it? "It is an example of that boldness of induction upon which ontology is based."[2] Yes, this reasoning, taken with its true point of departure, is an induction, although, to our thinking, there is no boldness about it. It is simply the chief process of reason, that which finds the majors; that which in our opinion logic does not bring sufficiently to the front; that which the best minds see dimly, which they even describe, as our author does here, but which they dare not frankly introduce into logic as an exact process, intimidated

[1] Saint Anselm, p. 533. We are considering only the philosophical part of M. de Rémusat's book. Were we considering the historic and religious part, we should be compelled to make certain reserves.

[2] Page 535.

as they are, despite the authority of Aristotle and all great
philosophers, by the time-honored prejudice that reason has
but one process, the syllogistic.[1]

Saint Anselm's argument, taken as a whole, is, in our opinion, a little masterpiece, containing in its simple form a great
wealth of ideas: it is the key to ontology, psychology, and
logic. Let us try to turn this key and see what it hides.

Let us see what occurs in the soul which attains to the
idea of God,—that chief major of all philosophy.

In the first place, every soul always feels the attraction of
the Sovereign Good. Moreover, it sees all things, in a certain
degree, in the light of God. All desire for any finite Good
whatever implies some desire for the Sovereign Good. The
vision of any finite being whatsoever implies a certain degree
of vision of the infinite Being. The attraction of the desirable and the intelligible, the divine sense, this is always the
beginning.

But this sense and this vision of God which is given us, or
at least offered us by everything desired or known, is implicit.
The soul sees as if it did not see; it feels as if it did not feel;
it has eyes and sees not, senses and feels not. Why? Because there is an obstacle, a double obstacle,—the obstacle
which results from the necessary limitations of the finite,

---

[1] Re-read from this point of view the last chapter of De Rémusat's book.
In those remarkable pages, full of good sense, penetration, elevation, ingenious
and truthful insight, the writer seems to consider in turn, from without, all
the phases of a leading idea of which he never gives a complete description,
and which he develops with some hesitation. What would be the living bond,
the precise unity, the solid axis of all this chapter? It would be this proposition, understood as we understand and set it forth in this work: "There is
in the human mind, besides syllogism, another process quite as exact, which
leads up from effects to causes, and from the finite to the infinite." But what
is there to prove clearly that this process is an exact one? This. This process is applicable and applied to geometry, whose mainstay it is. For several
years back this important observation has been made, both in France and Germany. Little by little, those who devote themselves to philosophy will pay
heed to it.

and, besides, the sickly obstacle of a guilty and debased life. "For the sense of my soul," says Saint Anselm, "has become hardened, and, as it were, stupefied by the ancient languor of sin."[1] In a sickly soul there must first be a certain moral condition, a sacrifice of evil as an obstacle, and, moreover, another sacrifice in humility, which is the sight of and regret at the narrow confines of finite nature. There must be this double sacrifice before the divine sense can become explicit in us. But, moreover, we must have recourse to reason, to make up for the degradation and obscurity of that inner sense. Reason, or rather ratiocination, reproduces, with toil and complication, what the divine sense, were it perfectly active, would give us at once.

Reason, therefore, makes it clear to us that the desire for a limited good is only the beginning of the desire for a sovereign good, and that the sight of finite beings is only the beginning of the sight of the Being which is infinite. Why? Because my reason cannot conceive of a limited good without conceiving a greater one, and a greater yet, and thus it speeds until it reaches a term which it attains at a single bound, and where it necessarily pauses; namely, *the idea of a being such that none greater can be conceived,*[2] of a first, supreme and absolute Being, upon whom all being necessarily rests, as my thought rests and pauses in him alone. But this simple ideal postulate once established, this simple name of a Being such that none greater can be conceived, being merely mentally expressed, does not the mind clearly recognize that which it saw implicitly, and does not the inner sense of the soul support that light with all the living force which is within it? Does not the soul

---

[1] Proslog., cap. xvii.

[2] Id quo majus cogitari nequit (Contra insipientem, cap. viii.).

Invenisti eum esse quiddam summum omnium, quo nihil melius cogitari potest (Prosl., cap. xiv.).

instantly believe in the actual existence of the Being such that none greater can be conceived?

Here, then, are two moments, — the one which, starting with the desire or the sight of limited good, conceives the name and formula of the Being such that none greater can be conceived, that is to say, simply Being; and the other which instantly recognizes under this single name, actual and real existence, as being necessarily contained therein, since we cannot say: Being is not.

If we ask Saint Anselm how we arrive at this idea of the Sovereign Good, he replies that we arrive at it by the sight of limited good (*de minoribus bonis ad majora conscendendo*). We pass from the idea of a Good such that a greater one can be conceived (*ex iis quibus majus cogitari valet*, CONJICERE *id quo majus cogitari nequit*), that is to say, from the idea of finite good (*quod initium et finem habet*) we rise to the idea of infinite good (*quod nec finem habet nec initium*). All lower good, in so far as good, has some likeness to the Sovereign Good (*omne minus bonum intantum est simile majori bono inquantum est bonum*). There is, therefore, a point of support to aid us in arriving at the idea of the infinite (*est igitur unde possit conjici quod majus cogitari nequeat*). Reason reveals this to every rational mind (*cuilibet rationali menti*). But if any Christian deny it, continues our holy doctor, we must remind him of the words of Saint Paul: "The invisible perfections of God are visible in the created world."[1]

This is the real basis of St. Anselm's argument, as the eminent writer whom we have quoted, very truly remarks. The argument is not an empty one, as is so constantly repeated, as Leibnitz and Kant believed, — Leibnitz, who labors to provide it with a point of support, and Kant, who strives to destroy the whole argument. Would that they had understood Saint Anselm!

[1] *Contra insipientem*, cap. viii.

In general, much trouble might be saved if, in studying
the human mind, great men were only considered in their
totality.   By a comparative study of their various works, we
should arrive at the living idea which filled their mind, at
the object which they saw.   Then, above all errors of text,
distractions of mind, and padding between patches of light,
we should see clearly the general form of their thought, and
recover that phase of the immutable truth which their genius
perceived.   Then we should comprehend the harmony of
great minds and how — always excluding the sophists who
gaze into darkness, and the fools who speak without looking — all minds which see, supplement and sustain, instead
of contradicting, each the other.

III.

Thus, according to Saint Anselm, the sight of finite beings
and the desire for transient goods, leads us to the idea of
and desire for the Supreme Good and the infinite Being.
But, once more, how and why does this idea of the Supreme
Good and the infinite Being imply the actual and real existence of that Being whom the mind conceives ?   This must
be fully understood, for this is the kernel of the argument.
Here is the plain and simple answer.   It is because an idea,
— an idea properly so called, is a particular view of the object.   Modern pantheists assert that the idea is the object.
Those who have no philosophy, on the contrary, believe that
an idea can have no object.   The truth is midway.   "We
do not perceive nothing," Malebranche constantly reiterates.
There can be no idea without an object ; but no idea in man
is his object.   The idea is a particular view of the object.   In
God alone is the idea identical with its object.   But what is
the idea, properly so called ?   It is neither the sensation
nor the image of it which remains in the memory.   The idea

has reference only to the universal, the permanent, the true in itself, the essential; it is therefore a particular view of God. But the sight of a thing implies its existence. It is thus, Saint Anselm says, I have the idea of a Being such that none greater can be conceived, that is, of an infinite Being; therefore that infinite Being exists; for you see him, in a certain sense, so soon as you think of him. For if he did not exist, he would not be such that none greater could be conceived. Far from being infinite, he would be nought. If you could conceive that being, such that none greater can be conceived, does not exist, you would simultaneously conceive the truth of two contradictory terms.

Now, there is a singular syllogistic form, which shows this contradiction, and it is the argument of Saint Anselm.

I have the idea of a being such that none greater can be conceived.

But if this being did not exist, he would not be greater than any that can be conceived.

Therefore it is a contradiction to affirm that the Being such that none greater can be conceived does not exist.

This singular argument proves the existence of God under a mathematical form and with mathematical precision. For it starts with a notion which exists in the mind, like that of the triangle, and deduces from this notion that of necessary existence, as from that of the triangle we deduce the necessary properties of the triangle. And yet it does not end in an ideal, abstract God, but in a real God. This is due to the fact that the argument is at the same time *a priori* and *a posteriori*. It proves that God is because he must be, and also because we see his existence. This argument holds good only of God, for the very reason that God is the only necessary Being. Outside of God the ideal and the real are separate. In him real and ideal are identical. And this is what Aristotle seems to show us when, speaking of the double series of the desirable and the intelligible, he says that the first desirable and the first intelligible are identical.[1]

But let us see more explicitly by what process reason rises from created things to God.

Since nothing exists or subsists save through the presence of the creative and preservative Being,[2] we can understand how, in seeing the created world, we must, according to Saint Paul, see something of the Creator. More yet, — all that we see, we see by the light of God (*quidquid video, per illam video*).[3] Lastly, the soul is a mirror in which God is seen.[4]

But if I see in all things both the creature and the light of God, — if I see at once, in some measure, the absolute perfection of God and the relative qualities of his creatures, — I must separate, in all my thoughts and sensations, those two things which are so absolutely different; I must distinguish that which shows me God, and that which shows me his creatures. What can I affirm of God? Of all that I can affirm of created things, what is there which befits the wonderful nature of God?[5] I am amazed if among the words applicable to beings created out of nothing I find any which can be worthily applied to the creative substance of all. Let us see, however, what reason will tell us on this point.

Here comes in the rational process to which we have already referred, and to which we shall have frequent occasion to refer: we must efface bounds and limits. We must efface, as Descartes says, all that partakes of imperfection and nothingness. As it is impossible to say that the supreme substance is something the non-existence of which

[1] Metaph., lib. ii. cap. vii.

[2] Monol., cap. xiii.

[3] Prosl., cap. xvi.

[4] Monol., cap. lxvii.

[5] Ibid., xiii.

would be, in any sense whatsoever, better than existence;
so, too, it must necessarily be all whose existence is better than non-existence: for it alone is the Sovereign
Good. We must therefore suppress every attribute of the
supreme essence which is less good than its negation, just
as we must affirm its every attribute which is better than
its negation.[1] Therefore we should affirm its life, wisdom,
beauty, goodness, omnipotence, beatitude, eternity, and every
other attribute which may be always and in every case
better than its negation. Now, this logical choice, almost
unintelligible in its theoretical statement, is practised spontaneously by every pure and religious soul, at every instant
of life.

It is accordingly by considering the works of God, but
above all by viewing itself, that the soul sees God, or at
least his image or reflection.[2] "For," says our Doctor, "it is
evident that we cannot see in ourselves that supreme nature,
but can only see it through an intermediary; it is certain that that which can best raise us to a knowledge
thereof is the sight of the created being most like it. . . .
So that the rational soul which, on the one hand, can alone
among created beings rise to the search after God, is also, on
the other hand, the very object in which it may find traces
of that which it seeks."

"We may therefore say of the soul, with perfect truth,
that it is to itself a mirror wherein it sees the image of him
whom it cannot behold face to face."[3]

Reason, adds Saint Anselm, transfers to God the attributes which it finds in the soul, but it does not transfer
them as they are. It speaks of them in the same terms, but
those terms have two meanings: one meaning relating to the
creature, another meaning relating to God; and the meaning
relating to the creature, that petty meaning (*tenuem signifi-*

---

[1] Monol., cap. xv.   [2] Ibid.   [3] Ibid., cap. lxvii.

cationem),[1] is only the image, and, as it were the enigma, of their meaning in God.

By summing up the foregoing, we see how complete Saint Anselm's idea was. Nothing is wanting: the divine sense, the attraction of the desirable and the intelligible; the obstacle to that attraction; the state of degradation of the divine sense in the soul; the need for moral preparation, for cure, in order that the divine sense, God's image in us, which includes the memory of God, and which leads to the knowledge and love of God, may be in some measure developed; the effort of the thought and will to develop that sense and derive light and love from it; the external point of departure of this task of reason, in the sight of finite beings, limited goods; the flight of reason from that which is limited to the Being which is without limitations; the crossing of the gulf between the world and God; the scientific operation which divides that which befits the Infinite and that which could never befit him; the fundamental process which finds the truth; the syllogism which more explicitly reveals the truth found, — we encounter all this at one and the same time in the thought of the holy Doctor.

IV.

It remains to determine what sort of knowledge Saint Anselm believed he should acquire by this exercise of the reason. He tells us, in the admirable summary which concludes his philosophical work from which we quote, —

"Hast thou found, my soul, all that thou hast sought? Thou hast sought God. Thou hast found that God is the Being such that none greater can be conceived: that he is life itself, light, wisdom, goodness, everlasting beatitude, blessed eternity; that he is all this, everywhere and always. For if thou hast not found

[1] Monol., cap. lxv.

God, how canst thou say that he is all which thou hast understood
with such complete certainty, such absolute truth ? But if thou
hast found him, why doth not thy heart feel the great God whom
thou hast found ? Why, O God, why doth my soul not feel thee,
if my soul possesseth thee ? Can it be that it hath not found
him whom it hath recognized as light and truth ? How hath it
understood this, if it be not by seeing thy light and thy truth ?
Can it understand aught of thee, save through thy light and
truth ? If it hath seen light and truth, it hath seen thee. If it
hath not seen thee, it hath not seen light and truth. But perhaps what it hath seen is indeed light and truth, although it hath
not yet seen thee thyself. It hath seen thee in a certain fashion,
but it hath not seen thee as thou art (*vidit te aliquatenus, sed non
vidit sicut es*).[1] My God, my Creator, my Regenerator, tell my
soul, estranged from thee though it be, what thou art, above and
beyond what it hath seen, to the end that it may one day learn to
see thee purely.

"Verily, Lord, that light wherein thou dwellest is an inaccessible light, and nought can penetrate it, so far as to see thee thyself. I therefore do not see it, — it is far beyond me ; there is no
proportion between it and me ; and yet by means of it I see all that
I see : even as my feeble sight sees by the light of the sun all that
it sees, although it cannot gaze at that light in the sun itself."

Thus this knowledge of God, acquired by reason, is a vision
which is still problematic, — a vision in a mirror. Reason
entereth not into that inaccessible light which shows God
directly and immediately. But if that light be inaccessible
to the forces of nature, man may be raised to it by the favor
of God (*quæ inacessibilis est viribus nostris, sed acceditur
ad eam muneribus divinis*).[2] Saint Anselm, therefore, distinguishes, as do all the Fathers, between the two modes, natural
and supernatural, indirect and direct, in which the soul may
see the light of God.

It is thus that he distinguishes between knowledge which
is purely human and knowledge which is purely divine. But

[1] Prosl., xiv.   [2] Homil., iv. in Ev. sec. Matth.

in practice he clings particularly to that knowledge, at once human and divine, which is the fruit of reason working in the light of revelation. This is expressed by those beautiful words so often quoted, which are, as it were, the motto of all Saint Anselm's works : —

"I long to possess, in so far as possible, the intelligence of the truth, O my God, of that truth which my heart loves and believes. I seek not intelligence to the end that I may believe, but I would believe to the end that I may have intelligence. I believe things which I could never comprehend if I did not first believe them.[1] ... Thanks to thee, O my God, that which at first I believed by thy grace I now see by thy light; so that if I should cease to believe that thou art, O my God, I could not cease to know it."[2]

So that, according to Saint Anslem, truths at first received through faith become so luminous that we can no longer help seeing them, even independently of faith. Faith, therefore, is the root of knowledge. "But if the true order exacts that Christian mysteries be received through faith, before reason undertakes to discuss them, so too we should be, it seems to me, guilty of negligence if, when we are established, we did not seek eagerly for the intellectual possession of that which we believe."[3]

And, in our opinion, this is incomparably the best way to arrive at philosophical discoveries. The example of Saint Anselm himself is a proof of this. Saint Anselm, in fact, is the stimulator of the great Scholastic movement, which is of all historic movements that which has done most to develop human reason. Moreover, Saint Anselm is perhaps the first of all the philosophers to handle methodically the idea of the infinite, that lever of science. If ideas required a genealogy, and if every clear-sighted mind did not perceive them in the light of God, there would be strong reasons for thinking

[1] Prosl., cap. i.
[2] Ibid., cap. iv.
[3] Cur Deus homo., lib. i. cap. ii.

that Saint Anslem's metaphysics form, in the development of the human mind, the first perceptible germ from which the invention of the infinitesimal calculus was afterwards to be developed. Saint Anselm's great idea, the formula which constantly recurs in his writings, is this: "The being such that none greater can be conceived." Now, this formula is not merely synonymous with the word *infinite*, it is a definition of it. The *infinite* is a word often used, which will often be used again, in a vague or false way, to the point of confounding it, as did the ancients, with the indefinite. Now, Saint Anselm's formula is the proper definition of the infinite, such as our reason can conceive it. The indefinite, in fact, is such that we can always conceive of something beyond it. The infinite, on the contrary, the infinite alone, is such that we can conceive of nothing beyond it. It is that absolute limit of which Leibnitz speaks, which is above and outside all size, which increasing size cannot attain, and which itself cannot increase. Now, faith, completely reasoned out, become evident, faith in the existence of the real and actual infinite, is the highest of all ideas, and the strongest of all scientific motives. It is, as it were, a type of truth, a general method of discoveries. This idea teaches us, in all things, to push reason to its farthest limit, to refer every contingent notion to its eternal exemplar, to seek out what may be the divine idea to which every object corresponds, as being its transitory and partial image; in fine, to study his creatures in God, as when geometry searches in the infinite for the laws and secret nature of finite forms.

The Church pays the following amazing testimony to Saint Anselm's philosophic work: "His writings show plainly that he derived from Heaven the form of doctrine by which he defends our faith, and which has been followed since by all theologians who apply the Scholastic method to sacred things." [1]

[1] Brev. Rom., April 21, lect. vi.

What is this form of doctrine? It is plainly that great Christian method, that complete process of thought which seeks Faith through Intelligence, and Intelligence through Faith. Saint Anselm, more exactly than the Fathers, gives his law to the school, and founds the admirable theologic and philosophic instruction in which the two principles of light, reason and faith, always radically distinct, remain profoundly united. And this is that which was derived from Heaven, and which earth needs, — as, I hope, may be understood in proportion as philosophy revives.

CHAPTER VI.

I.

WE may say that Saint Thomas Aquinas is to Saint Augustine what Aristotle is to Plato. We may also say that Saint Thomas includes Augustine, Aristotle, and Plato.

Saint Thomas Aquinas, as a philosopher, includes all the substance of his three great predecessors. But his mind is that of Aristotle. There are two kinds of mind, corresponding to the two processes of reasoning. Every mind employs both processes; but in almost all, one of the two prevails. Some move particularly by means of syllogistic identity, others by means of dialectic transcendence. Plato and Saint Augustine proceed mainly by means of *transcendence*, Aristotle and Saint Thomas by means of *identity*.

It is clear that Saint Thomas Aquinas must have deduced and wrought chiefly by syllogisms, since the majors were given him. That which Plato, Aristotle, and Saint Augustine found in philosophy, he had not to search out. Certainly he verified their postulates with more scrupulousness, profundity, and precision than any other man without exception. But still, his work was chiefly one of deduction, and he had reached that point of intellectual effort to which Plato alludes when, after describing one of the two processes of reasoning, that which, from the point of departure taken as primary cause, deduces its consequences by syllogisms, he passes to the other process, and says that reason, by its dialectic impulse, seizes the primary cause, not contained in the point of departure, then, thus possessing the idea and that which is dependent

upon it, it descends from idea to idea towards all the consequences of the chief idea. Such is the most customary field
of Saint Thomas's syllogisms. It is not only syllogism applied to the postulates of the senses and to abstract notions,
but it is chiefly syllogism applied to ideas, which is Plato's
distinguishing feature. This has never been sufficiently
noticed. An eminent mind, a partisan of Plato and Saint
Augustine, who did not fear to call Saint Thomas Aquinas
a destroyer of Philosophy, was led to this error from lack of
grasping the above distinction. There is here, according to
Plato, all the difference that there is between the two regions
of the world of intelligence, and, according to Saint Augustine, all the difference that there is between heaven and earth.
Saint Thomas Aquinas reasons in heaven, not on earth; he
deduces, but he deduces from heaven, not from earth.

So much for the syllogistic side of the argument. But
every mind necessarily makes use of both processes of
reasoning. Aristotle practises, and, up to a certain point,
describes both. Now, we may assert that Saint Thomas
Aquinas uses, far more than Aristotle, the chief process of
Philosophy. Saint Thomas, moreover, did not misunderstand Saint Augustine, as Aristotle misunderstood Plato, by
rejecting his dialectic; he set aside nothing in his glorious
predecessor; and that process of rational ascent, advancing
from the sensation to God, so well described by Saint
Augustine, is practised, mentioned, and also described by
Saint Thomas.[1]

There is in philosophy, in regard to the method, the same
difference between Aristotle and Plato that there is between
Lagrange and Leibnitz. Lagrange is blind and unjust in
respect to Leibnitz; he does not admit his principles; he is

---

[1] Alia rationalis scientia *dialectica* quæ ordinatur ad acquisitionem inven-
tivam, et alia scientia *demonstrativa* quæ est veritatis determinativa. 2ª, 2ᵐ, q.
51, 2, ad 3ᵐ.

willing to retain merely the results, which he claims to reach strictly by a better method. "He desires to base the entire differential calculus upon simple algebraic identities," employing for this purpose "one of those metaphysical paralogisms into which the greatest masters are liable to fall,"[1] and depending, to attain this end, upon a general principle, which is false in certain cases.[2] Instead of this, there is, between Saint Thomas Aquinas and Saint Augustine, only the difference that there is between Newton and Leibnitz, minus the dispute. Newton made the same discovery as Leibnitz, but without expressing the idea of infinite smallness; his idea is less distinct than that of Leibnitz, but it is the same, and he recognized it. Now, if Saint Thomas, upon this point, obscures Saint Augustine, it is in a yet more transparent manner, as we shall see.

II.

Saint Thomas Aquinas, in the question of the existence of God and its proof, starts with a main idea from which he never deviates ; it is that of Saint Paul : the invisible God is seen in his visible effects. We see that this is the principle of the proving of the infinite through the finite.

Henceforth, if any one object that the existence of God cannot be proved, because the proposition *God is*, is an identical and self-evident proposition, Saint Thomas confesses that it would be so to those who might know God in himself, but not to us, who only know him through his works.

If any one object that the existence of God is a truth superior to reason, and that faith alone can attain to it, he

---

[1] Cournot, Elementary Treatise on the Theory of Functions, vol. i. p. ix, French edition.

[2] This was proved by M. Lefébure de Fourcy in his lectures on the infinitesimal calculus.

denies it, and declares that reason is capable of perceiving and proving God through his works.

These two objections removed, Saint Thomas proceeds to prove the existence of God by his works.

We quote the whole of this argument. It is the second question in the Tʜᴇᴏʟᴏɢɪᴄᴀʟ Sᴜᴍ, which we translate literally, word for word. The reader will thus get an idea of one chapter in that famous Sᴜᴍ, — that abridgment of Theology written for beginners, as Saint Thomas Aquinas says.

"QUESTION II. — DOES GOD EXIST?

"This question includes three : 1. Is the existence of God self-evident? 2. Is it capable of proof? 3. Does God exist?

"Aʀᴛ. I. *Is the existence of God self-evident?*

"Those who hold that it is, proceed thus : —

"1. It is self-evident that God exists. For we call self-evident that which we know necessarily and naturally, like first principles. But, as John of Damascus asserts, every mind knows naturally that God exists. Therefore the existence of God is self-evident.

"2. Moreover, all that is instantly certain, so soon as we know the meaning of the terms, is self-evident : such is the evidence which characterizes, according to Aristotle, the first principles of proof. When you know what the whole is, and what the part is, you at once know, by this very knowledge, that the whole is greater than the part. But so soon as we know the value of the word *God*, we at once know that God is. For that name signifies, ' That which has nothing superior to it.' But that which is both real and intelligible is superior to that which is merely intelligible. Hence, God being intelligible, since you possess the idea, it follows that he is also real. Therefore the existence of God is self-evident. [This is Saint Anselm's proof.]

"Moreover, it is self-evident that truth is; for if you deny that truth is, you grant that it is not; but if truth is not, it is true that it is not. Therefore there is something true. Therefore truth is. Now, truth is God himself. ' I am the Way, the Truth, and the Life,' says the Word. Therefore it is evident that God is.

"On the contrary, we grant that none can conceive the opposite

of that which is self-evident, as Aristotle declares in regard to the
first principles of proof. Now, as a fact, we can think the opposite of the proposition : 'God is,' as we see in the Scriptures;
'The fool saith in his heart, There is no God.' Therefore the
existence of God is not self-evident.

"I reply to all this that a truth is self-evident in two ways :
1. In itself absolutely, and not relatively to us.   2. In itself, and
at the same time relatively to us.   A proposition is self-evident
when the attribute is included in the definition of the subject, as
follows : 'Man is an animate being.'   For the idea of 'animate
being' is included in the definition of 'man.'   If, therefore, every
one knew both the attribute and the subject of a proposition, that
proposition would be self-evident to all.   This is the case with
axioms whose terms are words familiar to all, such as 'being,' 'non-
being,' 'the whole,' or 'the part.'   But if any one is ignorant of either
subject or attribute, the proposition, evident in itself, is not so to
him.   Thus it happens, says Boethius, that there are truths evident
in themselves to sages only, such as : 'That mind is not subject
to space.'   I say, therefore, that the proposition, 'God is,' taken
in itself, is evident, since the attribute and the subject are identical.   For God is his very being, as we shall show.   But because
we do not know what God is, the proposition is not for us directly
evident, but requires to be proved by intermediaries more familiar
to us, although in themselves less clear, — I mean the sensible
effects of God's power.

"This established, we must reply to the first objection : that we
have, it is true, naturally within us, a sort of confused and general
knowledge of the existence of God, since, in fact, God is our sovereign Good; since the desire for the sovereign Good is natural, and
what we desire naturally, we also know naturally.   But this is not
exactly knowing the existence of God ; as, when I know that some
one is coming, I may not therefore know the man who is coming,
although I see him coming.   And, indeed, all wish for perfect happiness ; but some believe that perfect happiness lies in wealth,
others in pleasure, and so on.

"We reply to the second objection that those who hear the
word God, may not understand thereby the Being than whom
no higher can be conceived, since there are some who have
thought that God was a body.   But admitting that all under-

stand by the word 'God' the Being than whom no higher can be conceived, it does not follow that we admit that such a Being, although he be intelligible (he is this, since we think of him), therefore exists in the nature of things. And we cannot maintain that he is necessarily real, unless we grant that there is, in the nature of things, a being such that no greater can be conceived. And this is precisely what those who deny God do not grant.

"As for the third objection, it is plain, in general, that there is something true; but it is not evident, relatively to us, that there exists a first truth.

"ART. II. — *Can we prove the Existence of God?*

"Those who deny it, proceed thus : —

"1. We cannot prove the existence of God, for it is an article of faith. Now, faith is not capable of proof, for proof yields knowledge; but faith refers to things which are not seen, as the Apostle says (Epistle to the Hebrews) : therefore, the existence of God is not capable of proof.

"2. Moreover, the middle term of a demonstration is the essence of the subject. But we know of God, not what he is, but only what he is not, as John of Damascus says. Therefore, we cannot prove the existence of God.

"3. Moreover, if we could prove God, it would only be through his effects. But his effects bear no proportion to him, since he is infinite and his effects finite, and there is no connection between the finite and the infinite. A cause cannot be proved by an effect disproportionate to that cause. Therefore we cannot prove the existence of God.

"On the contrary, we cannot ignore what the Apostle says : The invisible God is seen in his visible effects. This would be false, if we could not by his effects prove that God is, for the first thing to be perceived of a being is to perceive that it is.

"I reply that *there are two kinds of proof,* — the one called proof *on account of which* (*propter quid*), which starts from the cause, from that which is intrinsically prior; the other called proof *because* (*quia*), which starts from the effect, and is prior only relatively to us.[1] When a certain effect is clearer to us than

---

[1] These are the two proofs mentioned by Plato, one of which starts from the principle and deduces its consequences, while the other reaches the principle by starting from a postulate which does not contain it. Repub., book vi., close.

its cause, we proceed to the knowledge of the cause by starting
from the effect. Now, every effect is sufficient proof that its
individual cause exists, when we are more familiar with these
effects than with their cause. The effect depending on the cause,
it is certain, if the effect exists, that the cause pre-exists. Thus
the existence of God, which to us is not self-evident, is proved by
its effects which we know.

"To the first objection it may be answered that the existence
of God, and other truths concerning God which may be known to
us through natural reason, as Saint Paul says in his Epistle to the
Romans, are not articles of faith, but preambles of faith. Faith
presupposes reason and natural knowledge, as grace presupposes
nature, and perfection presupposes the perfectible. Nevertheless,
nothing prevents the reception of that which is intrinsically capable of proof and naturally capable of being known as an article of
faith by those who do not understand the proof.

"We reply to the second objection that when we prove a cause
by its effects, we cannot start with a definition of the cause, but
must depend upon the effect ; and this is especially true in regard
to God ; because, to prove that a thing is, we must start with the
signification of its name, and not with its definition, — the definition coming after the proof of existence. Now, as we shall see,
the names of God are borrowed from his effects ; when, therefore,
we prove God by his effects, we may take the meaning of one or
other of his names as our middle term.

"We reply to the third objection : From effects disproportionate to their cause we can gain no complete knowledge of that
cause, but every effect is sufficient to prove *that* its cause exists.
Therefore the effects of God's power can prove to us that God is,
although they cannot acquaint us with all that he is.

"ART. III. — *Is there a God?*

"Those who deny this, proceed thus : —

"It seems that there is no God. If one of two opposites
be infinite, the other is not. But the word *God* means infinite
good. Therefore, if God were, there would be no evil. Now,
actually, there is evil. Therefore God is not.

"2. Moreover, that which can be explained by a few principles,
does not depend on a greater number. Now, all that we see in

the world may be explained by two principles, on the supposition that God is not. All material things may be referred to a single principle, — nature ; all spiritual things may be referred to another principle, — reason and will. It is unnecessary to suppose another principle, — God.

"On the other hand, it is written : ' I am that I am.'

" I reply that the existence of God may be proved in five ways.

" Motion is the first and most manifest.

"It is an assured fact, and we see, that there is motion in the world. Now, every object in motion is moved by some other. Nothing can be moved, if it be not in potentiality relatively to the movement imparted to it ; and nothing could move save as being in act, — motion being only the passage from potentiality to act. Clearly, nothing can be changed from potentiality to act, save by that which is in act. Just as the fire, actually burning, makes the wood, which was burning in potentiality, actually burning, and thereby moves and changes it. Now, it is impossible that one and the same thing should be at once actual and potential in one and the same respect, but only in different respects. That which is hot in act is not hot in potentiality on the same point, but upon that point cold in potentiality. It is therefore impossible that one and the same object, from one and the same point of view, can be at once moved and motor, — that is to say, that it can move itself. Therefore, all that is in motion is moved by some other thing. Therefore this motor, if it be itself in motion, is in its turn moved by another, and that other by still another. But there must be a pause ; we cannot go on thus to infinity, for there would be no prime motor ; if there were no prime motor, there would not be any motor, since secondary motors only move by the prime motor, as a stick is only moved by the hand. There must therefore be a primary motor which no other moves. Every one understands that such a motor is God.

" The second proof is that of the efficient cause.

" We find in visible things a series of efficient causes, each of which produces the other ; but we find nothing, and we can find nothing, which is its own efficient cause, since such a cause would be before being, which is impossible. Now, it is not possible to reascend endlessly from cause to cause, for in the sum total of the series of causes, the beginning is the cause of the middle, the middle of the end, whatever may be the number of terms. But if we remove the cause, we remove the effect. Therefore if there were no first efficient cause there would be no middle or end to the series. But if there were an infinite series of efficient causes, there would be no first one, and therefore there would be neither a last effect, nor middle efficient causes, which is manifestly false. Therefore, there must be a first efficient cause, which all call God.

" The third proof is that of the possible and the necessary.

" We see beings who may be or not be, since there are corruptions and generations. Now, it cannot be that that which is such can endure forever, for that which may not be, in a certain space of time ceases to exist. If, therefore, all might not be, it would follow that there was a time when nothing was. But in that case there would still be nothing now, for that which is not, does not begin to be, save through that which is already. If, therefore, nothing was, nothing can ever have begun to be; therefore there would be nothing, — which is false. Therefore all beings are not merely possible, and there is a necessary being. Now, that which is necessary·has in itself or outside itself the cause of its necessity. But there cannot be an endless series of necessary·beings, external necessities, any more than there is an endless series of efficient causes. We must therefore establish the fact that there is something necessary itself, having no other cause for its necessity, but being the cause of all which is necessary. Now, the being necessary in itself is God.

" The fourth proof is that of the degrees of perfection.

" We find more or less, and degrees of goodness, truth, nobility, and all other qualities of things. But the more and less can only be applied to various beings variously approaching a sovereign type ; as, for example, warmth is that which partakes more or less of absolute heat. There is therefore also a being who is supremely good, supremely true, supremely noble, and who thence is the Supreme Being. For, as Aristotle says, that which is supremely true is supremely. Now that which is supremely endowed with all perfection, of whatsoever kind it may be, is the cause of all degrees of perfection of the same kind, as fire is the cause of all heat. There is, therefore, a being who is the cause of the being, of the goodness, of the perfection of all being, and that being is God.

"Lastly, the fifth proof is drawn from the government of the world.

"We see certain intelligent beings, such as bodies, tend to an end, since they do, usually or always, and in the same way, that which leads them to a desired goal. Therefore it is not accidentally, but rather in consequence of an intention, that they attain that end. But having no knowledge, they have no individual intention, and advance to their end only as directed by an intelligence which possesses intention, as when the arrow is directed by the hunter. There is therefore an intelligent being who orders nature and guides it to its end. We call this God.

"Let us answer the first objection in Saint Augustine's words. God, being supremely good, would by no means suffer the presence of evil in his work, if he were not so all powerful and all good that he can make good proceed from evil. The infinitude of God's goodness endures if he permits evil only in order to produce a greater good.

"To the second objection we reply that as nature, which acts in that intention, advances towards its end only through the manifest intention of a superior mind, we must refer to God, as prime cause, all that nature effects. So, too, that which acts through intention should also be referred to a higher cause than human reason or will, because those two powers are variable and defectible. Now, everything variable, everything defectible, presupposes a first principle immutable and intrinsically essential, as we have just shown."

III.

Throughout this little treatise by Saint Thomas Aquinas upon the existence of God, in all his proofs and arguments there is one leading idea, — namely, the invisible God can be proved through his works. Now, this is precisely the basis of true demonstration, that which rises from the sight of the finite to the infinite, the proof which is familiar to every one, — to Plato, Aristotle, Saint Paul, Saint Augustine, all thinkers, to poets and the people.

Moreover, St. Thomas Aquinas clearly distinguishes be-

tween the proof which moves from cause to effect, which
deduces, which derives a consequence from a principle by
means of syllogism, and that which reascends from the
effect to the cause not contained in the effect, which advances
from finite effect to infinite cause.

He knows the objection to this point, and presents it
vigorously (Art. II., ad. 3ᵐ). " We can only," he objects,
"prove God through his works. Now, his works are wholly
disproportionate to himself, since he is infinite and his works
are finite, and there is no proportion between finite and infinite." He replies, "That an effect, disproportionate to its
cause, cannot reveal its entire cause, but can prove that it
exists."

He asserts, by the way, that those who say that there is
no God, do not accept actual infinity ; that is to say, the being
so great than none greater can be conceived (Art. I., ad. 2ᵐ).

He refutes Saint Anselm's proof, regarded as purely syllogistic and *a priori*, by the same remark that there may be
minds who deny actual infinity, and consequently do not
accept Saint Anselm's major.

Saint Thomas Aquinas therefore is perfectly aware that
this argument, to be complete, should be a proof at the same
time *a priori* and *a posteriori*, the proof of the existence of
God being the only one capable of combining these two extremes, because God is the only being at once ideal and real,
whose ideality is identical with reality, — which Saint Thomas
expresses perfectly in that statement, whose importance is
not understood : His being is his essence (*suum esse est sua
essentia*) ; that is to say, his ideality and his reality are identical. Every other being has his idea in God, and his reality
is distinct from his idea, as the finite is from the infinite.
God, who alone is infinite, is identical with his ideal, which
is himself. Therefore the proof of the existence of God is
both rational and experimental.

To establish this proof, we must know *a posteriori* that there is a Being such that none greater can be conceived. How can we know this *a posteriori?* By what effect, what experience, are we to reach it? By the path traced out by Saint Anselm, as we have seen, and followed by Descartes when he said, "I am an imperfect, incomplete being, dependent upon others, ceaselessly tending and aspiring towards something higher and better than I am;" and Descartes concludes from this experimental postulate the existence of actual infinity. And this by an intellectual and moral impulse which clings to the inner attraction of the sovereign Good. Saint Thomas shows the existence of this attraction in the soul (Art. I., ad. 1^m), when he explains the remark of John of Damascus which is brought to bear against him, — That all men know God naturally. We have, he says, a confused knowledge of him in our desire for happiness. Now, this confused knowledge is the experimental basis of distinct knowledge; it is the chief effect upon which reason relies for rising to God. This desire for happiness, this attraction of the sovereign Good, is the sense of infinity naturally existing in all men, if they do not destroy it by their own perversity.

IV.

For a better knowledge of Saint Thomas's theory of the method which rises to God, we should read his comments on Saint Paul's great words : "The invisible God is seen in his works." This divine text, as we have already seen, contains all the ideas of Saint Thomas upon this subject. Saint Thomas explains it thus.

Saint Paul is speaking of those men "who changed the truth of God into a lie, and hid that which may be known of God, which God had showed unto them. For the invisible things of him from the creation of the world are clearly seen, being understood by the things that are made, even his eternal power and Godhead."

In fact, says Saint Thomas, —

"Knowledge of the true God of itself leads us to the Good, but it is captive and bound by wilful love of injustice."

"These men, therefore, possessed to a certain extent the true knowledge of God; for what we may know of God (*quod notum est Dei*), that is, what man may know of him through reason, shone within them, was showed unto them by some inner faculty, by the intrinsic light of the soul."

"Not that, in one respect, God may not be unknown to man in this life, according to the mysterious inscription found by Saint Paul, — *Ignoto Deo*. We do not know *what God is*. In fact, our knowledge of God begins with the spectacle of the world in which we live, with the sight of those sentient creatures whose limitations can in no wise represent the divine essence. On the other hand, however, the sight of his creatures leads us to know God in three ways, as Dionysius shows in his book on the *Divine Names*.

"First, by causality (*viam causalitatis*). For all creatures being liable to change and imperfection, we must needs refer them to a perfect and unchanging principle. And this teaches us that God is."

"Secondly, by excellence (*viam excellentiæ*). For when we refer all creatures to their beginning and cause, it is a beginning which they do not contain, and a cause which absolutely transcends them, and thence we know not only that God is, but that he is above all."

"Thirdly, by negation (*viam negationis*). For this cause transcends all its effects; we must deny of it in a certain sense that which we see in created beings; and it is thus that we say of God that he is *infinite and immutable*, his creatures being finite and variable."

"God therefore, as Saint Paul says, made himself manifest."

"Now, God makes himself manifest in two ways: first, by shedding inward light upon our soul, and then by showing us the outward signs of his wisdom and power, — created beings. God thus made himself manifest to all men, both by this inward light and by his creatures, in whom we may read, as in a book, the knowledge of God."

" But, more exactly, what do we learn of God from these postulates? The invisible perfections of God, says Saint Paul,—that is,
his essence (*per quæ intelligitur Dei essentia*) ; but not in his unity.
We find traces and images of him in his creatures, which show us
partially and by their multiplicity that which is one in God, and
through this our intelligence considers the essence of God under
the forms of a goodness, a wisdom, a power, which are not such in
God."

" Secondly, we know his creative power, — that he is the beginning of all things."

" Thirdly, we know his divinity ; we know that he is the end to
which all beings tend."

" The first knowledge, that of the essence, is acquired by negation ; the second, by causality; the third, by excellence."

" What is the nature of this knowledge ? The Apostle tells us :
we see these things by intellect (*intellectu conspiciuntur*). In
fact, we know God by the intellect, not by the senses or imagination, which have not that power of transcendence which rises
above material things : and God is a spirit."

Such is the commentary on Saint Paul's words. It shows
us clearly the method of Saint Thomas Aquinas. Created
beings are the starting-point; the active force is reason, the
light which God sheds within the soul, — the process to
which he gives three names (*causalitatis, excellentiæ*, or
eminentiæ, negationis), and which leads us to perceive that
created beings, being subject to change and imperfection,
do not exist of themselves; that is to say that God is,
and that God, existing of himself, is neither subject to
change or imperfection, this process consists in perceiving
perfection (*excellentia*) in imperfection, in *denying* (*via negationis*) the limits of the finite qualities which we see.

Saint Thomas very aptly observes that to do this we must
rise by means of intellect (*transcendere*) above that which
imagination and the senses can give us. This is precisely
the process of transcendence to which we have so often referred, and which is defined by the words: *The way of excel-*

lence and *of negation* (*viam excellentiæ et negationis*), — a process which he calls elsewhere the *way of eminence* and *of elimination* (*via eminentiæ, via remotionis*), and of which he says: "These negations do not mean that he lacks that which we deny of him, but that he possesses it in excess (*hæc non removentur ab eo propter ejus defectum, sed quia superexcedit*)."

But Saint Thomas perfects this doctrine and touches its depths, in his comments upon the rest of the same chapter of Saint Paul's Epistle.

Saint Paul shows how the knowledge of God, which is given us, is not accepted; it is in us, but we smother it.

It is iniquity that smothers the knowledge of God within us. Saint Paul has already declared this, it is his first remark: "They held the truth in unrighteousness. . . . They are without excuse; they knew God, and *they glorified him not*. . . . But they became vain in their imaginations, and their foolish heart was darkened. . . . Professing themselves to be wise, they became fools. . . . They changed the truth of God into a lie, and worshipped and served the creature and not the Creator."

"*Glory*," says Saint Thomas, "is nothing but the light itself of the divine nature." Men smother it within them, and become vain in their imaginations. The human spirit escapes vanity only by resting upon God; so soon as it ceases to rely on God it is vain: the mind is empty and the heart darkened; the light of the spirit no longer illumines the heart; that heart becomes more and more foolish; it has lost that light of divine wisdom which alone can give us true knowledge of God. The eye loses sight of objects when the rays of the sun cease to give this to it; so too he who turns away from God, finding his support in himself, and not in God, loses the light of the mind. What does the man who does not ascribe to God the glory of God, that is, the divine light which falls upon him, do with that glory? He ascribes it to created beings; he sees its cause in nature or in himself. He attributes to the image that which only exists in the original, reversing everything, and making that which is secondary first. . . . The same reversal is immediately wrought in that soul which puts God below the world, from opinion and affection: its reason, which is divine, also places itself below the appetites, and falls into that *reprobate mind* (*sensum reprobum*) of which the Apostle speaks, which is the very opposite of nature, as is proved by the strange and unnatural vices to which it falls a prey. And all this because, having true knowledge of God through the light of reason, together with the sight of created beings, man does not accept it nor explain it, preferring to remain in vice.

Such is the commentary of Saint Thomas upon this grand text of Saint Paul.

All this is clearly the very foundation of the truth in regard to the question: Why not prove God explicitly? The elements of the knowledge of God are, everywhere and always, given to us, within us and outside us: within us, God himself enlightens us; outside us, he also enlightens us, by giving us a book which is his work, the world. Why do not men read this book? Their vices prevent them; this is the real obstacle. Saint Thomas, as well as Saint Paul, analyzes this mystery of iniquity; he says: It is *a reversal* (*converterunt primum in ultimum*). Theoretically, man believes himself to be the source of that light which God never ceases to shed upon him, or else he believes the material world to be its source, and that reason comes from the senses. This is a reversal. Practically, he subjects his reason to the sensual impulses which nature excites within him. Another reversal. Sense is reversed. Man overturns and reverses everything, in practice and speculatively. We shall see, in the course of this work, whether the doctrine of scientific atheism, as it is formulated to-day, be not *the doctrine of reversal* exactly and methodically applied to philosophy. This curious intellectual and moral phenomenon should throw a flood of light upon a multitude of moral, logical, and psychological questions.

Thus, in order to rise to God, we must first conquer the obstacle, as all true philosophers say. Then only are we able to take the spectacle of the world as our point of departure from which to rise to God ; then reason displays its powers, and the process which ascends to God is carried out. Then only do we wake from that guilty folly to which Saint Paul refers, and of which Saint Thomas says elsewhere : " Such folly is sinful " (*stultitia est peccatum*).

As for the process as a whole, we find in the writings of Saint Thomas a multitude of passages which show us how he understood it; notably these statements: "God is all things infinitely (*Deus est omnia eminenter*); God is in act that which in things is only potential (*Deus est actualitas omnium rerum*); All of being, goodness, and perfection to be found in any creature whatsoever, exists pre-eminently in God (*Quidquid entitatis, bonitatis, perfectionis est in quacumque creatura, totum est eminentius in Deo*) ; " and through his creatures we know God, by applying to the good qualities which we see, a process of elimination which deprives them of their limitations (*ad cognoscendum Deum oportet via remotionis.*)

V.

Everything has not been said regarding the theory of the knowledge of God as Saint Thomas Aquinas states it. Hitherto we have shown him as speaking after Aristotle's method and somewhat after Plato's fashion. He will now speak wholly like Plato and like Saint Augustine. Saint Thomas not only knew the first of those two regions of the

world of intelligibility distinguished by those sublime minds;
as a Christian and a theologian, he must have known the
other. He did know it; and we must own that he distinguishes both regions, and describes them with a precision
and exactness equalled by no other theologian or philosopher
whatever. Therefore the name of the Angel of the School,
applied to Saint Thomas, will endure.

The reader will recall what Saint Augustine says of
reason attaining to its end and becoming *power* (*ratio
perveniens ad finem suum . . . virtus vocatur*). This final
end of reason is the sight of God. Transcending the vision
of those absolute truths, which are but the eternal and certain shadow of the divine essence and the living truth, reason
finds, as Plato and Augustine say, truth itself, or the sun itself, which makes these other truths apparent. Saint Thomas
knows and discriminates so fully between these two degrees
of intelligibility that he usually makes separate questions
of them ; and the reader who does not effect a reconciliation,
sometimes takes Saint Thomas for a rationalist, — that is, for
a mind arrested at natural philosophy, which does not go to
the end, nor even so far as Plato when he speaks of the term
of the dialectic (τέλος τῆς πορείας). Now, Saint Thomas goes
farther than Plato upon this point, — as far as Saint Augustine; and he is more exact on this point than even Saint
Augustine, who is far more exact than Plato.

"There are," distinctly says Saint Thomas, "two degrees
of divine intelligibility (*duplici igitur veritate divinorum
intelligibilium existente*). There are, relatively to us, two
modes of divine truth (*duplex veritatis modus . . . duplicem
veritatem divinorum*)."

This is fundamental: THERE ARE TWO DEGREES OF DIVINE
INTELLIGIBILITY.

"Reason," he says elsewhere, "has a double term and two
degrees of perfection: a first degree, to which natural light

leads us, and a second degree, to which *the supernatural light*
is our guide." The reader must not judge this latter statement without fully comprehending it and knowing the idea
to which it corresponds in the thought of the theologians
who employ it.

Thus there are clearly two degrees of divine intelligibility
to which our intelligence may attain. But wherein does the
distinction lie ?

The distinction, according to Saint Thomas, is that which
Saint Paul makes: " For now we see through a glass darkly
(*per speculum*) ; but then face to face (*tunc autem facie ad
faciem*)."

Saint Thomas comments on this text in the same strain
as all commentators who come after him. " Now," says an
esteemed author, " we see God, not in himself immediately,
but indirectly, by reflected rays ; . . . then we shall see him
directly, perfectly, in his divine essence. . . . I shall see God
himself, as I am myself known of God." This is the thought
of Saint Thomas, whose admirable commentary upon Saint
Paul's grand expression we must quote entire. He says, —

" What is this sight through a glass, and what is this sight
face to face ? "

" We may see," he replies, " either light itself (*ipsa lux*), which
strikes the eye itself (*quæ presens est oculo*), or else its reflex
image, as when we perceive the white color of an object."

" Now, God sees himself in the first way. His essence is directly present to his intelligence, since his intelligence is his
essence (*in Deo idem est sua essentia et suus intellectus, et ideo
sua essentia est præsens suo intellectni*)."

" As for us, we know God in this life, by seeing his invisible
beauty in his creatures. The whole creation is like a mirror to
us. The order, beauty, and grandeur which God imparts to his
works teach us to know his wisdom, truth, and divine infinity.
This is the knowledge which has been called seeing through
a glass."

And now what is it to see him face to face?

"When we look into a glass, we do not see the thing itself, but its image; and when we look face to face, we see the thing itself just as it is. When, therefore, the Apostle tells us that in heaven we shall see God face to face, he means that we shall see the essence of God."

"Even as God knows my essence, I too shall know God in his essence."

"Those who say that we shall never see God, save by similitude, say what is false and impossible. . . . To say that God can only be seen by the image and reflection of his light, is to say that we cannot see the essence of God. But the soul itself is an image of God; the sight of the soul, wherein migratory man sees God, would therefore be no more enigmatic and specular than that clear, direct vision promised to us in glory. . . . And then the natural desire of mankind to reach the First Cause and behold his very self would be idle and vain."

Here certainly is light, full noonday, thrown upon what we must call the central point of Philosophy. Recall Plato's distinction between *the sight of divine phantasms, shadows of that which is,* and the sight through the intellect of *the Good itself such as it is.* Recall the same distinction as made by Saint Augustine, almost in the same terms.

Saint Thomas quotes and comments on these passages from Saint Augustine's works. In this *specular* sight, he says, in this first degree of intelligibility, it is indeed eternal truths that we see (*rationes incorporales et sempiternas*); these truths are higher than the human soul, since they are immutable (*quæ nisi supra mentem essent, incommutabiles profecto non essent*): Saint Augustine rightly speaks thus. But these truths, as we see them, are not God himself. "We see them in God, since they are eternal." Yes; but only in the sense that we see them in his light, — that is, by the natural light of reason, which is a participation in the divine light. Saint Augustine, to whom some very inopportunely take exception here, expresses himself perfectly when he says: "These intelligible spectacles only become visible to us as illumined by their sun, which is God. Just as in order to see an object with our eyes, it is not necessary to see the substance and body of the sun, so, too, to see the intelligible of this degree, it is not necessary to see the essence of God."

In this lower degree of the intelligible world, without seeing the essence of God, we still know God through our natural reason. When Saint Augustine says: "The eye of the soul is diseased, and it cannot gaze unblenchingly at this excellent light, except it be purified by the justice of faith," he refers to the sight of the essence of God. But when Saint Paul says, "That which may be known of God is manifest in them," he refers to that knowledge of God which is given to us by reason, without faith. Assuredly that reason rests upon sensible postulates which cannot show us the divine essence, since these visible effects are in no wise adequate to their cause, which is God. But yet, as these effects would not exist unless their cause existed, they prove to us that God is, and they teach us that he must be, as the cause of all, superior to all. We know that he is nothing of all that which he has created, but that all which we deny of him must be denied, not because he lacks that which we deny, but because he possesses it in excess.

Such is, according to Saint Thomas, the first of the two degrees of the world of intelligibility. The second is probably distinct therefrom.

Saint Thomas speaks of this second degree particularly in that question in the Sum: *How may the human mind know God?* (1ª, q. xii.) We give the headings of the articles into which he divides this question: —

1. Can the created intellect see God in his essence? Yes.

2. Does the created intellect which sees God's essence, see it *by any image or likeness?* No.

3. Can God's essence be seen by the material eye ? No.

4. Can created intellect see God's essence by the unaided powers of its own nature (*per sua naturalia*) ? No.

5. Does created intellect require the intermediation of any created light in order to see God's essence ? No.

6. Can God's essence be seen more or less perfectly ? Yes.

7. Is seeing God's essence the same thing as understanding God ? No.

8. Does the soul which beholds God's essence see everything in that essence ? No.

9. Does the soul see what it sees in God's essence, under any figure ? No.

10. Does he who sees God's essence, see in God, at a single glance, all that he sees therein ? Yes.

11. Is it possible, in this life, to see God's essence ? No, save it be by a miracle.

12. Can we, in this life, know God by our natural reason ? Yes.

13. Can we have, in this life, a knowledge of God deeper than that which our natural reason can give ? Yes.

Here we have this great distinction settled with a clearness and vigor which the ancients could not apply to it. There is the same difference between these two degrees of divine intelligibility that there is between the heaven and the earth.

But then — and this seems to result from what has just been established in regard to the question cited — it would follow that of the two degrees of divine intelligibility, one would be only for this world and this life, and the other for heaven and the life to come. Thus Plato and Aristotle must have been under an entire illusion when they spoke of the highest degree of divine intelligibility as capable of being grasped in this life, although with great difficulty and dimness.

Let us distinguish. Yes, according to Saint Thomas, as well as according to Saint Paul and all Christian theology, the clear vision of God's essence, save in certain rare and miraculous cases, is reserved for the life to come, for the heavenly home.

But it must be understood that in this higher of the two degrees of divine intelligibility — the one which gives us, not shadows, images, phantasms, and likenesses of God, but his essence — there are also two degrees : one to which the soul will only attain after its struggle, its labor, and its consummation, when it has reached its goal and gained the peace and rest of the heavenly home (*in patria videntium*) ; and the lower, which the soul attains during its progress (*in via videntium*). And these two degrees of the same light may be distinguished by these terms : *the light of grace* and *the light of glory (lumen gratiæ, lumen gloriæ)* ; or else, *the light of faith and the light of vision (lumen fidei et lumen visionis)*, — faith, according to Saint Thomas Aquinas, being but the beginning, still dim and unskilled, of the direct vision of God and his essence. "Faith, as to the assurance which it gives, is knowledge, and may be called science and vision. Faith is an assured beginning of the beatific vision of God. Faith belongs to the same order as the vision of the heavenly country."

Saint Thomas invariably declares faith to be the beginning of the intrinsic knowledge of God, as distinct from that reflex and abstract knowledge given by the natural light of reason.

While the natural light of reason is created truth (*veritas creata*), that is to say, the divine light reflected by a created object, — or, if you prefer, an image of unrevealed truth reflected in us (*similitudo veritatis increatæ in nobis resultantis*), — the object of faith, on the contrary, is uncreated truth, original truth (*objectum fidei, veritas prima, veritas increata*). " Faith, when it is virtue, raising human intelligence above its proper light, unites it to truth itself as it exists in the divine intelligence, truth which is the uncreated itself (*ipsius rei increatæ objectum*)." Undoubtedly, we must carefully distinguish between faith and supreme vision ; but they both have the same object. The object of supreme vision is original truth, in so far as luminous ; the object of faith is original truth in so far as obscure. It is neither God's creatures, men or angels, whose testimony leads us to believe, nor the images under which we believe, that are the object of faith, — it is God himself, with the knowledge of whom the assent of faith brings us into unity. Original truth is indeed, in itself and first of all, the object of faith (*veritas prima est primo et per se objectum fidei*).

We quote a fine passage from Saint Thomas Aquinas upon this subject ; it includes everything : —

" Light, during our earthly pilgrimage, is given to us in two ways : sometimes in a lesser degree, and as it were in faint rays. This is the light of our native intelligence, which is a participation in the eternal light, although remote, defective, comparable to darkness mingled with a little light ; which gives man that reason, the shadow of intelligence itself, whose feeble radiance gives birth to a diversity of opinions to be destroyed by the direct radiation of light. Sometimes light is given in a higher degree, in more abundant clearness, and *which brings us as it were face to face with the sun.* But there our sight is dazzled, because it beholds that which is beyond us, beyond human understanding ; and this is the light of faith."

Such, therefore, is the beginning of the second degree of divine intelligibility ; it is faith, the beginning of the knowledge which we shall have in heaven (*fides quædam prælibatio brevis quam in futuro habebimus cognitionis*).

We have here a fine distinction between the two degrees of divine intelligibility, that one may be obtained by the search of reason, and that the other transcends all efforts of human reason. It is this second degree which is the object of faith, and "although reason by faith cannot wholly grasp it, yet a high degree of perfection is given it, if it can grasp it in any way, through faith." Profane philosophy does not enter here, and it is of this that Saint Paul speaks when he says: "God hath revealed unto us by his Spirit what none of the princes of this world knew." "The princes of this world," says Saint Thomas, "are the philosophers." Philosophers suspect and know by conjecture and reasoning the existence of this region, but they do not enter it; and, as Saint Thomas says, "Certain of them see the light, but are not in the light." And he lays stress on Isaiah's vigorous words: "Seeing many things, thou observest not." (*Qui multa vides, nonne custodies ?*)   (Is. xlii. 20.)

Thus, in brief, the doctrine of Saint Thomas Aquinas is this: God is light; man may see the light which is God, directly or indirectly. These are the two degrees of divine intelligibility. Naturally he sees only the second degree; that is to say, the reflection or image of uncreated truth in the mirror of created beings, or the mirror of the soul. This is what is called the natural light of reason. But there is a higher degree of light for which the human mind has some natural desire. The human mind would fain see *the First Cause itself in itself.* This sight is the sight of the essence of God, the direct sight of the light which is God. This is why this degree is called that of supernatural light, God being above and beyond all nature. But there are two degrees of lucidity, in the supernatural degree itself; there is the confused, implicit, dazzled, and unpractised vision: this is faith, *the light of grace ;* and there is clear vision, supreme vision in *the light of glory.* The one is offered to man during his journey through this life (*in via videntium*); and the other awaits just men and saints at the end of their journey in the heavenly home (*in patria videntium*).

VI.

Do not understand, I beg, all these terms, *faith, grace, glory, natural light,* and *supernatural light,* as being more than names applied to the intelligible objects described; let us for a moment forget their theological meaning. We say that at any rate we have here an exact description and a complete guide to that world of intelligibility into which Plato looked. Saint Thomas is as superior to Plato in exact knowledge of the world of intelligibility as Kepler and Newton are to Pythagoras in astronomy. Pythagoras indeed thought that the stars must form a heart, of which the sun, the source of light, was lord and centre; so he said. But Kepler and Newton said: Yes, these worlds revolve about the sun in curves whose geometric nature is as follows; they are attracted towards that centre by a force whose law is as follows. Here, moreover, you have the speed and weight of each of these worlds.

Such is the distance between the conjecture and instinct of genius, on the one hand, and on the other revealed and exact knowledge. I rank Plato very high, but I consider Saint Thomas Aquinas as even more above Plato than our knowledge of the physical world is above that of the Greeks. Plato worked almost alone, amidst the gloom of the antique world; Saint Thomas worked beneath the sun of Christianity, sustained by the labor, the experience, and the wisdom of innumerable witnesses of the light, — just as our modern science, the fruit of a common industry, is enlightened by all which is shown it by thousands of eyes, increased by all that hundreds of thousands of hands can bring to it.

But Saint Thomas Aquinas is not understood! There are in him heights, depths, and precisions which contemporary intellect is far from suspecting, and which may perhaps be

understood several generations hence, if philosophy is re-
vived, if wisdom reappears among us.   Aristotle says somewhere that probably the arts and philosophy have been
discovered and lost several times over; that this is the cause
of those fragments of antique wisdom brought down to us by
tradition.   I believe this also, but in a different sense.
Philosophy was discovered by Plato and Aristotle, by Saint
Augustine, by Saint Thomas Aquinas, by the seventeenth
century, but was lost in the intervals.   To-day, among us,
it is evidently lost.   We read ancient monuments without
understanding them ; we do not know the language in which
they are written ; we do not penetrate their meaning.

The centuries lose wisdom or find it again, just as a man
may lose or find the truth, at different periods of his life,
according as his soul is dissolved in sensual pleasure and
fallen into the night of the senses, or steeped in virtue and
lifted towards the intelligible.   When a man renounces
wisdom, he does not therefore forget the discourse which
divine wisdom has held with his soul, the words which it
has graven on his memory : but those words have lost their
aureole, their life, their charm, their meaning ; they are
withered remnants, which thought, whose abode is elsewhere,
rolls along in its course because they are there ; but she no
longer uses them or believes in them.   Such is the state of
contemporary thought in regard to the noble philosophy of
the past and the wisdom of the great ages; it possesses all
their monuments, but has not their intelligence, and still less
their faith.

CHAPTER VII.

PART FIRST.

FROM Saint Thomas Aquinas we pass to the seventeenth century. In the interval, the human mind has apparently undergone a great change: on all sides Aristotle is rejected ; the Scholastic system and Saint Thomas Aquinas himself are held in less esteem, and this among the wisest and most learned. Clever intellects exclude and despise the philosophy of the past. Men desire to see for themselves ; they ardently search after truth, rather than the mere tradition of truth. They have resolved to find true knowledge; the mind takes a fresh flight, and, by a generous effort, sheds upon this noble age the greatest flood of human light ever known. We shall now see whether this light be other than the light of the past.

The mind of man will doubtless extend itself to fresh objects, and shine with more lustre in certain directions; but its laws will remain unchanged. Its former acquisitions will become deeper; it will complete and verify what it had already found in past ages, and, according to an admirable expression of the Holy Scripture, *their knowledge shall be renewed ;* but we shall see that the light has not changed, and that the renewed knowledge is, in fact, ever old and ever new.

I.

The seventeenth century should be treated as a single man, or better, as a choir of voices. Never were the har-

mony and unanimity of great minds more apparent, despite
certain easily corrected dissonances. True, these noble
geniuses count as nothing Spinoza, that questionable spirit,
and, with the exception of Leibnitz, who was far too amiable,
have nothing to say to Locke, an opaque intellect. The
seventeenth century did not take the absurd in earnest, but
set sophists on one side, and practised, in philosophy, the
great literary precept: *Hoc amet, hoc spernat*, " Know how
to love, and how to scorn," — an important characteristic of
truly philosophic minds or ages, which, because they know
the true, also know the false, and because they are luminous, drive away darkness. Night alone is favorable to the
equality of systems and to a common respect for error and
truth. The seventeenth century, on the contrary, is exclusive in the light, and firm in the unity of truth. From
this centre, it radiates light and strength and the wealth of
its harmonies. Would that I might reproduce something of
this in these pages ! My readers would then feel that if the
mind of man is destined to take another step forward, the
next great century, still more united in its view of the truth,
still more fully divided from the false, will witness the birth
of certainties of which we have lost sight, of unanimities for
which we have ceased to hope, and of some beginning of
that luminous peace which is to unite sciences and minds
in God.

All the philosophers of the great century sought God before anything else, knowing that he is the first truth and
the universal light. Certainly it was not to *demonstrate* the
existence of God that these men, full of practical sense as
they were, meditated their demonstrations. But they
knew that there would be found the centre of all philosophy, the foundation of metaphysics, the vital question
of method, the science of the soul, the point of contact between logic and morals, the basis of physics, and the essen-

tial meaning, so long sought for, of geometry. Kepler, the oldest of these pleiades, worked in science, discovered the heavens, only that he might "frame a tabernacle for his God therefrom." The others had the same purpose: Descartes, Pascal, Malebranche, Fénelon and Bossuet, Leibnitz, Clarke and Newton, Thomassin and Petau, the latter twain too little known, because they wrote in Latin: all seek God in every direction of thought; and all these voices are truly united in one and the same tone, one and the same song; their subject is Being and infinite perfection; and everything is combined in this wondrous symphony, from Theology, with its dogmatic decisions, to mathematics themselves, by the marvellous invention of Leibnitz.

Let us cast a comprehensive glance at the proof of the existence of God given by all these great minds. We will listen to each of them in turn.

The mystics shall begin, — I mean the true mystics, those whom Bossuet calls, "Safe mystics." [1]

All mysticism is contained in this motto: "Not only hear, but feel and suffer, the divine." [2] It is of this degree of inner contemplation that Saint Bonaventura says: "Not only to see divine spectacles, but to taste divine savors." [3] The mystic school is a school of divine experiments.

I do not hesitate to affirm that the distaste for abstract and isolated reasoning, and the need of experiment, which characterizes the modern scientific movement, was first made manifest among the mystics, and probably comes from them. The "Imitation of Christ" popularized this feeling; then the ardent piety of the Jesuits and the saintly spirit of the close of the seventeenth century rooted it in men's souls. Saint Philip Neri, Saint John of the Cross, Saint Theresa,

---

[1] Mystici in tuto.

[2] Non solum discens, sed et patiens divina.

[3] Non solum ad tuenda spectacula, sed etiam ad gustanda divina solatia.

Saint Francis de Sales, the pious school of Condren and Olier, and a multitude of ascetic writers of that period, spread abroad a feeling of contempt for abstract reasoning and "dry light," as Bossuet expresses it, and they urged men's souls to the direct perception of reality, to knowledge of life by personal experience. They apply this process of realism to the knowledge of God and the soul; others later on were to apply it to the knowledge of nature.

Upon this basis of practical piety, the effort of genuine thinkers stands out in bold relief: after the saints come the sages. The latter develop the profound truth grasped by the mystics; they descend into their own souls, and seek there for traces of God. Descartes, meditating on the soul, marks the way by these words: "I am an imperfect, incomplete thing, dependent upon another, ever tending and aspiring towards something better and higher than I am; but the great things to which I aspire are actually and infinitely possessed by him on whom I depend."[1]

Here we have the finite and the infinite face to face. The finite seen in ourselves as such by the direct experience of life, and the infinite grasped in the finite by a contrast of experience, and by the impulse of reason, which, without deviation or turn or discourse, conceives and declares the infinite.

Here we have the whole dialectic method. The entire, chief process of reasoning is contained here: the soul, a bounded thing, regarded as finite and imperfect, furnishes a starting-point: desire for the perfection which we do not possess, but would fain have, is the motive spring; hence results the flight of reason towards its object, — the absolute and actual infinite.

But Descartes and others bring out features which their predecessors of the Middle Age merely indicated. This is the advance in the proof of the existence of God. For

[1] Third Meditation, close.

. instance, they explain two things which Saint Thomas
stated, but possibly without bringing them into sufficient
juxtaposition, and which include the whole process: —

1. God is all things *eminently* (that is, *infinitely*). All
the being, goodness, perfection, found in any creature whatsoever, all this is in God in an infinite degree.[1]

2. To know God, we must employ a process of elimination.[2]

They all say with Leibnitz: "The perfections of God are
those of our souls, but raised to infinity." They all say
with Fénelon: "Destroy limitations, and you will dwell in
the universality of Being." Take the finite, destroy its
limitations, and you have that which corresponds to it in the
infinite. And they determine this process to such a point
that they apply it to geometry, and renew the aspect of
mathematical science by the application. We shall now
endeavor to make this clear by details.

DESCARTES.

I.

I will not say, —

"At last Descartes comes, and, the first in France,"

founds philosophy by restoring freedom to human reason.
I do not know who was the founder of philosophy, and ·
human reason had been free for many centuries: Jesus
Christ set it free, with the entire man.

But without exaggerating the influence of Descartes, it is
very evident that he imparted a great and fertile movement
to his century.

I must confess that I never greatly admired his Discourse
on Method. I see, moreover, as all admit, and as the Index

---

[1] 1. Deus est omnia eminenter. Quidquid entitatis, bonitatis, perfectionis
est in quacumque creatura, totum es eminentius in Deo.

[2] 2. Ad cognitionem Dei oportet uti via remotionis.

has decided, that Descartes is open to correction. But it is impossible to regard him as a sceptic and a wicked spirit. Such a spirit is to be excluded, not corrected. Clearly, the methodic doubt of Descartes is merely a vigorous defiance of scepticism. "I am called a sceptic," he says somewhere, "because I have fought sceptics. I am called an atheist, because I have proved the existence of God." Descartes claimed to sound the active powers of reason, and to reveal its resources; this certainly is one of the most useful tasks which could be undertaken for the benefit of mankind. Descartes understands what Fénelon says later: "There is far greater lack of reason than of religion in this world." He knew — as we may also conclude from a passage in the works of Saint Thomas Aquinas — that attacks upon reason are still more dangerous than attacks upon faith, because they ruin both at the same time, — that is to say, the sacred edifice, and the ground on which it stands. He labored to prepare the way for that future prophesied by Leibnitz: "A time will come when men will devote themselves to reason far more than hitherto." He showed in this work a matchless energy, an' invincible determination, and a faith which made him victorious.

To begin with, he proceeded at once to the heart of philosophy, to the basis and origin of reasoning, which is God; and there he stood fast almost throughout his career. Pascal was unjust when he reproached him with a wish to do without God in his physical researches. Descartes was even then pursuing in matter the laws, that is, the traces, of God. He abstracted, but he did not deny.

Descartes took up again, stated precisely, and simplified the proof of the existence of God, — that living proof which is, as we have already said, the act and fundamental process of the rational life. If the way in which Aristotle set forth his proofs made them dry and inapplicable in practice, it is not so with the work of Descartes. Many minds have been powerfully impressed and uplifted by the mighty impulse of his vigorous reasoning; and we might quote women, even in this century, whom the reading of Descartes has led to the most ardent piety, by the direct certainty and the species of intellectual perception of God derived therefrom by those who understand what they read.

II.

The true Cartesian proof of the existence of God rests upon what we may call natural prayer. Natural prayer is the impulse of the soul, which feels that it is limited and imperfect, towards the infinite which it conceives and desires. This prayer, or this impulse of the soul, which rises to God through desire and thought, and which proves his existence by thinking of and desiring him, is contained in these words, which we quote in full: " Not only do I know that I am an imperfect, incomplete thing, dependent on another, ever tending and aspiring towards something greater and better than I am, but I also know that he on whom I depend possesses in himself all those great things towards which I aspire, the ideas of which I find within myself," and that he possesses them "not indefinitely and potentially alone, but actually and infinitely, and thus that he is God." [1]

These profound words contain the conditions of the true proof in the most precise and explicit form : (1) the point of support, which is the finite being whom we see and whom we are; (2) the moral condition, or the motive spring, — namely, the moral life, which consists, speaking exactly, in constantly tending and aspiring towards something better and greater; that is, in yielding to the charm of the supreme Good ; (3) the process, that is, the advance of reason from disdain of the imperfect to the idea of infinite perfection.

[1] Descartes, Third Meditation, near close.

"There are but two ways," says Descartes, "in which we can prove that there is a God, — namely, one by his works, and the other by his essence."[1] That is to say, there is the experimental proof and the rational proof, — the proof *a posteriori,* and the proof *a priori.* We have already explained that the two proofs combined form the unassailable proof.

Now, in the words of Descartes already quoted, the two proofs are in one. It should be so, because God is the Being in whom ideality and reality are identical.

Descartes, it is true, afterwards elaborates them separately, and sometimes, perhaps, seems to lose sight of their unity; nevertheless, he does not break the connecting link, they are always united in his thought.

He states the first one thus: "The existence of God is demonstrated by his works from the mere fact that his idea is innate in us."[2]   .

He states the second thus: "We may prove that there is a God from the mere fact that the necessity of being or existence is included in our notion of him."[3]

Let us try to set forth the double rational and experimental proof contained in this double proof, to show the profound unity of the two, and their absolute certainty when we do not isolate them.

III.

We are not now demonstrating; we are showing, we are setting forth, we are striving to place these truths before the eye of the mind, — the mind which will see and comprehend them.

I think, I am. My thought is imperfect, because it hesi-

---

[1] Reply to the First Objection, i. 395.
[2] Medit., i. 293.   [3] Ibid., iii. 72.

tates, doubts, and mistakes; my being is imperfect, limited, finite; I see it and I feel it.

What is it to see and feel that my being is finite? It is to see, in seeing the finite, the infinity by contrast.

My whole being tends and aspires towards something greater and better than myself; and not only does it now aspire thus, but we see plainly that it will always thus aspire, — that is, it always aspires towards something greater than any given greatness. But something greater than any given or assignable greatness is infinity. Thus, my life is a tendency towards the infinite.

It is evident that this is true of every upright mind and healthy will. A perverse will, a corrupt mind, far from tending towards the infinite, tends towards lesser being, or nothingness: all true philosophers have noted this. There is a moral as well as an intellectual condition for this conception of the mind and this tendency of life towards infinity.

But this condition presupposed, it being no other than a healthy state of the moral and intellectual being, that moral and intellectual being, finite and imperfect as it is, conceives, from the very perception of its own imperfection, perfection; and it is drawn towards the perfect being by the very centre of its own being and the root of its life. Moreover, this is only what Aristotle says when he speaks of the first motionless motor which moves everything by its attraction, — the attraction of desirability and of intelligibility.

The attraction of the sovereign Good is felt by all men: every philosopher, every theologian, every man who uses his reason, sees this and says it. It is a truth at once *rational and experimental ;* it is a moral law, as real and scientific as that of the universal attraction of bodies.

God is at the same time desirable and intelligible, — two qualities which are but one in him: as desirable and as intelligible, he attracts all souls; and this actual effect of

13

God within us is called either *the attraction of the sovereign Good*, the *natural and universal desire for happiness*, or *the natural knowledge of God*, or else the *innate idea of God*, or yet again, the *divine sense*.

The last expression is the simplest, most complete and exact; it includes and amends the others: the others are somewhat exclusive, and refer either to the intelligible alone, or to the desirable alone ; this, from its complex meaning, is relative to both aspects.   Like sensation itself, which is, as has been remarked, both *representative* and *affective*, the *divine sense* implies two elements, — an element of knowledge and an element of love ; the divine sense is both intellectual and moral, its cause being both intelligible and desirable, — as we are both intelligence and will.   Moreover, the divine sense implies these elements, but does not explain them ; it gives a vague attraction and a confused idea, as Saint Thomas Aquinas observes ; it is, as Aristotle says, a power close at hand, ready to burst forth, but only bursting forth when the obstacle is removed.   God, by his presence, makes us this gift, which is innate, continual, universal. The gift has been made : it is put into our hands ; it remains for us to accept it with our reason and our freedom ; it remains for us to render explicit within us, by reason, the confused idea of God, and by freedom, the vague attraction towards God.   The corrupt spirit, the perverted intellect, changes the confused idea into a thousand monstrous errors, — into general idolatry.   A perverted will changes the vague attraction into corrupting passions.   We have our choice ; there is the act, both rational and free, which we must call the fundamental act of both intellectual and moral life.   From the finite being which he sees, which he is, which exists up to a certain point, but not beyond it, man may infer Being or nothing.   Stimulated by the *divine sense*, which urges him towards the Absolute from the one side or the other, man decides the direction in which he will be urged, and chooses his own conclusion. One man concludes in infinite Being, another in non-being; one asserts the existence of Good, the other, of evil; one says God, the other, nothing. This is what actually, historically, takes place in the bottom of every man's heart.

In this inner history of the soul's relation to God we should always read and study the proof of the existence of God. There we find it at once and inseparably moral and intellectual, rational and experimental, and conceive of God felt through his effects in the living reality, and seen by the essential idea which he puts within us.

It is therefore clear how the idea of infinite, necessary Being is actually developed in the mind as soon as the will yields to the moral attraction which implies it, and how this idea comes, by virtue of that infinite, necessary Being which shows itself as intelligible, after having made itself felt as desirable.

And here, as Descartes says, is the point "chiefly to be considered, and upon which all the force and all the light, or the intelligence, of this argument depend."[1] In fact, God himself makes himself visible in his idea. In a certain way it is God that we see. Henceforth we are sure that he exists, since we see him. Herein lies the depth and solidity of the proof.

Descartes and all the great school of the seventeenth century, in harmony, moreover, with the philosophy of the past, maintain that, in the idea of God, it is God who shows himself, and that in a certain sense we see him. "*The idea is the thing itself conceived,*"[2] Descartes constantly says, — an excellent phrase, which implies this axiom, accepted by Descartes, "All that is ideal is real, all that is real is ideal:" a profound truth, but one which should be thoroughly un-

[1] Vol. i. p. 375.   [2] Ibid., p. 370.

derstood, for we may carry it to an absurd conclusion, as
the Germans do at the present day.

IV.

Descartes and the seventeenth century, we say, concede
that in the idea of God it is, in a fashion, God whom we
see. In what fashion? This is the only question. Is God
seen directly *in himself?* Or is God seen indirectly *in the
soul?*

Descartes grasps the truth in regard to this question.
Malebranche and others go too far. What is the idea of
God, according to Descartes? Is it God? Is it ourselves?
It is both God and ourselves, seen at the same time; or
rather, it is my soul, seen in the light of God: I see my soul
directly; I see it in the light of God, without which everything is invisible, and I see God, who is that light, but by
a reflected ray.

Descartes maintains that *the idea is the thing itself conceived,*[1] which he explains thus:—

"The idea of God is God himself, existing in the understanding,
— not, it is true, formally, as he is intrinsically, but objectively,
that is, in the way that objects usually exist in the understanding.
This existence in the understanding is not a mere nothing.[2]   It is
not something feigned by the mind, not, as the saying is, an imaginary being; it is something real which is distinctly conceived,
and which, certainly, requires some cause other than the understanding for its conception.   Thus we must regard the objective
reality which exists in the idea of God; its cause can only be an
actually existing God.   Yes, for the very reason that we have
within us the idea of God, in which all conceivable perfection is
contained, we may very clearly infer thence that this idea depends
upon and proceeds from some cause which actually contains in itself all this perfection; namely, an actually existing God."[3]

[1] Vol. i. p. 370.   [2] Ibid., p. 371.   [3] Ibid., pp. 373, 374.

All this is true, unless it be that Descartes does not explain with sufficient distinctness that, in the idea of God, it is the light itself of God which we see wholly in the soul, or the soul which we see in the light of God. He comes closer to it in what follows: "This idea is imprinted in a similar fashion upon every human mind, . . . and therefore we suppose that it belongs to the very nature of our mind, and certainly not improperly; but we forget one thing, which we ought chiefly to consider, and on which all the force and all the light or intelligence of this argument depends, which is that *this faculty of having in one's self the idea of God could not be in us if our mind were only a finite thing, as it actually is,* and if it had not, as the cause of its being, a cause which was God,"[1] that is to say, infinite. This is of the utmost importance. Thus we see something finite and something infinite; any perception which we have of the infinite is an effect of which God is the cause, or rather it is God himself, thought.[2] It is God indirectly perceived, God seen, not in himself, but in the mirror of the mind. Descartes explains his meaning still better: "And, in fact, it is not strange that God, in creating me, should impress me with this idea, to be as it were the Maker's mark stamped upon his work; and neither is it necessary *that this mark should be anything different from that work itself;* for the mere reason that God created me it is very credible that he should in some measure make me after his own image and likeness, *in which the idea of God is contained, and that I should know him by the same faculty by which I know myself.*"

Descartes therefore plainly understands it thus: the idea of God is God and myself, — or rather it is my soul seen in the light of God; this idea implies a finite element, which is my soul, and an infinite element, which is the light of God, whom I see, and in which I at the same time see my soul by the same faculty.

[1] Vol. i. p. 375. [2] Medit. III. (close).

Hence it is evident that "this idea is not something feigned or invented, dependent only on my thought, but that it is the *image* of a true and immutable nature." [1]

And let no one say that Descartes here falls into a familiar trap, and treats the idea of God degradingly, by calling it an *image.* Descartes is as far from this as possible. Hear what he says further: "Assuredly I do not think that this idea is of the same nature as the images of material things painted in phantasy; but, on the contrary, I believe that it can only be conceived by the understanding, and that, indeed, *it is only that very thing which we perceive through its means* (by means of the understanding), *either when it conceives, or when it judges, or when it reasons.*" [2]   This is both exact and true.   The very light of thought — I mean the light which illumines my thought, and without which I cannot think — is God himself.   Malebranche would be satisfied with this, and we should not concede him an iota too much.

Descartes develops this still further elsewhere: "The rule which I have established — namely, that the things which we conceive very clearly and very distinctly are all true — is only secúre because God exists, and is a perfect being, and all which is in us comes from him; whence it follows that *our ideas or notions being real things,* and proceeding from God, in all wherein they are clear and distinct they can be no other than true."

Thus, according to Descartes, it is in our soul that we see God: this vision of the soul, the image of God, actually enlightened by God, without which it would not be visible, is the idea of God.   Our idea of God, therefore, includes the direct vision of our soul enlightened by God, and the indirect vision of God who enlightens the soul.   The idea of the perfect Being is placed in us by the perfect Being.   The idea of the perfect Being is an effect which transcends the power of

---

[1] Vol. i. p. 316.   [2] Ibid., p. 425.

an imperfect being: I can conceive it, but only under the influence of the perfect Being. I can see in a glass the sun which is not actually there, but I could not see it if the sun did not exist, and did not cast its image into the glass. The idea of God is God seen in the mirror of the soul, — a comparison so true, so profound, so exact, that none who do not understand it can know what an idea is.

V.

Having said this, let us again take up Descartes' two proofs, — his proof *a priori* and his proof *a posteriori*.

1. I have the idea of a perfect Being, therefore he exists; for this idea implies his existence.

2. I have the idea of a perfect Being, therefore he exists; for he only could have placed this idea in me.

In themselves, and properly, these two proofs are true, and each sustains itself separately. In fact, relatively to us, they form but one, and are mutually sustained.

The first, which is Saint Anselm's proof, to which Descartes with justice clings so closely, is true in itself; for it is true that God is the necessary Being. If he is the necessary Being, that means that it is of his essence actually to exist; his being and his essence are identical, as Saint Thomas Aquinas shows; in him real and ideal are identical; his idea is his being; whoever knows what God is, sees that he is by essence; whoever knows what every being, other than God, is, sees that those beings do not exist by essence, that is to say, *are not* necessary. The true idea of any being whatsoever, except God, implies the possibility of that being; the true idea of God implies, rigorously speaking, his necessary existence, his actual reality, as the idea of a triangle implies the equality of the three angles to two right angles.

From the very idea of perfection and infinity, as Descartes

constantly repeats, it follows that this perfect and infinite Being exists: the idea of infinite Being implies that of necessary existence. For what is the meaning of the words, "The perfect and infinite Being?" They signify absolute Being, that is, Being itself. For to speak of Being simply, is to speak of Absolute Being, as Saint Augustine truly remarks. Now, would it not be the most violent and absurd of all contradictory propositions to say: Being is not? Therefore, Being is, that is, the absolute, perfect, and infinite Being, that is, God, is.

Descartes confesses, and we must admit, that at first sight this argument, that the mere idea of the infinite and perfect Being implies the idea of necessary existence, seems a sophism to those who do not fathom it. The reason, 'he says, is this: "We are so accustomed in all other things to distinguish *existence* from *essence* that we do not consider how it appertains to the essence of God rather than to that of other things. . . . But we must make a distinction between *possible* and *necessary* existence, and observe that possible existence is included in the notion or idea of all things of which we conceive clearly or distinctly, but that necessary existence is included in the idea of God alone." [1]

Therefore the existence of God is at once an actual truth, a reality; and a rational truth, a necessary idea *a priori*, which is not true of any other existence. Not only does God exist, but he *must* exist, which is not true of any other being. It is as much a necessity, says Descartes, as the fact that the three angles of a triangle equal two right angles. It is just as necessary, and even clearer, says Descartes, and he says truly; for the proposition, Being is, is clearer than that the three angles of a triangle equal two right angles. It is plain that Being is; and Being is God.

All this, therefore, is intrinsically true; but is all this a

[1] Vol. i. p. 390.

proof relatively to us, to every mind, to man as he comes into this world? As Saint Thomas Aquinas remarks, if we do not already know what God is, if we have not his true idea, how can we know that his essence implies his existence, as the idea of a triangle implies the equality of the three angles to two right angles? We must first have his idea, true, real, and living, that is to say, enacted and caused in us by him. He gives us that divine sense which implies the true idea, — *divine sense, natural rational faith, or innate idea,* as so many gifted minds express it; *confused knowledge,* as Saint Thomas says; *vague thought,* as Leibnitz says: this is the germ given by God. But how is this germ set free? Ordinarily, it is set free by the word of another: another mind, by its word, is the father of mine, and sets in action that divine sense which is the first potentiality of the idea of God. This proximate potentiality passes into act under the influence of speech, if my mind responds to it; that is to say, if my reason, by the power which is in it, rises to the meaning of the word. And reason has this power naturally, because it is the light which illumines every man coming into the world, and because, starting from God, it 'seeks God. But the moral obstacle must not arrest it in this spontaneous energy of its impulse towards the infinite. If, therefore, the spirit, under the inner influence of the divine sense and the outer influence of the word, responds, by an act of moral and intellectual consent, to the light which God shows it, and which is God, the mind then has the true idea of God, in which it can clearly see, by a throng of reasons, that existence is implied.

Thus it is that Descartes' two proofs are actually inseparable to us, and constitute but one. The proof of the existence of God, derived from the idea alone, is clear and proved to us only when we have the idea of God. Now, the obtaining of this idea of God supposes an experimental postulate, and also a moral condition, which is the starting-point of the second proof.   At the same time, the moral and experimental condition does not suffice.   It is essential that the divine sense, or, if you prefer, the real attraction of the desirable and intelligible, felt by the soul, should come into the light; our reason must take possession of it.   Seeing this faint light of the implicit idea of God,— that is to say, seeing our soul, wherein God shines,— reason must distinguish the light from the glass, God from the soul, the infinite from the finite, and the perfect from the imperfect; to the end that it may assert the infinite at the same time that it sees the finite.

Theoretically, the dim idea of infinity passes into light by the following degrees.   We feel at first, simultaneously and obscurely, the finite and the infinite, God and the soul, life itself being only the harmony of the two; soon we see clearly the finite, but not as such, not as imperfect; then the dim sense of the infinite, or perfection, leads us to see the finite, or our soul, as imperfect; the sight of the finite as imperfect leads us to a clear conception, by contrast, of infinity and perfection.   And this knowledge of perfection, or of God, bears in itself the double assurance of the exist-ence of its object, first because it is experimental, then because it is recognized, when once it is possessed, as being necessarily rational, so that the opposite statement implies contradiction.

Thus, to sum all this up once more, I see God in my soul as in a glass; this sight is experimental, like sensation; this sublime sense of God, to produce an actual emotion, requires a moral condition; this emotion, in order to pass into light, supposes an act of reason.   This act of reason divides the infinite from the finite, and the light, which is God, from the mirror wherein it appears, which is ourself.

VI.

It remains for us to clear up a single point. Did Descartes regard this act of reason as a simple, spontaneous act, a sort of direct intuition of which nothing more can be said, or is it performed by some process which may be described? According to Descartes, there is a process, although this process is by no means complicated. This process is Plato's dialectic; it is that of which Saint Thomas says: "To know God, we must employ a process of elimination."

Just as the will, under the charm of desirability, through regret at its own imperfection, desires perfection, so too the intellect, in the light of intelligibility, at the sight of the finite, by the negation of limitations, raises itself to the idea of the infinite. The assertion of all that is positive in the finite, with the negation of its limitation, an assertion which raises this negation to the infinite, — such is the process.

Descartes aptly remarks that this process gives, at one stroke, not only the existence of God, but moreover the knowledge, in so far as we can obtain it, of what God is.[1] "We also acquire, through proving in this way the existence of God, the advantage that we are made acquainted, by the selfsame means, with what he is, in so far as the weakness of our nature permits; for in reflecting upon the idea which we actually have of God, we see that he is eternal, omniscient, omnipotent, the source of goodness and truth, the creator of all things, and in fact that he possesses in himself all perfection, or the absence of all imperfection."[2]

And this by the following process: "According to the trains of reasoning just made, to know the nature of God, in so far as my own is capable of so doing, I had but to consider, concerning all the things any idea of which I found in

---

[1] *Principles*, p. 235. [2] *Ibid.*, p. 239.

me, whether it was or was not a perfection to possess them;
and I was assured that none of them, possessed of any imperfection, was to be found in him, but that all the others
were."[1] He asserts all perfection and denies all imperfection. He denies of God all those negative ideas "which proceed from nothingness; that is to say, which are in me only
because something is lacking in my nature, and it is not
wholly perfect."[2] I deny those negative ideas, which are
only in me "inasmuch as I have defects."[3] I affirm the
real and positive idea of God, or of a supremely perfect
Being. I deny the negative idea of nothingness, that is,
"of that which is infinitely removed from any kind of
perfection."[4] I efface all limitations in whatever I find in
me that is positive. I see my knowledge grow; but it
will always be limited; I must destroy my limitations in
order to conceive of God's actual infinity. For "although
my knowledge may increase more and more, nevertheless
I know that it can never be actually infinite, since it will
never reach so high a degree of perfection as to be incapable
of greater increase. But I conceive of God as actually infinite to so high a degree that nothing can be added to the
sovereign perfection which he possesses."[5]

We see, therefore, what there is in us that is positive, and
we raise it to the infinite. "Thus, the idea which we have,
for instance, of the divine understanding does not seem to
me to differ from that which we have of our own understanding, save only as the idea of infinite number differs
from the idea of binary or ternary number; and it is the
same with all the attributes of God, some vestiges of which
we recognize in ourselves.[6] ... And we know that none of the
things which we conceive to be in God and in ourselves,
and which we consider separately in him as if they were

---

[1] Vol. i. p. 151.   [3] Ibid.   [5] Ibid., p. 283.
[2] Ibid., p. 278.   [4] Ibid., p. 295.   [6] Ibid., p. 422.

distinct, because of the weakness of our understanding and because we experieuce them so in ourselves, belong to God and to us in the way which is called in the schools *univocal.*[1] That is, we must in some sort transpose them from ourselves to God in conceiving their "immensity, simplicity, and absolute unity."[2] "Unity and immensity we conceive without ourselves possessing them, but God himself impresses them upon us, like the workman's mark stamped upon his work."[3] Upon which Descartes very aptly remarks that this process gives us a certain precise knowledge of what God is. Doubtless, according to Descartes, I do not comprehend the infinite, but I apprehend it. "For to apprehend clearly and distinctly that a thing is such that it is unlimited at every point, is clearly to apprehend that it is infinite."[4] Now, thoroughly distinguishing between the *indefinite* and the *infinite,* Descartes adds this most important assertion: "And there is nothing which I cau properly call infinite, save that in which I can find no limits at any point; in which sense God alone is infinite."[5]

Such is the description of the speculative process: in seeing the finite, to efface all limitations, and thus affirm to infinity everything positive found there.

As for the practical and total process, Descartes himself describes it thus: "I will now close my eyes, stop my ears, I will efface from my very thoughts all images of material things, or at least — because this can hardly be done — I will esteem them false and empty, and thus communing with myself alone, I will try to become better acquainted and more intimate with myself."

"I am a thing that thinks, that doubts, that affirms, that denies, that understands some few things, that is ignorant of many, that loves, that hates, that desires, that desires not."[6]

---

[1] Vol. i. p. 412.
[2] Ibid.
[3] Ibid.
[4] Ibid., 385.
[5] Ibid.
[6] Ibid., p. 263.

This is the beginning of the Third Meditation, wherein we recognize exactly the process of the ascetics and contempla-tors, who say, "Forsake the exterior; leave the world of sense, enter into yourselves; know yourselves; know your miseries; and from the knowledge of your miseries rise higher: go to God." This is the course of prayer.

Thus Descartes saw plainly how the human mind ascends to God.

VII.

We perceive but one break in all this. Descartes says nothing of the great distinction between the two regions of the world of intelligibility, nor of what Pascal, Plato, and Saint Augustine call the last step of reason. This is because Descartes had resolved, as he often says, not to touch on theology, but to keep to pure philosophy.

We all know the active faith and ardent piety of Descartes; and if Christina of Sweden, his pupil, could quit a throne to return to the bosom of the Church, that rare strength of conviction was in part derived from the lessons of the philosopher and Christian whom she admired. Therefore Descartes knew whither reason must lead us. But he had his views. This energetic friend of truth wished to conse-crate his life to reinforcing all truth, by essaying to educate reason taken in itself.

Like his methodic doubt, this rigorous separation of the purely rational order was on his part a manœuvre: in that great contest which the spirit of truth wages with the ever-recurring shadows of doubt, ignorance, and unbelief, he tried to oppose reason alone to the enemy. At this period, men were beginning to attack faith in the name of reason, and reason in the name of faith. Protestants and Jansenists had almost denied reason and the order of natural knowl-edge. Others — *free thinkers,* as they were called — denied faith. The structure of Scholasticism, that admirable combination of divine and human light, was attacked on both sides. Aristotle was pursued into the bosom of the theology with which he had meddled, and even into reason itself, — reason and faith being frequently wounded, under pretext of reaching Aristotle.

Very well ! said Descartes, — destroy this temple, and it will be rebuilt ; overthrow everything, and it shall be lifted again. When everything is dashed to the ground, will it be less true that we think and that we exist ? Now, with that one truth, all others can be restored. The entire order of rational truths will be re-established, reason will be restored, and reason, again raised up, will soon recover the grand foundations of faith, and accept the whole order of divine truths.

So Descartes thought ; but it is not generally known that at the same date many theologians, on their side, were effecting the same movement. "Make a clean separation of the two orders," was the cry; "give up that lawless use of scholastic theology which attempts to explain our mysteries to the faithful. Our mysteries are inexplicable." We find a very curious indication in this respect in Régis.

" This disorder," he says in his concordance of faith and of reason, — " this disorder, which proceeded rather from theologians than from Theology, *had prevailed in past centuries, but it has at last been remedied in ours*, where we see theology more purified, *and treated with greater dignity than formerly*. . . . Less heed is now paid to argument than to authority. . . . The historic bases of Christianity are proved, like truths of fact, and thereby those who have admitted them are brought even to belief in the Trinity and all the other mysteries. . . . Philosophic proofs are no longer mingled with them. . . . It is to this point," adds Régis, " that the University of Paris [the Sorbonne] has

reduced the chief part of its Theology. It is only to be
desired that it may keep on as it has begun; for which
there is reason to hope." [1]

Without dwelling upon the astonishing fact of an opinion
which sees *disorder, lawless use,* and a *lack of dignity* in that
Theology of past ages which gave us Saint Thomas Aquinas,
the Angel of the School and the prince of Catholic theologians, let us confine ourselves to showing that the Cartesian
philosophy did on its side what the Sorbonne did on its own.
There was an effort to divide, more than had been done in
the past, the two orders of reason and faith, which, each
in its sphere, have in themselves their proper authority.
Philosophers and theologians agreed to free themselves mutually,— to maintain apart the two authorities and their
proper consistency: well knowing that the maintenance of
either of the two was enough to save the whole. Both,
besides, were equally anxious for the triumph of theology
and of philosophy: the Sorbonne was as jealous of the
triumph of reason as Descartes, in his substantial piety, was
jealous of the triumph of faith. But men were very glad
to oppose unaided reason to the mystic evil scepticism of
Jansenism and Protestantism; and to the *free thinking* of
paltry rationalists, faith alone with its divine authority.

And yet, what has happened? These tactics, which were
well meant, but which, as Régis aptly remarks, were novel,
— being neither those of the Fathers nor of the Middle
Age,— produced very different results from what were expected. Bossuet foresaw the mischief when he wrote to a
disciple of Descartes and Malebranche: "I see a great
contest making ready against the Church, under the name of
Cartesian philosophy. I see more than one heresy springing
from its bosom and its principles, which are, *in my opinion,
misunderstood.*" More yet, Bossuet points out the mischief

---

[1] Régis, Concordance of Faith and Reason, book iii. ch. xxviii. p. 370.

as already accomplished: "From those same principles, misunderstood as they are, another formidable evil is visibly gaining ground; for on the pretext that we should only accept what we understand clearly, — which, reduced to certain bounds, is very true, — every man takes the liberty to say, I understand this, and I do not understand that; and upon this basis alone, he approves or rejects whatever he pleases, — without thinking that besides our clear and distinct ideas, there are others, confused and general, which nevertheless contain truths so essential that by denying them we overthrow everything. Upon this pretext a freedom of opinion is introduced which leads men to advance boldly anything that they may think, without regard to tradition."[1]

Thus, upon the plea of Cartesianism, those who pique themselves on their philosophy ensconce themselves in their reason and their clear ideas, and from that shelter judge of everything, — authority, tradition, and faith.

But, on the other hand, the theologians forsaking proofs and philosophical reasons, and "seizing the highest thing," as Régis says, theology became more and more obscure, particularly in the eyes of those who wished nothing but light. Saint Augustine said, "I exhort your faith to the love of intelligence." The Middle Age took for its motto, "Faith seeking intelligence." Saint Thomas Aquinas said, "Theology may receive from philosophy a grander manifestation of her dogmas." A means of manifestation was therefore lost, — that is to say, a means of introducing into the mind of men the revealed divine light.

So that these tactics produced but one result. They had, in a certain sense, divided one from the other, faith and reason, and had permitted the enemy to cut off *the right and left wings of truth*, as has ingeniously been said.[2] The

---

[1] To a Disciple of Malebranche. Letter to Father Lami.
[2] Father Lacordaire.

army of truth, thus reduced, must lose a battle. The consequences have been before us for a century. The eighteenth century, seeing faith and reason march separately, flung itself between them, isolated them, and ruined faith in the name of reason. This done, the enemy turned against reason itself; and, as we know, philosophy was at once ruined by the rebound, — since it is plain that what is called the philosophy of the eighteenth century is merely the absence and ignorance of all philosophy. And what shall we say of the final consequences of this great rout; namely, the formal and radical negation of reason in all its postulates, the premeditated and avowed destruction of logic in its necessary laws, — a mystery of intellectual death and decomposition which has been preparing for fifty years, and which now bursts upon us! For, as we see, reason is attacked in all its laws, as well as in all its postulates, as directly and as radically as faith was attacked; the very foundations of logic are denied, and the leader of this vast sophistic movement exclaims: "The time has come to transform logic;" and it is indeed transformed, by destroying the antagonism of affirmation and negation, whose identity is proclaimed, — which destroys logic itself, with every trace of theoretic and practical reason.

May this history be a lesson to our age! Let us return to the tactics of the Fathers and the Middle Age; or rather, let us have no tactics. Let us confine ourselves to not parting that which God hath joined together. Certainly human light, reason, is as different from divine light, faith, as man is inferior to God, the creature lower than the Creator. · The advance of philosophy and theology in the seventeenth century, and the decisions of the Church, have made a greater distinction than ever between the two orders of the natural and supernatural; and nothing is more necessary, and at the same time more fruitful, than an exact and precise knowledge of this radical distinction: but this is precisely where all Christianity rests upon the mystery of the two natures of Christ, infinitely distinct, but closely united in the unity of his person. So, too, as has been said, the true knowledge of Christians should rest upon the union and mutual communication of the two lights, otherwise radically distinct. This union constitutes the great knowledge, "at once human and divine," which all the Fathers and all the great theologians seek; which Saint Gregory Nazianzen calls the highest philosophy; and without which, says Origen in regard to Saint Gregory Thaumaturgus, who approves of it, true piety can never possess all its power.

PASCAL.

I.

In this admirable concert of illustrious voices which teach us to seek God through reason, Pascal develops and sustains an idea which is one of the most beautiful and most essential to the truth of the whole. Not that by his melancholy and his moans he does not sometimes make a discord with the others, but it is an indispensable discord, which must be understood and brought into the general harmony.

Pascal insists upon the practical side of the rational search for God; he shows us particularly its real condition, which, if it be fulfilled, suffices; which, if it be wanting, renders the rest impossible, and actually arrests all passage of the mind towards God.

Pascal knows that the reasoning which rises to God requires, as its motive-spring, a moral condition, and that the point of support of the proof is not only the experimental knowledge of our existence, but also that of our imperfection. He knows that the knowledge of our imperfection implies some sense of perfection, and that this divine sense of the perfect and the infinite is developed by moral rectitude, and obliterated by depravity of will, as is proved by these words of Scripture: "The fool saith in his heart, There is no God." The fool, that is, the man deprived of the divine sense by his folly, lacks any real starting-point for the proof of God. He cannot understand that proof if it be offered to him; his mind neither receives it nor produces it. The side of his reason which is capable of attaining the actual infinite, does not work, for lack of a motive-spring; the other side is active and entire, but the former is paralyzed by an obstacle, — that obstacle which Aristotle saw in the sensuality, intoxication, and blind torpor in which we live.

We see how important it was to develop vigorously this part of the truth, amid those great minds who raised the glory of human reason to such a height, by their doctrine and their works.

Pascal, moreover, seems to counterbalance Descartes, who devoted himself wholly to natural philosophy, and not to Theology; who sets faith apart, and makes so strong a distinction between "the two orders of divine intelligibility" as to isolate them. Pascal incessantly urges the mind towards the higher of the two orders, scorning the lesser. He rushes with all his might towards the term of the process, as Plato would say, and forgets the intermediaries. He knows that the last step of reason is a surrender to faith, and he hastens thither. He goes at once to the last depths, to the centre of the soul, which he calls the heart, then directly from the heart to God, — to the God of Christians, to the supernatural knowledge of God through Jesus Christ.

Thus, on the one hand, we have the moral condition indispensable to the flight of the mind towards God; on the other hand, the necessity for attaining the supernatural goal; the vanity of purely natural knowledge of God: such are the points to which the energetic eloquence of Pascal is devoted.

II.

Pascal's scepticism, in reality and in its intention, is not genuine scepticism: it is scarcely more than the sentiment expressed by Bossuet: "Ill befall the barren knowledge which does not turn to loving and betray itself!" it is scarcely more than the development of Bacon's words: "Human intelligence is not a dry light (*Intellectus humanus luminis sicci non est*)." For if that light be dried up, by isolating it from the heart, from feeling, from the divine sense, Pascal fails to understand how it can reach to the knowledge of God. "The heart," he says, "the heart has its reasons, which reason does not know."[1] Now, in his eyes, "it is the heart that feels God, not the reason. This is faith: God perceptible to the heart, not to the reason."[2] Moreover, Pascal sees an element of freedom in the use of this heart-sense, the beginning of the knowledge of God. "I say that the heart loves the universal Being naturally and itself naturally, according as it applies itself thereto; and it hardens itself against one or the other at its own choice. You reject one and retain the other: is it reason that leads you to love?"[3] This is indeed the core of the question: the heart's free choice in regard to God's natural attraction in the soul decides everything, and guides our mind towards God or turns it from him.

But what does Pascal understand by the heart?

We must know the original but deep significance which he gives to the word. To him the heart is the chief of the soul's faculties, implicating the roots of intelligence and will, — that which, in the soul, adheres directly to the first principles of the desirable and the intelligible, that is, the heart. On the other hand, to Pascal, most frequently at least, reason means ratiocination, and ratiocination means syllogism. Hence we can understand what follows: —

[1] Edit. Faugère, ii. 172.   [2] Ibid.   [3] Ibid.

"We know the truth, not only through the reason, but also through the heart: it is the first principles of this latter sort that we know, and it is in vain that ratiocination, which has no share therein, strives to combat them. . . . The knowledge of the first principles is as steadfast as any of those which our ratiocinations give. And it is upon such knowledge of the heart and instinct that reason should rest and should base all its discourse. Principles are felt, propositions are inferred ; and all this with equal certitude, though by different ways. And it is as absurd for reason to require of the heart proof of its first principles as a requisite for consenting to them, as it would be absurd for the heart to demand of reason a feeling for all the propositions that it proves, before it will receive them."[1]

We see that Pascal here describes inner facts which all philosophers have seen, only he calls "heart and instinct" what some call "direct perception of evidence;" others, "spontaneous knowledge;" others, "natural faith;" others, "the sense of the desirable and the intelligible;" and we understand how and in what sense he criticises reason: he wishes, like all sceptics of a dogmatic bent, to humiliate, not intrinsic reason, but reason isolated, mutilated, separated from its source in the soul and from its source in God.

Besides, Pascal does not deny that there is a natural and rational knowledge of God, independently of Christian faith ; but he says that this knowledge is barren, barren of salvation. "All those," he says, "who seek God without Jesus Christ, can never find such light as will afford them true satisfaction or genuine fruit. For either they do not advance so far as to know that there is a God, or if they do, it is in vain."[2] He therefore confesses that we can reach this natural knowledge ; he points out three modes of knowing God, — as a heathen, as a Jew, and as a Christian. "The divinity of Christians does not consist of a God who is merely the author of geometric truths and the order of the elements; that is the lot

---

[1] Edit. Faugère, ii. 108.　　　[2] Complete Works, ii. 307 (Lattaye).

of the heathen. It does not consist merely of a God who exercises his providence over the life and welfare of men, to give a happy length of years to those who adore him; that is the share of the Jews. But the God of Abraham and Jacob, the God of Christians, is a God of love and consolation: he is a God who fills the soul and heart which he possesses." [1]

Pascal, therefore, clearly distinguishes between natural and supernatural knowledge of God. But he points out the dryness and sterility of the natural knowledge. "If a man," he says, "should be persuaded that the proportions of numbers are immaterial and eternal truths dependent on a first truth in which they subsist, and which is called God, I should not consider that man had made great progress towards salvation." [2]

Pascal does not deny the legitimacy of the metaphysical proofs of God; he only remarks, with the world in general, upon their extreme difficulty, and their almost absolute in-utility in practice, — at least, when they are given under certain forms. Who does not see the perfect justice of the following observation? "The metaphysical proofs of God are so remote from human reasoning, and so complicated, that they strike us but little; and if they should serve some persons, it could only be during the moment that they see that demonstration; but an hour later, they fear lest they were deceived. Besides, this sort of proofs can only guide us to a speculative knowledge of God." [3]

It is plain enough that Pascal refers here to certain proofs which he calls metaphysical, *which are so remote from human reasoning, and so complicated, which only guide us to a speculative knowledge*, which have nothing common, popular, experimental, about them, — nothing which rests upon the divine sense and the moral side of the soul;

[1] Complete Works, ii. 306. [3] Ibid., p. 305.
[2] Ibid., p. 202.

hence, what can be truer than this criticism? Let us recall Aristotle's proofs, as stated by Saint Thomas Aquinas.

Pascal wishes the knowledge of God always to rest both upon the mind and upon the entire soul; if it rests on the mind alone, in his opinion it is only an idol. " Men make an idol of truth itself; for truth without charity is not God, it is his image, and an idol which should neither be loved nor worshipped," — words of wonderful depth.

Lastly, it seems to me impossible to regard Pascal as a genuine sceptic, if we weigh the following passages: " We must learn to doubt where it is requisite, to assume where it is requisite, to submit where it is requisite. He who fails to do this does not understand the power of reason.[1] . . . There are two excesses, — to exclude reason, and to admit nothing but reason.[2] . . . It is your assent to yourself, and the firm voice of your own reason, not that of others, which should lead you to believe." [3]

III.

From what precedes, it follows that in reality Pascal's doctrine concerning the knowledge of God is this: —

God is perceptible to the heart naturally, but the soul destroys or increases this divine feeling, "according as it applies itself, and of its own volition." When deprived of this feeling, the soul has no power to rise to the idea of God; and the arguments which it then accumulates afford it no useful light or assurance. On the contrary, with this feeling, which is developed in the soul in proportion as it becomes more familiar with its selfishness and poverty, the least argument at once raises the mind to God. In this case, "all our reasoning is reduced to yielding to emotion." In the former case, "reason acts slowly, and with so many

[1] Edit. Faugère, ii. 347.   [2] Ibid., p. 348.   [3] Ibid., p. 351.

different views and principles which it must always consider, that it continually grows drowsy, or goes astray for want of seeing them all at once. It is not so with feeling; it acts in an instant, and yet is always ready to act." [1] Plainly, Pascal has here in view the two processes of reason; and he shows the clumsiness, slowness, and complications of the syllogistic process, when used to reproduce what the dialectic process, although perfectly exact, seizes by a rapid, almost simple impulse, comparable to a prayer or an emotion.

Then, beyond all this, Pascal feels keenly that there is another degree of the divine intelligibility, and that in practice the true knowledge of God, serving for the salvation of the world and of every soul, is that which faith in Christ Jesus develops in us.

Such, I believe, is the solid basis of Pascal's philosophy. But it must be confessed that it is not easy to grasp a system among the scattered fragments which we know as his works, since we find manifest contradictions in that maze, where doubts and opinions, questions and assertions, objections and replies, are blended.

We see clearly that Pascal undertook to correct that purely syllogistic semi-reason, paralyzed in its best part, set apart from life, emotion, the heart, and all faith, whether natural or supernatural, indifferent to all guidance, destitute of rule or principles, limping, and blind to the infinite, even in geometry, as it asserts. When, therefore, this puny reason becomes arrogant, he humbles it, he overthrows it; and that is only just.

But it is quite as plain that Pascal, being a Jansenist, was liable to mistake, and was mistaken in regard to the relations between faith and reason. In the first place, he allows natural reason but too little light, and the will but too little

[1] Complete Works, vol. ii. p. 362.

liberty. He knows no healthy and upright reason but that
which rests on emotion and affection ; and at the same time
he admits of no other love of God but that supernatural
love, the gift of grace, which is charity. Moreover, he not
only says that the supernatural light of faith is a gift of
God, superadded to reason, — he believes that this gift is
arbitrary on God's part; that nothing can prepare us for it ;
that no effort can avail, even indirectly, to make us less
incapable of it, and that God refuses it to souls which labor
with all their might, by reason and by freedom, to remove
the obstacle ! " We utterly fail to understand the works of
God," he says, " unless we accept it as a principle that God
blinds some, and enlightens others.[1] No man ever believes
with a true and saving faith, unless God inclines his heart;
and *no man, when God inclines his heart, can refrain from
thus believing.*"[2] He also allows himself elsewhere to be so
far carried away that he writes these almost blasphemous
words: "Neither discourses nor books, neither our sacred
Scriptures nor our Gospel, neither our most holy mysteries,
nor alms, nor fasts, nor mortifications of the flesh, nor mira-
cles, nor the use of sacraments, nor the sacrifice of our body,
nor all my efforts, nor those of the whole world combined,
can do anything at all to *begin* my conversion, if thou dost
not add to all these things the most extraordinary aid of thy
grace."[3] So that between the two worlds, between the two
degrees of the divine intelligibility, one of which, however,
supposes the other, according to Plato and Saint Thomas Aquinas, there is no possible intermediary but an arbitrary decree
of God and a most extraordinary effort of his grace ; and
neither the proper use of reason and liberty, nor recourse to
the sacraments, nor reading of the gospel, nor all our efforts,
be they what they may, aided and preceded by that universal

---

[1] Thoughts (Paris, 1714), p. 47.   [3] Ibid., p. 303.
[2] Ibid., p. 177.

grace which God sheds like his sun upon all men, — absolutely nothing can avail to begin the soul's return to eternal life. And in speaking thus, Pascal imagines that he is following Saint Augustine, while Saint Augustine teaches this: "Do you think that man can believe if he desire it not, or that he can abstain from believing if he desire to believe? That would be absurd. Therefore faith is in our power. . . . But, as the Apostle says, all power comes from God. . . . God gives us the power to believe, without imposing upon us the necessity. . . . Faith, therefore, is in our power, since we believe if we choose, and if we believe, it is because we choose." [1]

Such is sectarian blindness. A man may rely upon Saint Augustine while he teaches the exact opposite of his doctrines. In this respect, in what concerned sects and their quarrels, no one was more sincerely blind and hasty than Pascal. It was a matter of temperament and character as much as of zeal and conviction.

Look at Pascal's portrait, sketched by Domat, in his *Corpus Juris*, with such striking truth. Never did face better express a whole history. At a single glance you read in those features the courage, tenderness, terrors, and tears of that generous heart; the vigor and sombre enthusiasm of that splendid genius, as well as the strange error which showed him an abyss ever yawning at his feet; and this other error, far worthier of pity, in which, without being responsible for it, I hope, he slandered the purest of men.

MALEBRANCHE.

I.

"France is not sufficiently proud of her Malebranche," said De Maistre. Others have called Malebranche the Christian Plato. And, indeed, if Plato brought all philosophy to

[1] De Spirit. et Litter., pp. 54, 55.

the search and the vision of eternal ideas, which are God, to what did Malebranche bring all philosophy, if not to see everything in God?

What the Gospel says, " The Word is the light of men ; " what Saint Augustine adds in his commentary on this passage, " This light of men is reason ; " all Descartes' efforts to show that the idea of God proceeds from God, is God conceived, and even that every idea, every opinion, every act of the understanding, is, or supposes, a certain perception of the light which is God, — is eagerly grasped by Malebranche, developed with matchless fulness and untiring zeal, maintained with contagious conviction, penetrative lucidity of reasoning and style. No man, so much as he, has shown the presence of God in reason.

All the resources of his style, undulating with light, all the power of the lofty poetry at his command, although a systematic foe to imagination, all the rigor of his geometry, all the perfection and the impetus of the most ardent faith, and all the genuine warmth of a soul as loving as it was clear-sighted, — all these resources are used, not in abstract demonstration of the existence of God, but in manifestation of God as the Word present in the soul. And this Word Malebranche calls sometimes " Reason," and sometimes ". Jesus Christ."

Let us hear what he says. He begins his Christian Meditations with this prayer : —

" O Eternal Wisdom ! I am not my light to myself, and the bodies which surround me cannot enlighten me ; intelligences themselves, not containing in their being the reason which renders them wise, cannot communicate that reason to my mind. Thou art alone the light of angels and of men ; thou art alone the universal light of minds, — wisdom, eternal, immutable, necessary. Oh, my true and sole Master ! show thyself to me ; make me see light in thy light. I address myself to none save

thee ; I would consult only thee. Speak, Eternal Word, word of
the Father, word which has always been spoken, which is spoken
now, and which will be spoken forever. Speak, and speak loudly
enough to make thyself heard, despite the noisy confusion which
my senses and my passions make in my mind.

"But, O Jesus! I pray thee to speak in me only for thy
glory, and to make me know only thy greatness. . . . Make me
know, O Jesus! that which thou art, and how all things subsist
in thee. Pervade my mind with the splendor of thy light, con-
sume my heart with the ardor of thy love, and grant me in the
course of this work, which I write solely for thy glory, expressions
clear and true, vivid and breathing, worthy of thee, and such that
they may increase in me and in those who deign to meditate
with me the knowledge of thy greatness and the sense of thy
benefits ! "

II.

Let us try, then, to mèditate a little while with Malebranche. He listens, he questions, and the inward master
answers him.

Master. " Dost thou not feel that the light of reason is ever
present to thee, that it dwells within thee, and that when thou
retirest within thyself thou dost become completely illumined
therewith ? Dost thou not hear that it answers thee when thou
dost question it, when thou canst question it by a serious attention, when thy passions and senses are reverent and silent ?

"Retire into thyself, and hear me. . . . Thus doth truth speak
to all those who love her and who with ardent desire implore her
to feed them with her substance : —

" I feed minds with my own self ; . . . I give myself wholly
to all and wholly to each. I have created them to make them
like unto myself, and to feed them with my substance ; and they
are the more rational the more perfectly they possess me." [1]

Soul. " What, my Jesus, is it thyself who dost speak to me in
my most secret reason ? It is then thy voice I hear. Thou
comest to shed light in an instant through my soul ! What!

---

[1] Meditation II., Nos. 11, 12, 13.

It is thou alone that enlightenest all men! Alas, how dull was I when I believed that thy creatures spoke to me, when thou didst reply! How vainglorious was I when I fancied that I was a light unto myself, when thou didst enlighten me! . . . Oh, my only master, may men know that thou dost penetrate them in such manner that when they believe they answer themselves and converse with themselves, it is thou who dost speak with them and hold converse with them! Yes, light of the world, I understand it now: it is thou who dost enlighten us, when we discover any truth whatsoever; it is thou who dost exhort us, when we see the beauty of order; it is thou who dost correct us, when we hear the secret reproaches of reason; it is thou who dost punish us or console us when we feel that deep remorse which rends our interiors, or those words of peace which fill us with joy.[1]

"May those who know thee as a God ever attent upon them, acting in them, enlightening them, entreating them, correcting them, consoling them, render perpetual thanks to thee for the benefits they receive at thy hands, so that they may deserve fresh favors, and that thou mayst at last make them worthy to possess thee forever. May those who, unconscious of the secret operations by which thou actest in us, do not know the author of their being, nor him who gives them every moment fresh motion and life, seek their benefactor with all their strength, with love, eagerness, and persistence, and may they tend an altar to the *unknown God*, until thou dost reveal thyself to them.[2]

"As for me, Lord, I implore thee to teach me that mode of consulting thee which is ever rewarded by a clear and evident knowledge of the truth."

Master. "Thou already knowest in part that which thou dost ask. I have already told thee, but thou dost not reflect thereon. Dost thou not remember that I have often answered thee as soon as thou hast desired it? Thy wishes, therefore, suffice to force me to answer thee. True, I desire to be entreated. But thy desire is a *natural prayer* which my mind frames in thee. It is the actual love of truth that prays, and that obtains the sight of truth."[3]

---

[1] Meditation II., No. 15.   [3] Meditation III, Nos. 9 and 10.
[2] Ibid., No. 19.

This is the beginning of these wonderful Meditations. What follows, although placed in the middle of the work, may be regarded as their conclusion.

"I confess it, my only Master, and I wish to consult thee solely concerning the truths which are necessary to me to lead me to the possession of true good. The time is short, death draws near, and I must enter such an eternity as I shall have deserved. The thought of death changes all my views and interrupts all my plans. Everything vanishes or changes its aspect when I think of eternity. Abstract knowledge, brilliant and sublime as you may be, you are but vanity, and I forsake you. I will study religion and morals; I will work to become perfect and happy, and quit the weary task which God has given to the children of men, all that empty knowledge of which it is written, that those who acquire it, instead of becoming wise and content, but add to their labors and their cares."[1]

We feel it to be our duty to give this quotation to show the genius of Malebranche and the practical result which he attained. In fact, Malebranche believed thoroughly in the inward converse of the soul with the universal Word. He did not merely state these things as speculative rules, he practised them habitually.

He took literally and accepted, as a philosopher, Christ's words in answer to those who asked him, "Who art thou?" "I am the beginning of all things, I who speak with you." Malebranche considered that these words contained the very principle of philosophy. The universal Word naturally speaks always to all men. This inner appeal of God, and our natural capacity for understanding its meaning, is reason. According to Malebranche, he who does not know this, knows nothing of philosophy. From this point of view any other knowledge than that of the Word itself seemed to him fruitless. We see that, like Plato, he regarded the abstract sci-

[1] End of Meditation IX.

ences, brilliant and sublime as they might be, as merely the
shadows of that which is, and as divine phantasms. He
wishes to pass from the shadow to the reality, which gives
us the profoundly philosophic meaning of the beautiful and
devout words just quoted..

III.

As for the proof itself of the existence of God, as Malebranche understands it, we find germs of it in the preceding
passages.   But here it is in plain terms, —

"God[1] is *He Who is;* that is to say, the Being which contains
in its esssence all the reality and perfection to be found in all
beings ; the Being infinite in every sense, — in a word, Being.

"Our God is Being, without any restriction or limitation. He
includes in himself, in a manner incomprehensible to the finite
mind, all perfections, all true reality possessed by created and
potential beings. He includes in himself whatever there is of
reality or perfection in matter, the last and most imperfect of
beings, but without its imperfection, its limitation, its nothingness; for there is no nothingness in being, no limitation in the
infinite of every kind."

Thus, "our God is all that he is wherever he is present,
and he is omnipresent." Malebranche does not take the
pains to conclude otherwise, or to add : As God is Being,
and can be none other, and as Being necessarily exists,
therefore God exists.

This is Saint Anselm's proof, and Descartes' *second* proof,
that which he sums up thus: We have the idea of God,
therefore he exists, for that idea implies his existence.

But to this proof Malebranche instantly makes answer,
through the mouth of the adversary, with the objection which

---

[1] Conversation between a Christian Philosopher and a Chinese Philosopher,
ii. 365 (Paris, 1837).

might be expected: We admit that the idea of infinity includes the idea of Being; "but we deny that infinity exists."[1]

This is the same objection made by Saint Thomas to Saint Anselm's proof: "The atheist," said he, "denies the very fact that infinity exists."

Malebranche answers this objection with Descartes' *first* proof: I have the idea of God, therefore he exists; for he alone could inspire me with that idea.

"This," says Malebranche, "is a very simple and very natural proof of God's existence, the most simple of all those which I could give you.

"To think of nothing and not to think, to see nothing and not to see anything, is the same thing. Therefore all that the mind perceives directly and immediately, is or exists. . . . All that the mind perceives immediately, really is. For if it were not, in perceiving it I should perceive nothing, therefore I should not perceive.

"Now, I think of the infinite: I perceive the infinite immediately and directly. Therefore it exists."[2]

To this the opponent answers, —

"I admit that if the immediate object of your mind were the infinite, when you think of it this would necessitate its existence; but then the immediate object of your mind is only your mind itself. . . . Thus it does not follow that the infinite exists absolutely and aside from us merely because we think of it."

Malebranche replies, —

"That which does not exist cannot be perceived. To perceive nothing and not to perceive anything, is the same thing. It is therefore evident that, in a finite mind, we cannot find sufficient

---

[1] Conversation between a Christian Philosopher and a Chinese Philosopher, ii. 365.

[2] Ibid., pp. 365, 366.

reality to see the infinite in it. Heed this well. Is not your idea
of space alone infinite ? Your idea of the heavens is very vast, but
do you not feel that your idea of space infinitely exceeds it ?
Does not this idea assure you that whatever impetus you may
give your mind to traverse it, you can never exhaust it, because
it has actually no bounds ? But if your mind, your own substance, does not contain sufficient reality to find out the infinite
in extent, this or that infinite, a particular infinite, how can you
see in it the infinite in every kind of being, the infinitely perfect
Being, in a word, Being ? "

Thus, " nothing finite containing the infinite, the very fact
that we perceive the infinite, necessitates its existence. All
this is based on the simple, evident principle that nothing
cannot be directly perceived, and that to see nothing and not
to see nothing is the same thing." [1]

Malebranche, therefore, understands this proof thus : In
his opinion the idea of God is an immediate knowledge, an
experimental perception of God ; it is God himself who by
his presence gives us his idea, or rather, all ideas. " This,"
he says, " is how I understand it. The infinitely perfect
being containing in himself all reality and perfection, he
can, *by touching us with his efficacious realities*, that is, by
his essence, reveal or represent to us all beings. I say, *by
touching us ;* for although my mind be capable of thinking
or perceiving, it can only perceive that which touches or
modifies it, and such is its greatness that none save its Creator can act immediately in it. God is the life of intelligences and the light which illumines them. . . . He contains
in his essence the ideas or archetypes of all beings, and
reveals them to us. . . . But gross and carnal men do not
comprehend this." [2] And, indeed, " the perception with
which the infinite touches us is so slight that you regard as

[1] Conversation between a Christian Philosopher and a Chinese Philosopher,
ii. 366.

[2] Ibid., ii. 371.

nothing that which touches you so slightly, . . . like children who think that the air is nothing, because their perception of it is unconscious."[1]

These two demonstrations, the one through the idea itself of the infinite, as involving the idea of necessary existence, the other through the idea of the infinite considered as *an effect of God*, as Descartes expresses it, and as a vision of God present, — these two demonstrations combined constitute the entire Cartesian proof, both rational and experimental, as we have stated it. Add to this the *cosmologic* proof, of which we are about to speak, and we shall have the complete, manifest, universal proof of God's existence such as mankind, wise or ignorant, philosophers or poets, have united in seeing and describing.

IV.

In the same Dialogue, Malebranche thus presents the cosmologic proof: "The proof which you have just given me of God's existence," says the interlocutor, "is very simple, but it is so abstract that it does not wholly convince me. Have you none which is more concrete?" "I will give you as many as you please, for there is nothing visible in the world which God has created whence we cannot rise to the knowledge of the Creator, provided that we reason correctly."[2]

In fact (we here abridge Malebranche's long exposition), any object whatsoever, seen by us, proves God, because no object can be seen save through God and in God.

According to Malebranche, God brings about in us directly and immediately all our ideas and sensations. He effects

[1] Conversation between a Christian Philosopher and a Chinese Philosopher, ii. 366, 367.

[2] Ibid., p. 368.

them by his presence and his contact in the same way that he effects in us his own idea, the idea of the infinite.

Here Malebranche confounds two truths. He believes that our natural idea of God is the direct and immediate vision of God himself. According to him, at least as he develops it in his "Search After Truth," the sight of created beings and the sight of our soul are but a sight of God; we therefore see only God, who effects within us, by the occasional cause of our soul and the world, the impressions, the sensations, the emotions which we attribute to the world and our soul. Malebranche does not say, with Saint Paul, "We see God through his creatures;" he says the opposite, — "We see his creatures through God." He seems to forget the passage from the Scriptures: "No man has ever seen God." And, indeed, have we, such as we are and are born into this world, a "direct and immediate" vision of God? Who can believe this? But we understand Saint Paul; we understand that when we see nature and our soul and all creation, we really gain a certain indirect and implicit view of God, since he is the light which enlightens us, without which nothing would be visible.

Malebranche confounds the two degrees of the divine intelligibility: here lies all his error. He attributes to reason, that is, to the natural vision of God in the mirror of the soul, characteristics which only belong to the supernatural vision of God in his essence. "The dogma of the beatific vision, profoundly meditated," says Balmès, "sheds floods of light upon philosophy. Malebranche's sublime dream may be only a reminiscence of his theological studies."[1] It could not be better expressed. Yes, the dogma of the supernatural vision of God bathes philosophy in light, since it reveals the final perfection of reason, and at the same time its limits; its natural range, — its range: it is a certain perception of the

[1] Filos. fund., i. 27.

Word; its limits : it is only the indirect perception thereof; its final perfection: it may be called to see directly the source of light, the essence of God. This is where Malebranche becomes confused. He dreams in a sublime dream that in his natural reason he already has the direct, immediate vision of God himself. Like Pascal, he goes at once to the goal; but while Pascal, in gazing at the supreme goal, neglects and despises the intermediary, Malebranche does the exact opposite, and fancies that the intermediary is the goal. He confounds, let us once more repeat, the two degrees of the divine intelligibility.

For if now, upon this plea, any one enter against this great mind a charge of pantheism, I answer that in the seventeenth century I recognize no pantheist but Spinoza, — Spinoza, whom Malebranche calls "that evil spirit, the miserable Spinoza." Spinoza was a pantheist, — consciously, by choice. Spinoza loves the error; Malebranche detests it. Spinoza sets up falsehood and develops it; Malebranche sees and upholds truth, but in some details expresses himself unhappily. This has occurred, on one point or another, to the best and greatest intellects. The philosopher who strives for truth and is accidentally mistaken, is radically different from the sophist who strives for error and accidentally speaks the truth.

Malebranche saw clearly and brought to light this truth, — that in every idea, every vision, every intellectual action, there is the light of God, and that nothing is visible save in the light of the divine sun. Have we not seen this doctrine in Saint Augustine and Saint Thomas Aquinas ? It is a supreme truth. But Malebranche does not fully grasp the relation of the light to the soul and to objects, although he distinguishes the three terms perfectly.

As for the proof of God's existence, Malebranche gives it to us entire. 1, He takes his point of support in experience,

in the vision of the soul and of the world; 2, he sees and
describes admirably the divine impetus, the sense of the
infinite, the sense of God, — of God who gives us his idea
by touching us; 3, he sees the obstacle to the development
of this proximate power "in gross and carnal men who do
not comprehend it." He therefore knows the moral condition
of the proof; in his Treatise on Morals, he develops it in all
forms, — notably in chapter xi., to which he gives the title,
"*In what Sort we must die to see God and be conjoined to Reason*," which recalls Socrates' profound words: "To philosophize is to learn to die." "4, As for the process itself by
which we may rise to God, it is found in these words: There is
nothing visible in the world which God hath created, whence
we may not rise to the knowledge of the Creator, provided we
reason correctly; . . . since he contains all true reality to be
found in all created and potential beings, even in matter, but
without their imperfection, limitation, and nothingness."

Let us repeat, in closing, that Malebranche, by his classic
style, which gains truth an entrance to the human mind,
rendered philosophy the immortal service of showing, better
than any other man before him, the presence of God in reason.
It was essential that in the seventeenth century this fundamental truth should be as loudly asserted as the impotence of
human thought when isolated from its source in God. Now,
these two truths, of which Pascal and Malebranche each
maintained one, — sometimes even excessively and discor-
dantly, — Fénelon was charged to maintain together, and
to bring the dissonance into a strong accord.

FÉNELON.

I.

We have already said, the best of all philosophers are
the theologians. Saint Augustine is deeper and more ex-

act than Descartes in matters of philosophy, because he is more of a theologian. Fénelon and Bossuet are more exact than Malebranche and Pascal, because the latter two are no great theologians. As for Fénelon, let no one doubt that he is an admirable theologian. In his dispute with Bossuet on divine love and the soul's relations to God, he teaches Bossuet more things than Bossuet teaches him, although Bossuet was the victor.[1] As a philosopher, Fénelon is the most exact of all the philosophers of the seventeenth century. The great philosophic idea of that century was the idea of the infinite. Upon this point Fénelon is the most complete, explicit, and sure of any. Strange to say, he knew far more about the metaphysics of the infinite than Leibnitz himself, the inventor of the infinitesimal calculus. Moreover, he avoids all exaggerations, both that of Pascal and that of Malebranche, the eccentricities of Leibnitz, and many others beside. In every particular his genius is well balanced, compounded as much of heart as of mind, of reason as of religion, of impulse as of good sense; in everything he preserves a happy medium, and that completely central human voice, of which it was so well said: " Fénelon's voice is neither a man's voice nor a woman's voice, but, like the voice of wisdom, it has no sex."[2]

II.

In his Treatise on the Existence of God, Fénelon gives all the proofs of the existence of God at length, consecutively, and methodically. He develops in due order, 1, the proof through the sight of the material world (cosmologic proof); 2, the proof from the sight of the soul (psychologic proof);

---

[1] This is shown in the fine work by the learned M. Gosselin, entitled, "The Literary History of Fénelon."

[2] Joubert's Thoughts, ii. 108.

3, the proof called metaphysical, based on the nature of
the idea of God. He demonstrates briefly the existence
of God from the spectacle of nature; then he states with
greater amplitude how reason and freedom, which exist in
us by the presence of God, prove God; and how the idea
alone which we have of the infinite, gives us immediately, by way of direct consequence, the idea of necessary existence.

In this treatise Fénelon corrects, particularizes, and
completes the exclusive points of view of Pascal and
Malebranche.

Pascal scourged reason, declaring it usually incapable of
advancing to God. Malebranche deified it, and said : Not
only does reason demonstrate God, but it is God himself
that we see directly and immediately when we reason ;
reason shows God, because it is God. Féuelon develops
perfectly and simultaneously what Pascal and Malebranche
maintain, each for himself, far too exclusively. Let us see
how he combines them into a whole which is the truth.

In searching for the proof of God's existence in the spectacle of our mind and the analysis of reason, he sees, first,
in the mind of man, that double character of pettiness
and grandeur clearly to be found there, and which strike us
at the first glance ; he sees the perfection and imperfection,
the constant disappointments and the infallible rule, the
evident limitations of the finite, the visible traces of the
infinite : he everywhere asserts that in reason we find both
God and ourselves.

We must quote these splendid passages, which should be
taken in their literal sense.

Having first described the weaknesses of our thought, he
shows the idea of the infinite therein, and exclaims, —

"Oh, how great is the mind of man ! He bears within him
matter to amaze and infinitely to surpass himself, his ideas are

universal, eternal, and immutable.[1] Those unbounded ideas can never be changed, altered, or effaced in us; they are the very foundation of reason.[2]

"Behold the mind of man, weak, uncertain, limited, full of errors. Who hath put the idea of the infinite — that is to say, of perfection — into a subject so limited and so full of imperfection?" Who hath placed in me that idea of the infinite which is "the true infinite of which we have the thought?"[3]

This idea is in me, but it is no part of me. Th· ·, fixed and immutable ideas, which are the basis of ɪ ·ᴄᴀson, are not a part of me.

"This fixed and immutable will is so inward and intimate that I am tempted to take it for myself; but it is superior to me, since it corrects me, sets me right, puts me on my guard against myself, and warns me of my own impotency. It is something which inspires me every hour, if I do but hearken to it; and I am never deceived save when I hearken not to it.[4]

"This inward rule is what I call my reason, but I speak of my reason without grasping the force of that expression.[5]

"Truly, my reason is within me, for I must unceasingly return into myself to find it; but the superior reason which corrects me in case of need, and which I consult, is not mine, and does not form a part of myself. That rule is perfect and unchanging; I am changeable and imperfect. When I err, it preserves its rectitude; when I am undeceived, it is not it that returns to the goal; without ever itself straying from the goal, it has authority to recall me and compel me to return to it. It is an inward master that commands me to be silent, to speak, to believe, to doubt, to confess my errors or confirm my judgments; this master is omnipresent, and his voice is heard from one end of the universe to the other, by all men as by me.[6]

"Thus, what seems most our own and to be our very essence, I mean our reason, is least peculiarly ours, is what we should account most borrowed. We unceasingly and obviously receive a

---

[1] First Part, chap. ii. No. 52.
[2] Ibid.
[3] Ibid., No. 53.
[4] Ibid., No. 54.
[5] Ibid.
[6] Ibid., No. 55.

reason superior to ourselves, as we unceasingly breathe the air, which is a foreign body, or as we unceasingly see all the objects about us in the light of the sun, whose rays are bodies foreign to our eyes.[1]

"In all things we find, as it were, two principles within us : the one gives, the other receives; the one lacks, the other supplies; the one errs, the other corrects; the one is prone to fall, the other lifts it up. . . . Every man feels within him *a limited and inferior reason*, which goes astray so soon as it escapes entire subjection, and which can only be rectified when it again submits to the yoke *of another superior, universal, and immutable reason.* Thus, everything in us bears the mark of an inferior, limited, shared, and borrowed reason, which requires another to correct it at every turn.[2] . . .

"Now, doubtless, the man who fears the correction of that incorruptible reason, and who goes astray from not following it, is not this perfect, universal, and unchanging reason which corrects him in his own despite.[3] . . .

"There are then two reasons to be found within me, one of which is myself, the other is superior to me. That which is myself is very imperfect, faulty, uncertain, prejudiced, headstrong, subject to error, changing, hasty, ignorant, and limited ; in fact, it possesses nothing that is not borrowed. The other is common to all men and superior to them; it is perfect, eternal, immutable, ever ready of access and ready to rectify all minds that err, — in fine, incapable of ever being exhausted or divided, although it is freely given to all those that desire it. Where is this perfect reason which is so near me, and yet so different from me? Where is it? It must be something real; for *nothing* cannot be perfect or render imperfect natures perfect. Where is this supreme reason? Is it not the God whom I seek?"[4]

Such is this superb analysis of reason, the best which has been made; and at the same time the most certain, most immediate, and most beautiful demonstration of the existence of God.

[1] First Part, chap. ii. No. 56.　　[3] Ibid.
[2] Ibid., No. 57.　　[4] Ibid., No. 60.

Fénelon completes this point of view by analyzing the will as he has before analyzed the intelligence. Just as he finds in us an inferior and a superior reason, the double light which Saint Augustine called "the illuminating and the illuminated light," and between which Malebranche also makes a distinction in more than one place ; so, too, he sees in our will two faces: "On the one hand I am free, on the other I am dependent.[1] I am dependent on a first Being even in my own will, and nevertheless I am free. What is this dependent liberty, this borrowed freedom ?"[2] Dependence reveals the nothingness from which I come, that is to say that I am a secondary cause and a finite being; my freedom, which I cannot doubt, is a greatness which comes from the infinite.[3]

Here we have everything in man clearly distinguished.

And here we have inferior reason scourged and contemned when it sets itself apart, as Pascal contemned it; we have infallible and supreme reason deified as Malebranche deifies it: both points of view are equally true; but Fénelon combines them without confusing anything, without exaggerating anything.

III.

Fénelon understood what few fully understand even now, — namely, that the marvellous thing which we call our reason, "without penetrating into the extent of this word," is God and ourself; or, more exactly speaking, it is a relation of God to us, in which, on our side, we may be found lacking, by turning away and isolating ourselves. Fénelon knows that our ideas exist in God and in us, pertain to God and to us. He knows the true theory of intellectual vision, which Malebranche perceives but incompletely: it is

---

[1] First Part, chap. ii. No. 63.
[2] Ibid., No. 69.
[3] Ibid., No. 69.

that of Plato, Saint Augustine, and Saint Thomas Aquinas, who (I will say it, however much metaphysicians may mistrust images) held fast to truth by an image, by depending upon the poetry of God, and comparing intellectual vision to physical vision,—a comparison of which Kant took excellent advantage on an important point, and of which philosophers will yet make greater use when they have acquired the true principle and practice of comparative science.

We quote this comparison, as used by Fénelon.

"There is a sun of spirits. . . . As the natural sun lights all bodies, so the sun of intelligence lights all minds. The substance of a man's eye is not the light; on the contrary, the eye borrows, every moment, the light from the rays of the sun. Just so, my mind is not the primitive reason, the universal and immutable truth, — it is only the organ through which that original light passes, and which is lighted by it. . . . That universal light discovers and represents all objects to our eyes; and we cannot judge of anything save by it, even as we cannot discern any body save by the rays of the sun." [1]

This is the precise truth that Malebranche describes imperfectly and inexactly. The soul, in its actual state, does not see God directly, it sees itself, and it sees its ideas in the light of God, as the eye sees objects in the light of day; but to see daylight is not the same as to see the sun itself directly, although the daylight proceeds from the sun; to see the colors and forms of objects is not the same as seeing the sun, although forms are only visible by means of the sun, and colors are only the light itself of the sun, broken, refracted, and partially reflected by objects. So, too, it is impossible to say that every idea, all vision, all knowledge, are immediately and directly the vision of God, although we can have no idea without God, and all knowledge implies

[1] First Part, chap. ii. No. 58.

God, as all vision through the eyes implies light, — both the source of light and its presence.

This Malebranche does not recognize. Malebranche's lofty intelligence is dazzled by the most admirable of truths, — namely, "that if we do not see God in some manner, we shall not see anything;"[1] that we see everything, without exception, in the light of God, and that in a certain sense we see God in all vision, spiritual or corporeal. But Malebranche believes that this necessary vision of God, which all vision and all thought imply, "is the direct and immediate vision of God;"[2] that we see nothing, even material bodies, save by seeing their ideas, which exist in God, and which are' God.[3] So that it is no longer possible for him to distinguish between the two degrees of the divine intelligibility. This' distinction is the capital truth that he lacks. He half perceives it when the objection is offered; but if he for a moment forsakes his error, it is only to return to it speedily. "No," he says, "we cannot conclude that spirits see God's essence, from the fact that they see all things in God in this manner. . . . For we see not so much the ideas of things, as the things themselves which the ideas represent; for instance, when we see a square, we do not say that we see the idea of that square which is united to the mind, but only the square which is on the exterior. . . . We do not say that we see God by seeing truths, but by seeing the *ideas* of those truths. . . . To our thinking, we see God when we see eternal truths; not that these truths are God, but because the ideas on which these truths depend exist in God."[4]

Malebranche here renounces his error, and teaches no

---

[1] Search after Truth, book iii. part ii. chap. vi.
[2] Ibid., chap. vii.
[3] Ibid., chap. ix.
[4] Ibid., book ii. chap. xi.

other than the theory of Plato, Saint Augustine, and Saint
Thomas,[1] which is the truth. But he does not stand fast;
his dazzled condition carries him away, and in the selfsame
pages he maintains — it is his ruling idea — that "God
shows all things to spirits simply by desiring that they shall
see what is most central in themselves; that is, that which
in him is in relation with those things and represents
them.[2] . . . It is," he says, "only God that we see with
direct and immediate vision. It is only he who can enlighten the mind by his own substance. . . . We know
things by their ideas, — that is, in God. . . . It is in God
and by their ideas that we see bodies and their properties,
and therefore our knowledge of them is very perfect; . . .
for when we see things as they are in God, we always see
them in a very perfect manner."[3] Saint Thomas says no
more than this of the beatific vision of the essence of God.
To see things in a very perfect manner, as they are in God,
— in their very ideas, which are God, — is the vision of
God's essence. Malebranche's error, therefore, plainly consists, as Balmès has observed, in his failure to distinguish
the beatific vision from that natural and indirect vision of
God without which we can see nothing. As a theologian,
he can evade this objection only by contradicting himself
and momentarily deserting his system. He grants, in the
sixth chapter, that in natural knowledge what spirits "see
in God is *very imperfect*, and God is very perfect." Having thus answered the objection, he asserts in chapter vii.
"that it is in God and by their ideas that we see bodies,
and that we have a *very perfect* knowledge of them." This
is what may be called in Malebranche a dazzled bewilder-

---

[1] Omnis cognoscens, cognoscit implicite Deum in quolibet cognito. —*Verit.*,
q. xxii. 2, 1ᵐ.

[2] Search after Truth, chap. vi.

[3] Ibid.

ment. But Fénelon here seems to us to see the whole truth, without confusion or exaggeration. He asserts everywhere that "it is the light of God that reveals objects to us, and that we can judge of nothing save through it. This same knowledge of individual things, where God is not the immediate object of my thought, can only be acquired in so far as God gives to the creature intelligibility, and to me actual intelligence. It is therefore in the light of God that I see all that can be seen." [1] Fénelon does not say, as Malebranche does, that in everything we see God directly and immediately, but only that we see everything in the light of God. He does not speak of direct vision, and this is the great point; if he speaks of immediate vision, he makes a distinction: "The immediate object of all my universal knowledge is God himself, and the single being or created individual . . . is the immediate object of my single knowledge." [2] But how is God himself the immediate object of my general knowledge, — for instance, of the idea of the infinite? "Who is it that put the idea of the infinite in a subject so limited? . . . Let us suppose that the mind of man is like a looking-glass. . . . What being was able to imprint within us the *image* of the infinite, if the *infinite* never existed? . . . This image of the infinite is the true infinite of which we have the thought. . . . If it were not, could it be engraved on the very essence of our minds?" [3] Accordingly, our idea of God is not the direct vision of God, but it is *an image* of God, — that is, a vision reflected in the mirror of the soul. Here we again meet with the doctrine of Saint Thomas Aquinas, — natural vision of the truth is, in the soul, the reflection (*refulgentia*) of uncreated truth. For if Fénelon goes so far as to say

[1] Treatise on the Existence of God, part ii. ch. iv. No. 58.
[2] Ibid., No. 60.
[3] First part, chap. ii. No. 53.

that, when we see the truth, "it is God himself, infinite
truth, that is revealed immediately to us, with the limitations under which he may communicate his being,"[1] he
understands it as he has just explained it: God graves his
image in our soul, he reflects himself in the mirror of the
soul. This is the very doctrine of Descartes.

So that, to sum up the whole, in Fénelon's simile the idea
of God is the image of the sun in the mirror: all general
knowledge is the full rays of that image; the light of God
reflected in the soul is then the immediate object of intellectual
vision. As for special knowledge, it is like the vision of bodies by sunlight; I see bodies by their colors, partial, decom-
posed rays of the universal light that makes bodies visible.
But, in that very case, the eye sees something of the sun.
"Thus," says Fenelon, "our ideas are a constant mixture of the
infinite Being of God, who is our object, and of the limitations
which he always gives essentially to each of his creatures."[2]

IV.

The reader will now better understand the admirable
demonstration of the existence of God derived from the
theory of reason. Fénelon proves God from the spectacle
of the human mind as we prove the sun from light. He
sees, in our mind, the contrast between "a weakness which
strays and an infallibility which corrects, an insignificance
ignorant of its own thoughts, and an unlimited fund of ideas
which nothing can efface or alter." From the sight of this
weakness he learns that we are not the infallible; from the
sight of this insignificance he learns that we are not the
infinite or the unlimited fund of ideas, but that all this is
God, or an effect of the presence of God. He concludes from
this that God exists. It is thus that the sight of darkness

[1] Part ii. No. 53.   [2] Ibid., chap. iv. No. 54.

informs us in regard to light, tells us that it exists, in itself, independently of objects, since they are only visible by it, and are effaced when it ceases to lend its aid.

No one has known or developed better than Fénelon the conditions of the true proof of the existence of God. The point of support, in reality, takes up the whole of the first part of his treatise. He does not drop it when he proceeds to the metaphysical proof through the intrinsic idea of the infinite and necessary Being. As for that sense of the divine and that divine impulse which raise us to God and call us to the light, it is described in these charming words : —

" Where is that pure, sweet light, which not only enlightens the eyes that are open, but which opens the eyes that are closed ; which heals diseased eyes ; which gives eyes to those who have none wherewith to see ; in brief, which inspires us with a desire to be enlightened by it, and which makes itself loved even by those who fear to see it ? " [1]

Fénelon perceives the obstacle in these clouds of our passions on the divine sun ; he sees the diseased eyes closed to the light ; he therefore knows the moral condition and the proof of the existence of God.

As for the process by which our mind rises from the sight of the finite to the knowledge of the infinite, Fénelon describes it perfectly. He says, —

" God is veritably in himself all that there is real and positive in the human mind, all that there is real and positive in material bodies, all that there is real and positive in the essences of all possible creatures, of which I have no distinct idea. He has all the being of the body, without being limited to the body ; all the being of the mind, without being limited to the mind ; and the same of the other possible essences. He is all being in such a manner that he has all the being of each of these creatures, but

---

[1] Treatise on the Existence of God, part ii. chap. iv. No. 58.

16

without the limitation that bounds it. Remove all bounds; remove all the difference which confines being to species : you retain the universality of being, and, consequently, the infinite perfection of Being by itself.[1]

"And when I conceive it thus in that kind which the School calls *transcendental*, which no difference can ever cause to lose its universal simplicity, I conceive that it can equally derive from its simple and infinite being, minds, bodies, and all the other possible essences which correspond to these infinite degrees of beings."[2]

In short, for what properly concerns the result of the process, and the idea of the infinite which it should give, I find it nowhere given with precision and completeness save in Fénelon alone. Here is a passage in which he himself sums it up : —

"I could never conceive of more than *a single infinite ;* that is to say, other than the being infinitely perfect, or *infinite in every kind.* Any infinite which was infinite in but one kind would not be a true infinite. To speak of a genus or species is plainly to speak of limitation, and to exclude all ulterior reality, — which establishes the fact of a finite and limited being. To restrict the idea of the infinite to the limits of a genus shows that we have not considered it with sufficient simplicity. It is clear that it can only be found in the universality of being, which is the being infinitely perfect in every kind, and infinitely simple."[8]

Nothing could be more important than these words. This we shall see later.

In short, Fénelon corrects Pascal and Malebranche; and he gives Descartes exactness and completion.

V.

Fénelon being our subject, we may be allowed to say a few words more concerning him.

[1] Treatise on the Existence of God, part ii. chap. v. No. 66.
[2] Ibid., No. 67.
[8] Letters on Metaphysics, letter iv. 3.

Errors may be found in the writings of every man of the seventeenth century. I ask if any be found in Fénelon?

Not that in asking this question I forget the matter of Quietism, and the just condemnation which concluded it. I have it in mind. But did Fénelon submit to that condemnation? Did he burn his book? Yes; consequently he yielded to the truth. If he yielded to the truth, he was not mistaken. This we must admit, unless we mean to impute to him the erasures in his manuscripts, and reproach him with the pages which he flung into the fire. Let us learn at least to appreciate the greatness of a mind capable of sacrificing the first forms of its thought. Such a mind is great, because it is greater than itself. The sacrificer of the false, who immolates it in his own mind, is not a victim of error, but a martyr to truth; and he rises, by virtue of the sacrifice, above himself to the truth which is God. "Leave self, to enter into the infinity of God!" exclaimed Fénelon. Now that which he has said, that he has done.

Consider, amidst the great geniuses of the seventeenth century, this admirable intellectual character, his perfect proportions, his firm attitude in the truth. Fuller and more luminous than Descartes in regard to the theory of ideas and reason; incomparably more exact that Leibnitz as to the theory of the infinite; avoiding the bitter melancholy of Pascal, who seems to curse nature, as well as the brilliant exaggeration of Malebranche, who believes that our natural reason is the very vision of God; more absolute, more clear-sighted, than most in his opposition to pantheism and the sophists; firmer and more decided in regard to the error of Jansenism than even Bossuet, who sometimes seems to waver; truer than Bossuet, too, in regard to the theory of ability and liberty, and the great question of the relations of Church and State; holily animated with a pious and generous belief in the future and in the progress of the world,

— a faith very rare at that time, and perhaps as rare now; admirable for his mystic learning, which he taught to Bossuet day by day, until he made an accomplished master of that sublime pupil;[1] more amiable, more attractive than all others through the happy equilibrium of his courage, his intelligence, and his goodness, — the only man, in short, besides Saint Vincent de Paul, whose aureole has remained visible to all eyes through the lapse of two centuries: consider all these features of perfect human beauty, and see if these glorious pre-eminencies do not seem to realize in Fénelon the words of Scripture: "He who humbles himself shall be exalted."

When shall we learn what sacrifice is, in things of the spirit, and what it can do? "Our will is finite," says Bossuet; "in so far as it restricts itself to itself it gives itself limits. If you would be free, release yourself. Cut away, retrench. Have no will but that of God." This is the moral sacrifice. Now we may, by copying these words, say also: "Our intellect is finite; in so far as it restricts itself to itself, it gives itself limits. If you would be free, release yourself. Cut away, retrench. Have no thoughts but those of God." Behold intellectual sacrifice!

Fénelon cut away and retrenched. "If your right hand offend you," says the Gospel, "cut it off and cast it from you." Fénelon cast far from him thoughts full of error and danger; but the fund of truth which was in his soul, and which those imperfect and faulty formulas curtailed and impaired, was set free by the action of the Church, to diffuse itself into the human mind. True orthodox mysticism, theologically perfected, dates from that period. That is to say, before Fénelon's effort to systematize mystic science the writings of the most saintly authors contained inexactitudes on this head, not of intention, but in expression; so

1 See the "Literary History of Fénelon," by the Abbé Gosselin.

that the chief point of mystic theology, the final word of true wisdom, was then, and then only, defined and fixed. We know that Fénelon's effort attracted the attention of Bossuet, who was very justly moved; Fénelon's vigorous and luminous defence taught Bossuet the science; Bossuet, well armed by his opponent, urged on the contest. The con-test was judged by the Church : the false side of Fénelon's thought, or at least of his words, was corrected in the most just and delicate way ; nothing that he had seen, felt, or written of the truth, was touched, — in short, Fénelon's sur-render ended all in peace, in unity, and in truth.

Peace! peace in unity and in truth! when will these good things be granted to us? When shall we advance towards this goal? "Quarrelsome race of men !" exclaims Saint Chrysostom. Quarrelsome race indeed ! Yes, we are born to quarrel, dissension, and division. Not only does human-ity form two camps and two cities, for and against God, for and against the truth, but, not to mention here the sophists and the criminals, behold the history of the good and of those who have pursued the truth with upright spirit. Behold them all in presence of the sun : each is bathed in its rays; but each considers his soul and its thought in that light, instead of considering the light itself in the soul and the thought; each limits, modifies, and di-versifies the light, chooses the rays each according to its proper color, and instead of understanding that all tints are but the same light, suppose that the colors are contradictory, — as if the vivid purple of dawn should deem itself contra-dicted by the dazzling whiteness of noon, or the dark violet of the evening clouds. I am well aware that Plato divined the necessary unanimity of the wise, and said, " All wise men agree." Meantime, Plato and Aristotle are divided, Saint Augustine and Saint Jerome do not always agree. Saint Thomas and Saint Bonaventura give rise to two schools that

contend for centuries. See Pascal opposed to Descartes
and the Jesuits, Descartes to Aristotle, Fénelon to Malebranche, Newton to Leibnitz, and Bossuet to Fénelon; see
all these glorious couples struggling, often even in the sharp-
est anger! But in reality, as Saint Augustine affirms of
Aristotle and Plato, they differ owing to accidents which are
overcome by him who sees the true harmony of these
beauteous tints in the unity of light. Moreover, the separation between Plato and Aristotle is incomparably deeper
than that of the shades of philosophic doctrine in the Christian Fathers; when we weigh things well, we find that these
very shades are far less pronounced in the Middle Age
than in the Patristic age; and in the seventeenth century,
the sophists always excepted, the divisions are even less
marked. This is undoubtedly because the two Cities, among
men, are continually closing in and becoming stronger, each
in its own unity.

But under what influence and by what cause does the
unity of righteous hearts and docile minds thus increase, if
not because, since Plato and Aristotle, he who has been
called the Prince of Peace has arisen, and the Angel of
Peace has cast upon the earth the beginning of unity?
That part of humanity truly united to God has assumed a
visible centre, as astronomers say that they perceive in the
heavens, in the formation of worlds, a period when the
vague cloud, the raw material of the stars, assumes a centre
and labors to acquire regularity, roundness, and unity. God
then lays, as Genesis says, "a firmament in the midst of the
waters."[1] So too, a time has come in history when God is
placing, in the bosom of the ever-changing and scattered
mass of mankind, the centre of attraction which strives for
the increasing union of men in God.

Do we not see, in this supreme question of the soul's

---

[1] Dixit quoque Deus, Fiat firmamentum in medio aquarum. — *Genesis* i. 6.

relations to God in love, that Bossuet and Fénelon, who, by themselves, were forever divided, were only reunited by the power and authority of that centre, and brought their difficulties, unjust on both sides, to it, — Bossuet sacrificing his ignorances little by little, under the ascendency of Catholic theology and the tradition of the saints which Fénelon opposed to him, and Fénelon yielding wholly by a single effort at the first warning of Unity, to the voice of the representative of him of whom he himself had said, "It is in this centre that all men meet, from one end of the world to the other"?

Thus, there is in the world a uniting force and a visible basis of unity. May peace then come in unity and in truth!

Deign, O God, ever to attract us more and more, both by thy secret power and by the firm though gentle authority of the visible centre of thy eternal unity! Grant that by considering self less, we may see thee more, — may lose sight of our diversities, and contemplate thy unity. May we be at length permitted to divide light less; may the partial tint of our souls impair less the whiteness of the ray; may our mind, despite its insignificance, and through the disinterestedness that comes from thee, love and seek the universality and immensity of truth, and may our defects and our limits at least never turn to negations and blindness. Give us, with the charity of the heart, that of the mind. Grant that, as Saint Ignatius says, a Christian may ever be more ready to accept than to reject the word of his brother. Grant that in spite of the difficulty of language and the imperfect form of human thought, we may learn to reascend through the word of another to the pure origin of the ray which has produced this word and this thought. Grant that by this charity of mind we may learn to leave self behind and reach out after the lights of others, and grasp in intellectual struggles the aspect of truth which is opposed to us, and which we lack.   Grant, above all, that we may be docile to the intellectual unanimity of our Fathers, and to the supreme authority of the holy inspiration that directs thy Church; to the end that by docility, humility, and charity, men may attain to some communion of minds on earth, and, being united, understanding one another in God more and more, may approach that eternal goal of which Saint Augustine says: "We shall then all see the thoughts of all; we shall see God in our own intelligence; we shall see him in that of others." [1]

[1] De Civitate Dei, lib. xxii. cap. xxix. 6.

CHAPTER VII.

PART SECOND.

PETAU AND THOMASSIN.

EVERY one knows that Leibnitz wrote a Theodicy, Fénelon the Treatise on the Existence of God, Bossuet a book On the Knowledge of God and self; that Descartes, Malebranche, and others cleared, deepened, and developed the proofs of God's existence, and the way that leads the mind to the knowledge thereof; but scarcely any one knows that there also appeared in the seventeenth century two Latin Theodicies, each of considerable length, — equivalent to eight or ten volumes like ours, — and that these two works are masterpieces of philosophic depth and learning.

Two great minds, scarcely inferior to the greatest, — Petau and Thomassin, — brought together in these admirable works all the substance of the fathers and the ancient philosophers, in regard to the Theodicy; then, with wondrous art, they worked up and grouped the precious materials in the light of their individual reflection. I know no books where original thought is better blended with the thought of others, where the intuition of genius is more perfectly supported by the power of tradition and the weight of authority; and when Thomassin says, "Thus decree the patricians of thought and the fathers of religion;" when he goes on to proclaim these decrees, all luminous in the light of his expositions, — we see that he is himself one of those patri-

cians, one of those fathers, voting with the rest, and uttering his vote in a voice worthy to be heard with the most
illustrious.

Thomassin lived nearly fifty years after Petau, who died
about the same time as Descartes. His work is longer than
that of the famous Jesuit, more complete, perhaps still more
philosophic and more original. As it would be little else
than a repetition to speak in equal detail of two such similar
works, we will pay special attention to that of Thomassin.
We will merely give an analysis of one of Petau's chapters,
which will suffice to show the bearing of his mind.

We will take the chapter on *Demonstrative Theology;* that
is to say, the process by which reason rises to God.

We give an abridged translation [1] : —

"Demonstrative Theology treats of what are commonly known
as *attributes;* attributes which are divided into affirmative and
negative attributes. We shall deal with them in general in this
chapter, then in detail in the ensuing chapters.

"This division into positive and negative properties is usual
only with the ancient theologians : it is owing to the fact, as Saint
Cyril observes, that we know in two ways that which it is fit that
we should assert regarding the divine substance : we know God
from what he is, and from what he is not. Saint Dionysius, in his
Mystic Theology, has done more than any one else to point out this
twofold way : 'We must,' he says, 'posit in God all affirmations
which are true of all things, and they are true of him, because he
is the cause of all; but then we must deny them, because he is
superior to all, and we should not suppose that these negations are
contrary to those affirmations; and certainly the First Cause is
superior to these negations, being superior to all negation and even
all affirmation.' The same author remarks elsewhere that the
Scripture adopts sometimes one and sometimes the other of these
two modes: for it sometimes calls God *Reason, Mind, Substance,
Light and Life;* sometimes designates him by very different terms,
as when it declares that he is *invisible, infinite,* and *incomprehensible,*

[1] Theologicorum Dogmatum, lib. i. cap. v.

and by other terms which express, not what he is, but, on the contrary, what he is not.

"This is elegantly summed up by Saint Gregory Nazianzen in the words: 'End of all, thou art one, thou art all that is, being neither one nor all.' [1]

"Theology, therefore, seeks God by this twofold process of affirmation and negation; but negation, according to Saint Dionysius and other Fathers, is more potent here than even affirmation, which he explains as follows in his celestial hierarchy. 'It is,' he says, 'because in denying his identity with the things we see, we speak truly, and thus attain, although indirectly, *his substance raised above all other substance, and his infinity incomprehensible to the mind as to all speech.*'

"In fact, these negations, as Saint Dionysius says elsewhere, *in no way signify that there is in God any privation of that which they deny, but, on the contrary, excess and plenitude.* To say of God that he is not substance, means that he is infinite substance; to say that he is not life, means that he is supreme life; to say that he is not thought, means that he is sovereign thought.[2] This is supported by Saint Maximus when he remarks that negations are more efficacious than assertions in God.

"Nevertheless, if negative statements are superior in exactness to affirmative ones, still the latter should be maintained; the two should be combined and modified one by the other. These negations and affirmations are not contradictory, but, on the contrary, they support and complete one another. And, as Theodore Abucara says, positive properties should be attributed to God, as well as negative ones, *in such manner as to transfer to God all the perfections of our souls, taking away, by negation, all that proceeds from accident or fault.*[3]

"This is very well shown by John Cyparissiotus when he develops the thought that *negation is far from refusing to God what affirmation attributes to him.*

"Very far from this, affirmative statements, positive notions, are, by these negations, extended and made perfect: *negation wipes away and removes* everything in the affirmation which is gross, nar-

---

[1] Tu finis cunctorum, unus, simul omnia, nullus,
  Non unus, non cuncta.
[2] Dion., cap. iv. *de Divin. non.*   [3] Theod. Abuc., opusc. tert.

row, or borrowed from the creature whence it proceeds; the idea
remains, purer, more transparent, worthier of God. As if marble,
says Saint Dionysius, contained innate statues : the hand of the
artist need only remove that which conceals them, and could un-
veil these hidden beauties by removing that which is not they.
This Maximus makes still clearer by his charming comments. He
says that there are two sorts of natural cameos, — those which the
artist takes from the lump without adding anything, and which he
draws by removal; and those which Euripides calls *innate forms*
(αὐτόμορφοι) : as when Nature herself creates a design in a precious
stone. Such was that cameo of Pyrrhus mentioned by Pliny,[1]
where the Nine Muses and Apollo with his lyre were engraved, not
by the hand or art of any man, but by Nature herself, which had
so disposed the forms and shades of the stone as to produce these
figures, and even to give each of the nine sisters all her attributes
in minute detail. In this case, the artist, without touching the
material itself, had only to remove the waste and smooth off the
roughness to reveal the innate masterpiece. This comparison admirably befits the notion of God shaped in us by the process of
theological elimination, — a process which Plotinus believed to be
universal, because we know in general the nature of a being if we
take everything accidental from it. ‘ To know any nature,’ he says,
‘ we must see it in its purity : knowledge is prevented by accidental
additions to its essence. Therefore we should seek the essence by
eliminating the accidental.’[2]

"All this agrees with the thought of Aristotle, who gives us his
first category, not by a positive, but by a negative definition.
Ammonius discusses and understands it in the same way. Alcinous
compares this process of rising to God by negation and elimination, to the geometric process which rises to the idea of a point by
eliminating the sensible forms of extension, passing from a solid
body to the surface, from the surface to the line, and from the line
to the point.

"In short, this process is peculiarly applicable to the idea of
God. For, as a Platonist, Herennius, observes in an unpublished
book, affirmations define, circumscribe; negations alone have an
infinite extent ; only negation has the power to rise, from beings
restricted in their limitations, to the illimitable Being whom nothing can circumscribe."

1 Book xxxvii. chap. i.   2 Plot. Enn., i. 7, c. ix.

Such is this chapter of Petau's Theodicy.

Assuredly the chief process of reason, which rises to the infinity of God, which is, moreover, the universal process for the knowledge of all intrinsic truth, was never described better, never more completely or more profoundly analyzed, than in this splendid chapter.

How is it that this fine work is unknown; that it is not in the hands of every one who makes a study of philosophy; that the Theodicy can be discussed without a knowledge of it?

II.

Thomassin writes Latin as Malebranche does French, if we make a slight reservation in regard to purity of classic taste. Sometimes, in Thomassin's rapid composition, strange excrescences of language and brilliant barbarisms slip in. But the wealth, lucidity, and elevation of style are the same in Thomassin and in Malebranche. As prodigiously learned as Malebranche was not, he is no less original. In both, the central idea, the philosophic cult, is the same: it is the worship of the Everlasting Word considered under both its phases, — both as the Universal Reason which enlightens all men, and as the Incarnate Word, the Saviour of mankind.

In both points of view Thomassin's motto is this: "Christ comes at all times" (*Christus venit semper*). As Reason, he enlightens every man coming into this world; as Saviour or Incarnate Word, he also comes for all, and acts from the beginning, according to the words of Scripture which speak "of the Lamb slain from the foundation of the world."

Hence the vigorous eclecticism of Thomassin, which, in the light of Catholic truth, and supported by the steadfast basis of dogma, refers to Christianity, as its peculiar property, all fragments and vestiges of truth which at any time and in any place the Universal Word has sowed in the mind of

men who have cultivated and followed their reason. Thomassin takes everything in good part, when it is not utterly
impossible; he rejects but little, accepts much. His broad
genius is generously hospitable; he can always find room for
every man. He rejects none but the vicious and the impious;
all who have been serious and sincere in their search for
truth are received. After Saint Augustine, Plato more than
any other, and all that relates to Plato, is dear to him.[1] The
whole train of Neo-Platonists is well received, and his goodness is not sufficiently on its guard againt Plotinus, who generally is half a sophist. He practises, even to excess, the words
of Saint Paul: "Charity believeth all things." Nor ever
does this abundant and perpetual hospitality inconvenience
him. He remains free in the midst of the multitude; he
contrives to live at once with all and with himself. He is
always conversing, but never stops meditating; and while
entering into the thoughts of others, he never abandons his
own. By the pertinency of his questions, and the comparison which he constantly evokes between the universal and
the individual mind, he attributes to some, even often the
best, more intellect than they possess. He is well aware
that all the world has more intellect than any individual;
therefore he brings all the world as near together as he can.

The mutual penetration of free thought and tradition, of
theology and philosophy, was never carried farther. No
man ever labored more for the reconciliation of all truths,
the reciprocal illumination of each order of things by all the
others. It was his aim to take up the sum total of human

---

[1] We know that there are two ways of judging Plato : we may take him in
a good or in a bad sense. We believe the former to be the truer way, and on
this subject we agree with the good Franciscan monk who printed at Bologna,
in 1627, a book entitled, "Christianæ Theologicæ cum Platonica comparatio,
auctore Livio Galante, sacri Seraphici ordinis Theologo." On the frontispiece,
the author engraved a rose. That rose is Plato. Upon the rose, to the right,
is a bee ; at the left, a spider. Above the bee are the words, *hinc mel ;* and
above the spider, *hinc venenum.* Now, Thomassin is a bee.

intellect; to survey and compare its entire sphere; to recover, by placing himself at the centre of that sphere, its lost unity and forgotten harmonies; to bring down from the central point the universal light of the Word, or catholic truth, in all the circles and upon all the points of the sphere; to create the true encyclopædia, and apply it to the education of minds.

Besides his great theological work, which is really an admirable comparison of theology and philosophy, he left behind as monuments of his labor four fine works, even less known than his Theological Dogmas, — "Christian Methods of Studying and Teaching Philosophy;" "Grammar;" "Historians;" "Poets."

Lastly, Thomassin elaborates his views in regard also to "the mode of referring to God even physics and natural history, which is one of the finest parts of Philosophy, most important, useful, and instructive." It is certainly high time to follow these hints of genius given us by the seventeenth century, if we desire to renew science, letters, and philosophy, to re-establish education and instruction, to restore public reason, and through reason, religion.

But let us return to our subject, which is Thomassin's Theodicy.

III.

This work, which forms the first part of the Theological Dogmas, is divided into ten books, — each of which is about the length of Fénelon's Treatise on the Existence of God, and which bear the following titles: I. On the Existence of God; II. On the Unity of God and his Goodness; III. On God considered as Absolute Being, as Truth, Beauty, Love, and Life (where Ideas are treated of); IV. On the Simplicity of God; V. On the Immensity, Immutability, and Eternity of God; VI. On the Vision of God (how souls see God); VII. On the Knowledge and Will of God. The last three books are purely theological, and treat of predestination.

This Theodicy, which is the work of the Fathers of the Church summarized by a man of genius, is probably the most complete, scholarly, and philosophic work regarding God ever written.[1]

We have now particularly to analyze the first book, which treats of the existence of God. This book contains all the profundities and all the aspects of the question, which is amply discussed in its pages by the philosophers and the Fathers.

All, according to Thomassin, who quotes them, recognize first in the soul the innate idea, or at least the natural idea of God, — a sort of anticipated knowledge, or rather conscious-ness, of God, impressed by God upon the new-born soul, or, if you prefer, which the ever-present God never ceases to offer it by revealing himself.[2]

All see this innate germ of knowledge of God in the in-nate desire for the sovereign Good.[3]

They also see this implicit knowledge of God in that light which distinguishes the just from the unjust, — a natural law written upon every heart.[4]

They see it in reason itself, which cannot exist without an actual relation of the soul to God; which, first of all, repre-sents God by his necessary forms, — first principles, axioms, the ideas of the infinite and of perfection; and which also sees God himself implicitly, by seeing what it sees, and every time that it judges. There is the nature itself of the rational soul which carries in its essence the idea of God (*divinam lucem animæ inessentialem*),[5] and there is the actual and living relation of the soul to God, which shows it God immediately (*inmediatis cum Deo mentis congressibus*).[6]

---

[1] Tardy justice has at last been done to this almost unknown genius by M. Lescœur's fine work on Thomassin's Theodicy.

[2] Dogm. Theol., de Deo, lib. i. cap. i. § 1.

[3] Ibid., cap. v. [5] Ibid., cap. viii. § 1.

[4] Ibid., cap. vi. and vii. [6] Ibid., cap. viii.

Then, in the knowledge that our soul has of itself, knowledge that implies other forms of knowledge not given by the visible world, and, moreover, far clearer to us,[1] Thomassin shows us a firmer and surer point of support, whence we may rise to God, than the sight of the whole world could afford.[2]

Yet this rational knowledge of God, which we find naturally in us, rather teaches us that God is, than shows us what he is.[3] That is to say, it is indirect rather than direct.

Moreover, the existence of God is also proved by all creation. It is demonstrated by that upward course of the mind which advances from the things which are seen to those which are not seen.[4]

Necessary geometric ideas, taken in themselves, also prove it.[5]

Both the Fathers and the Philosophers agree in recognizing these three ways of proving the existence of God: 1. The gradation of beings (cosmological proof); 2. Intelligence and the innate desire for the Good and the Beautiful (psychological proof); 3. Necessary ideas taken in themselves (metaphysical proof).[6]

We therefore find here once more, both in Thomassin and in all those whom he consults, the two proofs *a posteriori*, from the sight of our soul and that of nature, and the proof *a priori* from ideas taken in themselves.

Thomassin considers the metaphysical proof *a priori* good; but he does not in any way separate it from the proof *a posteriori*, and the basis of his thought is as follows : —

That, in reality, the starting-point for all knowledge of God, all efficacious and actual proof of his existence, is that

---

[1] Dogm. Theol., de Deo, title of cap. xvi.
[2] Ibid., cap. xvii.
[3] Ibid., cap. xviii.
[4] Ibid., cap. xxii.
[5] Cap. xxiii. and xxiv.
[6] Cap. xxv.

fact which is commonly known as the innate idea of God,
but that it is essential to search into it and to describe it in
a more philosophical manner.

IV.

Now, we have here the profoundly original, and, to our
thinking, fundamental theory of what has been called *the
innate idea of God.* It is given by Thomassin in the title
of his nineteenth chapter, and elaborated throughout the
chapter : "Higher, more central than the intelligence, there
is a mysterious sense that touches God, rather than sees
or conceives him." (*Supra vim intelligendi est sensus
quidem arcanus quo Deus tangitur, magis quam cernitur aut
intelligitur.*)

In this chapter Thomassin posits and describes the most
profound of philosophic facts, which throws light on all
psychology, gives the Theodicy its true basis, and reveals
the true force of intelligence and will.   It is what Aristotle,
without describing it, calls the attraction of the desirable
and the intelligible.

We do not hesitate to say that this point, which is the
introduction in philosophy to true and necessary mysticism,
is the chief point which philosophy has pursued from the
beginning, without which it can never be completed, without which it would lack all root, by which it will be perfected, transformed, and organized.   This truth is perhaps
that perceived by the actual leader of German philosophy,
Schelling,[1] when he says that God can never again be only a
rational being to philosophy, but must also be *an experimental being,* and he sees a transformation of philosophy in this
new postulate.   "It is in this direction," he says, "that philosophy is on the eve of yet another great revolution, which,

[1] When I wrote these lines Schelling was still living.

so far as the substance of things is concerned, will be the last." [1]

We believe these words well founded, and we say that Thomassin handles and describes the fact to which they relate better than any one. Moreover, Christians only will fulfil this prophecy.

Thomassin therefore posits and asserts the existence of a ' divine sense in the soul, a sense of divine contact, distinct from the necessary ideas also existent in the soul, which are a sort of vision of God. According to Thomassin, the soul is conscious of material bodies, is conscious of itself, is conscious of God. Here we have the sum total of sensitivity, which is thus divided into *outward sense, inward sense,* and *divine sense.*

But the divine sense, note it well, can only give from this contact with God an implicit knowledge and love of God, — a double element, which must be developed and directed in us by reason and liberty.

Thenceforth we know God as we know the world. Sensation gives our knowledge of the world an experimental, but confused and obscure basis : reason adds to this its lights; so, too, the divine sense gives an experimental basis for the knowledge of God, obscure and confused though it be; and reason adds its lights. While we actually have this obscure sense of the substance of God, we have, on the other hand, a clear idea of the evident, necessary, absolute, and immutable truths which also proceed from God, which are a sort of vision of God. Let us add these lights to the obscure sense ; let the moral and affectional element implied in that sense be the mainspring and give the impetus; let reason proceed according to its law, according to that simple and natural process which seeks through all things nought save the uni-

---

[1] System of Transcendental Idealism, appendix to Cousin's Philosophy, p. 393.

versal, the absolute, and the infinite affirmation, that is, God; then the genuine demonstration of the existence of God, rational and experimental, ideal and real, *a priori* and *a posteriori*, as certain as experience, as accurate as geometry, as beautiful as poetry, as simple as intuition, as living as prayer, is effected in the soul.

V.

But let us continue, with Thomassin, the analysis of the innate idea of God, or rather the analysis of that fact which has been called the innate idea of God and which Thomassin sometimes calls the natural presentiment of God (*naturalis de Deo anticipatio*), sometimes the anticipated consciousness of God (*anticipata Dei notitia*), or innate knowledge of God (*innata Dei notitia*), or natural knowledge of God imprinted on the human mind (*notitia Dei naturaliter mentibus informata*).[1] Thomassin makes a more profound and complete analysis of this natural divine postulate than any other philosopher has ever done. Malebranche and many others regard it simply as a vision of God, and make a mistake in their description and appreciation of this sort of vision; the mystics regard it merely as a secret sense by means of which God inspires and touches us; Descartes considers it "the mark of the Maker stamped upon his work." Thomassin combines these three points of view. According to him the natural divine postulate is alike our own soul, the image of God, and the image of all; it is our own soul seeing God in necessary and eternal ideas; it is our own soul touching God through that mysterious sense which is, as it were, its root. We must quote his analysis: —

The inward divine postulate consists "in those ideas which our essence implies; in the very nature of our soul, which in

---

[1] Cap. xx. and xxi.

a sense and in its measure is all things, and which, therefore, as it develops, and, so to say, deploys its constituent fibres, perceives all intelligibles."[1] It consists "in the commerce and kinship of the soul with the intelligible, whose omnipresent splendor shines upon it. Had the soul no ideas either accidentally impressed upon it, or substantially implicated and essentiated in it, — nevertheless, as it is an intellectual eye, it has only to open and look about to behold the omnipresent and ever resplendent intelligibles."[2] It consists, lastly, "in that secret, incorporeal contact wherein the soul, by its centre and unity, touches God, and feels rather than sees him."[3]

In the same place Thomassin also accepts Descartes' phrase, "the Maker's mark stamped upon his work," and, he adds, that he accepts all these elements of the natural divine postulate provisionally in this form, until he can present the subject more precisely, in the proper time and place. He does this in the third book of the Theodicy, where he treats of God considered as truth, as the substance of the eternal ideas, and as love. It is there that he actually develops what was merely suggested in the first book, when he treats of the divine sense and expresses himself as follows: "Intelligence and will in man correspond to God considered as Truth and Love. But the unity itself of the soul, its deepest centre, should correspond, in man, to the unity itself of God, — that principle which is conceived as in some sort anterior to Truth and Love."[4] That is to say, in sum, that a triple postulate, which he calls the divine touch, the vision of intelligibility, the love of the beautiful, corresponds in the soul to God considered as Power, Truth, and Love. The whole third book of the Theodicy is devoted to the development of the latter two elements of the divine postulate. Here, considering God as very Being, very Truth, and very Love, he first shows him, in so far as the source of ideas, manifest in the intelli-

[1] Lib. i. cap. xx. § i.   [2] Ibid.   [3] Ibid.   [4] Ibid., cap. xix. § v.

gence. Here Thomassin speaks of God visible and present
in reason, in quite as explicit a way as Malebranche himself.
"There is," he says, "naturally in all men some perception of
truth. We see the first principles and all the immutable rules
of reason in the light of eternal truth. Truth is sole mis-
tress of all minds that see it ; those that we call our masters
are only monitors.[1] It presides over the reason of every
man ; all consult it to know that which is, to dissipate
doubts, to correct the will, and to regulate life." We seem
to hear Fénelon saying almost the selfsame words twenty
years later. Thomassin continues : " Ideas shine forth in
the light of supreme truth, which is the Word of God. . . .
Ideas exist in the divine understanding, in God himself.
There we must posit them, and there Plato and the Platonists posited them ; the Fathers of the Church agree in
admitting this. . . . Ideas exist in God, they are the Word
itself, say the Fathers ; all wisdom, all theology, and all
philosophy depend upon their contemplation. . . . We see
ideas through the immediate and permanent presence of
truth in the mind."[2] We plainly hear Malebranche and
Fénelon in these words. Thomassin develops these things
throughout the larger part of his book with a power of
analysis and fulness of wealth which Malebranche had
merely to translate. But Malebranche did not translate,
he wrote the same things out of his own store; thus we
have two witnesses to the same truth.

Having considered God as Truth, Thomassin next considers him as Love, and shows us the divine postulate in us
under the form of love : " Our innate knowledge, our innate
desire for the supreme beauty, is the origin of all love in
us.[3] God is love, and we possess God just as intimately, as

---

[1] Lib. iii. cap. v.
[2] Lib. iii., headings of several chapters.
[3] Lib. iii. cap. xxii., heading to § 5.

constantly, as familiarly, as we have love for him and for our brothers. Love in us, all true virtue in us, is the divine form which stamps itself upon our soul, and stamps itself there perpetually. God is the eternal law of love, by which he himself lives, and by which he causes all intelligent natures to live." [1]

Such is the genuine, complete, truly philosophical analysis of the complex psychological fact which has been vaguely called the innate idea of God. God exists, the soul exists : the soul is conscious of all that exists ; it is conscious of the existence of God through the mysterious basis of its existence ; endowed with intelligence, — that is, intellectual vision, — it knows certain things to be absolutely and eternally true, which is in a certain sense the vision or perception of God ; endowed with will, it desires to love, it seeks beauty, it seeks somewhat of the moral law of love, — which is in a certain sense the desire for God, who is supreme beauty.

VI.

And here let us observe that this implicit divine postulate, in which we have noted three elements, — the touch, the sight of, and the desire for God, considered as being, as truth, and as love, — is essentially one, like the soul, like God himself. God may be known both by the clear surface of thought, where evident principles and axioms are, and by the hidden depth of feeling, if always those two extremes are united by a living movement which shows their identity and restores them to unity, — a movement which is at the same time instinctive, rational, and voluntary. This is the foundation of what we are beginning to understand, — that the demonstration of the existence of God, starting from necessary ideas taken in themselves, if it be isolated, is in

[1] Lib. iii. çap. xxxiii., heading to § 2.

danger; but that it must rest upon that which rises to God through his operations in the soul,—in short, that a decisive affirmation implies a voluntary element and an act of freedom. The same holds good of the natural knowledge of God as of the supernatural knowledge, to which Christ refers in the Gospel when he says, "*No man can come unto me except it be given unto him of my Father,*"—which signifies that the Son, the eternal Word, the world of ideas, visible in the flesh, appeals to man from without, and that the Father, the principle of Being deep hidden in the secrecy of the soul, attracts him inwardly; swayed by that attraction and that light, the will which craves love, but is free to choose between universal love and the other love, self-love, decides and chooses either God or an idol.

Let us add two other remarks by Thomassin himself:—

"I cannot," he says, "omit indicating here two points of the utmost importance.

"In the first place, it is not particularly the germ of innate knowledge, it is that of the innate love of the beautiful, which true philosophers follow as a means for rising higher. The reason of this may be that if our affections always rest upon some vague knowledge of the object, still, all men are surer of their love than of their knowledge, and are very conscious that they love beauty and happiness without knowing what those things intrinsically are. The knowledges natural to the soul are in some sort inert, are not felt, and are found only by reflection. But our affections unfold spontaneously, often tumultuously, and there is no mind so coarse, so uncultured, as not to perceive them.

"Moreover, these philosophers have doubtless found it more useful to begin by using our feelings and affections, and to lift our heart gradually to the Eternal and Divine, than to attempt the same transition by starting from the necessary ideas naturally given to all. And this because love, in reality, guides and persuades men better than thorny arguments. Moreover, it is far better to attain an end by love than by speculation, since the touch of the heart and its ardent embraces make us feel and enjoy God

far better than the intellect. All the more so because that same
love purifies the eye of the soul and gives it the power of divine
contemplation."[1]

VII.

We have thus seen what, according to Thomassin, constitutes the true substance and basis of the proof of the existence of God. Let us now look at the process which illustrates
that substance and all these implicit postulates.

I translate: —

"Although it be given to us to conceive of God through our
natural and innate ideas of justice, truth, wisdom, goodness, supreme, eternal, immutable beatitude, yet these ideas are but symbols, attributes transferred from our soul to God. Our soul sees
all these things in itself, only finite and imperfect; wherefore when
it transfers them to God, it removes their defects and invests them
with immutability and infinity. We make use of these symbols
to describe God; and we are impelled to do this by that deep
sense in which Nature makes us feel that there is a God: that
is, a supreme, incomprehensible, ineffable being, nothing beyond
whom can be conceived, who can be equalled by nothing of which
we can conceive; to whom, consequently, we must attribute
all conceivable perfections, — perfections which, because of his
ineffable excellence, we must at once withdraw as unworthy and
insufficient."[2]

Here Thomassin was defending himself against Plotinus
and the false Alexandrian mysticism, as well as certain of the
ancient Fathers, some of whose expressions contain traces of
Alexandrianism. Thomassin, as is his wont, carries tolerance
to excess; he lets these authors say what they will; then he
twists and turns their utterances and gives them a rational
meaning. He does not hesitate to quote those mystics who,
applying in a wrong sense that process of reason which rises
to the infinite by denying the limitations of the finite, sub-

[1] Lib. i. cap. xxv. §§ 6 and 7.   [2] Ibid., cap. xviii. § 11.

tilize and deny everything, and to form the idea of God, not
only wipe out limitations, imperfection, contingency, but
take to denying God even positive qualities, even beauty,
even being, even unity. Thomassin allows Pachymerus to
speak, and he exclaims : [1] "Well, if I may make so bold, God
is neither beautiful nor good." Then comes Victorinus Afer,
who declares that God is not even unity, and that he may be
said to be without existence, without substance, without intelligence, without life.[2] Still, Victorinus, as a Christian,
that is to say, preserved from absurdity by faith, cannot stop
there, and instantly adds : "We give him these privative
titles, not as terms of privation, but as terms of transcendency ; for all which can be named by human speech is inferior to him." [3]

Thomassin resumes, and adds : —

"Thus Victorinus *strives to purify* Platonic theology (Neo-Pla-
tonic), and to adapt it to Christianity. He denies all the concrete
names which may be given to God, as all implying some limitation
or imperfection, even the words for existence, substance, life, and
unity, because God is far higher than the ideas conveyed in those
words ; but, to him, all these negations mean only one thing, — the
transcendency, the ineffable excellence, of God and of his qualities.[4]
Thus these negations are, after a fashion, nothing but affirmations
raised to the superlative degree.

"Moreover, these very words, the imperfection of which we reject, signify him, praise him, admire him in his vestiges and effects,
as Cause and Creator of being, mind, unity, and all things." [5]

Nevertheless, we must confess that Thomassin sometimes
sins through excess of tolerance for the Alexandrians and
those Christian authors who have borrowed from them; or
at least, in regard to the comparison or relation of the finite
and infinite, he is far less exact and explicit than Bossuet and
Fénelon, who were both made exact by the great controversy,

---

[1] Lib. ii. cap. vi. § 4.   [3] *Loc. cit.*   [5] *Loc. cit.*
[2] Ibid.   [4] Lib. ii. cap. vi. § 5.

whose result Thomassin could not know, as he died before that date.[1]

Several conditions were requisite before philosophy could attain precision on this chief point of metaphysics. Not only was the wonderful controversy between Bossuet and Fénelon requisite, the most admirable dispute recorded in history; not only was the decision of the Catholic Church as judge of the contention requisite, — it was also requisite that Leibnitz should apply these ideas to geometry; it was requisite that the truth in regard to this point should become geometrical; it was also requisite that the relation of all these things should be understood, and that the same truth touching the relation of the finite and the infinite should be encountered alike in metaphysics, theology, and geometry. This is not yet thoroughly understood, and it is what we are trying to explain. If we succeed in doing so, it will be a decided philosophical advance.

We shall deal with this point more at length in speaking of Bossuet and Leibnitz.

VIII.

But first we must consider Thomassin from another point of view. Did he, as well as Plato, Saint Augustine, and Saint Thomas Aquinas, know the two regions of the world of intelligibility? What did he say of it?

Thomassin was perfectly familiar with that fundamental distinction, and devoted much thought to it. After Saint Thomas, he perhaps wrote better of it than any other philosopher. We must not forget that this distinction of the two regions of the world of intelligibility corresponds to what the-

---

[1] Thomassin died in 1695, and the condemnation of the "Maxims of the Saints" did not take place till 1699. Moreover, his "Theological Dogmas" appeared in 1680, 1684, and 1689.

ologians and Christian philosophers call natural light and supernatural light, or *the light of reason* and *the light of grace.*

Now, as we know, in the seventeenth and even from the sixteenth century, the hottest of the philosophical combat was waged in regard to nature and grace, reason and faith, liberty and divine power. This was the contested question between Catholics and Protestants; the Protestants denied, by the mouth of Luther and Calvin, reason and liberty, — that is to say, one of the two orders of things, — the Catholics maintaining both. It was also the question at issue between Jansenists and Jesuits, between Fénelon and Bossuet, — the Jansenists almost annihilating reason and liberty, and Fénelon, with the Quietists, expressing himself inexactly and in the direction of the negation of the human act, the natural side of life. Now, Thomassin stood in the centre of the fight. A member of the Oratory, but free from Jansenist passions, moreover one of the broadest and most conciliatory of minds, he had profoundly studied the great question of God's relations to the soul, of the natural to the supernatural, the finite to the infinite; and he must have grasped this distinction of the two regions of intelligibility, which is a particular case of the general question. A profound psychologist, who seems to have sounded all the spheres of the soul, — even that spot so remote that the senses do not suspect its existence, as Bossuet expresses it, — he must have seen in the soul that region of necessary and immutable truths, the sight of which, however, is not the actual sight of God. Indeed, he describes this degree of the intelligible, which he distinguishes from the other, in many places in his Theodicy; and from this distinction he derives consequences and applications of the greatest fertility and of the utmost importance to the highest theology, as we shall proceed to show briefly.

"Where do we see," he says, "the unchanging laws of

logic, geometry, numbers, and morals? Most assuredly, in eternal wisdom (*in æternæ veritatis sinu*); and yet it is not outside of the soul (*extra animam non esse*). All the doctors of the Church agree about these two things, which seem to be opposites. But they reconcile them thus: the rational soul is indeed enlightened by the simple truth of God, but it receives that light tempered according to its proper form and degree" (*ita et circa intelligentiam et veritatem Dei simplicissimam versatur anima rationalis; sed ejus lumina pro suo gradu et modo temperata recipit*).[1]

The question is even better put elsewhere.[2] "How can these truths, these laws, these first principles of dialectic, of arithmetic, of music, of ethics and other sciences, be eternal and immutable, if they are not of divine substance, since save God it is very plain that there is nothing eternal or immutable? But, on the other hand, how can it be God himself, since we see that they are multiple, and not simple? . . . It is very probable that these truths are rays shed down into us (*condescensiones quasdam*), and tempered for us from the eternal and immutable light of the Word, which is lowered to rational natures, which suits itself to their capacity, and allows the simple ray to be refracted in them."[3] Thomassin fully understands that this light, thus tempered and lowered, "constitutes our reason."[4]

Farther on, he expresses the distinction between the two regions in a way which is as profound as it is simple: "That incorruptible wisdom, that justice, that sanctity, which shines over the soul, is a certain ray of God, who reveals and stamps himself therein, *not such as he himself is, but such as they are*, in such manner as they may convey the divine; he shows them that he is, not what he is."[5]

---

[1] Lib. i. cap. xxvi. § 7.

[2] Vol. ii. p. 263.

[3] Tract. de Trinitate, cap. xxii. § 7.

[4] Lib. iv. cap. xi. § 11.

[5] Ibid., cap. ii. § 12.

Nothing can be more profound than these words. The light of the lower region of the world of intelligibility is God, — *God revealing himself to human souls, not such as he himself is, but such as they are.* The other light, therefore, must be God revealing himself to human souls, not such as they are, but such as he is himself. This is indeed always the simple distinction between the two degrees of the light, — the light of God seen in us, the light of God seen in God.

Thomassin sees perfectly that the first degree of the world of intelligibility is that natural contemplation of which Saint Gregory of Nyssa says : " That which thou canst see and comprehend is the degree in which thou canst contemplate God in thyself![1] These are truths *essentiated, consubstantiated, incarnated,* with thy soul."[2] They are copies, resemblances, images, of that which exists in God (*simulacra, similitudines, et quasi imitamenta*), says Saint Gregory of Nyssa ; and Thomassin dwells upon this, and calls this region of intelligibility the simulachre of God and his brilliant imitation (*Dei simulacrum et divinitatis fulgidissimum imitamentum*). We therefore indeed recover here " those divine phantasms and those immutable shadows of him who exists eternally." Thomassin quotes and repeats the very words of Saint Augustine (*spectamina illa æternarum rationum*), and thus sums up his description of the lower degree of the intelligible. " We must," he says, " maintain tenaciously (*mordicus*) these two things ; namely, that those immutable spectacles of eternal principles which never cease to illumine the rational soul, and are naturally allied to it, — that all these incorruptible forms of wisdom, justice, and beauty exist in God, live in God, radiate ideas and types from that

---

[1] Lib. v. cap. ii. § 18.
[2] Naturæ quasi inessentiaverit, sive consubstantiaverit et incorporaverit. — *Ibid.*

source, and are engraved upon the rational soul, without abiding there (*non immigrando sed inscribendo*); so that when we are asked if we see immutable principles either in God or in the soul, we must admit both at the same time, in the sense that we are well aware that they can only appear in the soul if the eternal ideas that exist in God are graven in the soul, and that we do not presume to see them in God, unless it be at so incredible an interval that our whole sight of them becomes enigmatic and symbolic."[1]

In short, this degree, as we constantly repeat, with all those who know anything of the interior of the soul, this degree of the intelligible is a mirror in which we see God by his rays (*nimirum hæc specula sunt, in quæ radios suos Deus ejaculatur, in quibus videtur*).[2]

But then, what is the other degree of the intellectual world, that wherein we see, not merely that God is, but what he is, — where we see himself; a knowledge which the impious man cannot possess, while he is capable of the other? This knowledge, says Thomassin, is supernatural; the other, only natural. He quotes and approves of the author quoted by Saint Bernard, who teaches "that the knowledge of God by the immutable laws of wisdom and truth is natural, but to know that which God actually is, is a peculiar gift of *divine grace;* that these two degrees are distinct, and that in the lower we do not know what God is in himself.[3] But to know what he who is, is in himself, is impossible, unless we attain to it through the sense of luminous love."[4]

These are the same two regions pointed out by Plato, Saint Augustine, and Saint Thomas, in one of which we see the phantom or image of him who is, while in the other the soul contemplates him who is.

---

[1] Lib. iv. cap. xii. § 9.
[2] Ibid., cap. ii. § 18.
[3] Ibid., cap. § 11.
[4] Ibid.

But we said that Thomassin makes a happy and fertile application of this distinction to the highest theology. We know no more admirable theologian in this respect. In his eyes, one of the regions is that of the universal Word naturally enlightening all men born into this world; the other is that of the incarnate Word, supernaturally giving itself for the salvation of the world. The one is reason, the other is Christ. Like Malebranche, he knows the relation of these two names. He shows the identity of the two in their principles, that is to say, in God himself; then he shows us their relation, their necessary agreement, and above all the means and condition of the passage of one to the other. Of this we shall speak in its place.

BOSSUET.

I.

Bossuet plainly played a greater part as theologian than as philosopher in the grand movement of the human mind which makes up the seventeenth century. Bossuet, like all great minds, thought but little of what he called the *purely philosophical*. No mind of the first order — not Plato, Aristotle, Saint Augustine, Saint Thomas, Descartes, or Leibnitz — ever made any pretensions to pure philosophy. Pure philosophy is an invention of professors and sophists. Truly great and practical intellects simply love and seek the truth in all directions and without abstraction. This is particularly true of Bossuet. He sought the truth everywhere, — in theology, philosophy, history, and physiology. He had to a high degree the instinct of comparative science and of the unity of the human mind. He applies and compares theology to everything, and all things to one another. His ideas are like his style, which, says Joubert, makes use of all our idioms as Homer does of all dialects. All ages and all doctrines were ever present to him, as were all things and all words.

The human mind, says Pascal, is like the mind "of a universal man, in whom the effects of ratiocination are ever increasing, because the whole race of men, throughout the course of so many centuries, should be regarded as one man who exists eternally and learns continually."

Now, such minds as Bossuet, Fénelon, Leibnitz, and a few others, are the real links in this ideal unity; they, more than ordinary intellects, possess the life and unity of the great human mind; they express and develop it, often unconsciously.

This mind of the universal man pursues and maintains the unity of its tasks even when the individuals themselves are ignorant of it, and is harmoniously and simultaneously displayed more frequently than we think. The glorious light of the seventeenth century offers us the most striking instance of this. It is thus that Bossuet and Leibnitz revealed and determined the general idea of the great century, each by an unexpected application, whose relation to the whole they perhaps did not see themselves. Bossuet applied the general idea to theology, and Leibnitz to mathematics.

II.

Bossuet's work, a work truly immense in its depth and its results, is the reciprocal application of philosophy and theology. "Theology," says Saint Thomas Aquinas, "may receive somewhat from philosophy,[1] not as to its fundamental truths, but in regard to the development and fuller manifestation of its proper postulates." Moreover, what is all theology but an application of philosophy to religion? Has it not been said — and justly said — of Saint Thomas Aquinas

[1] Iᵃ q. 1, art. 5 ad 2ᵐ.

that he merely translated the simplicity of the Gospel into
philosophy?[1] Theology is developed, as Saint Vincent de
Lerins says, from age to age and from century to century,
and the wisdom, intelligence, and knowledge of mankind and
of the Church itself become more and more exact and luminous; the holy and sacred gift remains the same; but the
idea which men form of it becomes broader, more analytical,
more scholarly. Now, Bossuet, by his labors, his struggle,
and his victory over Fénelon, made clear an important point
in mystic theology which had never been determined, and
upon which the Church pronounced judgment by condemning
Fénelon's book. And what is this point? It is the great
and universal question of the relation of the finite to the
infinite, regarded from its most practical, most telling, and
most useful side for mankind. Instead of the *infinite*, let us
say God; instead of the *finite*, the soul; instead of *relation*,
love. How is the soul united to God through love? This
is the question which Bossuet reduced to exact terms, and
whose solution he established by a decree of the Church.

Is not the connection of this question with that of the
proofs of God's existence clear? How can the mind attain
to God through reason? How does the will reach God
through freedom? How is the soul united to God through
the divine love? These three questions, although not identical, are analogous. It is possible that one and the same
universal idea may be applied to all, and that one and the
same general metaphysical formula includes them as special
cases. This is our belief.

In fact, what is the process by which reason proves and
knows God? We have already said that this process consists in asserting in the infinite, by the negation of limitations, all the being, all the beauty, and all the positive
qualities of which we see any trace in the world, and of

[1] Amelotte, Life of P. de Condren (preface).

which we find in ourselves any idea. And this is actually the process employed by philosophy, by poetry, and by common-sense to prove and to know God.

Now, even at the present day, in spite of the philosophy of all ages, and, what is more, in spite of the common-sense of the human race and the poetry of all souls, sophistry, ever active, denies to reason the legitimacy of this process. You see, says the sophist, limited being, that is, being and its limitation; why do you assert infinite Being, which destroys limitation, and why, on the contrary, do you not assert that the infinite has limitations, which would destroy Being? Who tells you that this is not the absolute truth? You freely choose, between Being and nothing, but without reason. Why this choice?

This is the final question between sophistry and philosophy.

Now, in the seventeenth century, the false mystics put the same question in theology. They put it so subtly that Fénelon himself was wanting in precision, and did not see the whole difficulty, nor all the vastness of the abyss dug by false mysticism. The question was this: Must the soul annihilate its own being in order to find God through love? Must it efface its ideas, destroy its powers, and suppress its faculties? or rather, should it be the reverse? Should it develop its powers, its faculties, its ideas; should it unfold all its being by annihilating and pushing back its limitations, to its utmost ability?

We see the relation, or rather the metaphysical identity, of the two questions.

Bossuet, with steadfast firmness, with the ardor given by the perception of truth, and the consciousness of a great danger to be repelled, begins against false mysticism, against what he calls *wilful annihilation*, that warfare which, despite the passion that men may mingle with it, is his finest title to glory, and the greatest service rendered in that century to the human mind and the inner life of souls.

What should be annihilated ? *We should annihilate the* *limit, the boundary, the obstacle, not the Being.* Such is the general law for the rational knowledge of God, as well as for the moral growth of the soul in God, the supernatural union of the soul with God in the Holy Ghost, and the transition from the finite to the geometrical infinite. So that mystic theology, through Bossuet's labor and the decision of the Church, was echoed even in speculative philosophy, and confirmed its method.

All the war upon Quietism, the whole of the noble book upon *States of Prayer*, the book entitled *Mystici in tuto,* and the other, *Schola in tuto,* were intended to combat, as Bossuet himself expresses it, "*the pernicious meanings which some persons give to the words nothing and annihilation ;* " [1] to confound those false mystics who annihilate man in order to unite him to God, as Pantheism annihilates man before God.

The repose of which the true mystics speak, says Bossuet, " is an act; it is the most perfect of acts, which, far from being inaction, sets us wholly in action for God."

That death of which the true mystics speak, is not the annihilation of our soul or its faculties, it is the annihilation of the egotism which confines it within narrow limits.

That passive contemplation of which they speak, far from excluding, as Molinos says, "Not only every image from the memory, but also every idea from the mind," is, on the contrary, a powerful mental act, a simple thought wherein all the infinite perfections of God are combined in one whole, in so far as it is permitted to human weakness.

The generous indifference of the saints is not the annihilation of liberty and will, " it is, on the contrary," says Bossuet, " the expansion and dilatation of a heart which has no other will but that of God. Our will, so long as it is confined to

[1] Vol. viii. p. 3.

itself, limits itself;" let it aggrandize itself, set itself free, and become free by willing like God !

Bossuet had before him Molinos' theory of annihilation, that theory which destroys man, in order that God may be all, — a theory which modern German pantheists continue. Molinos said,[1] " Annihilation, to be perfect, is extended to the judgment, actions, inclinations, desires, thoughts, and the entire substance of life." Elsewhere : " The life, rest, and joy of the soul lie in considering nothing, desiring nothing, wishing nothing, making no effort." Elsewhere : " The soul should be dead to its wishes, efforts, and perceptions, willing as if it did not will, understanding as if it did not understand, having no inclination even for nothingness." Elsewhere : " An inner soul is lost when it turns towards reason. Its only reason is to have no regard for it."[2] Elsewhere he speaks of nothingness with even greater affection: " Array yourself in this nothingness, make it your food and your abode." " Bury yourself in nothingness; this God will be your all."

But, what was far more dangerous, Bossuet had to combat a multitude of inexact expressions, used by many orthodox mystics, quoted, commented on, and collected by Fénelon, to such a point that the most enlightened minds might well hesitate in regard to the precise doctrine of the relation of the soul to God in prayer. Bossuet raised the entire question, and obtained a decision which fixed this most important point, and was given with that sort of mathematical exactitude which marks all the pronouncements of the Church.

But here is not the place to develop this point. It is enough to indicate it, and to show its relation to the Theodicy and to the proof of the existence of God. Let us come to the Theodicy itself.

[1] Instruction in regard to States of Prayer, book iii. (beginning).
[2] Molinos, Guide, liv. iii. ch. viii.

III.

Bossuet's work on philosophy begins thus : "Wisdom consists in the knowledge of God and self. Knowledge of self should raise us to the knowledge of God."

In these first words Bossuet points out the course of his proof of the existence of God.

He begins, like all men, with the spectacle of creation :

"All that shows order, accurate proportions, and means adapted to produce certain ends, also shows an express purpose; consequently, a fixed intention, a regulated intelligence, and a perfect art.[1]

"If art be requisite to observe this harmony and accuracy, so much the more is it necessary to establish them.

"Thus, by the term nature we understand a deep wisdom, which develops in order and according to accurate laws all the movements which we see.

"But of all the works of nature, man is undoubtedly the one in which the design is most continuous."

Bossuet states this point at length, and from the light of a deep knowledge of physiology he concludes, regarding the life of the body, what Descartes, Malebranche. Fénelon, and others say of the intellectual life, that that life implies God, — that God is present in it.

"It therefore appears," he says, in conclusion, "that this body is an instrument formed and subjected to our will by a power external to us ; and every time that we make use of it, — whether to speak, to breathe, or to move in whatsoever fashion, — *we should always feel God present.*"[2]

Thus the body and its life not only prove the existence of God, they also imply his presence. Bossuet adds, —

"But nothing so serves to raise the soul to its Author as the knowledge it has of itself and of its sublime actions.[3]

[1] Vol. x. p. 77.   [2] Ibid., p. 81.   [3] Ibid., p. 83.

" We have already observed that eternal truths are the object of the understanding.

"These eternal truths, which every understanding always perceives the same, by which every understanding is regulated, are something of God, or rather are God himself.

" We need, therefore, only reflect upon our own actions in order to understand that we proceed from a higher principle.[1]

" For from the fact that our soul feels itself capable of understanding, affirming, and denying, and that, moreover, it feels that it is ignorant of many things, that it often errs, . . . it sees, in truth, that it has within it a good principle ; but it also sees that it is imperfect, and that there is a higher wisdom to which it owes its existence.[2]

" In fact, perfection exists rather than imperfection, and imperfection presupposes it, — as the lesser presupposes the greater of which it is the diminution. . . . Thus it is natural that imperfection should presuppose perfection, from which it has, as it were, degenerated ; and if an imperfect wisdom such as ours, which can doubt, be ignorant, and err, still exists, — so much the more should we believe that perfect wisdom exists and subsists, and that ours is but a faint spark thereof.

"We therefore know by ourselves and our own imperfection that there is an infinite wisdom which never errs, which doubts nothing, is ignorant of nothing, because it has full comprehension of the truth,— or rather, because it is truth itself."[3]

This is what we have called *the act and fundamental process of rational life*, — that is to say, the assertion in the infinite, by the destruction of limitations, of every positive quality or finite perfection shown to us by nature or our soul.

And not only, according to Bossuet, does the sight of our imperfection, joined to the possession of eternal ideas, prove the existence of eternal truth, higher than we are, more subsistent than we are, — that is to say, the existence of God, — but, moreover, the sight itself of eternal ideas implies the sight of God and reveals his presence.

[1] Vol. x. p. 83.   [2] Ibid.   [3] Ibid.

The presence of God alone is the divine impulse that lifts our mind to God ; Bossuet knows this, and asserts it amply. For, he says, —

"We see these truths in a light superior to ourselves. . . . It is in it, in a certain manner incomprehensible to me, — it is in it, I say, that I see these eternal truths ; and to see them is to turn to him who is unchangeably all truth, and to receive his light.[1]

"And when I actually receive that impression, when I actually understand the truth which I was capable of understanding, what befalls me, if not to be actually enlightened of God and rendered like unto him?[2]

"We must therefore understand that the soul, made in the image of God, capable of understanding the truth, which is God himself, is actually turned towards its original, — that is, towards God, where the truth appears to it in so far as God is pleased to make it apparent.

"It is an amazing thing that man should understand so many truths, without at the same time understanding that all truth proceeds from God, that it exists in God, and that it is God himself. But he is enchanted by his senses and his deceitful passions ; and he is like one who, shut in his closet, where he is busied with his affairs, uses light without heeding whence it comes."[3]

Here, therefore, Bossuet points out the *obstacle* to the light of God, and the need for the moral condition for the knowledge of God and the proof of his existence. Then he adds, —

"We have seen that the soul, which seeks and finds in God the truth, turns towards him to conceive of it. But what is it to turn towards God? . . . God is always and everywhere invisibly present. The soul always possesses him inly, for it is through him that it subsists. But to see, it is not enough that light should be present, — we must turn towards it, we must open our eyes to it. The soul also has its way of turning towards God, who is its light, because he is truth ; and to turn to that light — that is, to truth — is, briefly, to desire to understand it. . . . The soul is upright through this desire."

[1] Vol. x. p. 82.,   [2] Ibid., p. 85.   [3] Ibid.

Bossuet understands that the soul begins to rise to God *through this desire*, and he points out *that divine sense* which is the simultaneous attraction of the desirable and the intelligible. He sees that the first love and the first knowledge of truth mutually imply each other; and that this double natural postulate is increased by our concurrence and our purity. He says, —

" The love of truth supposes some knowledge of it. God, therefore, who has made us in his image, — that is to say, who has made us to understand and love the truth after his example, — begins by first giving us the general idea of it, *by which he urges us to seek for full possession of it*, to which we advance in proportion as love of truth is purified and kindled within us."

IV.

Behold, then, God demonstrated both by the spectacle of nature and by his effects in us. But Bossuet also gives the other demonstration, — God demonstrated by his idea taken in itself; which is Saint Anselm's proof. Only he does not separate this *a priori* proof from the other, which is *a posteriori;* he does not divide the purely rational proof from that which is also experimental; he blends them, one with the other, — he combines the two, as is proper. And it seems to us that the argument is stated by Bossuet with singular energy : —

" And indeed, among those eternal truths that I know, one of the most certain is this, — that there is something in the world which exists of itself, consequently which is eternal and immutable.

" If there were a single moment when nothing was, then nothing would eternally be. Thus nothingness would forever be all truth, and nothing would be true save nothingness, — an absurd and contradictory thing.

" There is, therefore, necessarily something that exists before all times and from all eternity; and it is in this eternal that these eternal truths subsist."

It is plain that Bossuet does not rely here only on the pure idea of the necessary Being, and that he blends with that argument an experimental postulate, — namely, that something exists; and Leibnitz also does the same, as we shall see, when he reproduces this argument. Still, we must note that Bossuet declares the hypothesis of nothingness to be *absurd and contradictory.* Therefore his argument is clearly *a priori.*

This argument is so much the stronger in our eyes because we accept the principle, so fully established by Descartes and Fénelon, which necessarily results from the idea of the infinite, — that is, that there is but a single infinite; that that which is infinite in one sense is so in every sense; and that that infinite is God, aside from whom there can be nothing infinite.

Now, it is certain that something exists from all eternity, otherwise there would be nothing; but that which exists from all eternity is infinite in duration; therefore it is so in every sense; therefore it is God.

If any one object that the world has existed thus eternally, we reply that the world, being manifestly finite in several senses, cannot be infinite in one sense, — namely, in duration; for otherwise it would be infinite in every sense.

Moreover, in the Elevations on the Mysteries, Bossuet develops his thought in regard to the necessity of Being, that is to say, of eternal, infinite Being; and he seems to foresee modern follies, and the silly bandying by sophists of the words *Being* and *Nothing.*

" Whence comes it," he says, " that something exists, and that it cannot be that nothing should exist, if not because Being is better than nothing, and because nothing cannot prevail over Being or prevent the being of Being? . . . O God! one loses himself in such great blindness, the impious man loses himself in the *nothingness of God*, which he prefers to the *Being of God !*"

Here we clearly find the proof *a priori* and the proof *a posteriori* at the same time distinguished and conjoined.

V.

We now come to a page by Bossuet, one of the finest that he ever wrote, in which he sets forth the practical process by which the soul rises to the knowledge of God. In it we again encounter all our ideas regarding this chief process of reason.

Considering our reason and its power, proved by the creation of the arts and sciences, he exclaims "That all this would be impossible, that man could not rule the world, if he were not bound to God, the creator of the world; if he had not in himself, *in some part of his being, some art derived from that first art, some fruitful ideas derived from those original ideas,* — in short, some likeness, some tincture, some portion of that working mind which made the world." [1]

" Yes," he says, "there is a divine light within us : a ray from thy countenance, O Lord! has been imprinted on our souls. It is there, . . . the first Reason who shows himself to us *by his image.*"

This could not be better expressed. Moreover, it is the exact doctrine of Saint Thomas Aquinas. The reader thoroughly understands, from what precedes, that our reason is the first Reason revealed to us *by his image;* that it is God who enlightens us to make us visible to ourselves, we who are his image.

But it is not enough for the soul to see itself and the world in that light, it desires to know that light itself.

[1] Sermon on Death, p. 210.

"So," says Bossuet, "all this is nothing; and here is the most admirable feature of the divine likeness. God knows and contemplates himself; it is his life to know himself; and because man is his image, he wishes also that *he* should know him."

That is to say that it is not enough for the soul to know something, — for instance, itself and the world, — and that it should be, through self-knowledge, a certain image of God who knows all. To know the soul and the world, this is nothing. Since God knows God, our soul also must know God. We must make use of that light which renders us rational by impressing itself upon us, and which shows us, in its radiance, all that the mind sees; we must make use of it to rise higher, to inquire after the light itself, and to know what it is.

And how can we become acquainted with it, when we do not perceive it directly? How can we become acquainted with it, it being eternal and infinite, while we are conscious of nothing that is not limited, and see nothing that is not subject to change? Bossuet goes on as follows: —

"Eternal, immense, infinite Being, exempt from all materiality, free from all limitation, destitute of all imperfection! What is this miracle? We who are conscious of nothing that is not limited, see nothing that is not subject to change, where did we learn to comprehend this eternity? Where have we dreamed of this infinity? O Eternity! O Infinity! says Saint Augustine, that our senses do not even suspect, where didst thou find entrance to our souls?"

How admirably the difficulty is here stated! In what way can the mind pass from that which is subject to change and limitation, to the infinite, to the eternal? Bossuet adds, —

"So, too, if we are all body and all material, how can we conceive of pure spirit? And how could we ever invent that name?"

Without making any explicit distinction between these two analogous questions, he answers that we conceive of pure spirit, because we are ourselves a spirit, and are not all body and all material; then we conceive of pure, eternal, infinite spirit because, being allied to a principle higher than man, the soul is conscious of a secret virtue in itself which teaches it what the eternal spirit is, by means of negation, by saying to it of every imperfect conception: It is not that.

According to Bossuet, we should not believe that, by this indirect means, we know nothing of the pure, eternal, infinite spirit of God. We know of it all that it is not. He says, —

"I know what may be said in this place, and justly, that when we speak of these spirits, we do not fully understand what we say; our feeble imagination, unable to sustain so pure an idea, always offers it some little body to clothe it. But after it has made its final effort to render them very subtle and very delicate, do you not feel at the same time that a celestial light issues from the *bottom of our soul*, which dissipates all these phantasms, however aërial and refined we have been able to figure them? If you urge it still further, and ask it what it is, *a voice will rise from the centre of the soul:* 'I know not what it is, but nevertheless it is not that.'"

Is not this the negative theology of the Alexandrian Fathers, so well described by Petau and Thomassin? Bossuet finds it again here in the actual life of the soul. He speaks of it elsewhere, like Thomassin; like him, he sees its source in *the bottom of the soul,* in *the centre of the soul,* — expressions full of meaning, which superficial psychology understands not.

But what follows is admirable : —

"What power, what energy, what secret virtue does that soul feel within itself to correct and contradict itself and to dare to reject all that it thinks!"

This is precisely what Thomassin says : —

"There is a *secret virtue*, a *secret sense* (*arcanus sensus*), by which the soul feels God when it has not yet seen him, and which shows it that all which it sees is not he."

Bossuet adds, —

"Who does not see that there is within it a *hidden spring* which does not yet act with all its strength, and which, although it be constrained, although it has not yet freedom of motion, plainly shows, by a certain vigor, that it is not wholly bound to matter, and that it is, *as it were, attached by its extreme point to some higher principle. . . .*"

This hidden spring of which Bossuet speaks is an intuition of genius. Whoever does not know this hidden spring, is utterly ignorant of the human soul. The soul of man is evidently bound to matter, which is beneath it and touches it; but it is not wholly bound to it, and it touches something else than mere matter, — it touches God, who is higher than it; it is joined to him by its extreme point, or, as Plato says, it is suspended from him by its root; and this necessary union with God gives the soul a secret virtue and a hidden spring, by means of which it rises to heights beyond itself, towards the infinite and eternal, to conceive thereof. Plato also speaks of these soarings and these wings of the soul.

But note this. This hidden spring does not yet act with full force; it is constrained, it has not yet freedom of motion. And moreover, in our present and natural state, this spring is soon relaxed, and the soul speedily returns to its phantasms. "I confess it," adds Bossuet, "we do not long maintain this noble ardor; these fair ideas soon become clouded, and the soul is quickly replunged in material things. It has its weaknesses, its languors, and — let me say it, for I know not how to express myself — it has incomprehensible grossnesses, which, *if it be not otherwise enlightened*, almost force it to doubt what itself is."

These words complete the truth on this point. That is to say, Bossuet points out here that distinction of the two regions of the intelligible world which all minds of the first order have perceived.

In the lower, which is still sublime, the mind does not see the eternal, the infinite, save through contrast and negation. "I know not what it is," says reason, "but it is not that." At the sight of all the phantasms, shadows of him who is, the mind says, " It is not he," — which it could not do, as Bossuet, Thomassin, and the others understand, if it did not already bear within it the celestial radiance at the bottom of the soul, the voice at the centre, the hidden spring, the sense of the infinite, the divine sense, which alone can lead it to say, "That is not he."

But this degree is imperfect; we see nothing in it save by contrast, negatively and indirectly. We feel that the hidden spring is constrained, and has no freedom of motion ; it falls back more easily than it darts upward; and the soul is quickly replunged in material things, *if it be not otherwise enlightened.*

The soul requires the other light, the light of the other region of the intelligible world, the direct light, no longer seen by its shadow, but by itself. Those who are acquainted with our soul are well aware that it can find rest only in this direct vision.

Let no one say that all these expressions, such as "secret virtue," "centre of the soul," "hidden spring," "bound by its extreme point to some higher principle," are only images, without philosophical precision. The meaning of all these terms is clear enough, precise enough, luminous enough. All this means that God and the soul exist ; that the soul, which is conscious of itself and of the material bodies under it, is also conscious of God, who is above it, and that the divine sense leads it to know God, as the external senses lead us to know bodies.

In the first place, this divine sense, which in our present and natural state is far from having all its strength, all its movements, or all its perceptions, is yet sufficient to teach us that which God is not, and to inform us by contrast, in the presence of limited and transitory things, that he is eternal and infinite.   But this conclusion, though absolutely sure, is abstract; it establishes the fact that God is ˙eternal and infinite, but it does not show us the eternal, infinite essence.   The divine sense then regrets that it does not see this, and desires to see him whom our reason knows to be eternal and infinite.   For so much that degree of light and that region of the intelligible world serve, wherein, Plato says, the mind sees divine phantasms, the shadows of God, but not God.   This first region makes us desire the other, — that which reveals God himself; that where our soul is otherwise enlightened, as Bossuet says; and where, in the potent and vivifying light, ardor is sustained, languor is cured, incomprehensible grossnesses are overcome, and the soul learns no longer to sink itself in material things.

LEIBNITZ.

I.

"The soul is the mirror of the universe," said Leibnitz; and perhaps no man has so well verified the profound thought as its author himself.   His genius is indeed a sort of universal mirror, in which everything paints itself with the richest profusion.

Only, it must be said that useless things were sometimes mirrored in that fair glass, and that its surface was not without flaw.   Various irregularities at times impair the truth of its images.   But it is only necessary that the eye should place itself in front of those singular points known as the universal *mathematical language* and the *pre-established harmony*, to enjoy the sight of the finest, greatest, most brilliant reflector of light that ever existed.

Leibnitz, then, could not fail to bear within him the great idea on which, throughout that century, the human mind brooded, inspired by the mind of God, — namely, the idea of the infinite, the relation of infinite being to finite beings, and the mode of transition from the one order to the other. Only, while Bossuet, helped by Fénelon, saw these things in the living relation of the soul to God, Leibnitz saw them in geometry, and laid down the laws of the comparison and the passage of the geometrical finite to the geometrical infinite.

This does not mean that Leibnitz was the legislator of the idea of the infinite in metaphysics, — far from it; this idea bewilders him to such a degree that he sometimes (almost incredible to relate) asserts the actual existence of the infinite in nature and in matter; and sometimes, alarmed by the outcries of the geometricians of that day, he deserts, as Fontenelle blames him for doing, the geometrical infinite itself, thus reversing the whole truth, — saying yes where he should say no, and *vice versa*.

And yet Leibnitz's chief title to glory — an immortal title, and one of the grandest ever won by the mind of any man — is the fragmentary chapter of a work which he meditated, and which he called *de Scientia infiniti*. This chapter contains the discovery of the infinitesimal calculus, — the most potent lever ever given to human thought with which to uplift the world; a discovery whence proceed the marvels of our physical sciences, and whence other marvels will yet proceed. Newton also discovered this lever, but he gave it to us in an involved form which was both less scientific and less practical. Leibnitz presents it to us in its true form, in its inmost nature, which is the comparison, the relation, the rational passage, of the finite to the infinite.

Let us say at once that this process is merely a particular case and a special application, to the geometrical infinite and finite, of the universal process of reason in its passage from the contingent to the necessary, from the particular to the universal, from the world to God, and from the finite to the infinite. This will be more fully developed in the course of the present work.

II.

Did Leibnitz understand all the metaphysical significance of his discovery? Did he see its relation to the proof of the existence of God? Did he see its relation to the theological question of the love of God, the true and false mysticism, argued between Bossuet and Fénelon? We think he did. He says in his New Essays:[1] —

"This is not the place *to suggest the true means of extending the art of demonstration beyond its ancient limits,* which have hitherto been essentially the same as those of the region of mathematics. I hope, if God gives me the requisite time, *to show some attempt at this, by making effective use of these means, without confining myself to precepts.*"

Elsewhere, in a letter to Wagner, on logic, he writes: —

"By logic, I understand the art of using one's reason, and not only of judging that which is established, but also of finding out that which is hidden. . . . But I must confess that all systems of logic known up to the present day are barely the shadow of that which I desire, and which I see afar off. . . . I hold it as certain that it is possible to carry this art of using reason incomparably higher, — I seem to see it, I have a foretaste of it; but *had it not been for mathematics, I should have found it very hard to reach it.* I discovered some principles upon this subject while still a novice

[1] New Essays, book iv. ch. iii. § 19.

in mathematics, and, towards my twentieth year, printed somewhat concerning it; but now I see how obstructed the road is, and how hard it would have been for me to force a passage, *without the help of the deepest part of mathematics.*" [1]

All this applies very well to the infinitesimal calculus, which extends the art of demonstration far beyond its ancient limits; which is not confined to rules, but makes effective use of itself in mathematics first, then in metaphysics, to which it is also applied, as has never been sufficiently noted. And it certainly appears as if it were to the infinitesimal analysis that Leibnitz alludes here, for, three pages later, [2] it seems to him that *scientific knowledge* will be carried much farther than in the past; "that considerable progress will be made in time; that we only lack the art of using our materials, small beginnings of which I do not despair of seeing, since infinitesimal analysis has given us the means of allying geometry and physics." And if he here appears to speak only of physical sciences, we must observe that shortly before he remarks "that logic can demonstrate as well as geometry, and that the logic of geometricians is an extension or particular promotion of general logic." [3] If, therefore, Leibnitz understands, as we see, that the logic of geometricians is only a particular extension of general logic, if he knows that the art of demonstration in general has ordinarily had the same limits as those of the mathematical region, if he can see that the infinitesimal analysis has vastly extended the limits of that region, how could he fail to conclude that this fresh extension of the logic of geometricians extends the power of general logic in the same proportion ? And how can these fail to be the true means of extending the art of demonstration, which he claimed to possess, and effective proof of which he promised to give some day ?

[1] Opera Philosophica, Erdmann's edition, p. 419.
[2] New Essays, book iv. chap. iii. § 24.   [3] Ibid., chap. ii. § 9.

But let us not anticipate. The subject before us now is the proof of God's existence as given in the Theodicy of Leibnitz.

III.

In his Theodicy, Leibnitz, with that superabundant intellectual variety which characterizes his genius, accepts all the demonstrations of the existence of God. However, he retouches them all, not finding any of them completely enough developed. "I hold," said he, that "the possibility and the existence of God are demonstrated in more than one way. I believe that nearly all the methods used to prove the existence of God are good, and would be of service, if perfected."

Leibnitz, therefore, accepts, with Aristotle, the proof of God's existence derived from the fact of motion; and he works it over again, hoping that it is then raised to mathematical precision. In the title of his curious dissertation on the combinatory art, we find these words: *Demonstration of the existence of God, brought to mathematical precision.*[1] This demonstration starts from the fact of motion (*aliquod corpus movetur*), and claims to deduce from that fact, with rigorous exactness, the existence of *an incorporeal substance of infinite virtue.*

Elsewhere,[2] Leibnitz sees a demonstration of the existence of God in Aristotle's assertion "That there is in us an agent superior to our reason, and which is God." He only fears that Aristotle by this understood that *universal active-intellect* which would be one and the same in all men, and would alone survive at death. But he sees, at any rate, in this assertion a testimony to the universal light which enlightens all men, which speaks to us when we have the certainty of some immutable truth, and which is God.

---

[1] Works of Leibnitz, Dutens' edition, vol. ii. p. 239.
[2] Ibid., p. 264.

He also accepts as good, Saint Anselm's proof, reproduced by Descartes, deduced *a priori* from the idea of necessary being. He considers it "very beautiful and very ingenious," but he sees in it "a void to be filled." "I hold the middle ground," [1] he says, "between those who take this reasoning for a sophism, and the opinion of Father Lamy, who takes it for a complete demonstration."

"Saint Anselm," he says elsewhere,[2] "congratulates himself, and not unjustly, upon having found a way to prove the existence of God *a priori*, from his own idea, without recourse to his effects. And this is closely the form of his argument: God is the greatest, or, as Descartes puts it, the most perfect of beings; or rather he is a being of a supreme grandeur and perfection which contains all the degrees. This is the idea of God. Now, see how existence follows from this notion. It is something more to exist than not to exist, or rather existence adds a degree to grandeur or perfection, and, as Descartes declares, existence is itself a perfection. Therefore that degree of grandeur and perfection, or rather that perfection which consists of existence, exists in that supreme, all-great, all-perfect Being; for otherwise he would lack some degree, contrary to his definition; and consequently that Supreme Being exists. The Scholastics, not excepting their angelic doctor, scorned this argument, and have passed it off as a paralogism, — in which they were very wrong, and Descartes was quite right to restore it. It is not a paralogism, but it is an imperfect demonstration, which supposes something which should also have been proved to make it mathematically evident, — that is, it is tacitly supposed that this idea of the all-great or all-perfect Being is possible, and does not imply a contradiction. And it is something gained that by this remark we prove that *supposing God were possible, he exists*, which is the privilege of the only divinity. But it is to be desired that skilful persons might finish the demonstration with the exactness of mathematical evidence, and I believe I have said somewhat elsewhere which may aid in the task."

---

[1] Leibnitz's Works, vol. ii. p. 254.

[2] New Essays, book iv. chap. ix. § 7.

These improvements on Saint Anselm's proof are indicated by Leibnitz in an answer to the "Journal des Savants."[1]   He says:—

"In the first place, God should not be defined as the Supreme Being, or the Perfect Being, but as Being in itself (*Ens a se*). Hence, if such a being be possible, he exists.   Those who would deny this proposition would deny the possibility of *being in itself*. But note well that this very expedient serves to show that they are wrong, and fills the void in the demonstration.   For if *being in itself* be impossible, all beings through another are so also; since after all they only exist through the *being in itself:* thus nothing could exist.   This reasoning leads us to another modal proposition, equivalent to the preceding one (*if necessary being be possible, it exists*), and which, combined with it, completes the proof.   We might state it thus : *If necessary being does not exist, there is no being possible*.   It seems as if this demonstration had never before been carried so far; and yet I have also labored elsewhere to prove that the perfect being is possible."

We shall touch on this other work of Leibnitz later.   But let us first note that he recurs here to precisely the true point of support for proving the existence of God; he again and inevitably bases what is called the rational proof *a priori*, upon the ground of experience.   For if, to finish the demonstration and to fill up the void, we must say that *if the necessary being does not exist, no being is possible*, that means that the necessary being exists, because there are possible beings who actually exist under our eyes.   This again helps to establish what we have called Descartes' second proof, the proof of God from his idea taken in itself, upon the first, the proof of God from his effects.   Moreover, is not the idea itself, as all philosophers observe, the first and chief effect of God in us?   And this is the place to observe that what is usually called Saint Anselm's argument is only, as we have

---

[1] Works, vol. ii. p. 254.

seen, Saint Anselm's argument cut in halves. Men forget that if, in the *Proslogium*, he *deduces* from the notion of God his existence, he, in the *Monologium*, by *induction* gains the notion of God from the sight of created beings.

Moreover, those are mistaken [1] who suppose that Leibnitz claimed to put Saint Anselm's argument and the entire proof of God's existence into a single formal syllogism. By this syllogism Leibnitz plainly intends to prove but one of the two modal propositions which should, he says, be added to Saint Anselm's argument to fill the void in it.

Here is the syllogism : —

" The being whose essence implies existence, exists if he be possible, that is to say, if he have an essence (this is an identical axiom, which needs no proof).

" Now, God is the Being whose essence implies existence (this is the definition).

" Therefore God, if he be possible, exists (necessary conclusion)." [2]

Clearly this is not a demonstration of God's existence, since the conclusion itself is not this, *God exists*, but this other, *God, if he be possible, exists*.

To this proposition, *God exists, if he be possible*, which in fact rigorously proves that syllogism, *must be added*, as Leibnitz says, the other proposition, *If necessary being do not exist, no being is possible*. These two together, as Leibnitz asserts, fill the void in the isolated ontological argument, and complete the demonstration.

Thus Leibnitz, far from compromising by this alteration what he believed to be Saint Anselm's proof, as is commonly supposed, far from exaggerating its abstract character, has, on the contrary, placed it on its true basis, by introducing

---

[1] Cousin, in his sixth lesson on Kant, p. 238, and Saisset, in his "Manual of Philosophy," p. 242, both fall into this error.

[2] Dutens, vol. v. p. 361.

into it a concrete element, and resting it on the solid foundation of reality.[1]

IV.

We now come to the work undertaken by Leibnitz to prove that perfect being is possible. We find in the summary of his doctrine written out for Prince Eugene,[2] from § 36 to § 45, —

36. "But there must also be a *sufficient reason* for contingent truths of fact; that is, for the series of things diffused through the world of creatures, where the resolution into particular reasons might run into unlimited detail, on account of the immense variety of natural objects and the infinite division of bodies. There is an infinity of figures and of movements, present and past, which enter into the efficient cause of my present writing, and there is an infinity of little inclinations and dispositions of my soul, past and present, which enter into the final cause.

37. "And as all this detail only involves other anterior or more detailed contingencies, each of which again requires a similar analysis in order to account for it, we make no advance, and the sufficient or final reason must be outside of the sequence or series of the detail of contingencies, however infinite it may be.

38. "And thus it is that the final reason of things must be found in a necessary substance, in which the detail of changes exists eminently only, as in its source, and this is what we call God.

39. "Now, this substance being a sufficient reason of all this detail, which is everywhere connected, *there is but one God*, and *this God suffices*.

40. "We may also judge that this supreme substance, which is unique, universal, and necessary, having nothing outside of itself which is independent of it, and being the simple continuity of pos-

---

[1] Leibnitz has so little idea of giving a proof of the existence of God here, that, on the contrary, he asserts, in this very same place, that there is another part of the question to be demonstrated, — namely, the possibility of the existence of God. See the Letter to Bierling, vol. v. p. 361.

[2] Works, vol. ii. p. 25, from § 36 to § 45 inclusive.

sible being, must be incapable of limitations, and contain all of reality that is possible.

41. "Whence it follows that God is absolutely perfect; perfection being nothing else than the greatest of positive reality taken exactly, setting aside the limitations or bounds in that which is limited. And there where there are no bounds, that is, in God, perfection is absolutely infinite."

42. "It also follows that creatures have their perfections from the influence of God; but they have their imperfections from their own nature, incapable of existing without limits, for it is by this that they are distinguished from God."

43. "It is also true that in God is the source, not only of existences, but also of essences, so far as they are real, or of that which is real in the possible; this is because the understanding of God is the region of eternal truths, or of the ideas on which they depend, and because without him there would be nothing real in the possibilities, and not only nothing existing, but also nothing possible."

44. "And yet if there be a reality in the essences or possibilities, or, indeed, in the eternal truths, that reality must be based upon something existing and actual, and consequently in the existence of the necessary being, in whom the essence includes existence, or with whom it is enough to be possible in order to be actual."

45. "Thus God alone — or the necessary being — has this privilege, that he must exist if he be possible. And as nothing can prevent the possibility of that which includes no bound, no negation, and consequently no contradiction, this also suffices to establish the existence of God *a priori*. We have also proved it by the reality of the eternal truths. But we have just proved it *a posteriori*, since contingent beings exist, which can only have their final or sufficient reason in a necessary being who has the reason of his existence in himself."

In these statements Leibnitz therefore claims, as he says, to include three proofs of God's existence, — 1, the proof *a posteriori*, by the existence of contingent beings (§§ 36–41); 2, the proof from the reality of eternal truths (§§ 43, 44); 3, the proof *a priori*, based on the fact that God is

possible, and that he exists if he is possible (§ 45). The
first is Descartes' first proof, God known by his acts; and
the other two belong to Descartes' second proof, God known
by his idea. And this second, we see clearly here, continually rests upon the first.

Leibnitz first asserts, in this remarkable summary, that it
is useless to analyze contingents, — "we make no advance;
and the sufficient or final reason must be outside of the
serial detail of contingencies." This is the substance of
any demonstration of God's existence, — which, at bottom,
may be reduced to this simple argument: There are finite
beings, therefore there is an infinite being; in other words,
there is something, therefore God exists, — a train of reasoning which is in no way a syllogism, but which is the work
of the other process of reason; that which, far from advancing, like the first, from identity to identity, advances
from finite to infinite, and that without intermediary, since
there is none.

And it seems to me that here Leibnitz had an intuition
of the identity of the metaphysical process, which finds
necessary immutable being at the root of contingents, and
of his infinitesimal analysis, which finds at the bottom of
the variable increments of a geometrical postulate the fixed,
absolute, infinitesimal element that corresponds to it, and
that is its source, although it may be infinitely distinct from
it. Does he not immediately add that "the final reason of
things must exist in a necessary substance, *in which the
detail of changes exists eminently only, as in its source*"?
I ask all geometricians, is it possible to give a better definition of the infinitesimal geometrical element, compared to
the variable increments of finite greatness which correspond
to it, than to call it the necessary element, *in which the
detail of changes exists eminently only, as in its source?*

However this may be, we again encounter here, and with

much precision, all the details of the process which, at a single stroke, demonstrates God and shows us his attributes, — to destroy limitations, remove bounds, assert *all positive perfection, by setting aside limits and bounds,* in order to obtain *absolute, infinite perfection,* and the reality of all potentiality, as Saint Thomas Aquinas says (*Deus est actualitas totius possibilitatis*).

The famous editor of Leibnitz very aptly remarks, like ourselves, that we have here an exact process, which has its name and its.laws; he calls it *via eminentiæ vel perfectionis,* and describes it as follows,[1] in a precise and perfect way:

" This process, which rises to the attributes of God, is called the process of eminence, or perfection. It consists in removing the limitations of the perfections seen in finite beings, and then attributing them to God, — thus advancing in thought from the finite perfections of created beings to the infinite perfections of God. Only, we must be careful to grasp in our attributes that which is actually there and is properly real ; otherwise we might attribute imperfections to God. This process is distinct from the other, called that *of causality,* which considers the effects of God's attributes, and rises from these effects to their cause."

At bottom, these two processes, logically distinct, come to the same thing, since every finite perfection of created beings is at the same time the finite image and the finite effect of the infinite perfections of God.

Leibnitz develops his thought still farther in the same place, in these beautiful words : —

" To love God, we need only behold his perfections, — which is easy, *because we find their ideas within us. The perfections of God are those of our souls, but he possesses them without bounds ;* he is an ocean of which we have received but a few drops ; *there is within us some power, some knowledge, some goodness, but they are all entire in God.* Order, proportion, harmony, enchant us, — paint-

[1] See Bilfingeri Dilucid. Philosoph., sect. v. cap. iii. § 418. Dutens, Works of Leibnitz, vol. i. p. 38.

ing and music are specimens. God is all order, he always observes precise proportion, he makes universal harmony ; all beauty is an effusion of his radiance."

Elsewhere, [1] —

" We are instantly aware of substance and of spirit by becoming aware of ourselves, and that the idea of God exists in ours by the suppression of the limits of our perfections, as extension, taken absolutely, is included in the idea of a globe."

Elsewhere, [2] —

" When we think of ourselves, we think of being, of substance, simple and composite, of the immaterial and of God himself, conceiving that what with us is limited exists in him without limit."

We see that among the seventeenth-century philosophers, Leibnitz stated mathematically the process by which our mind rises from the finite to the infinite, from limited beings to God; he applied it to geometry. Not Leibnitz, but Fénelon, gained the clearest and most complete idea of the infinite. But Leibnitz gave its final precision to the process which knows the infinite.

V.

As to formal proofs of the existence of God, Leibnitz, truly, sometimes seems to offer them too exclusively as a work of pure reason, isolated from all experience, and he thus exposes them to the criticism of Kant. And yet, if we penetrate to the root of his thought, and reunite the various points of view upon this subject, scattered throughout his writings, we see plainly that he knows the experimental side of the proof, its moral condition, and the existence of that divine sense, without which it could never be effected in the mind.

[1] Theodicy, § 4.   [2] Monadology, § 30, p. 395.

What is his grand and beautiful theory of innate ideas, what his constant allusions to *confused knowledge* and *indistinct thought?* "What are these ideas which exist in us, not always so that we perceive them, but always so that we may draw them from our own store and make them perceptible?"[1] Is it not precisely the same to have an innate idea of God, as to have what we can and should call the divine sense?

"There are," he says elsewhere,[2] "innate truths which we find within us in two ways,— by light and by instinct. . . . There are in us instinctive truths which are innate principles, which *we feel*, and which we approve in spite of everything. We have no proof of them, although we acquire it when we yield to that instinct." This could not be better expressed; those principles which we approve without having a proof of them, recall Pascal's words: "The heart has its reasons, which reason does not know." Only Leibnitz adds to this that reason may become acquainted with them later. Leibnitz sees perfectly that the instinct which urges us to happiness, which is only the attraction of the supreme Good, or the divine sense, is an innate principle, which we do not know in a luminous manner; that, however, this principle established, we may derive from it scientific consequences,[3] then founded *on internal experience*, or on *confused knowledges.*[4]

Leibnitz, like all philosophers, distinguishes between " correct and genuine reason, and a pretended reason corrupted and abused by false appearances."

He knows, and calls attention to, that violation, or rather that reversal, of the true powers of reason, which denies to reason the power of giving any idea or definition of the attributes of God.[5] He knows that abuse of the grand process of

---

[1] New Essays, book iv. chap. x. § 7.   [3] Ibid., § 1 and 2.
[2] Ibid., book i. chap. ii. § 3.   [4] Ibid.
[5] Works, vol. i. p. 66: Disc. on the Conform. of Reason and Faith, No. 4.

reason which, instead of annihilating all limits in the sight
of finite creatures, annihilates beings themselves and their
limited attributes, and is thus raised, not to being, but to
nothing. He sees the affinity between this strange dialectic,
the pantheism of Spinoza, and the errors of quietists and
false mystics.[1] He sees that the "deification of the mystics"
leads to Spinoza's doctrine, and starts from the false dialectic
which destroys the positive and not the negative. "The
destruction of that which peculiarly belongs to us," he says,[2]
"carried so far by the quietists, may also be disguised im-
piety."   He compares this quietism with the quietism of
Foë, "who, feeling death close at hand, declared to his disciples that he had hidden the truth from them under the
veil of metaphors, and *that all might be reduced to nothing,
which he considered the primary principle of all things.*"

It thus plainly appears that Leibnitz saw more or less
distinctly the affinity which exists between these questions:
the proof of the existence of God, discussions of Quietism, the
idea of the geometrical finite and infinite, and the advance
of the healthy reason, which, moreover, he by no means
separated from the heart, instinct, feeling, and morality.

It even appears that his philosophical motive, like that of
all true philosophers, is moral, and that historically his mind
advanced from the search for justice to the search for truth.
"I had," he says, "a greater leaning towards ethics . . .
than familiarity with speculative philosophers; but I have
learned more and more how much ethics are strengthened
by the solid principles of true philosophy; therefore I have
studied them ever since with more application, and have
entered upon rather novel meditations. . . ."

We cannot better close this article than by a quotation
from the introduction to the New Essays.   He says: —

[1] Disc. on the Conform. of Reason and Faith, p. 71, No. 9.
[2] Ibid., No. 10.

"Since then I seem to see a new aspect of the interior of things. This system seems to unite Plato and Democritus, Aristotle and Descartes, the Scholastics with the moderns, theology and morals with reason. It seems to take the best from every side, and then afterwards to go farther than any one has yet gone. . . . I find in it an amazing uniformity and simplicity, so that it may be said that it is everywhere and always the same thing, nearly in the degrees of perfection. I see now what Plato meant when he took matter for an imperfect and transitory entity; what Aristotle meant by his Entelechy; what the promise is that even Democritus, like Pliny, made of another life; just how far the sceptics were right in inveighing against the senses; how animals are automata, according to Descartes, and yet how they have souls and feeling, according to the opinion of the human race; how we should explain rationally those who lodged life and perception in all things; . . . how the laws of nature (a good part of which were unknown before this system) originate in principles superior to matter, although, nevertheless, everything takes place mechanically in matter. . . ."

This system is the system of universal harmony, the abuse of which led to the singular idea of *pre-established harmony*, but the truth of which is expressed in these profound words : "We must know that harmony, metaphysics, ethics, and geometry exist everywhere." We have just seen that theology also exists everywhere, according to Leibnitz. So in matter, in mind, finite beings, in God, infinite Being, it is the same thing, nearly to the degrees of perfection, — infinite perfection in God, and finite in his creatures; but by virtue of the universal harmony we can read in the lower order the truths of the higher order, — we can read God in nature, as Saint Paul said, and as the human race has ever done.

CHAPTER VIII.

HERE we close the study of the theodicies of the philosophers of the first order We have seen that all prove the
existence of God in the same way. All allude to the moral
obstacle which hides the light from the soul, and which must
first be removed ; all speak of that inward and divine sense,
that charm of the desirable and the intelligible, which, when
the obstacle is removed, becomes the mainspring of reason ;
all find the fulcrum of this impulse of reason in the spectacle of created things, the world or the soul; all understand that this starting-point is in no sense a principle from
which reason can deduce God, but merely a starting-point
from which reason rises to the principle of all things, which
contains no point of departure; all understand or dimly perceive that this process differs wholly from syllogism, and that
it is one of the two essential processes of reason, that which
finds the majors, and not that which draws the consequences;
all describe this process as an act of reason, which, beholding
finite being, the world or the soul, sees, through contrast and
regret, even more than through resemblance, the necessary
existence of the infinite in this finite, and knows the infinite
through negation in denying the limits of all finite being and
all bounded perfection.

It is clear that, as Descartes says, this process gives us at
once the proof of the existence of God and the knowledge of
his attributes. For God cannot be proved save in so far as
he is proved as gifted with his essential attributes, without

which we should have proved the existence of something else, but not of God.

We need not, therefore, in this Theodicy, undertake to write a special treatise on the attributes of God. The demonstration of the existence of God .gives us all at the same time.

And yet, before we close this study and finish the proof of the existence of God, — a proof in regard to which two weighty considerations remain to be stated, — we must first show that reason may throw light upon and develop tho idea of God, and know his attributes, in two ways. It may either acquire them all, starting from the spectacle of created beings, by this principle: "The perfections of God are those of his creatures, without their limitations;" or else, a single one of God's attributes being given, it may deduce all the others from this by means of identity. We have hitherto constantly referred to the former of these two methods; we must now briefly take up the second.

When Plato describes the dialectic process which, from the sight of things, rises to grasp the principle above all things, he adds that once in possession of the principle, reason possesses all that touches that principle, and may advance from consequence to consequence, and from idea to idea, without again relying upon the sight of sensible objects. This is what we desire to say here. In possession of a single one of God's attributes, reason possesses all the others, and can deduce them from the first, by syllogism, as we deduce from an algebraic figure, by means of identity, advancing from equation to equation, all which the given formula implies. It is undoubtedly to this that Aristotle alludes when he asserts that the exact process of the geometricians applies to intelligible things.

However this may be, that attribute of God which implies all the others, is what scholastics call the *metaphysical es-*

sence of God. Only it was useless, it seems, to disagree upon
the question as to which of God's attributes should be called
his metaphysical essence; since clearly every attribute which
characterizes God is a formula whence we may deduce all the
rest. The teaching of theology on this point is evident,
namely: "That no real distinction can be admitted between
the attributes of God, nor between God and his attributes."
Therefore each attribute of God being, in essence, identical
with every other and with God, reason may derive all the
others from each one, and take each one among them as the
metaphysical essence of God. It is this principle of the absolute identity of all that is in God, which the sophists so
abuse in their system of identity; instead of reserving this
principle for God, who alone is simple and absolutely identical in himself, they apply it to all, God and the world being
classed together.

Thus, every postulate that implies the infinite is the metaphysical essence of God, and may serve reason as a principle
for the obtainment of God's attributes. One attribute of God
being given, to take it as a principle and deduce the other
attributes from it, by means of syllogistic consequence and
algebraic identity, is a task often essayed by Saint Thomas
Aquinas; for instance, in the beginning of his Philosophic
Sum, and in the beginning of his Ninth Opuscule, which is
an abridged Theology. In both places he first proves the existence of God from the fact of motion. By applying to this
fact the dialectic or inductive process which gives the majors,
he infers the existence of immutable being. Then from immutability, taken as the metaphysical essence of God, he
deduces all the divine attributes.

This deduction may be effected in several ways. We may
at the start establish a first attribute, be it what it may, from
this first deduce a second, from the second a third, and so on, as
Saint Thomas Aquinas does. Again, we may establish a first

attribute, and from it derive all the rest as rays around a centre. We may combine these two methods and deduce each attribute in succession either from that which was taken as the principle, or from those already deduced. This exercise should be given in logic several times to every student of philosophy. It is the simplest and best exercise in pure ratiocination which can possibly be proposed. There is a true algebraic identity in the deduction, to those who can take the words strictly and in their absolute simplicity. The thesis of God's attributes is unique in this respect, from the very fact that here every point leads to every other, and we know in advance that there is identity everywhere. Only it is not always easy to grasp, to see, and to express the identity clearly.

Here is an instance of deduction, starting from the attribute of God contained in the words of Scripture : "*I am that I am.*" From the idea of Being, or, if you prefer, from this proposition, "Being is," we will first deduce what are called the metaphysical attributes of God.

To do this we must take everything with mathematical precision. We suppose it to be true — purely, simply, and absolutely true — that Being is, — a proposition, moreover, which is the clearest of identical propositions, and, as it were, the criterion of rational evidence.

Besides, it is plain enough that when we speak of *Being,* simply and absolutely, we refer to absolute being, and not to relative beings. This results from the very nature itself of language. The pantheists abuse words, and found their systems upon this abuse, when they at the same time designate both absolute Being and relative beings by the word Being.

1. This established, if Being is, simply and absolutely, it is not a finite being, for finite being is up to a certain point, and not beyond it. It is only within limits and under pe-

culiar conditions; it is not simply and absolutely. Therefore, the Being which is is not finite therefore it is infinite.

2. Let us follow the deduction rigorously. Let us set aside the habit of seeing everything partially and relatively. If Being is infinite, it is a strict identity to add that it is infinite in every sense. It is well to add this, merely because we have a weakness for falling back upon our limited, partial, relative imaginations. Let us reject these customary distractions; we are in algebra; we must take things strictly and simply. It is obvious, I say, that if Being is infinite, that means identically that it is infinite in every sense, since if it ceased to be infinite in one sense, it would be finite in that sense, it would not be the infinite. Where there is a limit in any sense whatever, in that point and in that sense it would cease to Be; therefore it would not be Being, as we have stated.

Therefore, if Being is, it is infinite in every sense.

3. If Being is, it is all that is possible; otherwise it would not be absolutely. It is all that is possible; it is this infinitely; since if it were not infinitely such possible it would have, in that mode of being and in that sense, a limit beyond which it would not be. If it is, it is infinitely all that is possible.

4. If Being is, it is immense and eternal; this is the same argument as for the infinity. If it were not eternal, this would imply that there would be a time when it would not be; if it were not immense, this would imply that there would be a place where it would not be. It *would therefore not be* purely, simply, and absolutely. Moreover, we see clearly that eternity and immensity are two attributes identical with infinity.

5. If Being is, it follows that it is necessary. The question, *Why is there anything?* is irrational. From the very fact that Being is, it follows that it cannot cease to

be. The question is, like this statement, fundamentally absurd: "If God did not exist, we should have to invent him."

Being is necessary because it is.

There was never a possibility of choice between Being and nothing, from the very fact that Being is eternal. Therefore there never was, and there never could be, any chance for the non-existence of absolute Being. It could not be that Being should not be; as it could not be that nothing should be: these two propositions are contradictory in terms. While these two others: Being is, and Nothing is not, are two identical propositions, expressing one and the same necessary truth: Being is, it is necessarily. If you can conceive a doubt as to the possibility of the non-existence of being, it is because you have not the idea of Being, and do not know the force of the word.

Whence it also follows that all which is not absolutely Being, need not have existed: all which has not existed from all eternity is capable of non-existence, and is only contingent.

6. If Being is, it is by itself. For if it were not by itself, it would not be absolutely, it would be relative being, and the Being by which it would be would be Being by itself,— that is to say, God. Moreover, if Being is necessary, it follows that it is by itself; this is the same idea under two forms.

7. A very important and absolutely exact, although truly inconceivable deduction, — as are, for instance, various algebraic deductions in their geometrical application, — is that Being, since it is eternal and immense, is really present at all points of time and space. We conceive up to a certain point its immensity, its omnipresence at all points of space; but we cannot conceive its omnipresence at all points of time. And yet, if it is absolutely, it is equally at all times,

in every place; with God there is neither past nor future, — he sees and includes all in an eternal present. Past, present, and future coexist in the infinite, as the two extreme points and the centre of an infinitesimal element coexist in a single, simple, and unextended point.

8. If God exists absolutely, he is simple. For if he were not simple, he would be composite; if he were composite, he would have parts, — physical or spiritual parts, no matter which. If he had physical parts, one part would be in one point, another elsewhere; he would not be entire in every point; he would not, therefore, be absolutely in one of the points, nor absolutely in the other point, he would therefore not be absolutely. If they were spiritual, immaterial parts, they would be distinct attributes, one of which would not be the other, and would not be wholly he, — which hence would be limited the one by the other, and limited relatively to him; they would therefore be limited, and not infinite attributes. Hence he would not exist, in the sense of these limited attributes, save up to a certain point, not beyond it; he *would not be* absolutely. Therefore God, being unable to be in any way composite, is absolutely simple; therefore his attributes are necessarily identical each with the other, and with his essence. Therefore we can establish a strictly exact equation between all the attributes of God himself and his being and his essence, and we can say, with Saint Thomas Aquinas: "God himself is his essence.[1] In God, being and essence are identical.[2] God's intelligence is his essence.[3] His will is his essence.[4] God is his life;[5] God is his beatitude."[6]

9. God, therefore, is absolutely simple and absolutely one. He is unity itself. He alone is unity. No being has its

---

[1] Contra Gent., book i. cap. xxi.
[2] Ibid., cap. xxii.
[3] Ibid., xlv.

[4] Summa contra Gentes.
[5] Ibid.
[6] Ibid.

unity save in him. The infinite alone is absolutely one, for
the infinite alone is total; no created being is total, none is
absolutely complete. There is no concrete unity, save God,
which is absolute. Which ? a mass of matter ? Since
space is capable of infinite division, that quantity of matter
must be infinite to fill the volume, — that is to say, to contain an actually infinite number of points : which is impossible, since created being is finite. All created unity is
approximate; it is the image of unity, but not unity. An
atom is one only in its centre and by its centre, which is not
it. So with souls and ideas. Where is there an idea absolutely one, total, and full? Such an idea can only exist in
God; it is infinite, it is God.

Therefore absolute being is simple and a unit.

10. It is simple and a unit in itself; but it is also one in
the sense that there is but one absolute being. To state the
distinction between two absolute beings would be to state the
distinction between two identicals or two *indiscernibles,* says
Leibnitz. It would be to state two infinites. It would be
to state this formula: *the infinite plus the infinite,* — a
formula which has no meaning in algebra, and cannot be
stated ; or which would signify exactly the only infinite.

11. He who is, is immutable ; for what is change ? It is
to become that which you were not, or to cease being what
you were. But if the infinite becomes, if he gain anything
in any sense, then he was not in that sense, or from the
point where he begins to gain ; if he lose anything, he ceases
to be in that sense; he was not and is not absolutely.
Therefore, if he is he is immutable. Therefore he is actually all that he is. He is not in a state of growth, like us;
he is not, like us, partly in act and partly in potentiality.
He is all act. He is pure act, as Aristotle and Saint Thomas
Aquinas so well express it, — a formula which is one of the
simplest, most perfect, and most fecund to teach the knowl-

edge of God. If he is all act, he is all his potentiality deployed; he is all potentiality actually present, living.

12. Finally, unless we deny that there are finite and relative beings aside from the absolute Being, it is true that these finite beings, as incapable of becoming or of beginning if nothing existed, could begin only through the Being which already was. Therefore that Being had the power to produce all that which is produced; but since those beings which are were not, it follows that he produced, created, them out of nothing; but to produce that which was not is possible only to an infinite power. No finite power could produce anything out of nothing. Infinite power alone is capable of producing out of nothing. This is what these algebraic formulas symbolize: *Zero multiplied by any quantity whatsoever equals zero ; zero multiplied by the infinite equals any quantity whatsoever.*

Therefore absolute Being is also omnipotent.

II.

Thus far we have deduced from the idea of Being what may be called the metaphysical attributes of God, — infinity, immensity, eternity, necessary existence, undividedness, simplicity, unity, immutability, pure actuality, and omnipotence.

But all the philosophers or theologians see at least two distinct orders of attributes in God, — metaphysical attributes and moral attributes.

Those who distinguish three orders of attributes, metaphysical, intellectual, and moral, — those have still more clearly seen that which was to be distinguished.

When Clarke, having developed the metaphysical attributes, comes to the intellectual attributes, he begins in these words : "The hottest dispute between the atheists and ourselves rages about this proposition. And indeed, who does not admit the existence of an eternal Being, infinite power and origin of all things, whether this world be his work or be himself?" The spirit of atheism tolerates such a God, — a physical, geometrical, and mechanical God, who is infinitely all that which we find in nature and its laws. Between such a God and infinite intelligence lies a great void; intelligence is quite another aspect, and like another dimension, of being.

But this is not the only void which reason encounters here. Grant that the absolute, eternal, immense, immutable Being possesses intelligence; add to infinite power infinite intelligence, — freedom, will, and goodness would still be lacking.

Is this being of infinite power and intelligence free; does he will, does he love? This is again another order of things, another face, and a new dimension of Being.

And, indeed, there are minds which stop at the first dimension of Being, and ignore the other two; and there are those who accept the first and second, like Spinoza, while they reject the third, without which we have no more idea of God than we have the idea of a body, without the idea of the three dimensions.

In mathematics, unity, taken simply, geometrically represents linear unity, — an abstract thing; unity multiplied by unity, which is still unity, represents unity of surface, — an abstract thing; but unity thrice taken as factor, the product still being unity, represents unity of bulk, — a concrete thing. Unity taken as factor a still greater number of times, represents nothing more.

Thus, unity thrice taken as factor, neither more nor less, alone has a concrete geometrical meaning.

So, too, I say that the order of the metaphysical attributes, taken quite alone, is an abstraction of the mind, a selection from the complete, subsistent, and living being.

So, too, with the first two orders taken together. We must have all three. Being has its three necessary dimensions; and the formula of infinite being would be not only *the infinite*, but *the infinite multiplied by the infinite multiplied by the infinite*, — which is still simple unity, just as, algebraically, unity multiplied by itself is always unity.

Having said this, we must inquire whether the intellectual and moral attributes, as well as the metaphysical attributes, are deduced from the idea of Being.

It is certain that Clarke does not perform this deduction *a priori*. He again steeps himself in reality, returns to earth, redescends into his own soul, sees there freedom and intelligence, and thence, no longer by deduction, but by the inverse process, he transfers these things to God, raised to infinity.

In fact, it is thus that the mind usually proceeds, both for the intellectual and the moral attributes. We see the three worlds described by Pascal, — the world of bodies, the world of minds, and the world of love. We see the three rays contained in the ray of physical life, — the ray of force, the ray of light, and the ray of heat. We see the three rays contained in the ray of spiritual life, which not only is, but which loves and knows, and we transfer to God this necessary triplicity of all totality.

Yet Saint Thomas Aquinas deduces everything from the idea of immutable being, — even intelligence, freedom, goodness, and will. He proceeds by a method which Clarke regards as correct, but difficult, and of which he says: " I will not employ, to prove it, the reason that that which exists by itself must be invested with all possible perfections; the thing in itself is very certain, but it is of such a nature that it cannot readily be demonstrated *a priori*." [1]

Saint Thomas takes this method, and having demonstrated

[1] On the Existence of God, Clarke, chap. ix. prop. viii.

that God is infinite, he deduces from this that in God we must necessarily find all perfections which exist in all beings, and find them superabundantly. If this be so, he says, God must be intelligent.[1]

Now, although in Clarke's eyes this process of Saint Thomas differs from that which he himself employs, it is plain enough that the two processes are but one, and that Saint Thomas, as well as Clarke, in order to pass to the intellectual and moral attributes, not only deduces the idea of intelligence and goodness from the idea of immutable being by the way of identity, but goes back to experience and reality, to the human soul, and there again sees, as Saint Paul says, the invisible perfections of God through the spectacle of the creation.

The metaphysical — that is, abstract — attributes of physical things are, as their name shows, revealed by the sight of material bodies in the light of reason; the intellectual attributes are revealed to the mind by the mind; and the moral attributes by the heart, by the consciousness of freedom.

And yet, if we cannot rigorously deduce both his intelligence and his freedom from the idea of God's being (which, moreover, we do not hold to be impossible), this is due to the limitations of our faculties or of our actual knowledge. For it is certain, as Saint Thomas instantly adds, that God, being absolutely simple, is his own intelligence as well as his own being. In God, being and intelligence are identical; in him will is identical with intelligence as well as with being. Therefore, with sufficient penetration and sufficient knowledge, we might advance, by means of identity, from being to intelligence and freedom, or rather we should see that Being is absolutely, necessarily, simply, all this together.

---

[1] Opusc. ix. chap. xxi. and chap. xxviii.

III.

Whether we follow out the idea of being, taken in itself, or the knowledge of ourselves, transfigured by reason, we say: Being is intelligent.

Then, we at once see that all the metaphysical attributes of being are applicable to intelligence, which is identical with being, since it has already been proved that being is absolutely simple, and that all its attributes are identical. Therefore the intelligence of Being is Being itself, or Being itself is intelligence. Therefore, too, since Being is simple, infinite, eternal, immutable, wholly actual and omnipotent, its intelligence which is itself, has precisely these characteristics.

It is simple, not discursive, not composite, like our own. In it, everything is one in the distinction. It is infinite, and it extends itself to infinite being, and to all relative, possible, or actual being. It is eternal, that is, equally present at all times, knowing all in an eternal present. It is immutable and immovable, and can neither forget nor acquire. It is, therefore, all act; never passing, like our mind, from potentiality to act, from darkness to light. It is not a faculty, a power, a quality of being, it is Being itself, — it is its very essence. Far more, its present act of intelligence is its very substance.[1] And, finally, it is its omnipotence.[2] God, says Saint Augustine, — repeated by Saint Thomas, — does not know things because they are, but they are because he knows them.[3]

What does he know? In the first place, he knows himself wholly. God is the identity of the intelligible and the intelligent, as Aristotle expresses it, and Saint Thomas develops

---

[1] 1ᵃ, 1ᵃᵉ, q. xiv. a. 4.   [2] Ibid., a. 8.

[3] 15 De Trint., cap. xiii. 1ᵃ, 1ᵃᵉ, q. xiv. a. 8.

it,[1] quoting, as applicable to God alone, these weighty words: "The Being who knows his essence is identical with his essence."[2]

He not only knows himself, but he knows all which he has created, since, indeed, his intelligence, joined with his will, is the cause of creation. And there is in God not only the unitary idea of himself, but also the multiple ideas of divers things.

And what are these ideas in God? No one has so well expressed it as Saint Augustine, repeated by Saint Thomas: "Ideas are the principles or formal reasons of things, reasons stable, immutable, and independent of every principle other than themselves; eternal, subsisting in the intelligence of God. They are not born, and do not die; and yet they are the model of all which may be born and die, of all which is born and dies."[3] They are in God, and they are God. God sees them because he sees himself; but if he is simple, how can he see divers ideas in himself? He can, says Saint Thomas Aquinas; and thus: "He knows his essence, — he knows it, just so far as it is knowable. He can therefore know it not only in accordance with what it is in itself, but also in accordance with the partial resemblance which any one of his creatures may bear to it. But that which constitutes the species of a creature, is its degree of likeness to this divine essence. Therefore, when God knows his essence in so far as it is imitable by that creature, he knows it as the reason or idea of that same creature. Thus God sees in himself distinct ideas of things."[4]

---

[1] De Trinit., cap. xiii. 1ᵃ, 1ᵃᵉ, q. xiv.

[2] "Omnis sciens, qui scit suam essentiam, et rediens ad suam essentiam est rediens ad suam essentiam reditione completa."

[3] Lib. de divers Quæst., q. xlvi. — Iᵃ q. xv. art. 2.

[4] Iᵃ q. xv. art. 2.

IV.

Are there in God will, freedom, goodness, love? Does God's providence pervade the world?

I cannot help again asserting that the idea of being, fully explained, if we can set aside the habit of limiting and abstracting everything, of positing, even in being, the negation only fitted for nonentity, and of never wholly daring to maintain universal affirmation, — the idea of being, I repeat, is identical with that of power, intelligence, will, freedom, and love. Take away any of these things, and you destroy that which is. Is not this clear? Take away intelligence, take away love, take away freedom, which takes away love, — you blind the sight, you tear out the heart of him who was, and you so wholly deprive him of being that you then say: There is no God. You say this, and justly. There is no longer a superior Being above us; there is only an inferior being. We are superior to this shattered God, — incomparably superior; since we know, will, love. There is no longer an absolute being.

But independently of the possible deduction from being of goodness and love, reason establishes the fact directly, by its chief process, that God is infinitely good, free, and loving, since there are in us traces of freedom, love, and goodness.

God is free, he is good, and he loves; and all this, in reference to God's relation to the world, may be summed up in a single word which also implies his wisdom and his power, — the word "Providence," or the paternal government of the world.

I am well aware that the sophists of all ages regard these words as devoid of meaning. But in our opinion these very words are most full of meaning, while abstract words, even when exact, are empty.

If the sophists, on this subject, as well as concerning the words referring to it, see the opposite of what we see, this is a necessity, and is explained by that strange fact but too little known, — namely, that, as Plato and Leibnitz say, sophists are minds so perverted that they see everything inversely. In fact, they are minds which have by artificial means learned to see, not things themselves, but only their own abstract thought of them. These minds, therefore, are like eyes which have succeeded, by an artifice, in changing the nature of their vision, so that they no longer see objects themselves, but the images of these things on the retina. They would thus see all objects inverted, since the image on the retina is always inverted. Thus, I say, the sophists see invertedly. Hence, if we take the opposite of what they assert, we have the truth.

I ask how it is possible not to see that God governs the world by his providence. I ask to what degree of blindness and intellectual inversion a man must attain to say, with Lucretius, —

"Do not think that eyes were given us that we might see the world about us ; that our feet are flexible so that we may walk ; that strong arms, that two hands, opposite and skilful, were given us that we might use them. All that is thus interpreted, is interpreted quite wrongly ; it is all inverted. Nothing was given us that we might make use of it ; that which exists, that is what determines the use that is made of it." [1]

> "Lumina ne facias oculorum clara creata
> Prospicere ut possimus; et ut proferre viai
> Proceros passus, ideo vestigia posse
> Surarum ac feminum pedibus fundata plicari ;
> Brachia tum porro validis aptata lacertis
> Esse, manusque datas utraque ex parte ministras
> Ut jacere ad vitam possimus, quæ foret usus.
> Cætera de genere hoc inter quæcumque pretantur,
> *Omnia perversa præpostera sunt ratione ;*
> Nil ideo natum est a nostro corpore ut uti
> Possimus, sed quod natum est id procreat usum."

Is this credible ? Wherein does Lucretius differ here from one who should say, "Men think that their feet are below, and their head is above, but it is just the opposite"?

We must say frankly that a man must have lost his sense and forsworn his reason not to admit that our eyes were given us to see, our limbs to walk and act; not to understand that a deep knowledge and deep goodness, sustained by an infinite power, framed our bodies and this world, and left their mark and, as it were, their signature, upon the whole and on every detail. Let us leave abstract arguments; here are palpable realities.

Yesterday, I held in my hand a fragment of flesh taken by science from a corpse. It was a part of the aorta, taken from the point where that arterial trunk arises from the heart. I admired that door of the heart, whence life gushes with the blood throughout the body, — a door so constructed that it is always both open and shut; wide open and close shut: open to life which rushes forth, and closed to life which might try to withdraw. I felt that tissue, frail as a rose-leaf, but of matchless firmness; fitted to vanish, as if it did not exist, before the blood coming from the heart, and to reappear, inflexible, so soon as the tide pauses and makes a brief return towards the heart. The tiniest reflux itself collects the three portions of the barrier, adapts them by its motion, and closes them before it. But lest the slight web, too firmly united to the arch of the canal, should some day forget its task unseasonably, each fold of the valve is provided with a button which the reflux must needs grasp for its own restraint; and this delicate action is performed in my breast at every beat of my heart, quickening with emotion, adapting its rhythm to my thought, my necessity, my effort, — the impulse of my soul; growing calmer when I sleep, and resuming the mathematical regularity which rests and renews me. And this goes on within me for half a

century, — it may be a century, — giving me fresh life with
every throb, and sweeping away death in the intervening
space.

Now, the whole life of my body and all the mechanism of
my life, as to-day known to science, is made up of a mil-
lion such details, all bearing the mark of the Maker, after
the same fashion; moreover, all tend to the same purpose;
moreover, all these details, adapted to each other in the
unity of my life, are in their turn adapted to the unity of
universal life, and to millions of other marvels in the midst
of which I live.

Whence does the heart, whose every fresh impulse gives
me new life, derive that life? It comes to it from without,
— a perpetual source, which comes to us without our aid;
whose unfailing beneficence dwells in my own breast, affords
it its chief nourishment. Thousands of secondary forms of
nourishment are within my grasp; there is another life than
mine, which produces them and gives them birth about me.
I am hungry, and there is bread; and moreover, that bread
gives me life. And that hunger and that bread, and that
power given to the bread to support life, and the countless
means of attaining this end, — all this is again made up
of thousands of details, each adapted to the other, each of
which, taken separately, is a miracle, and the sum total of
which, we may well say, is the very sight of God's hands
and God's labor to nourish me.

Before I existed, and before the first man existed, God
formed this globe out of a previous vapor. He made it into
a rock, welded it with fire; he cooled this burning lava,
clothed the rock with water, and brought it within reach of
the sun. He traced upon the ocean, which covered everything, the plan for a palace and a garden, and caused palace
and garden to spring from the deep waters. Then, on the
arid soil of the garden he spread that fertile earth suited for

plants, and he ordered it to bring forth plants. The dwelling was magnificently adorned and richly provided with fruit and food ; there were, moreover, deposited beneath the ground instruments, and, in case of need, arms and treasures. God then created another marvel, — animated servitors, docile powers, animals.

And the plan of all this abode, in the eyes of science able to see, is clearly a plan traced by intelligent goodness for the education of a race of men.

When all was ready, there was a day like our present day, and measured by the same sun, — a day whose date is certain, although unknown ; there was a spot where man, who an hour before did not exist upon the earth, was placed.

In the midst of this mute and unintelligent world suddenly appears a being who stands upright, who speaks and thinks, and who, addressing the invisible, says: " My Father ! "

All this is thus, and we see it with our own eyes.

But who was the nurse and the mother of that nascent man ? Who taught the first man to walk and to talk ? There is no choice in the matter, — it was God.

God, like that poetic king of whom Virgil speaks, who bore his child in his arms, —

" Ipse sinu præ se portans,"

and who bound him to his lance when he crossed a torrent, — God, Creator and King of the world, at that transitional moment also bore his child in his arms and bound him to his sceptre.

Woe unto him who can think without emotion and admiration of that unique and marvellous moment in history, — of that birthday of the human race !

It is not a question of Providence here, — a word too abstract and too cold to express what I behold ! I see my beloved father and mother! I see the wisdom and the support of a father, the protecting love of a mother, — an eternal father and mother, who are God.

Shall I believe that this Father, who created me out of nothing, who placed me on this earth, who supports my life, who gives me intelligence and love, no longer watches over me? No; I believe and I see that which, thank God, is taught to the youngest child, and which the youngest child believes and understands: I believe and I understand, and cannot fail to understand, that his eye is ever upon me, that he sees my most secret thoughts, knows every motion of my heart; that in every throb of that heart he incites me to love him, and that, ever present and zealous, he labors at my celestial education, — even to the smallest details of the minutest actions of my life.

I see, I understand, and cannot fail to understand, that this is true of every man and of all mankind. When I know the philosophy of history, as I believe I now know that of my own life, I shall understand the providential march of God in the history of humanity, as I see it now in my own history; and if the history of the world be so slow, it is due to the cause which makes my own progress slow. Now, I know but too well what it is that has retarded my advance.

I shall then know that God co-operates in events as he co-operates in our thoughts and actions, and that he has a purpose in tracing out the plan of history, quite as much as in tracing out the course of the year. The purpose of the visible plan of the year is the harvest: is not the purpose of the history of the ages a harvest too?

Why do the ages move, if it be not to ripen the harvest to which the Gospel alludes, and to prepare the work of the harvesters whom the Father of the family shall send?

It seems to me that if we will leave abstractions, to look,

in accord with the nature of human vision, at what is before our eyes, we shall see, without any possibility of a question, God's visible presence in the world.

Yet I confess that there is a shadow over the picture, and a constant contradiction which leads many to doubt. This shadow, this contradiction, is death. Death poisons and destroys everything; death holds all else in check, and annihilates all God's gifts. Where, then, is Providence? Where is the Father? For death renders his work null.

Yes, if death be nothingness. But if it be immortality, as the life within us affirms, — which we should rather believe than that unknown shadow which affrights us, — then, on the contrary, death is but a final feature added to the perfection of the picture. It is the feature which explains all and justifies all; it becomes the light that transfigures the whole and gives it an eternal significance: for it is to the work of God what that chief act of my reason and my will is to the life of my heart and my intelligence, which, as Fénelon says, breaks and sacrifices, by God's help, the limitations of my intelligence and freedom, to enter into the infinitude of God.

This will be explained more fully when we come to speak of man's death and immortality, and also of the death of this world and its reconstruction, of which Leibnitz says: "This globe shall be destroyed and renewed whenever the government of minds demands it."

V.

Before concluding this study of the attributes of God, we must point out that to which we consider the philosophic and true distinction of those attributes into metaphysical, intellectual, and moral, corresponds in theology. This distinction corresponds to the dogma of the Trinity, if it be true that, as Saint Thomas Aquinas says, the distinction of persons depends, in the holy Trinity, upon the procession of the Word from the Principle which speaks it, and of Love from both. (*Beata Trinitas distinguitur secundum processionem Verbi a Dicente, et Amoris ab utroque.*)

Since non-Catholic writers abuse this divine mystery, and pantheists found their entire system on the dogma, — as, for instance, Lamennais' entire book is but a false application of it, and Hegel's whole system an absurd interpretation, — I do not see why Christians should be forbidden to consider in philosophy, together with Saint Thomas Aquinas, Saint Augustine, and others, the philosophical side of this dogma, and its possible applications to the knowledge of man and the world.

Here we will say but a word regarding it. We will say that if Christian philosophy be developed, — that is, if the only philosophy now possible and useful be called to bear its fruits, — the wise will at last learn that power, intelligence, and love, those three radical distinctions, are to absolute Being what the three dimensions are to the body, and that they constitute its unity, as the product of the three unities of dimension constitute the unity of the solid body; that they no more destroy its simplicity than the simplicity of the infinitesimal element of the solid body is destroyed by the fact that we are bound to distinguish in it the elements of the three dimensions; that, lastly, if it be true that in living organisms the highest perfection corresponds to the maximum of individuality or unity combined with the maximum of distinction in the organs, then in absolute life perfection consists in absolute unity, combined with absolute distinction. Now, absolute unity is simplicity, and absolute distinction is the distinction of person from person. If, therefore, the true philosophy be developed, we shall understand what certain theologians have said, — that the distinction of persons is, in God, the condition of simplicity, far from being its negation. We shall understand the words of Saint Thomas Aquinas: "Unity and transcendent plurality are identical;" and those of Saint Hilary of Poitiers: "Our God is not solitary, although he is one." We shall understand the truth of these comparisons and conceptions, and above all, their insufficiency; and we shall know the incomprehensibility of the mystery.

And while still sounding the immeasurable depth of the mystery by contemplation and study, we shall tend above all to adore and worshipfully imitate it. We shall see in it the source of all knowledge, of all virtue, life itself, and immortality. We have weighed all these words thoroughly. We shall see therein the heart of Christianity, the last wish of Christ: "May they be one, O my Father, even as we are one." We shall see therein both the perfection of every soul, and the organization of the world to come and of the ideal society of heaven, — which will be, according to the Saviour's prayer, a plurality of persons in one.

CHAPTER IX.

I.

WE have completed the demonstration of the existence of God, of God characterized by his attributes. But, as we have already declared, two fundamental points still await development, which will add singularly to the force of this demonstration.

In the first place we shall show, as we have repeatedly asserted in the foregoing pages, that the demonstration of the existence of God, which is merely the application to its proper object of one of the two essential processes of reason, is as rigorous as a genuine mathematical demonstration, as Descartes and Leibnitz also affirm; and that it is thus rigorous because it is nothing else than one of the two processes of geometry which correspond to the two general processes of reason. It is the infinitesimal process applied, not to the abstract geometrical infinite, but to the substantial infinite, which is God.

In the second place, we shall show that contemporary atheism, which is very consistent and very learned, is a demonstration *ad absurdum* of the existence of God, and that it is merely the chief process of reason reversed, and the infinitesimal geometrical process applied the wrong way.

And first, as for the primary point, Descartes lays great stress upon the mathematical precision of the demonstration of the existence of God. "When I think of it attentively," he says, "I clearly find that God's existence can no more be separated from his essence than the equality of its three angles to two right angles can be separated from the essence of a right-angled triangle." Elsewhere he says: "It is certain that I no less find in my consciousness the idea of a supremely perfect being than that of any figure or number whatsoever; and I know no less plainly and distinctly that an eternal and actual existence belongs to his nature than I know that all which I can demonstrate of any figure or any number veritably belongs to the nature of that figure or number: and therefore . . . the existence of God must pass in my mind as being a truth no less certain than I have hitherto esteemed all mathematical truths to be."

Thus thought Descartes. Leibnitz, as we have seen, thought the same. The two greatest mathematicians whom the world has known assert that the proof of God's existence is as rigorous as any mathematical proof.

Now, not only is the truth of God's existence, regarded from a particular point of view, of the same order as mathematical truths, although it is also experimental at the same time that it is ideal, — it is, I say, of that order, in that it is a necessary idea which cannot but be true, since God is the Being whose essence implies existence, as the essence of the triangle implies the equality of the three angles to two right angles. Not only is this so, but we shall show besides, as we have just declared, that the proof of God's existence, as men practise it commonly, poetically, and as true philosophers have developed it, is no other than a universal process, of which the pre-eminent mathematical process — the infinitesimal process of Leibnitz — is an individual case and a special application.

"Metaphysics, harmony, geometry, and morality," says Leibnitz, "exist everywhere." Therefore, according to Leibnitz, there is geometry in metaphysics, or rather there is a sort of *universal mathematics,* for which Descartes and Leibnitz sought, and the bases of which Leibnitz discovered. It is undoubtedly this idea which he pursued in his treatise entitled, *De Scientia infiniti.* Moreover, the whole seventeenth century is full of this idea of the infinite. Theology, metaphysics, mathematics, even the ascetic treatises of that period are full of it. All the thinkers of that time are in pursuit of it. Pascal, Fermat, Wallis, Descartes, dwell upon it. But Leibnitz, more than the rest, applies it to mathematics by the marvellous invention of the infinitesimal calculus, — a discovery which transfigures that science, and gives it the greatest impulse it ever received or ever can receive.

Let us see what the infinitesimal process of Leibnitz is. The idea is comprehensible without any special knowledge.

Mathematics treats of forms, motions, velocities, — that is, of the effects of force acting in space and time.

Now, the difficulty in mathematical research, "that is, in research into forms and motions, comes," as Lacroix says, "from the fact that there is continuity in lines and velocities."

And, in fact, how are we to reach continuity? How can we grasp, in forms or motions, the passage from one point to the following one? What is the point which follows another point? Is it the same point, or are there two points? If it be the same point, what can we say of the passage or relation of the one to the other? If it be another point divided by space, however small the interval may be, it is not the following point; for between any two points, divided by an interval, there is always a space infinitely divisible, — that is to say, capable of containing as many geometrical points as we like. This question is a labyrinth in which we are soon lost. Hence that book, mentioned by Leibnitz, entitled, *Labyrinthus de compositione continui.* And yet, in the analysis of forms and motions, we must be familiar with the law of transition from one point to the succeeding point, or else the continuity escapes us. But two consecutive points coincide, otherwise there would instantly be an infinity between the two. We must therefore analyze and find the relation between two contiguous points, distinct, although coincident, and grasp the law of transition from one to the other. We must analyze the indivisible, according to the expression of Leibnitz, who called his calculus, "the analysis of indivisibles (*analysis indivisibilium*)." But this analysis evidently issued from the analysis of finite quantities, and entered into infinity, — into the infinitely great and infinitely little, those two things which Leibnitz calls "the two extremes of quantity considered aside from quantity (*extremitates quantitatis non inclusæ sed seclusæ*)." One enters upon the indivisible or infinitely small in finding the relation between two coincident points, and enters alike upon the infinitely great and infinitely small in considering curves as polygons with an infinite number of infinitely small sides. Hence Leibnitz also calls his analysis: "An analysis of indivisibles or infinites (*Analysis indivisibilium seu infinitorum*)." It is essential, in a word, to posit at the base of the calculus the idea of the two actual infinites, — the infinitely great and the infinitely little, — an idea without which, Pascal says, no one can be a geometrician ; and this double geometrical infinite must be considered as actually existing, if we would grasp the essence of forms and motions. Hence Leibnitz really conceives of continuity. He conceives of two contiguous points distinct in their essence although coincident in space.

This is not all. How are we to grasp the relation of these two points ? Thus. By starting from the relation of two points considered as separated by a finite distance. By the ordinary geometry of finite quantities, we find the relation between two separate points ; we then assert that by annulling the distance between the two points, that is, by passing from the finite to the infinite by annihilating the interval, the obstacle to continuity, the essence of the relation remains, although it loses a variable part depending on the greater or less distance between the points, when they were separated by space.

Thus, while the ordinary analysis of finite quantities could not attain continuity, or the essence of the relation between the points, but merely attained, between two given points divided by a definite interval, a particular relation constantly differing according to the position and distance of the given points, the infinitesimal analysis finds the relation between any two contiguous points an invariable relation, always identical for the infinite series of all points of the given curve and for any curve of the same sort. This is what is called the law of the increase of magnitudes, anterior to every quantity of increase. It is the very law of the generation of forms of a given kind. We advance, by the infinitesimal process, from finite magnitude to infinite magnitude, — that is, to geometrical immensity in its infinite wealth and its absolute continuity. We attain immensity itself, — abstract immensity, not vague and indeterminate immensity, but intelligible immensity, full of its eternal laws, of the laws and ideas of all forms.

The infinitesimal process destroys the finite magnitude of forms, to obtain the laws and essences of forms realizable by magnitude. It suppresses the variable quantity, but preserves the immutable essence. Dimensions vanish, but the relations of dimensions remain, — relations which are invariable for every sort of conceivable forms.

To suppress the variable and retain the necessary in forms ; to bring the multitude of points back to simplicity, in order to destroy their accidental relations without destroying their essential relations; to return to the infinite by gathering magnitude and dimension into a single point, wherein subsists and wherein is discovered the law of generation for these multitudes, — such is the infinitesimal calculus. It is, briefly, if we may venture to say so, a re-ascent to the mathematical laws and forms as they exist eternally in God, independent of all size and all dimension.

Thus the infinitesimal mathematical process, like the Platonic and Cartesian demonstration of the existence of God, moves from finite to infinite, from contingent to necessary, from variable to eternal, from the individual to the universal;[1] and it proceeds in precisely the same manner, effacing all the limits of contingence and variation, disengaging the essence in particular realities, reducing accident to zero, and raising the essential to infinity.

Therefore the infinitesimal process of mathematics is precisely an instance and particular application of a universal, fundamental process, by which the human mind springs, with an action as sublime and as certain as it is simple, from any finite postulate to the infinite.

The same general process is applicable to the relation of finite to infinite, whether in geometry or in metaphysics. Now, applied to geometry, it produces marvels, and what it gives us is infallibly sure: is it possible that when applied to metaphysics it should produce only error?

I ask if it be rational to admit that a process innate in the human mind, actually practised, implicitly or explicitly, by all men; a process which is the foundation of poetry, that flower of truth; a process which all philosophers of the first rank have perceived or described more or less clearly, and which, lastly, by the progress of science, being also applied to geometry,[2] there reveals, by most amazing discoveries, the rigor of its certainty and the grandeur of its power, — I ask, I say, if it be permissible to admit that such a method is true only in geometry, and has been wrongly applied, from the beginning of the world, by common-sense, by poetry, by

---

[1] It is plain that in mathematics the mind does not leave *the abstract;* it moves from the *abstract finite* to the *abstract infinite.*

[2] To tell the truth, the process has been applied to geometry since the beginning of science, by the notion of *limits* and that of *infinitely littles,* but it has only entered into it fully and methodically since the time of Leibnitz and Newton.

philosophy, to the demonstration and study of the living infinite? This cannot be. There is necessarily solidarity between the two applications of the process, and its geometrical certainty confirms its metaphysical certainty.

The identity of the geometrical infinitesimal process with the fundamental process of the rational life by which God is demonstrated, has never been established. We state for the first time explicitly and directly this identity,[1] to the study of which we devote a part of our Treatise on Logic; and we there demonstrate what Descartes and Leibnitz assert without proving it, — namely, that the proof of God's existence has a mathematical validity. At the same time we introduce in theoretical logic the clearer knowledge of a truth which is not sufficiently developed therein, — namely, that reason has two exact processes, and not one only ; that syllogism is not the only form of reasoning ; that there is another radically different from the first, but equally sure ; and that these two logical processes correspond to the two methods of geometry, — the algebraic deductive method by means of identity, and the infinitesimal method, which gives the infinite by starting from the finite. We believe that Leibnitz knew this, but he neither said so clearly, nor demonstrated it. He insinuated something of it, but he was not understood. Perhaps this was what he was reserving for development in his work on "The Science of the Infinite."

The geometrical infinitesimal process, discovered as a methodical form of calculus by that seventeenth century which

---

[1] Wallis, Newton, and above all, Leibnitz, have said what is equivalent to this, but in terms which are not sufficiently explicit. I have answered the objections made to me on this point, in an Introduction to my Logic, which seems to me to close the discussion. Allow me to say that the objections made to me were, all and always, based upon the strangest of misunderstandings, — misunderstandings certainly not justified by the *sum total* of my statement, but to which I necessarily gave occasion by some obscure detail or some ill-defined word. In later editions, particularly in the latest one, I have tried to correct these blemishes.

was the father of sciences, transfigured mathematics, an infallible science, and made it a power and a glory. This process is verified by its geometrical and mechanical applications. It attains laws and forms which the analysis of finite quantities can in no way reach; it solves with incomparable ease problems which the analysis of finite quantities solves with difficulty; it is a new and transcendent method in all the significance and truth of the word.

Whence we may conclude, it seems to me, that this same process, when philosophy at last comprehends its universality, reach, and precision, will transform philosophy as it has transformed mathematics; will answer questions which long courses of deductive reasoning were unable to answer; and will make quick and easy, even for the simplest minds, the solution of problems which the greatest geniuses have solved with difficulty.

I allude to that fundamental operation of the rational life, that act of sovereign reason, which from every finite postulate springs to the infinite as the actual source and eternal model of the finite postulate that we see; which asserts the actual, infinite existence of all being, all beauty, all power, and all goodness of which we see any trace; which says, in its consciousness of being, of life, and of limitations: Remove these limitations; you have an infinite being, actually and infinitely living;— which says: "I know something, therefore an infinite intelligence exists; I love, therefore infinite love exists; I see limited space, transitory time, therefore infinite extension and eternity exist; there are traces of beauty, therefore there is a supreme beauty; there are traces of happiness, therefore there is a complete happiness and a felicity without bounds." Yes, these simple, common-place arguments, implicitly employed by all good hearts and right minds from the beginning of the world, make up a very simple, very potent and exact method, which scientists and sages, although glimpsing at it, have not thus far ventured to apply, for the very reason that it seemed to them at once too potent and too simple. I repeat that this infinitesimal method, identical with the corresponding mathematical process which is but a special application of it, will renew Philosophy whenever Philosophy at last chooses to take possession of it and boldly apply it in its fulness.

II.

We said in the beginning of this Theodicy that if there be a genuine proof of the existence of God, that proof must correspond to some common, daily, essential, and fundamental process of human reason; we have shown in the soul and human mind a universal tendency, which, ever desirous to enlarge, embellish, and raise to the infinite every trace of being, beauty, and goodness presented by the world, rises to God by this poetic process, which is but the impulse of reason. Most minds, even the simplest, reach God by this way. We have recognized that the proofs of God's existence given by true philosophers, from Plato to Descartes, are nothing but this common method translated into philosophic language. We have explained the essence of this process; we have asserted and shown, with Descartes and Leibnitz, that this proof is as rigorous as any mathematical proof; and lastly, we have shown that this vital and fundamental process of the human mind is a universal process, of which the infinitesimal mathematical process is merely a special application.

It now remains for us to understand how, if it be true that the demonstration of the existence of God be the simplest and most spontaneous as well as the grandest and most essential of the acts of reason; if it be true that philosophy has described, analyzed, and argued it with full details and precision, and that this demonstration has now clearly acquired mathematical certainty,—it remains, we say, for us to understand how there can still be atheists, how there always will be, and how there is, at the present day, a school of atheism which is far more scientific than the old-fashioned atheism.

In the first place, there are atheists because man is a free agent, and because there are wicked men.

In fact, the proof of God's existence is not only the act and fundamental process of the rational life, it is also the act and fundamental process of the moral and practical life. That is to say, the operation of the mind which proves God answers to a moral act of the free will which loves and adores God. These two acts answer to each other in such fashion that the moral act is the source, the point of support, the cause, of the rational act. For if the will refuse its action, reason cannot complete its own. The mind, when the heart does not adore God, cannot alone effect the true proof of the existence of God. It sees the reasons for it if they be pointed out, but does not believe them. It can repeat the lesson, if it choose to be a hypocrite, but it has no faith in God; and we find that the demonstration is only an argument without a basis, which, to a dry, abstract spirit, far removed from love and spontaneous worship, does not imply the reality of God's existence, but only the abstract idea of God.

So that, among men, those who reach God through love may reach him through reason ; those who do not reach him through love can only reach him through reason in seeming, or actually turn their reason against him : I do not say that they do not at the same time turn reason against itself, but they turn their reason against God, and deny him in their intelligence because they have denied him in their affection.

Let us study more in detail the origin of atheism.

To do this, we must first recall the proof of the existence of God.

We consider the beings who surround us, we contemplate the world and our soul. We see therein being and life, although limited; traces of beauty and goodness, mingled with contrasts and changes. But the imperfect goodness of this world leads us to comprehend infinite goodness; its borrowed beauty, absolute beauty. For this world speaks and proclaims God. This is what the soul of every man should comprehend in presence of this world, and such is the duty of his reason.

The duty of reason is to conceive the infinite through every trace of being, beauty, and goodness shown to us by creatures; and because they also everywhere show us limitations, void, evil, and imperfection, it is the duty of reason, as well as of will, to prevent us from pausing at knowledge or love in limited beings. To go beyond them, to seek the infinitely perfect being, manifestly different from all creatures, although evidently proclaimed by each, — such is our duty.

But it is here that men part, and either advance towards God or hold aloof from him.

Who has not often hesitated before the complex vision of things? Now, the order and beauty of the world compel the soul to admiration, praise, hope, and faith in that invisible being whom all things proclaim and reveal. Again, the disorder and evil, the misery and brevity, of the present, above all, death, trouble us, sadden us, drive us to distrust, complaint, and despair. In this hesitation, in this trial of reason and will, some, upheld by the legitimate instinct of human nature, — or, to speak better, by the contact of God with the root of the soul, — maintain within them their ideal, faith in the infinite perfection, substantial, actual, and living. Others, despite the horror felt by their soul and

22

the remorse of their reason, allow their ideal to be smothered
by the sight of chance, their faith by the sight of obstacle,
and, in answer to doubt, choose negation. These are the
two moral and intellectual races who divide the world.
There are minds and hearts which affirm, there are others
which deny. Herein lies the whole question: God or not;
yes or no.

Consider well that the choice is free. We are, by choice
and freely, for God or against God.

The choice between these two paths is offered to every
man, not only in his youth, but at every point in life. Every
movement of our consciousness, every impression received
from our fellow-creatures, may and should re echo from ourselves and our fellow-creatures back to God, if, repelling and
scorning the vanity, imperfection, and present misery of
things and of ourselves, a vigorous love of good — that is,
virtue — lifts our soul towards the sovereign Good, the
supreme perfection, transporting us from the finite to the
infinite, from the transitory to the eternal. This is what
Socrates meant by philosophizing, when he said: "To philosophize is to learn to die;" it is to learn to sacrifice accidental and transitory impressions, limited sensations, finite
and transitory joys, to attain the substance itself of which
these are the shadows. This progress towards the infinite
by the sacrifice of the finite is the right path, — the path
of goodness and truth.

But if all the moments of consciousness, if all the impressions received from our fellow-creatures, far from re-
echoing to God in our intelligence and affection, wrap us in
selfishness and sensuality; if every pleasure and every pain
nail us — to use Plato's vigorous expression — to the present
and accidental point of life; if, far from raising us to the
infinite and the immense, the present instant fixes us upon
a point of the finite; if it not only detach us from the con-

sciousness of God, but also from full consciousness of ourselves, from entire possession of our soul which is greater than the world, and reduce us to the proportions of a creature which is but a mere detail in the world, — this degradation, which can only occur because we freely prefer the possession of self to that of God, and the external possession of the senses to the full and entire possession of self, sensuality to reason, pleasure to virtue and freedom, — this continuous descent towards the lower, is clearly the false path, the path of evil and of error.

We are not sufficiently alive to the fact that man ascends or descends the ladder of life, as he may prefer, at every point in life. He tends, by each of his unbiassed actions, towards fulness of life or vacuity of life, — that is, towards an actual being more complete or more empty. We approach God, and *we are more;* we depart from him, and *we are less.* And this is the whole mystery of life, — to advance towards God, or to depart from him. We know not the perpetual and universal history of the world and of every soul. Meantime, the tremendous drama does not pause. We steadily advance either towards God or towards nonentity. "The wicked man sinks towards nothingness," says the holy Scripture.

This is why there are atheists.[1]

Assuredly there are fearful moments for the soul, when, having sunk in some sort to a lower state of being, — that is, to an enfeebled vitality, — it is tempted to absolute incredulity ; conscious of its degradation and decay, it is tempted to say, There is nothing but an empty void ; there is nothing, there is no God. Because it is moving towards

---

[1] Yet, let us not forget, there are men who are mental, but not wilful atheists, as there are Christians who have faith, dead faith, but have no love. So, too, it is very different to cherish a *dead atheism,* and to cherish atheism as the actual principle of life.

lesser being, it begins to believe in nonentity; just as, in the luminous moments of increasing life, the soul, conscious of growth and progress, conceives of being more and more, trembles with joy, and leaps by a mighty act of faith to the immediate certainty and absolute assertion of Being, — that is, infinite Being.

So that, in reality, the mystery of good and evil, of truth and error, consists in attaining, by free choice, to one of these extremes, to one of these two prime decisions, implicit universals, which are the foundation of every mind: *Being is*, or else *Being is not*, — a living, intimate, and incarnate double proposition, which every soul asserts at will and bears in its innermost core; of which the one, produced by free love of the supreme Good, is the very formula of evidence, *Being is;* the other, produced by that distaste for the supreme Good and that habitual choice of the lesser, which result from egoism, is the general formula of the absurd, — that is, the most concise and most absolute of all contradictory propositions, *Being is not.*

Once more, we have the two human tendencies, good and evil, truth and error; there are minds which affirm, because they love; there are minds which deny, because they do not love: absolute negation or absolute affirmation, Being or non-Being, God or no God, all or nothing.

Hence the noble words of Plato, which Leibnitz holds to be so true: "The philosopher and the sophist move in opposite directions: one advances towards being, the other towards nothing; and while the philosopher is dazzled by the too great clarity of his object, the sophist, on the contrary, is blinded by the darkness of his."

On this subject Leibnitz reports that the sophist Foë at the close of his life said to his disciples: "This is the basis of all things, — there is nothing; nonentity is the principle of all things." We know that India is full of this insensate nihilism. Greek sophists, Gorgias among others, taught it; Plotinus renewed it; and in our day a whole school of philosophy teaches it.

Thus there are atheists ; there have been such in all ages ; there will always be such, because evil plants radical incredulity and absolute negation in perverse hearts. Atheism, says Plato, is a disease of the soul before it is an error of the mind.

This is why there is a modern school of atheism more scientific than the ancient one.

It is because, as practical atheism is and can be nothing but the will itself directed in a sense contrary to the moral laws, so speculative atheism is only the reason directed in a sense contrary to the laws of logic; whence results this strange consequence, that in philosophy the theory of atheism is nothing but the demonstration of the existence of God taken inversely. The actual demonstration of the existence of God being mathematically exact, and having clearly become so by the labors of the seventeenth century, it follows that the actual theory of atheism, which is that same demonstration reversed, is in a certain sense exact, and, I might even say, true, — true, in that it entails at the close of the argument a manifest absurdity; which must be so, since a correct train of reasoning must reduce to an absurdity the hypothesis that there is no God.

Contemporary atheism proceeds as follows. To the sight of finite beings, who only exist up to a certain point, and not beyond it, to the sight of created perfections and their limitations, it applies in an inverse sense the process which rises to God. Instead of destroying the limitation and raising the perfections to the infinite, it destroys the perfections and raises the limitation to the infinite; and it thus succeeds in asserting that *absolute nonentity exists*, and that there is no other absolute being than this nothingness.

Whence it follows that "Being and Nothing are identical," or that "Being is Nothing."[1] These two propositions exist textually in Hegel's works, and he constantly repeats them. They are, as we see, the statement of absolute absurdity. This is inevitable. The process which, applied correctly, gives us truth itself, must produce pure absurdity when applied in a contrary sense.

Thus we have in contemporary atheism a demonstration, by means of the *reductio ad absurdum*, of the existence of God.

But what is truly monstrous, and what is peculiar to the present school of atheists, is that it clings with desperate determination to this radical absurdity, and intrenches itself in it. It asserts that the formula, "Being is nothing," is the principle of philosophy, and that, starting from this principle, logic must be transformed. "The time has come," says Hegel, "to transform logic;" and this transformation consists chiefly in denying *the principle of contradiction,* — that is, in maintaining that in all things we can and ought to assert at the same time for and against, in the same sense and in the same connection.

So that a new system of Logic, absolutely contradicting the old one, has been taught in Europe for the last forty years, successfully, brilliantly, — nay, more, with such raciness of reasoning that Logic, reversed as it is by this school, will come forth more fully developed than it was, because several points hitherto unknown, or undemonstrated, will be thus demonstrated to absurdity. This is an important fact, a solemn and critical moment in the history of the human mind. This fact, rich as it is in consequences and instruction, will be the object of minute study in our Treatise on Logic. We shall then see how modern sophistry, which has built up in the nineteenth century a powerful school

---

[1] Sein und Nichts ist dasselbe. — *Log.*, § 88 (*Encyclopædia*).

of atheism, is simply and precisely Descartes turned wrong side out, Leibnitz reversed.

III.

Let us close this first part of the Treatise on the Knowledge of God.

We have set forth the proofs of God's existence as they have been given in all ages.

These proofs are distinguished as the cosmological, psychological, and ontological proofs, according as our reason rises to God from the spectacle of nature, from the sight of our own soul, or from the idea of God taken in itself. But the first two form but one: it is God known through his acts; so that there are really, as Descartes says, but two proofs, — that which proves God through his acts, and that which proves him through the mere idea which we have of him.

But it is clear that the idea of God is only obtained from his acts, according to the sublime words of Saint Paul: "For the invisible things of him from the creation of the world are clearly seen, being understood by the things that are made, even his eternal power and godhead." Therefore, actually, there is but one proof of the existence of God, which may be thus defined: There is something, therefore God exists.

We have seen that if we truly possess the idea of God, we possess the proof of his existence; because then the proposition, *God is*, is merely an identical proposition in our eyes, as well as in itself. Everything, therefore, reverts to obtaining the idea of God through his acts.

We have seen the process employed to this end by reason, and we have also shown the moral requisite for the exercise of the process. The whole process, — permit us to summarize once more, — the entire proof, consists in rising from the finite to the infinite by the negation of the limits of the finite, and in proceeding thus from everything to God, because, according to Saint Thomas Aquinas, everything exists in God infinitely, or God is everything eminently. We apply to the finite this process of elimination, which gives us the idea of the infinite; that is, the idea of God, which, so soon as it is obtained, of itself proves that God exists.

This process has the precision of geometrical processes, since the infinitesimal process of geometry is itself but a special application of it to the geometrical finite and infinite.

But as the exercise of this process also implies a moral requisite, and the process, exact in itself, may be applied, if desired, in a contrary way, it follows that there may be atheists more logical and more consistent than ever before. It is true that, by the very power of this admirable process, the sophists, who apply it inversely, are led where they should go, to a manifest absurdity; that is to say, to the contradictory proposition, which may be stated thus : Being is not. They proceed thither, they cling to this statement : they assert and write literally : " Being is nothing (*Sein und Nichts ist dasselbe*)." So that modern atheism is nothing but a demonstration *ad absurdum* of the existence of God, a counter-proof of the direct demonstration. Either there never was a demonstration *ad absurdum*, or this is the strongest which has ever been given.

We have seen that this magnificent process not only proves the existence of God, but at the same time gives us his attributes; and that if all these attributes may be deduced by way of identity from the idea of infinite Being, each of them taken separately, they may also be obtained directly and seen, as Saint Paul says, by the chief process of reason, in every trace of beauty or goodness found in created beings.

We must have understood that this act of the human soul which sees in nature, in the visible world, or in the soul, God and his attributes, is the chief act, the fundamental process, of the rational and moral life; it is the pre-eminent act of reason and liberty combined; it is a joint act of intelligence and will, — a simultaneous work of discernment and morality; it is what should be called natural prayer, the impulse of the soul which moves from everything to God.

From this point of view, there is but a single proof of God's existence. Everything is that proof. Every being, be it what it may; every action, be it what it may, is that proof.

Why can I not make it perfectly clear? How can any man fail to see it for himself? How can any one fail to see that everything reveals God, that every thought leads to him, every sensation conducts us to him? Why must sensuality, which animalizes us and arrests in us, as in animals, every sensation at its first effects, without permitting them to be echoed back to the reason and heart; why must impurity, which swallows up and profanes sensation, to enjoy it; the stupid habit of life which ceases to gaze and to admire; that hateful education which withers and destroys our faculties, instead of elevating and transfiguring them; that narrow, blind, abstract, and ignorant rationalism, which clips the wings of the soul from earliest infancy, — why must all these causes destroy within us the divine sense of nature and life, and the innate germs of the sacred poetry which sees God in all things? If souls were less dead, all nature would lift us to the knowledge of God, to admiration, adoration, love! Every impression would be echoed back in the mind to God.

Touch any material body, be it only a stone. I say that this contact, in a pure and contemplative man, is echoed back through the body, the senses, the mind and soul, to God: the soul is conscious of Being, and, in Being, instantly of the Infinite. Yes, at the touch of wood or stone, the soul

should naturally exclaim: *He, God!* "Yes," says Bossuet,
"every time that we use our body to move in whatsoever
fashion, we should always feel God present." The soul
should thus mount, by wondrous undulations far swifter than
those of light, from world to world, from the world of the
body to that of the soul, and from that of the soul to God,
from the body, from this stone which it feels, — which it
feels to be neither God nor a free or rational mind, to the
intelligent being which is itself, and from this free and intelligent but still imperfect world to perfect and infinite being.

Such is the legitimate margin of a sensation, of any impression whatsoever, outward or inward, in undegraded man.
Who has not felt these things in some privileged moment?
Who does not understand, when he reflects, that it must be
so? The soundest and most incontestable philosophy, and the
most rigorous theology, teach that God is everywhere present, that God is in all being, really and substantially. Then,
if God be in the stone, in touching it I implicitly touch him.

Not only is God in all being, but he operates in all action
and acts in all movement. "God operates in every operative
being," says Saint Thomas Aquinas (*Deus operatur in omni
operante*). This is true of all movements of bodies or of
minds. God is necessarily at the foundation of every act of
thought or will. Heat, light, attraction, sounds, savors, perfumes, — all things which are forms of motion, are an effect of
God's presence, of God's contact with material bodies. The
light of the sun is the sun which God incites to shine. The
sun can no more shine without the impelling force of God,
than it can exist without his presence. In all being, in all
motion whatsoever, God is present as first cause, as motionless mover. To all who know the value of words, these are
identical propositions, which cannot but be true.

Thus when the soul, through the body, is conscious of any
being whatsoever, it receives a certain impression, of which,

after all, the first cause is God ; and if our soul possessed all
its natural refinement, it is to be supposed that it would at
once, by that swift circulation of vague thoughts and · imperceptible arguments, described by Leibnitz, conceive, in a more
or less explicit way, of the infinite and eternal power which
the finite and transitory being that it touches, implies from
the fact of its own creation.

Why can we not recall our earliest childhood, our first
vivid impressions, on beholding nature and life which have
but newly come to us! There would be more philosophy in
that passive wisdom of little children than in the books of
philosophers. It may be in this sense that Christ says:
"Out of the mouths of babes and sucklings thou hast perfected praise."

I remember, in childhood, before I had attained what is
called the age of reason, once experiencing this sense of Being
in all its vividness. A great effort against something external, distinct from myself, whose unyielding resistance
amazed me, led me to pronounce the words: "I am!" I
thought of it for the first time. Surprise grew into intense
amazement and into the most vivid admiration. I repeated,
with transport: "I am!... being! being!" All the religious, poetic, and intelligent foundation of my soul was
stirred and awakened at that instant. A penetrating light,
which I seem still to see, enveloped me. I saw that Being
is, that Being is beautiful, blessed, lovely, full of mystery !

I can still see, after the lapse of forty years, all these inner
facts, and the physical details which surrounded me.

Who has not, in his life, one of these transfigured memories
which time cannot impair? We see it still; we shall always
see it ! We see, amidst the dimness of surrounding and forgotten years, days, and hours, a place, a scene, a landscape,
a feeling, a thought, or a word. Be the visible detail, the
common basis, of these immortal memories what it may, light

envelops the scene. But study it with care, you will always find in these luminous depths an emotion which echoes even to God. That light, in fact, was God. It is God whom we recall. God is the foundation of the remembrance. When we have once dimly perceived him, he transfigures forever in our mind the objects and the veils through which we saw him.

This corresponds to that noble intellectual phenomenon, familiar to meditative minds, which may be called the transfiguration of words. Sometimes a word opens, particularly if it be a word used in the Gospel, and a flood of light pours from it, which is a living idea, proceeding from the fountain-head. At the heart of the idea there is a feeling, there is a soul, and at the centre of that soul is God. "The more a word resembles a thought, a thought a soul, a soul God," some one has said, "the more beautiful it is." This admirable remark aptly illustrates the relative passage from a word to God. Our soul, touched by this word, stirred, that is to say, moved, advances from the word to the idea, from the idea to love, and from love to God, by that marvellous movement of spiritual undulations of which the visible waves of light are but a feeble image. Thus every sensation, in a soul not degraded, should echo from the outward object to the soul, from the soul to God.

And it is in this sense that we can say: Everything is a proof of the existence of God. The Heavens, the Earth, Night, Day, the smallest creature and the feeblest motion, display God and celebrate his glory.

Part Second.

CHAPTER I.

TWO DEGREES OF THE DIVINE INTELLIGIBLE.

I.

THE reader who has followed us thus far will surely believe that in this arduous task of presenting a summary of Philosophy, our object is not merely to satisfy intellectual curiosity. Our object is first and foremost practical and religious. We desire to do our part in arousing in select souls the taste for wisdom, the passion for truth, and the effort for morality. Active search after goodness, light, virtue, is more than ever lacking in the souls of men. We do not watch, we do not pray, as Christ requires us to do. We sleep, as Saint Paul said (*dormiunt multi*). Life makes no effort, consequently no progress, consequently loses its true glory and fruitfulness.

Now, to our thinking, true philosophy is nothing but this effort to gain wisdom. That is the very meaning of the word; and it is in this sense that Cicero understands it when he says: "Philosophy, light of life!" Saint Gregory Nazianzen also understands it thus when he speaks of the "very lofty Philosophy." So also do Saint Gregory Thaumaturgus and Origen,[1] when they assert that without philosophy there is no true piety. So also Saint Augustine, when he says: "I consecrate my life to philosophy."[2] Lastly, when Clement

---

[1] Panegyric on Origen by Saint Gregory Thaumaturgus.
[2] Huic investigandæ inservire proposui. — *Contra Academ.*, lib. iii. 43.

of Alexandria asserts that before the coming of the Saviour philosophy was requisite to lead man to justice, and that now it leads him to piety,[1] it is plain that in speaking thus that Father means by philosophy, as we do, the aspiration of the soul towards wisdom, the labor of reason and of liberty, in every man, to gain light and virtue.

It is therefore in behalf of philosophy, thus conceived, that we labor. We desire to make it known, and to arouse it, if may be, in every soul. We know no other genuine philosophy than that philosophy — true aspiration towards all wisdom — which seeks religion when deprived of it, and glorifies it when found.

Let us note, in the words of Saint Clement which we have just quoted, the distinction which he makes between philosophy before the coming of Christ and philosophy after Christ. Here we again find the two watersheds in the history of the human mind, before and beyond the Cross; and, which is the same thing, the two states of human reason, according as it is deprived of faith or illumined by it, — which again responds to the great distinction between the two regions of the world of intelligibility, which all real philosophers have conjectured or known.

It is this supreme distinction which we desire, above all, to establish in philosophy, and it is this that marks the difference between the two parts of this Treatise on the Knowledge of God. "There are," says Saint Thomas Aquinas, "two ways of knowing God; there are two degrees of the divine intelligible, and the wise man should seek to know God in both these degrees."

Not that we intend to set forth, in this work, what Saint Thomas calls the highest degree of the divine intelligible: that would necessitate a statement of theology, the doctrine of

---

[1] Atque erat quidem ante Domini adventum philosophia Græcis necessaria ad justitiam; nunc autem est utilis ad pietatem.

faith; but we shall try, in this philosophical treatise, to make known the foundation of this great distinction, and the relation of reason to the two degrees of the divine intelligible.

We must essentially distinguish three things when we speak of philosophy, — namely, the abuse of reason, whence sophistry results; the purely human use of reason, or philosophy before faith, which is the duty of the mind destitute of faith ; and lastly, the use of reason enlightened by faith, philosophy both human and divine, which is peculiarly the philosophy of Christians and total wisdom.

It is indispensable to know these three states of reason, these three tendencies of the human mind, if we would avoid the one which leads to yawning abysses, and would not linger with the one which remains on the earth, which becomes corrupt if it does not advance, but which, when it advances, becomes, as De Maistre expresses it, the human preface to the Gospel, or, according to Baronius, the vestibule of the Church of Christ.

To speak precisely, there are actually but two tendencies of the mind, — the one towards God, the other away from God. For when the middle tendency, which seeks God in the limitations of human nature, is true to itself, aided by God, it mounts higher. God, by a new principle which he gives it, changes it into a divine virtue. But, on the contrary, when the purely human tendency is opposed to that which is superior to it, through this very fact it changes its own course; it turns round, belies its nature, becomes a sophistical and perverse tendency, and falls below the level of man, towards those degrees of debased intelligence which Saint James calls a carnal and diabolic wisdom.

The knowledge of these states of the human mind, of their relations, and of the causes which lead a soul from one to the other, which sometimes urge to its natural conclusion the effort after wisdom, and then raise it higher than man, and sometimes turn it back and convert it into a revolt against all truth, — this knowledge would surely suffice to put an end to all the intellectual scandals of the present day, both to those of lawless sophistry and those of the apparent strife between reason and faith. These scandals must be overcome · if we desire to see humanity, held back now for more than a century, resume its progressive march.

Let us therefore try to make these three states of reason known to all.

II.

First, let us descend into our own soul, and into the life of our own mind, to seek the initial elements of this knowledge. There is no one who has not hesitated between these three states, who has not been inclined to each in turn, or has not really passed from one to the other.

Unhappily, scarcely any one studies his own soul enough, or exercises what true observers call the discernment of minds. Still, as all these various movements constitute our daily history, I hope that if we succeed in describing them truthfully in these pages, they may be readily recognized by all.

First comes what is certain, and what each of us sees in himself.

There is something that speaks within us. Is it ourself? Is it something other than ourself? "Is it I, or another?" said Saint Augustine; "is it I and another at the same time?" This is not the question now. But what is certain is, that there is in us an inner conversation, which is not always made up of lucid discussion or finished speech and luminous thoughts, but oftener of vague thoughts, impressions, and sensations. There are clear and cold views; there are ardent and impassioned movements; there are secret impressions, implicit desires, almost imperceptible lights.

Now, amidst all these sensations, does your soul maintain a constant and habitual effort after wisdom, — that is to say, towards light and virtue ? Do you unceasingly tend and aspire towards something better and greater than yourself? Or do you live in an habitual and secret state of despair of attaining to truth and freedom ? Or again, formally consenting to this guilty despair, and turning it into a deliberate maxim, do you deny in your heart virtue, truth, the future of the soul, and do you turn all your efforts to the search after present joys ?

These are the two tendencies, — one towards God, and the other away from God. But the tendency towards God, the march towards wisdom, has two degrees.

Do you search anxiously ? Do you seek with doubt which is ever renewed in regard to the sum total of truth, although you may be certain in regard to some details, and you have flickering lights, sometimes bright and sometimes dim ? Have you no assurances save those which bestow no peace, — rational lights, as certain as geometry, but as cold as it; knowledges full of defects and regrets; persuasions ever seeking for more upon which to rest ? Do you feel a state of mental exile ? Do you see all the truth which you perceive, as being outside yourself, and remote, like a star in some other world, which does indeed send us a few of its rays, but does not warm us ?

If you seek thus, it is certain that you have reached the first degree of the tendency towards wisdom. That wisdom appeals to you, since you seek it; it appeals to you constantly, though indirectly, since it leaves you no peace, since it never ceases to show you the vanity of what you possess,

23

the imperfection and defects of all your knowledge and all your present virtue. You are like the Jews under the law, which makes sin abound, says Saint Paul, because it renders it visible; but you are not yet subject to grace, which will bring you light. But yet, if you persevere in your attempt, if your effort is maintained, if your faith in the light to come remains unshaken, you will have fulfilled the duty of that degree of life; you will have done what was in you, and you have reason to hope that God will not refuse to raise you to the higher degree.

That higher degree is known only to those souls whom God himself raises to it. Its chief characteristic is peace. When divine wisdom enters the soul, its first words are those of Jesus Christ when he entered the room at the Last Supper: "Peace be with you." It then seems to the soul that it is no longer alone. It seems as if the Truth said to it, "I, who spake to you from afar, am here with you (*Ego ipse qui loquebar, ecce adsum*)." The soul feels that it is founded, rooted, in a new principle, which it possesses, which exists in it, in which it exists. It no longer hesitates or shifts in regard to its principle, as in the foregoing degree, but it possesses it and is conjoined to it. It is no longer outside of its centre, ever impelled to hasten in order to approach it, but it is within that centre which attracted it. Its task and its motion change their nature. It was, as Saint Thomas Aquinas says, an oblique and discursive motion; it is now a sort of motionless motion, comparable to the motion of a sphere which is at rest by its centre, and in motion by its circumference. It was the course of a mind seeking its point of departure and its principle; it is now the expansion of an intelligence unfolding in the light, because it contains the principle of light. The love of wisdom no longer lies for that soul in seeking unknown wisdom (*Græci sapientiam quærunt*), but in glorifying the wisdom it has found, which

is self-given and which dwells within us (*nos autem prædi-
camus . . . Dei sapientiam*). Woe to them whose effort is
again relaxed, and who neglect the present wisdom, while
others still await the wisdom to come! If they withdraw
now, they will quickly fall to the lowest degree of that outer
darkness where all those dwell who despair of virtue and
truth.

Thus the soul sometimes turns its effort in a contrary direction, surrenders its will to evil, and its intelligence to error;
again, it indeed pursues wisdom, but without possessing its
principle; and yet again it possesses that principle, and labors
to display its light.

These three states of soul correspond to the states of philosophy, of which we find one in the sophists of all ages;
another in the great philosophers of antiquity, such as Plato
and Aristotle; and the other in the great Christian philosophers, such as Saint Augustine and Saint Thomas Aquinas.
Only as those who are capable of the most are capable of the
least, we see how Saint Thomas could write, besides his *Theological Sum*, his *Sum* addressed to the heathen, where he
starts with philosophy as it may be in the middle and purely
human degree. We see that, following his example and in
his footsteps, we should strive, in this work, to present philosophy on its seizable side to those who, destitute of the
gift of faith, can as yet bring to it only the effort of healthy
reason.

III.

But what can the causes be which drag minds down from
the middle to the lower degree, or which hinder them from
rising to the higher degree, or which, finally, permit the eternal wisdom to address to them the blessed invitation of the
Gospel: "Friend, go up higher."

Let us imagine a mind established in this middle degree, a mind in which we find the beginning of philosophical life; by this I mean the effort after wisdom. What is the duty of that soul? What is its law? Clearly this is its law, "Thou shalt seek with all thy soul, with all thy heart, with all thy mind, and with all thy strength." .But, I ask, who is there that fulfils this law? No man fulfils it, I might say with Saint Paul. No man advances towards wisdom with all his soul, all his heart, all his mind, and all his strength. Men devote a part of their powers and faculties thereto, but not all.

And, first, do you not find it easier to seek wisdom with your whole mind than with your whole soul and heart? Do you not feel that we may indeed devote our whole intelligence to the task, but not our whole will? Is not this the usual state of the soul? I speak of the best souls, those whom the beauty of wisdom attracts. They regard it as a bright ideal which they love to contemplate, but which they will make a part of their life — later! We see the good, but we follow after the bad. This is the history of humanity.

Thus, first, we may seek wisdom with our whole mind, but not with our whole heart, nor consequently with all our powers, since the heart is one of our powers, and indeed the chief of them. But, moreover, is it indeed true that we devote our whole mind to it? Do you not observe that it is very rare for our mind to spread its wings, and consequently put forth all its powers? By this I mean that it is very rarely that our mind takes a flight and leaves the earth to rise higher in search of the unknown. And this because the human mind is naturally self-sufficient. Man scarcely believes that there is anything absolutely unknown to him. Even minds whose evident poverty should most distress them, even those minds most destitute of light, those minds even above all find it hard to believe that there exists a light greater than themselves; they refuse to leave self behind by some vigorous impulse; they do indeed try to deduce what they do not know from that which they know, but they do not try to acquire those things of which they are wholly ignorant, because a secret pride leads them to declare that there is nothing of which they are absolutely ignorant. The mind is indocile in proportion as it lacks light, and farther removed from humility in proportion to its pettiness. To leave self behind, as Fénelon says, that we may enter the infinite of God, is a thing which minds without greatness refuse more stubbornly than others.

What can we say, save that the mind itself, in this case, does not seek wisdom with all its powers, and this secret disposition which maintains it in its present light and in the identity of its actual wisdom, deprives it of the chief of the two movements of reason, that which soars upward, leaving to it only that which deduces or infers.

All true progress is impossible to such a soul. Its will, its practical life, almost estranged from search and effort, never grows; its mind never discovers; it does not acquire any new principle, any fresh revelation; it amplifies what it possessed, and deduces consequences therefrom, but does not gain what it does not already possess, and does not arrive at any essential novelty.

In these inner facts of the soul you have the history of that average philosophy, purely human, purely speculative, and incomplete even in its speculation, which is locked up in itself, and does not attain to real wisdom, — to Christianity and its supernatural faith, that new and divine principle.

Nor is this all. As some one has said, Life must live, — that is, must grow and develop.

And this law of progress is so far necessary that, sooner than pause, life, when necessary, will move in an inverse sense, and will progress backwards.

So that, if the natural effort of the soul towards wisdom be constantly arrested from above, because of the decided refusal of the will to leave self behind and enter the infinite of God, there will come a time when wisdom, tired of attracting it in vain, will repel it.   Or rather, a time will come when the soul itself, tired of constant motion without ever reaching the end, of constant search without ever finding its object, and of constant oscillation, says Plato, between the lower and the middle regions, without ever penetrating the higher, — the soul, I say, will turn entirely, and change its course.   As it demands, first and foremost, happiness and novelty, it will try if, by letting itself fall, it may not find the happiness and life which it did not gain by an indolent effort to rise.   " There is nothing above," it will say to itself; " let us look below."

Such is sophistry, the carnal and diabolic wisdom of which Saint James speaks.   The soul then no longer merely stifles the inspirations of God, it turns them round ; and the hidden spring, which comes from God's immediate contact with the root of the soul, according to Plato, Bossuet, and others, being unable to raise it to God, hurls it downward.

We again encounter this latter feature in that purely human philosophy, which, not seeking wisdom with all its strength, and hence not attaining the end of reason, is at last wearied, and often turns back, is transformed, and becomes the exact opposite of philosophy, — the source of all those monstrous errors which should be regarded, distinctly says Saint Thomas Aquinas, as outside the pale of philosophy (*extraneas philosophiœ opiniones*).

Close examination would show how this fall results in the soul's failure to fulfil its law, — that is, to seek with all its heart, all its mind, and all its strength.

The soul begins by bringing its effort to bear upon the mind alone, not sufficiently sustaining the mind by the

heart and practical will. Hence, in the vigorous and profound words of the Gospel, "It *doeth* not the truth," it
merely looks at it. Hence comes all the mischief. The
soul, not working wisdom in itself, cannot grow in wisdom,
and limits itself to considering from the outside an abstract
ideal towards which it does not advance. At first it looks
and longs at the sight of this beauty, from which it is immeasurably remote. Soon it ceases to long; the charm of
the ideal lessens in proportion as we gaze without approaching and reflect without acting. Our knowledge is, after all,
but a reflection of our life. Knowledge is experimental in
its better half. If moral life grows less, how can intellectual truth increase? "For he that doeth truth, cometh to
the light," says the Gospel; "and every one that doeth evil,
hateth the light, neither cometh to the light." But, in truth,
from the very fact that we do not seek wisdom with all our
strength, with heart and mind alike, but rather with the
mind alone; from this very fact we no longer seek it with
our whole mind. The mind has its roots in the heart, and
necessarily clings to the will even in the unity of the soul.
There are sensations which the isolated mind cannot know;
the mind can deduce by itself, but it cannot soar by itself.
We lessen the upward flight of the intelligence in proportion
as we isolate it and as the whole soul does not assist it with
all its powers. How, then, can we expect such a mind to
rise to the highest region of the intelligible, and reason, so
ill supported, to attain the goal?

It can only vacillate between the lower and the middle
regions, become exhausted by this sterile toil, drop back,
invert its effort, and seek progress by its fall.

IV.

We will now show how, on the contrary, it is granted to the soul to rise from the medium and purely human state which seeks wisdom, to the divine, supernatural state, which possesses it.

To understand this, we must admit that wisdom seeks to bestow herself on all, and traverses the nations, as the holy Scripture says, to form friends of God therein. We must admit that this wisdom is God, and that it continually solicits every soul. "Eternal wisdom," says Saint Augustine, "never ceaseth to address every soul, to the end that it may attract and convert it." We must admit, what is plain, that the majority of men oppose an obstacle thereto in the bottom of their soul, and, what is no less plain, that the soul, in the middle state where we have imagined it, should unceasingly aspire and tend towards that wisdom which ceases not to solicit it, — that is, towards the attraction of the desirable and intelligible. The soul should not cease to groan and sigh, in view of the obstacle, the imperfection and vice which dwell within it, and which remove it from the light of God. Let us, however, suppose that this aspiration, beneath the attraction of God, by the good will of man, becomes ever more and more vivid and sincere, and that the soul, increasing its effort, more and more sets its heart upon it. Then it will be granted to it, by the anticipative goodness of God, to effect a first advance, that of understanding and feeling, better than it could before it began to struggle, that between it and wisdom lies the infinite, and that an effort a thousand times greater would not bring it any closer, — an immense although a negative advance, without which wisdom is never to be given. But if the soul possessed the secret of life, it would know that this deep and humiliating vision of its own insignificance is the sign of the approach of God. The soul has struggled, hoped, recognized its impotence, seen its infinite distance from God, and yet it still hopes; it understands that God desires to give himself, since he makes himself desired and sought; it therefore *does that which is in it,* — it removes, in so far as in its power, the obstacle to God's coming, which in fact forewarned it, and without which it could never have desired or sought or struggled or recognized its impotence, and far less hoped, in spite of the vision of its own insignificance. God therefore, so soon as he will, and he will as soon as the obstacle on man's side is removed, — God bestows himself, and the mystery of regeneration is fulfilled. God gives the mind and soul a new life, which is the possession of the very principle of wisdom, which is God. The soul passes from alarm to peace, from search to possession. God establishes it in a state which is the germ and the beginning of eternal life.

We have spoken of purely human philosophy; we have explained what arrests it; we also know what turns it aside and hurls it headlong. We have pointed out what constitutes its progress; then what transforms it, raises it above itself and above man. But this important point requires ample study. Now, as the true progress of healthy reason clearly is to attain its end, as Saint Augustine says (*ratio perveniens ad finem suum* [1]), as that end is a new light other than that which it at first possessed; as that light is no other than the supernatural light of faith, announced by Christianity, — it follows that we shall here enter upon a sort

[1] Let us not forget that these words of Saint Augustine can be understood only in the sense of Saint Thomas, when he speaks of reason which has attained its highest degree of perfection through supernatural light (*ratio perfecta lumine supernaturali*). Perfected reason, raised above itself, is reason which has attained its supernatural end, very different from its natural end. It is to the supernatural end that Saint Augustine alludes here.

of Treatise as to the relations of reason and faith ; or, if you prefer, the relations of reason to the highest degree of the divine intelligible.

There is a void in almost every treatise on philosophy : they lack a special chapter on the relations of reason and faith. This void must be filled up in future. Already Theology, on its side, extending its hand to Philosophy, has introduced, among its other divisions, a special treatise on the relations of reason and faith.[1]   Philosophy, in its turn, must follow that example.

This is what we now undertake.

[1] See Perrone's Theology: *Tractatus de Analogia fidei et rationis.*

CHAPTER II.

I.

THE distinction between healthy, right, and useful human philosophy, and sterile and hide-bound or perverse and introverted philosophy, is that true philosophy, in its full effort after total wisdom, may be called by the name given it by the Middle Ages, " Intelligence in search of faith." This work will reveal it more and more; and, to our thinking, we have already proved it by our studies of Plato, Aristotle, Saint Augustine, Saint Thomas Aquinas, and the seventeenth century. If it be true that all philosophers of the first rank — and notably Plato — make a distinction between the two regions of the intelligible world; if this distinction has its root in the very core of philosophy; if it be certain, as philosophers and theologians superabundantly declare, that one of these two degrees is the perception of absolute and necessary truths, as God impresses them upon our native reason, and which constitute that reason, while the other is the direct, immediate perception of the source which causes these truths to shine within us, that is, of God, viewed, not in a mirror, but in himself; if it be true that faith is the attempt at or beginning of that direct vision, as Saint Thomas Aquinas and Bossuet say, and that hence it is distinguished from the reason which, of itself, is incapable of this vision, and can only grieve after it and conjecture it, — if all this be true, it results that the healthy and right reason is that which seeks both regions of the intelligible, and pursues its double perfection, natural and supernatural, as Saint Thomas expresses it: it follows that the true philosophy is that which seeks, regrets, desires, waits for faith when it is without it, and which, when it finds it, takes firm root in it, develops it, raises itself above itself by this supernatural support, and bears, through this divine strength, fruits which it could not otherwise bear.

Let us, therefore, enter with attention and respect upon this study of the relations of faith and reason. What is reason? What is faith? What relation unites them? What can reason do without faith? What is its duty when faith is given?

It has not been sufficiently noted that Saint Thomas Aquinas, the most vigorous metaphysical genius, perhaps, who ever lived, the one of all writers in whom knowledge and sanctity, reason and faith, were best combined, wrote two principal works, the *Theological Sum* and the *Philosophical Sum*, and that these two works correspond exactly to the two states of reason and philosophy, to the two regions of the intelligible world. In the *Theological Sum*, the holy doctor, as a learned oratorian [1] observes, "merely translates the simplicity of the Gospel into philosophy;" it is philosophy after faith, or faith seeking for intelligence (*fides quærens intellectum*). In the *Sum* addressed to the Heathen, Saint Thomas himself declares that it being clearly the duty of the wise to traverse both regions of divine truths, that which reason attains of itself, and that which transcends its effort, he intends, in that book, to seek by the rational way all that human reason can attain of God. This is philosophy before faith; it is intelligence seeking faith (*intellectus quærens fidem*).

In the beginning of the *Philosophic Sum*, Saint Thomas states in these terms the distinction between the two regions

[1] Amelotte, Vie de Condren.

of the intelligible world, the two orders of divine truths, or rather the two modes in which it may be given to man to know God, — a double knowledge, which he who seeks wisdom should pursue impartially. He says, —

" Since there are men who do not accept the authority of revelation, we must have recourse to the use of the natural reason, to which every man is forced to submit, but which, however, in divine things has but a limited range.

" There is, in what touches God, *a double mode of truth.* There are, in God, truths which all the powers of the human mind cannot reach. . . . There are others which the natural reason can reach, such as the existence and unity of God, and those of similar nature, which philosophers, indeed, led by the natural light of reason, have demonstrated.[1]

" To scan the depths of the sovereign essence, and the transcendant side of the divine intelligible, is clearly beyond the human reason ; and this Aristotle himself seems to have understood when he asserts (Metaph. ii.) that in regard to the principle of the Being which, from its nature, is light itself, our intelligence is as the eye of the owl in presence of the sun." [2]

Saint Thomas adds, —

" There are, then, *two degrees of truth in the divine intelligible :* one attainable by the search of reason, and the other, which transcends its efforts." [3]

The holy doctor concludes, —

" It clearly results from what has just been said that the wise man should devote himself to these two orders of divine truths, one of which is accessible to the investigation of reason, the other of which transcends all that its zeal can attain. It is understood that when I distinguish two orders of truths in the divine intelligible, I fully comprehend that it is not so in God, who is single and simple truth ; this distinction relates only to the human understanding, which has two modes of knowing God." [4]

---

[1] Contra Gentes, cap. iii.
[2] Ibid., cap. iii. 3.
[3] Ibid. cap. iv.
[4] Ibid., cap. ix.

What Saint Thomas says here is of the utmost importance. In these passages, the two degrees of the intelligible are clearly distinguished one from the other. Man may attain to one by natural reason, such as it is, and he can only attain to the other through faith. This distinction relates to man only, not to God. In him there is one only truth, which is God. But man may know this truth in two ways. The two lights of which theology treats, the natural light and the supernatural light, are in God but one and the same light, variously received by man. And Saint Thomas asserts, as an evident fact, that the wise man should study both.

This distinction being clearly established, — with this important reserve, that it is not relative to God, but to man, that is to say, it being fully understood that the same God is the source of the light of reason as well as of the light of faith, and that in him there is but one light, — let us strive to know fully wherein reason and faith consist, what they are in regard one to the other.

II.

There is God, there is the soul. God is a light which enlightens the soul, and which the soul can conceive in two ways. But what is the characteristic feature of these two ways ? "The light of reason," says Saint Thomas Aquinas, "by which we know the principles of truth, is a light which God sheds within us; *it is an image of the uncreated truth which is reflected in us.*" [1]

This is what we have already frequently repeated, with Saint Augustine, Saint Thomas Aquinas, and Thomassin : reason is the light of God, seen in us, reflected in the mirror of the soul, in the words of Saint Paul. "The assurance of reason proceeds from a light which God gives us inwardly

[1] Verit., quæst. ii. art. i.

and by which he speaks in us.[1] 'God maketh the light of his face to shine upon us,' says the Psalmist. This is the light of natural reason, which is the image of God."[2] Saint Thomas, following Saint Augustine in this (it is, moreover, the constant doctrine of the Fathers, of the Theologians, and of the Holy Scripture), always insists upon this lofty origin of reason. To him, "reason is the impression made upon us by divine light."[3] To him, "the natural light, thrown into the soul, is the illumination of God."[4] To him, "the principles of practical, as well as of speculative reason, are natural data which exist in the soul."[5] But this vision in ourselves of the light of God, Saint Thomas calls, with Saint Paul, seeing in a glass;[6] it is absolutely distinct from the sight of the light of God in God, which is no longer specular vision, but rather vision through essence.[7]

"Doubtless," says Saint Thomas Aquinas, "when we see, by reason, certain immutable, eternal truths, which hence are beyond us, we may see that we see them in God, since we know nothing save through his light, and since reason is a participation in that light; for, says Saint Augustine, these intelligible spectacles are only made visible to us as illuminated by their sun, which is God. But even as in the world of bodies, to see objects beneath the sun, it is not necessary to see the substance and orb of the sun, so too with this intellectual vision through the reason, it is not necessary to see the essence of God."[8]

In telling us what reason is, Saint Thomas begins to make

---

[1] Verit., quæst. ii. art. 1.
[2] Comment. in Paul.
[3] 1ª. 2ᵃᵉ. q. xci. art. 2.
[4] 1ª. 2ᵃᵉ. q. ix. art. 1.
[5] Naturaliter nobis esse indita sicut principia speculabilium ita et principia operabilium.
[6] Visio specularis.
[7] Cognitio per essentiam.
[8] 1ª. q. xii. art. 11 ad 3ᵐ.

clear to us what faith is. Reason is like seeing the world beneath the sun, and faith, or at least that vision of which faith is an essay, a foretaste, an imperfect participation, is like seeing the sun itself.[1]

This again rests upon the noble text already quoted in our study of the Theodicy of Saint Thomas Aquinas: "Light, during our earthly sojourn, is given to us in two ways. Sometimes in a less degree, and, as it were, from a faint ray: *this is the light of our natural intelligence*, which is a participation in the eternal light, but remote, defective, comparable to a *shadow* mingled with a little light: which gives man that reason, the shadow of intelligence, whose feeble radi-

---

[1] The word *faith*, says Billuart, has several meanings. Sometimes, for instance, it signifies *consciousness* (what we call *natural faith*, or *divine sense*); sometimes it signifies the *teaching of the faith*, the *object itself of faith*; sometimes, again, it signifies that divine virtue whose principle is grace, whose formal object is God alone, whose formal motive is the wisdom and authority of God alone, whose material object is all that God has revealed, and whose rule is the Catholic Church alone. It is this virtue, taken in itself, considered as a supernatural gift, in the supernatural light which constitutes it, that Saint Thomas, transforming Saint Paul's phrase, defines as "A habit of the soul with which eternal life begins in us, and by which the intelligence clings to divine things which it sees not (*Fides est habitus mentis quo inchoatur vita æterna in nobis, faciens intellectum non apparentibus assentire*)." Still, Saint Thomas does not insist so strongly on the obscurity of faith that he does not also say : "Faith is, in a certain sense, knowledge and vision (*Fides etiam quodammodo scientia et visio dicitur*)." (Verit. xiv. art. 4.) And elsewhere : "Faith is an imperfect beginning of future knowledge (*Fides est quædam prælibatio brevis cognitionis quam in futuro habemus*)." (Verit., art. 2, ad 9ᵐ.) Saint Thomas also makes the word *faith* synonymous with supernatural light, when he says : "*That light which is faith*, is that which produces assent to divine truths; and it is hence that it is akin to perfection ; but we do not possess this light perfectly, intellectual imperfection subsists with faith (*Ex lumine simplici, quod est fides, causatur id quod perfectionis est*, assentire ; *sed in quantum illud lumen non perfecte participatur, non totaliter tollitur imperfectio intellectus*)." (Verit. xiv. 2 ad 5ᵐ.) It is in this sense that several catechisms define faith : "A gift of God and a supernatural light which makes us cling to the truths revealed by God." It is of course understood that here we are speaking particularly of the intellectual element of faith. There is a voluntary element of which we must never lose sight, and of which Saint Thomas says, *In cognitione fidei principalitatem habet voluntas* (Contra Gentes, 1. III. c. xl.).

ance engenders diversity of opinions which the direct radiation of light will destroy. Sometimes again we receive light in a greater degree, in more abundance, and we are brought, as it were, *face to face with the sun.* But then our eyes are dazzled, because we contemplate that which transcends human sense; and *this is the light of faith.*"

Whence it clearly results, as from our entire study of the Theodicy of Saint Thomas, that, in the opinion of the Angelic Doctor, there are two degrees of the divine intelligible, to which reason and faith correspond; that light, in itself, is one, but that the created spirit sees it in two ways, directly or indirectly. Or rather, it sees the likeness of it in itself,[1] the image and the reflection; and this reflected light is the light of reason. Or the created spirit may see light in God himself; it may see, no longer in itself, but in God, its source and its direct rays, as when an eye beholds the sun. And this direct light is the supernatural light, which begins in faith, although it only attains its consummation in the beatific vision.

This distinction between reason and faith, between natural and supernatural light, is that of all Christian theology. Let us recall that which we saw in our study of Thomassin. There we found precisely the same doctrine, and, as it were, the commentary of Saint Thomas. According to Thomassin, reason doubtless sees the truth of God; but it only receives the light thereof in a tempered condition, according as it can bear it in its present state. They are rays of the eternal light of the Word, but let down to us (*condescensiones quasdam*). These same rays constitute reason (*hoc sic inest rationi, ut hoc ipsum ipsa ratio sit*). It is God revealing himself to souls, not such as he is, but such as they are (*radius Deitatis ostendentis se, non qualis ipsa est, sed quales ipsæ sunt*). And, further says Thomassin, copying Saint Gregory of Nyssa,

[1] Similitudo veritatis increntæ in nobis resultantis.

24

who speaks as do Augustine and Plato, these rays are *simulacra*, images and imitations of God (*simulacra, similitudines
et quasi imitamenta*). Yes, he says, this is a simulacrum,
and a very luminous image of divinity. The spectacle of
eternal principles, according to Saint Augustine (*spectacula
illa æternarum rationum*), is God when he sends us his
light, and impresses it upon us; but it is not God himself
directly present (*non immigrando, sed inscribendo*); in a
word, says Thomassin, this degree of the divine intelligible,
according to Saint Thomas, is like unto a mirror in which
God shows himself by sending his rays into it (*nimirum hæc
specula sunt in quæ radios suos Deus ejaculatur, in quibus
videtur*).

In Thomassin's opinion, this doctrine in regard to the
nature of reason, namely, that it is only a certain aspect of
the Word, and that immutable, geometrical, logical, and
moral truths are seen in the light of the Word, — this doctrine is not only that of the Fathers and Theologians, it is
plainly that of Christ and the Holy Gospel.

Having characterized reason, Thomassin describes the two
degrees of the intelligible with which we are striving to
become familiar. "The first degree of knowledge," he says,
"gives us certain necessary truths, which are eternal, immutable; these are the eternal reasons, rays of the incorruptible
truth which is revealed always and everywhere to every
being endowed with reason.

"But if a spirit love to follow this light, to linger and
purify itself in its rays, then it in its turn becomes light;
it can receive true purity, and become the child of God,
worthy at last to see God." [1]

Thus, according to Thomassin, the first degree shows us
certain truths, immutable principles, which are the light of
the Word in the soul; but the second shows us God him-

---

[1] De Proleg. Theol., vol. iii. cap. ix. § 1.

self. Such are indeed the two degrees of the intelligible, of which one is the natural sphere of reason, but the other is supernatural, and is granted only to the regenerate, in that light whose beginning is faith. In a word, the first degree shows God in the mirror of the soul; and the second, God in himself.

Saint Augustine understands it no otherwise, as we have already shown. But he expresses it in a particularly forcible way when he calls the two lights " the illuminating light and the illuminated light (*lumen illuminans et lumen illuminatum*)." Reason perceives only the illuminated light. And direct vision, of which faith is the attempt, has for object only the illuminating light. This is what the great doctor teaches when, speaking of his human knowledge before faith (*cum deformiter et sacrilega turpitudine in doctrina pietatis errorem*),[1] he compares himself to a man who turns his back to the light, and his face to material objects. This comparison is the exact truth upon this point. " I delighted in these things," he says, "but knew not whence came all, what therein was true or certain. *For I had my back to the light, and my face to the things enlightened;* whence my face, with which I discerned the things enlightened, itself was not enlightened."[2] And it is not of sensible knowledge, properly so called, that Saint Augustine speaks here, but rather of rational knowledge; he refers to abstract, geometrical truths, immutable, necessary qualities, figures, and numbers (*de dimentionibus figurarum et de musicis et de numeris*). The natural light of reason, according to Saint Augustine, is therefore reflected light, while the other is direct. The latter the eye receives itself, coming from its source, and does not derive it from objects or abstract 'it from creatures.

Now, these comparisons are the deepest and clearest ex-

---

[1] Confess. I., lib. iv. cap. xiv. p. 31.   [2] Ibid., p. 30.

pressions of philosophy on this subject. Reason is a certain vision of God, this is great and positive. But it is not the direct, immediate view of the substance and essence of God. It is a vision of God by means of reflection; it is an image of God which the soul perceives by seeing itself.

This is clear, simple, and certain, intelligible to all, useful, fruitful, and the final word uttered by philosophers of the first order, and by theologians, in regard to the nature of reason.

The importance and fertility of this theory of reason lies especially in the fact that it also shows us that reason is something correlative to faith; so that when we know what reason is, we also know, up to a certain point, what faith is. If we comprehend that there are two modes of seeing God, — indirectly and in his image; directly and in himself, — we comprehend that, if reason be the first of these two modes in which man sees God, there remains the second. Every philosopher will admit this, and the theologian may then say, That second mode of seeing God is that which we call supernatural. The philosopher, if he be a true philosopher, will understand this. Moreover, we at once comprehend that reason, having attained its natural end, and contemplating these intelligible spectacles, illuminated by that divine sun which it does not see, may, as it did in Plato himself, recognize that even these are but divine phantasms, conjecture that the sun exists, and feel regret at not seeing it. Now, the beginning, imperfect and obscure, of this supernatural knowledge of God, is faith.

III.

This distinction is so fundamental and general that it recurs, by analogy, throughout the history of the development of man in relation to God.

Saint Paul, establishing, in the Epistle to the Hebrews, the difference between the two Testaments, between the law of Moses and Christian faith, had it in view. Re-read that Epistle. Throughout his constant comparison of the two Testaments, of law and grace,[1] we find the analogy of reason and faith.

In one, God spoke through the prophets (chap. i. 1); in the other, he speaks to us directly through his Son, who is God. One is the word of Moses, announcing God to us ; the other is God himself (chap. iii. 3, 4). We must transcend this first degree, which is weak, and does not move directly to eternal salvation. The law did not give perfection. But we have a better hope, that of union with God (chap. vii. 18, 19). The priest of the law is only frail man ; but that which comes after the law is the eternal and perfect Son (chap. viii. 28). In the Old Testament, God takes us by the hand ; in the New, God takes us by the heart (chap. viii. 9, 19). The Old Testament is only the image and shadow of celestial things (*exemplari et umbræ cælestium*) ; the New gives us celestial things themselves, heaven itself (*ipsa cælestia, ipsum cælum*). (Chap. ix. 23, 24.)

There are two tabernacles, one of which is called *the worldly sanctuary* (*Sanctum sæculare*), and the other the Holy of Holies (*Sanctum sanctorum*), (chap. ix. 1, 3). The latter was *behind the veil*. It is now *revealed*. Christ himself has become priest, to give us everlasting salvation by this greater and more perfect tabernacle, which is not made with hands ; that is to say, is not of this creation, but is supernatural (chap. ix. 11, 12).

Yes, the law had but a shadow of good things to come

---

[1] Not that we would maintain that there was no grace under the law and in the law, — a theory condemned by the Bull *Auctorem Fidei*. But this, far from destroying our analogy, confirms it, for we also think, as will be shown later, that, in real life, grace is continually blended with reason, even when reason works in its own peculiar domain.

(*umbram enim habens lex futurorum bonorum*); but the just shall live by faith (*justus autem ex fide vivit*). Faith is the substance of things hoped for (*est fides sperandarum substantia rerum*), (chap. x. 1; chap. xi. 1). Under the law there was a voice which spake on earth, there is now a voice which speaketh to us from heaven (chap. xii. 25, 27). And that voice will change the earth, the transitory abode of man, into the kingdom of God which cannot be moved.

IV.

This established, what can reason do without faith ? What is its duty in advance of faith ? We have already stated this at length in the words of Saint Thomas Aquinas. It can attain to the first of the two orders of truths to be distinguished in the divine intelligible. It can do this, it should do this; and, as an actual fact, according to the same learned doctor, these truths, — which are the existence of God, his unity, and others of similar nature, — have been demonstrated by various philosophers, illumined by the natural light of reason.[1]

Natural reason may, without the aid of supernatural revelation, know with certainty various truths, not only of the geometric order, but also touching God, and we must accept this theologic proposition: "Healthy reason, without the aid of supernatural revelation, may know with certainty various truths of the natural order, which we may call preambles of faith."[2] We style an error of the *super-naturalists* the error of those mentioned by Saint Thomas, who hold "that the existence of God cannot be discovered by reason, but must be received by the single means of

---

[1] Contra Gentes, cap. iii.
[2] Perrone, de Analogia rationis et fidei, prop. i.

faith and revelation." [1] This is an error, he says, and he refutes this error (*hic error*) at some length.[2]

That fanatical tendency which would deny to natural reason all power, whether to know God, or in general to know anything with certainty, has often striven to spring up in the Church, but has always been repelled, notably in Luther, Calvin, Baïus, Quesnel, and more recently in Lamennais.

"Was it not Luther," says Erasmus, "who wrote that all discipline, practical as well as speculative, is damnable; that all speculative sciences are sins and errors?" [3] Luther denied natural reason as well as free will.

According to Calvin, all the faculties of our soul are wholly infected by evil. Moral freedom, of which man makes his vain boast, is but a chimera. Man of himself can produce nought save vicious acts and sins. Thus all our natural faculties are accursed.[4]

According to Baïus, all the virtues of philosophers are vices, and it is a Pelagian doctrine not to admit any natural good, — that is, any good produced by the unaided powers of nature, and by the sole effort of philosophy.[5]

Quesnel claimed that any knowledge of God, even natural, even in heathen philosophy, can only proceed from God himself, and that, without grace, it produces only vanity, presumption, and opposition to God. [6]

Lamennais not only denied that reason has the power to know certain truths relative to God, he went so far as to refuse reason the power of asserting with certainty our own existence. "The rational certainty of our isolated existence," he says, "would suppose as equally certain the certainty of our reason and even its infallibility; for to *affirm that we*

---

[1] Contra Gentes, lib. i. cap. xii.
[2] Ibid., lib. i. cap. xii.
[3] Quoted by Perrone, vol. ii. p, 1393.

[4] Institut., book iii. ch. ii.
[5] 25–27, Baii.
[6] 41, Quesnel.

exist, is to express an opinion, and if it were possible to be mistaken in saying *I exist*, we should not be rationally certain of our existence. To hold that every man possesses an innate rational certainty of his existence, therefore, is to declare that we accept the Cartesian philosophy, with all its consequences. It is flinging ourselves into the midst of the inconveniences, contradictions, and absurdities inherent in that philosophy, which is as dangerous as it is stupid." [1] Surprising words, which fully justify Saint Augustine's remark: "It is really to be feared that some may come to distrust reason, or to detest it to the point of rejecting evidence itself." [2]

We know that this system has been completely refuted by Father Rosaven, with irresistible logic and great wealth of learning.[3]

Moreover, all these Lutheran, Calvinist, and Jansenist errors, and all this pseudo-Catholic pyrrhonism, which sees nothing but the wounds and sores of human nature, fails to recognize its resources, refuses it all light and all power, and deprives it of free will as well as reason, — all these errors have, in all times, been condemned by the Church. These sombre doctrines, as has been observed, are allied to Manicheism. Manicheism, that senseless flattery of the supernatural order, taught that nature is the work of Satan, that the order of grace alone is good, that the New Testament alone is true, and outside it and before it, all is false and bad, — even the Old Testament, even natural law, its dogmas and precepts.

The least traces of these fundamental errors are subversive, and it is not to be contested that the war upon reason

---

[1] Defence of the Essay, p. 192.
[2] De Magistro.
[3] Review of a work entitled, "Philosophic Teachings in regard to Christianity, by J. L. Rosaven, S. J. Avignon, 1833."

is an insult to the Word of God, which is revealed as light enlightening every man coming into the world. When the Gospel speaks of the light of men, that light of men, say the commentaries, which are accepted by Saint Thomas, is reason. The Church, too, has never ceased to watch over this point, and even recently (1849) one of the Provincial Councils of France, revised and approved by the Holy See, pointed out the error of writers who, " in order to aggrandize faith, depreciate reason excessively, thereby endangering the double foundation of reason and faith, and threatening to overthrow both." [1] This phenomenon is the opposite of that revealed by the history of sophists, who, attacking faith in the name of reason, end by denying reason. By dint of attacking reason in the name of faith, faith too will be wrecked, as the Council of Rennes declared.

From this point of view no one has ever fully noted and praised the part played by the Jesuits in the history of Christian philosophy, and the way in which their imperturbable good sense, in all ages, and in our own day, has always placed them in the foremost rank of the defenders of reason and human liberty. And, strange to say, if they have become unpopular, it is particularly because they upheld, in the seventeenth century, the cause of reason and liberty against the popularity of the Jansenists. [2]

V.

In general, what the Church reprobates is the negation of any gift of God, natural or . supernatural.

All orthodox theology on this head may be summed up in a few words spoken by the pious and learned Cornelius

---

[1] Council of Rennes, decree lxiii.
[2] See also the contemporary works of Fathers Chastel, Cahours, Daniel, etc.

à Lapide, in his parallel of the two wisdoms, — human wisdom by reason, divine wisdom by grace and faith.[1]

The judicious author begins by exalting the first, in order to put the second higher yet. He considers sound reason the guide of human life.[2] God, from the beginning, gave man, proportioning it to his nature, a noble and divine law, the expression of the eternal and living reasons which exist in God.[3] Only, by sin this wisdom is dimmed, mingled with errors and clouds, is deteriorated in many things (*fucata, nebulis errorum præstricta, sopita multis in rebus*). This is our reason, the source of natural wisdom.

But "if the profane wisdom of philosophers has been of so much use and glory to the world, of how much greater use and glory would that divine and sacred wisdom be, which transcends that of philosophers as much as faith transcends wisdom, grace nature, and heaven the earth!"[4] This is true; the fruits of reason, even in antiquity, are good, but those of grace and faith surpass them immeasurably.

"Wisdom's first title to glory is its origin. The origin of natural wisdom is nature, that is, God, in so far as he is and as he may be called creative nature, author and master of nature. But the origin of supernatural and divine wisdom is God, in so far as he is the author of grace and of all supernatural goods."[5] Such is the orthodox point of view. We have already proved it by Saint Thomas Aquinas. We will now show it by an even greater theological authority.

The authority of Saint Thomas Aquinas, whose *Theologic Sum* was placed in the Council of Trent face to face with Holy Scripture, would be the highest of all authorities, did there not exist a book, written by order of the Council of Trent, to be distributed throughout the world as the com-

---

[1] Heading of Commentary upon Ecclesiasticus, Antwerp, 1687.
[2] Rectamrationem quasi datam sibi a Deo facem, sibique viæ ac vitæ ducem.
[3] Commentary upon Ecclesiasticus.   [4] Ibid.   [5] Ibid.

mon catechism of Catholicism. This book, written principally under the influence of Saint Charles Borromeo, and published by Pius V., is called, in the preface to the work itself, "the work of the Church Universal" (*Universalis opus Ecclesiæ*). Now, this is the beginning of that Œcumenical Catechism : —

"Such is the nature of the soul and of the human intelligence that, although it may have discovered for itself, by dint of labor and care, many truths in the order of divine things, yet the greater part of those truths — those which lead to eternal salvation, the end for which God created man in his own image — cannot be seen by reason or known by natural light alone.

"The invisible perfections of God, as the Apostle teaches, his eternal power and his divinity, are visible to the intelligence through the spectacle of created things; but the hidden Mystery, known neither to the ages nor the generations, so far transcends human intelligence that had it not been manifested to the saints, to whom God by the gift of faith has revealed the riches and glory of his new alliance with men, no human effort could have attained that mystery, that wisdom which is Jesus Christ."

This is the beginning of the Roman Catechism. Farther on, in the body of the work, we find a complete parallel established between reason and faith. We need only quote it, reminding all Catholics that this is their catechism, as all supreme Pontiffs for three centuries back have given it to the entire Church. Here is the parallel:[1] —

"The great difference between Christian philosophy and that of the age lies in the fact that this latter, guided by natural light alone, taking as its starting-point visible things and the operations of God, only rises to the comprehension of the invisible perfections of God by slow degrees, with difficulty, after long labor, and thus arrives at the knowledge that God exists, and that he is the First Cause and Author of all things. But faith, on the contrary, so elevates and strengthens the vision of the soul

[1] De Symbolo Fidei, cap. ii. 6, 7.

that it enters heaven without effort, is there bathed in the light
of God, is able at first to contemplate the actual source of eternal
light, then all created things in that source; so that the soul
knows by experience, as the prince of the Apostles says, that it is
called to the admirable light of God, and it shudders with bliss in
its faith.

"God inhabits, says the Apostle, inaccessible light, which no
man sees or can see. Our soul, to reach the sublimity of God,
must be freed from the senses. This is impossible in the present
life by the unaided forces of nature.

"Nevertheless, God has not at any time left man without testimony of himself; he has filled the world with good things, says
the Apostle; he has given the heaven its dew, the earth its
fruitfulness, to all that lives its nourishment, to the heart of man
its joy. And this is what teaches philosophers to attribute nothing low to the majesty of God; to remove from his idea everything
material, all gross mixture; to attribute to him all good and all
virtue, in a perfect degree; to conceive him as the living and
inexhaustible source of all goodness, of all quality, whence all
perfection flows for his creatures; to call him wise, the friend of
truth, the principle of virtue, and to give him other names which
presuppose supreme and absolute perfection; finally, to call him
immense, infinite in his greatness, his power, and his action.

"Such are the great features of the knowledge of God, truly
conformed to the nature of God and to the authority of Holy
Scripture, which philosophy has discovered in the contemplation
of nature (*investigatione cognoverunt*). And yet upon this same
point we recognize the necessity of divine instruction, if we
note that faith not only gives, as has been already stated, to the
simplest and most ignorant, instantly and clearly, knowledge
which sages only obtained with time and effort, but that it also
imprints upon the soul a purer and more certain knowledge than
if the intelligence had acquired it by the labor of human thought;
moreover, that the light of faith opens to believers another order of
divine knowledge which the spectacle of nature could never give."

This then is the teaching of the universal catechism. The
whole question is here treated, regulated, and judged.

Our reason can by itself (*ipsa per se*) discover (*investigare, investigatione cognoscere*) many truths touching the knowledge of God, his existence, his perfections, and his infinity (*bonorum omnium perfectam vim . . . immensam et infinitam virtutem*). As for the other order of divine truths, those which relate to eternal life, reason, by natural light alone, can effect nothing.

Reason in one sense sees God, it contemplates him (*invisibilia Dei contemplatur*), but it is only through his acts (*ab effectibus*); it sees him in the things created by him (*ex rerum effectarum investigatione*). This is an indirect vision.[1] Christian wisdom, on the contrary (*Christiana philosophia*), whose principle is faith, enters heaven and contemplates the source itself of eternal light (*æternum ipsum luminis fontem*); our mind attains to God himself (*ut mens nostra ad Deum perveniat*), which is impossible in this life by the mere forces of nature (*cujus rei facultatem in hac vita naturaliter non habemus*). This therefore is the direct vision, knowledge of the source.

Once again, such is the teaching of Catholic theology in all ages upon this subject.

There is no motive for, and there is no possibility of, ranking reason either higher or lower, whether we rely upon reason or upon faith.

VI.

We have just seen that, according to Saint Thomas Aquinas and all orthodox theologians, and, finally, according to the greatest of all theological authorities, the catechism of the Council of Trent, natural reason, even in the individual, has capabilities, possesses its own certainty, and, by its own unaided effort, discovers and demonstrates truths known to theologians as *preambles of faith*, which form one of the two orders of the divine intelligibleness.

---

[1] Billuart, Dissert., i. art. ii. *Utrum sit Deus?*

But there are limits set by theologians to the power of reason even in the order of these natural truths which form its proper domain.

Saint Thomas, who so vigorously upholds the natural power of reason, nevertheless recognizes the evident limitations and weaknesses of which we all give testimony. He asserts that if men had no means save reason for attaining a knowledge of God, even in that of the two intelligible orders to which reason can attain, three things would result.[1] "First, few men would acquire a knowledge of God. Second, this small number of privileged philosophers would attain that knowledge only after much labor. Third, as error most frequently slips into the researches of human reason, truths, even rigorously demonstrated, would still leave doubts in the mind, *because we do not know the force of demonstration,* and because we actually see so many various systems."

These statements of Saint Thomas Aquinas require no proofs; they are but the simple expression of what every one knows and sees in himself, around him, and in the history of the human mind.

Now, there is, in regard to what natural reason can and cannot do, a very simple theological distinction, but whose profundity, I hope, we shall understand. Human, natural reason, without special help of grace, can do something, but it cannot do everything, even in the natural order of truths. This theology was formulated as follows: "Fallen man may, without the special help of grace, know certain truths of the natural order. The grace of God is essential to fallen man for a complete knowledge of the truths of the natural order." The first of these propositions is evident. The second is what Bossuet expresses so well in this fine phrase: "Human wisdom always falls short somewhere." Fénelon in his turn elaborates it thus: "Men, as an author of our day has very

---

[1] Contra Gentes, l. i. c. iv.

aptly observed, *have not sufficient strength to follow out all their reason.* Thus I am fully persuaded that no man, without grace, could have, of his own unaided natural powers, all the constancy, all the regularity, all the moderation, all the distrust of self, requisite for the discovery of those very truths which do not call for the higher light of faith, — in a word, that natural philosophy which would move, without prejudice, without impatience, without pride, *to the final end of human reason, is a romance of philosophy.* I reckon upon grace alone to guide reason, even in the narrow confines of reason, to the discovery of true religion." This, therefore, is clearly understood, and will be, moreover, developed further on.

VII.

There is, therefore, a fixed and precise limit to the power of purely natural reason. Reason, of itself, may do something, but it cannot do everything, even in the order of natural truth. By the nature of things, the sum total of truths escapes it.

But, yet once again, it may do something; it has its own certainty; it discovers, it demonstrates, with certainty, and knows, up to a certain point, several natural truths, such as the existence of God, his attributes, the moral freedom and spirituality of the soul.

Nevertheless, we must fully agree as to what natural reason, sound reason is, if we would avoid falling into that error which is known as *rationalism*. We must be on our guard against the sophistic ignorance which regards reason as independent of God and men, and as dependent on the individual alone.

In the first place, nothing in man is independent. His very being, his actual being, depends on God, as well as his life, his reason, and all his faculties. This all true philosophers know; all, we have seen, agree with Saint Thomas Aquinas, and declare that reason depends on the light of God. "Eternal wisdom," says Saint Augustine, "ceaseth not for an instant to speak to the rational creature;" and this constant and natural speech of God within us, is reason. The light of men, as the Gospel calls the Word which enlightens every man coming into the world, is the source of reason. Let us not forget this point, for we shall see its consequences.

More yet. As an actual fact, how does reason wake in every man? The Word of God in the soul is the true source of reason; also, in reality, the potential reason in every new-born man is roused by the speech of other men, by the expression of their already formed reason. Man, created rational, develops the germs of his reason, at first because God speaks to him inwardly in the natural light which he causes to shine upon his soul: this is the doctrine of Saint Thomas; and, furthermore, because the human race, by articulate speech, *warns him* — this is the expression of Saint Augustine — actually to hear the truth which he is capable of hearing.

So that reason is developed, in every man, in the same way as faith, according to what Catholic theology teaches in regard to the development of faith.

Faith comes primarily from God, it is a gift of God (*ex interiore instinctu Dei*); it is a supernatural light which man refuses or accepts at will. Secondly, according to Saint Paul, faith cometh by hearing (*fides ex auditu*).

"Faith," says Saint Thomas, "comes chiefly by this diffused light (*fides principaliter ex infusione*); but as for its determination, it cometh by the hearing." [1] "Two things are needful for faith, of which one is the inclination of the heart, which cometh not by hearing, but by grace; the other is the determination of the articles of faith, which cometh by hearing." [2]

[1] 4 d. q. 2, 2.   [2] Epist. ad Rom. x. lect. 2.

Thus God inspires within, God's Church speaks without; and under this double influence free man accepts or rejects this light, by a simultaneous act of intelligence and will.

So, too, with reason. It is, as it were, a luminous germ which God implants in every man; but articulate speech, supervening from without, develops the germ.

Only, it is very plain that in both cases the luminous germ which God sows in the soul is the chief element. Faith comes *chiefly* by the diffused light (*fides principaliter ex infusione*). This light of grace is properly the principle of faith. And as for reason, Saint Augustine and Saint Thomas point out in an admirable manner how adherence to the truth, the very foundation of certainty, comes from this inward light, by which God renders us rational.

" Go not without, enter into thine own self," says Saint Augustine; "it is in the inner man that truth dwells!"[1] "In all that the intelligence hears, what the mind consults is not the word which echoes without, it is the truth which presides within ; the word, perhaps, warns us to consult that truth which presides within."[2]

"The assurance of knowledge and intelligence," says Saint Thomas Aquinas, "comes from the evidence itself of that which is called certain."[3] "It is natural light that gives our soul the assurance of that which it knows in that light, — as, for example, the first principles."[4] "The assurance of what we know, therefore, comes from the light of reason, inwardly given to man by God, and by which God speaks in us ; it does not come from the man who speaks to us from without, save in so far as instruction refers conclusions to their principles, — which, moreover, would give us no certain knowledge, if we had not in advance the assurance of those principles to which the conclusions are referred."[5]

And this rational assurance, according to Saint Thomas Aquinas, is entire. "There is," he says, "a certain basis of

---

[1] De vera Relig., chap. xxxix.
[2] De Magistro, chap. ii. 18.
[3] 3 d. q. art. ii. q. 3.
[4] Contra Gentes, book ii. chap. cliv.
[5] De Verit., quæst. ii. art. i.

truth, with which no semblance of error can be mingled, — for instance, in first principles."[1]

Therefore, with reason as with faith, the chief part is always the inward light given by God, supernatural and natural alike.

Bossuet felicitously compares, upon this head, the generation of reason to that of faith.

"We must not imagine," he says, "that children, in whom reason is beginning to appear, because they cannot arrange and systematize their reasonings, are therefore incapable of feeling the impressions of truth. We see them learn to talk at a still earlier age; how they learn this, how they distinguish between noun and verb, substantive and adjective, they neither know, nor can we who have methodically learned it clearly explain it, so deeply hidden is it. We learn the language of the Church in much the same way. *A secret light leads us to it, in one estate as in the other, —there, in reason; here, in faith.* Reason is developed little by little, and faith infused by baptism does the same."[2]

Thus in both cases there is a secret light at the bottom of the soul, — in the one case, in reason; in the other, in faith. This light, in both cases, is the chief element. Then the language of mankind develops the germ of reason, and the words of the Church develop the germ of faith.

Three things are essential for the development of reason. We must have the soul, capable of knowing; we must have God, sole source of light, shedding his light upon the mirror of the soul, which at first is incapable of seeing it, as the eyes of the new-born child do not see the light of the sun; then mankind intervenes with speech, and the expression of reason already formed, which stimulates the soul to see, and develops, by a most mysterious generation, the obscure germ of reason.

Thus reason is developed. Is it absolutely impossible for

[1] 2 d. 25, art. 20.   [2] Conv. with Claude.

it to be developed otherwise? Cannot God arouse it by his own unaided purpose, without the help of the words of rational and talking man? It would be, to say the least, bold to assert this; or rather, it is plain that we cannot assert it, since, as an actual fact, God alone developed reason in the first man, even as, according to Saint Thomas and all theology, God can, of himself alone, and without the word of the Church, develop faith by revelation in an isolated man.

But let us confine ourselves to stating here that, save for exceptions, such is the law. Individual reason is not in man an absolute and independent power, invariable, immutable, self-subsisting, equal and identical in all; it depends, on the contrary, in its principle and in its development, in its source and in its course, not only upon ourselves, but upon God and the human race. Men impose upon us from the beginning, by the communication of language, a sort of ready made reason, more or less developed, more or less pure, but which contains necessarily all the essential elements of reason; they form us from without, while God unceasingly stimulates within us the living source of original, certain, eternal, infallible reason; and beneath these influences, the free and rational soul, according to its ardor or its sluggishness, its indifference or eagerness for light, its absorption or its effusion, clings more or less closely either to this original source, to this ready made reason, to its essential elements, or to its bastard developments.

From this point of view we can readily define sound reason, and perverse, corrupt reason, — in other words, the true philosophic tendency, and its opposite. We can take a new and very important step in this study of reason compared with faith, and in this analysis of the two degrees of the divine intelligible we shall better understand the progress of the mind towards both, and what we call the effort towards total wisdom.

VIII.

Man's law is this: "Thou shalt love the Lord thy God
with all thy heart, with all thy soul, with all thy mind, and
with all thy strength." This is the first commandment; and
the second, which the Gospel says is like unto it, is this:
"Thou shalt love thy neighbor as thyself."

I say that this double precept, which is the law for the
entire man, also contains the law of reason, and shows us
wherein it is sound and wherein it is corrupt.

In point of fact, rational and free man, placed between
God, the Father and Source of reason, and humanity, which
may perhaps be called the mother of reason, should fulfil
this law in order to maintain his reason sound and sane,
instead of perverting it. Is not this manifest? So soon as
the individual learns to despise humanity, in so far as the
nurse and mother of his intelligence, to consider himself
greater than it and its tradition; so soon as he ceases to love
with all his heart and with all his soul the charm of the
desirable and intelligible, the inner and enduring voice of
God, the source whence light comes to him,—just so soon
that man begins to corrupt and pervert his reason. Whether,
intrenching himself more and more closely in moral and
intellectual egotism, that man thus renders himself ever
more and more incapable, I cannot affirm positively, but I
feel at least that the source of his reason is far above him,
and consequently that the mind should hearken and obey
humbly; if he become accustomed to profane that source, as
being merely himself and dependent merely on himself; if,
which is more serious, he defiantly enter that source which,
nevertheless, is still divine; if he contend with light, and
seek malignly [1] for proofs of light and demonstration of evi-

---

[1] Insidiose. — *Eccli.* xxxii. 20.

dence ; if he take upon himself the mission of constructing evidence, of creating light by his own acts, instead of receiving it as the inspiration of his acts ; if he desire to make himself in some sort the author of his own reason, by taking up his position above first principles, instead of placing himself below them, — if, I say, a man enter upon this path, he has already acquired "that evil heart of unbelief" of which Saint Paul speaks,[1] which departs from the "living God." That soul, in the exercise of its reason, no longer depends upon the divine source of reason; in it, fallible reason, which receives and errs, as Fénelon says, has parted from the immutable reason which gives, lifts up, and illumines; in brief, that mind has departed from the living God.

That soul, therefore, as Scripture says, *is plucked up by the roots, twice dead.*[2] Not only it has not advanced from reason towards faith, not taken root in supernatural light, but it has broken off, as far as in it lay, the natural root of the light of God; it has lost that faith, that innate faith, the principle of reason, of which theology and philosophy speak. And this very thing is the origin of the great sophistical tendency whose excesses and follies, in all ages,[3] have soiled the history of the human mind, and which is precisely reason reversed, philosophy inverted. And, indeed, the attempt to reject God instead of seeking him, the attempt to conquer light instead of yielding to it, the desire to prove evidence by reasoning instead of throwing light on reasoning by evidence ;

[1] Hebrews iii. 12.

[2] Jude 12.

[3] In all ages we encounter the efforts and eccentricities of perverse reason. But it is remarkable that a complete development, theoretical and practical, of sophistry, properly so called, forming a school, and taking the absurd as its principle, has occurred only twice in the intellectual history of the western world, — first, in the time of Gorgias, and again in our own day, by the work of Hegel. We see the remains of it in the wretched sect of atheists and sophists, now (1864) the scorn of French literature, and whom I have made known in a book entitled "Sophists and Criticism."

the habit of rendering unknown that which is known, instead
of moving from the vision of that which is known to that
which is unknown; the incredible mania for aspiring to dig
under the roots to divide them from the earth, instead of
rising with them to their fruits, — is not all this precisely
the opposite to the rational procedure? Now, those who are
acquainted with the history of philosophy know that all this
is practised and has always been practised. And why? Because some souls do not observe in the intellectual order the
law which obliges us to love God more than all things else,
and our neighbors as ourselves. The mind, with secret and
habitual pride, thoughtless though it often be, desires to rise
above humanity and above God. This is an overturning, an
inversion, of all things. It is an imitation of Satan's sin, and
it is the source of the *devilish wisdom* [1] of which Saint James
speaks, which is nothing but an effort in a direction contrary
to wisdom, a task undertaken in aversion from God.

Reason in a man, therefore, sometimes learns to doubt its
own origin; and again it goes so far as to break. with its first
principle.

We find in a contemporary philosopher vigorous descriptions of these two degrees of intellectual ruin. These quotations will better explain to the reader the reality of this
frightful state. "*We believe,*" says Jouffroy, "that is a fact;
but have we any reason to believe what we believe? Is that
which we regard as truth really truth? This universe which
surrounds us, these laws which seem to us to govern it, and
which we torture ourselves to discover, that powerful, wise,
and just Cause which, *on the faith of our reason,* we attribute
to it; those principles of good and ill which humanity respects, and which seems to us the law of the moral world, —
may not all this be an illusion, a consequent dream, and humanity with all this, and we who dream that dream, like all

---

[1] James iii. 17.

the rest? Fearful question, terrible doubt, which rises in the lonely thought of every man who reflects!"[1]

Whence we see that he who describes this doubt, shared in it himself, at least at times, since he elsewhere calls "*a strange illusion,* that of modern philosophers who still persist in solving the impossible *problem of absolute truth,* and in dissipating by means of the human mind a doubt which, striking the human mind itself, can never be destroyed."[2]

But this is how the same thinker describes the intellectual state which supervenes when we overcome that doubt by negation, by the supposition that *no absolute truth exists.* "If our lips," he says, "can state this hypothesis, our intelligence cannot comprehend it. For if certain things exist, they exist in a certain manner, and there are certain relations between them; it is therefore absolutely true that they exist, that they exist in such manner, and that there are such relations between them. If, on the contrary, nothing exists, it is absolutely true that nothing exists. *In order that absolute truth should not exist,* certain things therefore must both exist and not exist at one and the same time; they must have and not have at one and the same time certain modes of existence; and there must be and not be at one and the same time certain relations between them, — which is a contradiction in terms. If everything exists, there is absolute truth; if nothing exists, there is still absolute truth. Whoever denies that there is absolute truth, denies at once reality and nonentity, or rather affirms the co-existence of these two things. The tongue itself refuses to express such an absurdity; it is forced to make that which is the opposite of existence, nonentity, exist!"[3] Jouffroy did not suspect that, while he wrote thus, all these absurdities, or rather these delirious ravings, were

---

[1] Jouffroy, Philosoph. Miscell., 2d edit. p. 187.
[2] Preface to Reid's Works, pp. 190–192.
[3] Jouffroy, Philosoph. Miscell., 2d edit. p. 210.

literally taught in Germany by Hegel, and that the most learned of all nations accepted that teaching.

Reason, therefore, may be corrupted among men in consequence of that *evil heart of unbelief which breaks with the living God* and with collective mankind, and which thus parts the mind from its proper principle and its necessary root.

This is corrupt reason. Then what is sound reason?

Sound reason is that of the man who, receiving, like every other mind, the light which enlightens all, practises the law in regard to that reason-God, as Bossuet says; in other words, loves it, and seeks it with all his strength. Sound reason is the reason of the man doing all that he can, in the mystery of the soul and of conscience, to surrender self to divine reason, its principle and source.

But wherein precisely does this surrender consist, which conjoins us, in the natural order, to the living God?

This must be studied in detail.

CHAPTER III.

WE must know that, even in the natural order, there exists a sort of faith which, by its inward authority, imposes assent upon our mind. There is an intellectual conscience, as there is a moral conscience; and just as the voice of the moral conscience is that of God, the voice of this intellectual conscience is also that of God. This point is of such prime importance that we cannot dwell upon it too long.

Let us see upon what theology, on the one hand, and philosophy, on the other, support themselves in affirming the existence of *natural faith*.

We read in the Scriptures these remarkable words: "In every good work trust thy own soul with faith; for this is the keeping of the commandments. He that believeth in the Lord taketh heed to the commandment."[1]

Clearly this does not refer to the faith whose principle is supernatural light, and whose rule is the Catholic Church; it refers to that faith whose primary cause is natural light, which enlightens all men in their conscience and reason.

The sacred text, say the commentators, does not allude here to theological faith, to Christian supernatural faith (*fides supernaturalis Christiana*), but to that which is the practical dictate of conscience (*fides quæ est practicum conscientiæ dictamen*), which may also be called *moral faith, particular practical faith* (*fides moralis et particularis*

---

[1] Ecclesiasticus xxxii. 27, 28.

practica), or the firm trust of the soul in God (*certa animi
fiducia in Deo*). As for theological faith, we cannot say of
it : " Follow with faith the movements of thy soul, *trust thy
own soul* with faith (*crede ex fide animæ tuæ*)." The object
of theological faith is very God and God alone, not the soul ;
while natural faith, the primary cause of reason, is addressed
to the soul enlightened of God. It is an indirect faith in
God.

Such is also the meaning of Saint Paul's words: " Whatsoever is not of faith is sin (*omne autem quod non est ex fide
peccatum est*)." The Church herself has decided this point,
for she condemned this proposition of Baïus : "All the works
of the infidel [that is, of those who have not supernatural
Christian faith] are sins." [1] Saint Paul, as is also shown by
the context, does not, therefore, refer to supernatural Christian
faith when he says, " Whatsoever is not of faith is sin."
Accordingly, he evidently referred to that *natural faith*
whose primary cause is the voice of God in the conscience
and reason.

Theologians often speak of natural faith under other
names. When the Scriptures say, " The wise man believeth
in the law of the Lord ; " and again, " The fool saith in his
heart, There is no God," — it is clear that the words *wise* and
fool signify the soul which has or has not that faith. So
when Saint Augustine says: "We have in the inward man
another sense far more sublime than the outward sense, it
is that which teaches us to discern between the just and the
unjust ;" it is plain that he alludes to what Perrone calls
" The faith which is the practical dictate of the conscience."
It is also clear that this latter theologian has in view the
same inward fact when, speaking of feeling in general, he
expresses himself thus: " We do not intend to refuse man
those feelings which the beneficent hand of the Creator has

[1] Omnia opera infidelium sunt peccata. — 35 *Baii.*

placed in the heart of man to lead him more readily and gently to truth, justice, and order. We admit a *rational sense* (*sensum rationalem*), which impels the mind to truth and enjoys it. We admit a *moral sense*, which, by its nature, approves that which is just and virtuous in itself, takes pleasure in it, condemns and detests evil. We admit a *sense of the beautiful*, which teaches man to love and enjoy all order and all beauty. He who would tear from the human heart this triple sense which God himself has placed in it, and which is born of that general and unconquerable charm of the desirable and intelligible which never quits the soul, — that man would mutilate human nature and deprive it of its most essential element." [1]

This sense which the charm of the desirable and intelligible, identical with God, awakens in us, is assuredly the divine sense; and this sense, which leads us to distinguish at once between good and evil, is that practical dictate of conscience which our author calls faith.

II.

But we find in the Scriptures a chapter which throws most beautiful and brilliant light on this question. Consider these divine texts with us for a moment: —

"God created man from the earth, and made him in his own image." Here we have the creation of man's body and of his soul, in the image of God.

"Then God turned man anew into this image, and clothed him with virtue like unto his own." [2] It is difficult not to see, in this second verse, the elevation of man to the supernatural life. The sacred author, having spoken of the creation, alludes directly after to this new creation, by which

[1] Perrone, Prælect. theol., vol. ii. p. 1330.
[2] Eccli. xvii.

God resumes his creature, converts him, brings him back to himself, clothes him with virtue like unto his own ; that is to say, endues him with his proper quality.

But soon the sacred text speaks of the knowledge and *sense* which God gives to man; and the distinction between the two orders, natural and supernatural, becomes fully evident.

" Counsel, and a tongue, and eyes, ears, and a heart, gave he them to understand. Withal he filled them with the knowledge of understanding, and showed them good and evil. He set his eye upon their hearts, that he might show them the greatness of his works. He gave them to glory in his marvellous acts for ever, that they might declare his works with understanding."

Evidently, the allusion here is to the natural light which teaches us to know God *through his works*. The allusion is to that knowledge which God gives the mind in creating it, which is reason, and to that power of distinguishing between good and evil, which is conscience. And, consequently, the *sense* with which God fills the heart, when he sets his eye on it, is that natural sense of which we speak, which makes man feel the greatness of God in his work, and teaches him to rise from created beauties to their Creator.

But what follows is manifestly of the supernatural order:

" Besides this, he gave them knowledge, and the law of life for an heritage. He made an everlasting covenant with them, and showed them his justice and his judgments. Their eyes saw the majesty of his glory, and their ears heard his glorious voice."

This added gift, this heritage of the law of life ; this everlasting covenant, this justice of God ; this sight of the majesty of God no longer in his works, but in his own glory which they see with their eyes ; the power to hear his very voice with their own ears, — all this is supernatural.

Thus, in these complete and connected texts we clearly perceive the strong distinction between that which is natural and that which is supernatural; and it is plain that the sense with which God fills our heart, when he sets his eye on it, at the same time that he gives us knowledge, is of the purely natural order, and that we must henceforth distinguish between a natural divine sense and a supernatural divine sense, as we distinguish between a natural and a supernatural knowledge of God, a natural and a supernatural love of God. Whence it would follow that each of the three powers of the soul may attain God in two modes, naturally and supernaturally, and that there is a complete parallelism between the two orders. Saint John says: "The Son of God hath given us a *sense* to know the true God." This supernatural divine sense, which is faith or its principle, corresponds to an essential element of human nature, to that natural divine sense to which the sacred text refers, and through which we know God by his works; and this natural divine sense is the natural faith of which Saint Paul speaks, the faith in which we must trust our soul, say the Scriptures, the faith which theology calls "the practical dictate of conscience."

Thus the word "faith" has, in theology, two meanings. We distinguish between supernatural Christian faith, whose principle is the light supernaturally given of God, and natural faith, whose principle is the light which, in his conscience and reason, enlightens every man coming into this world, — "natural human faith which is in the individual as it were the basis of human reason." [1]

III.

And now what do philosophers think on this point?
Philosophers use the word, in every instance, beginning

[1] On Grace and Nature, by the Abbé Rohrbacher, p. 96.

with Aristotle, to signify spontaneous, immediate adherence to the primary, indemonstrable principles of reason, whether speculative or practical.

The principle of demonstration, says Aristotle, is not demonstration (ἀποδείξεως ἀρχὴ οὐκ ἀπόδειξις), so too the principle of knowledge is not knowledge (οὐδ' ἐπιστήμης ἐπιστήμη). All knowledge being discursive, there is no knowledge of principles (τῶν ἀρχῶν ἐπιστήμη μὲν οὐκ ἂν εἴη).[1] Assured and primary principles are those which *create faith* of themselves, without borrowing their certainty elsewhere (τὰ μὴ δι' ἑτέρων ἀλλὰ δι αὐτῶν ἔχοντα τὴν πίστιν). When these principles are referred to, we cannot ask the why and wherefore (οὐ δεῖ ἐν ταῖς ἐπιστημονικαῖς ἀρχαῖς ἐπιζητεῖσθαι τὸ διὰ τί). Each principle, taken in itself, inspires faith (ἀλλ' ἑκάστην τῶν ἀρχῶν αὐτὴν καθ' ἑαυτὴν εἶναι πιστήν). We cannot demonstrate them, we have no knowledge of them, and it is impossible to say anything in regard to them (ἀδύνατον εἰπεῖν τι περὶ αὐτῶν), for the very reason that they are anterior to everything.[2] How are these principles known ? By experience, which arouses in the soul what was latent there (ἐκ δ' ἐμπειρίας ἢ ἐκ παντὸς ἡμερήσαντος τοῦ καθόλου ἐν τῇ ψυχῇ). The mind attains these principles by an *inductive movement* (τὰ πρῶτα ἐπαγωγῇ γνωρίζειν ἀναγκαῖον), by which very thing sensation reveals the universal in the soul (καὶ γὰρ καὶ αἴσθησις οὕτω τὸ καθόλον ἐμποιεῖ).[3] This inductive movement, which awakens the universal in the soul, is, as it were, an act of rational faith, which adheres to primary principles.

And indeed this necessary adhesion,[4] in intelligible light, to primary, indemonstrable principles, of which we have no knowledge, concerning which we can say nothing, and which sophists deny because they ask in vain for their demonstra-

---

[1] Post Analyt., 19.   [3] Post Analyt., 19.
[2] Topiq., i. 1, 2.   [4] Ibid.

tion, — this adhesion Aristotle calls *faith* (πίστις) wherever he speaks of it. He uses the very word which has since been elevated by the Fathers of the Church to mean Christian faith. Not that he understands by that word a blind opinion ; on the contrary, he regards it as an adhesion of the mind to evidence, in intelligible light. But is it not thus that Saint Thomas likewise understands it when he says, "Just as man, by the natural light of intelligence, adheres to principles, so too by the light of faith, divinely diffused in the soul, man adheres to the things of faith"?[1] And Thomassin understands it as Saint Thomas does when he calls faith adhesion to the evidence of primary principles.

The Alexandrine philosophers, urged on by the Christians, went farther on this road, and developed the germs which Aristotle and Plato contained upon this point. Proclus says many beautiful things of them, which Thomassin quotes and applauds. And Saint Athanasius, in his life of Saint Antony, aptly sets forth this doctrine. He relates that Saint Antony, in a journey to Alexandria, desiring to convert certain philosophers to the Christian faith, began by talking to them of philosophical natural faith, saying to them "That this faith is, of all modes of knowledge, the most certain (ἡ διὰ πίστεως ἐνέργεια . . . ταύτην εἶναι τὴν ἀκριβῆ γνῶσιν)." Then he formally put this question to them : "What is, in all things, and especially if it relates to God, the most perfect mode of knowledge? Is it by demonstration, or by the action of faith in the soul? And which is anterior to the other, — the action of faith, or rational demonstration ?" The philosophers at once replied. "The action of faith." The question was well put by Saint Antony, and the philosophers answered very aptly according to Aristotle and Plato.

But on this point a strange work has been effected in modern philosophy.

[1] 2ª. 2ᵃᵉ. q. ii. art. 3.

Descartes said, "*I believe* in the existence of the world, because God is truthful, and cannot deceive me." He went too far, and exceeded sound theology, as well as sound philosophy. He employed a subterfuge, an argument, in order to believe in the existence of the world; while that natural, rational faith referred to by Aristotle, and to which Descartes meant to refer, is immediate, and clings to its object itself, without any outside mixture of argument, — its object being precisely a primary, indemonstrable fact. But Descartes, introducing argument between that faith and its object, gives idealists and sceptics cause to deny the existence of bodies. Kant, indignant at this exaggeration, strove to re-establish the truth; he undertook radically to ruin that scepticism and idealism. To this end, he distinguishes abstract reason, separated from that rational, natural faith which makes it sound, solid, and straightforward; he distinguishes it from sound reason, from straightforward reason, which depends " upon that rational faith," so called by him in exact terms (*Vernunftglaube*), " which alone," he says, " can give human reason its bearings." [1]

But Kant, despite his mighty powers, is a clumsy, awkward, and confused master, who becomes embarrassed in the first half of his demonstration, loses his breath in the second, and who, by this distinction carried to excess, opens the way for all the series of sophists to which Germany has given birth. They take possession of precisely this reason, artificially abstracted from rational faith, as being reason itself, true reason, total reason, and they make use of it to destroy everything. And therein they justify Kant; since, starting with this reason out of its latitude, they actually end, as we now see, in denying the first principles, certain and undemonstrable though they be, whether of practical or of theoretical reason, to the point of expressly contradicting the axiom

---

[1] Was heisst sich im Denken orientiren. — *Opusc.* vi.

given by Aristotle as the last degree of evidence possible : "That there is no medium between affirmation and negation, and that it is impossible that one and the same thing should at the same time exist and not exist."

Meantime, calmer minds try to maintain common-sense. The Scotch patiently anlayze thought, and find indeed that there is everywhere, in the beginning, in what relates to primary facts and principles, an element of immediate, spontaneous, unreasoned adhesion, which they call faith. This fact, with its developments, is perhaps the only useful result of Scotch philosophy. But it is important. It is an effort to return to truth.

Nevertheless, it is by no means a discovery ; and our theology, as we have seen, had long been familiar with it. Even Aristotle had already comprehended it.

IV.

Here Thomassin is particularly to be admired. Whether considered as theologian or as philosopher, he has said everything that there is to be said on this capital point; and, to my knowledge, he is the only one. Let us recall his chapter entitled, "Deeper than intelligence itself, there exists in the soul a secret sense which *touches* God, rather than sees or hears him." Thomassin often reproduces this idea, for he prizes it, and justly. In his Treatise on God, he again expresses himself thus : —

"The soul,[1] by a sort of innate presage, so soon as it is freed from the distractions and defilements of the senses, and, restored to itself, has recovered its dignity, — the soul naturally suspects and *feels* the sovereign principle, indescribable and ineffable. It feels this by an intimate and secret contact,[2] which touches God, ever present in the centre of the soul to protect its life. But

[1] De Deo, lib. iv. cap. v. 7.   [2] Ibid., 8.

this immaterial and divine contact is the most mysterious point of the education of minds; we know anything of it rather by experience than by speech. Our soul proceeds, without any intermediary, from the sovereign principle; and it is the hand of God which produces it, touches it, moulds it, and forms it; and it, in its turn, — for all contact is mutual, — feels God and touches him, when it is not wrapped in the rough bark of low things, fastened to it by the attraction of a gross love."

But what is the name of this divine touch, this divine sense? It is faith, according to Thomassin, — natural faith, as the Alexandrian philosophers understood it, to whom Saint Anthony addressed himself; faith, as Plato understood it in the book of the Laws, according to Proclus, quoted by Thomassin. And here our author distinguishes several meanings of the word *faith*. He says, —

"There is that faith by which the loftiest souls, which have attained the peace of the highest beatitude, possess God and enjoy him, — a very different faith from that wholly human faith which binds us, through opinion, to unknown things; different, also, from that loftier faith through which our soul clings, without reasoning or proof, to the evident light and immediate certainty of first principles. That of which we speak here is anterior, superior, to the other two. Deeply hidden in the soul, it teaches us thoroughly that which we could not otherwise have known, because we could not have seen, and to accept what we cannot understand." [1]

"It is this faith which feels ineffable Being and sovereign Good rather than understands them." [2]

Thomassin quotes on this head very beautiful passages from Proclus, notably this: "Faith is the ineffable bond between all souls, all minds, and God. Faith is anterior to knowledge. Faith is that which leads souls into the hidden nature of God." [3]

---

[1] De Deo., book vi. chap. v. 11.   [2] Ibid.   [3] Ibid.

That is, there is in the soul, in the opinion of philosophers and theologians, whose views Thomassin sums up, a natural sense which feels God, a sense which some theologians and philosophers call faith. And this faith, this *divine sense*, is nothing but the sovereign use of one of the three functions of the soul, — *to feel, to know, to will.* The soul *feels* everything, — God, itself, and the world.

From all which precedes, we see that in philosophy as well as in theology we find allusions to a certain *faith* which is not supernatural Christian faith, which is therefore natural, whose principle is the voice of God in the conscience and reason, — a faith through which we must needs cling to the theoretical and practical first principles of reason ; a faith which, indeed, all minds do not possess, since there are actually those who deny all logical and moral laws, whether they deny them from explicit and avowed doubt, or from some obscure but determinate system, as was seen in Greece and is seen in Germany.

It is not an abuse of words to call faith, with Aristotle and the Scotch philosophers, the adhesion of the mind to the evidence of first principles, or to the evidence of primary facts. *To see* and *to believe* are not opposite things. To believe is not the opposite of to see, but to demonstrate and understand thoroughly. For instance, man sees the world without understanding it. Saint Augustine expresses himself very happily when he says, " He who has intelligence has also faith ; but he who has faith has not always intelligence." [1] Saint Augustine here points out this fundamental fact, — namely, that there is in all human light a root of faith ; that for man, faith exists with intelligence, with perception. Why ? Because man never possesses the *prius absolu* of anything, being only secondary and not primary intelligence. But when he sees and is bathed in light, he

[1] De Utilit. cred., cap. xi.

does not see everything, and his gaze does not pierce any
being, any truth, through and through. Even when he
shall see God face to face, says theology, he will not understand him.   Faith, in one sense, says Saint Thomas, will endure in that light; it will disappear as an enigma, but
it will endure as knowledge.[1]   Its substance will remain.
There will therefore *still be faith in vision*, as in the vision
of this world by our eyes there is faith, as in the evidence
of first principles there is faith, — and this because we do
not see the whole of anything; because we cannot see
God, or the world, or the principles of reason, to as great a
degree as God sees them.   In all things we start from a
light greater than ourselves, and from data which transcend
us, and which always leave us with questions unsolved.
Faith is essential to the being who receives light; faith is
the first acceptance of light, it is adherence to him who
gives it.   Faith is that region of reason of which Bossuet
speaks, — "that region unknown to man in his own actions
and in his own conduct, which is the secret region wherein
God acts, and the spring which he sets in motion."[2]

In this sense, therefore, we may, with Aristotle, call faith
the adhesion of the mind to evidence and to indemonstrable
first principles.

V.

Having fully established these two meanings of the word
faith, natural faith and supernatural Christian faith, let us
return to the question with which we started: What is
sound reason?

Sound reason is that which is not severed from *rational
faith*, its basis and its compass, without which, as some one
has aptly expressed it, it loses its bearings. "Faith," says
Saint Thomas Aquinas, "is, in the supernatural order, what

[1] 1ᵃ, 2ᵃᵉ, q. 67, 5, c.   [2] Vol. xxv. p. 394.

the evidence of principles is in the natural order."[1] This is admirable in its depth.

Thus sound reason is that which is not set apart from its source in the root of the soul, which is not set apart from that point of which Plato speaks, whence God suspends the soul to himself, which he calls the *root* of the soul.[2] Sound reason is that which clings to the charm of desirability and intelligibility, so called by Aristotle ; to those simple operations of the soul into which error does not enter, says Saint Thomas Aquinas ;[3] to that supreme, infallible reason which supports and corrects, of which Fénelon speaks ; to that inner sanctuary, that inmost core, that centre of which Bossuet and all the mystics speak, where the truth makes itself heard, where pure and simple ideas are collected and contemplated ; to that hidden spring of which Bossuet also speaks, " Which has not now all its pristine power, but clearly shows us, by a certain vigor, that it is rooted in some higher principle."

Sound reason is that which does not break with the divine sense, that divine touch, that secret sense, deeper than intelligence, and by which God is touched rather than understood or seen.

Sound reason, in fine, is that which, in every man, conjoined at some point to that of God and to the common reason of the human race, fulfils the law which consists in loving, even in the intellectual order, God and man.

And perverse reason is that which breaks with that necessary root of all its legitimate development, with that rational, natural faith whose existence we have just established. Corrupt reason is that which by some secret egoism confines itself to the unduly narrow limits of individual thought, makes of itself a cistern, instead of a channel of living water,

[1] 3 d. 26, q. 2, 2ᵐ, and 2ᵃ, 2ᵃᵉ. q. ii. art. 3.
[2] In Joann. Tract., xxvi. 2.
[3] Et in hac operatione animi non est error.

and cuts itself off from its source in God and from its human affluents.

Now, thanks to God, sound reason is that with which we are born, the Word, on the one hand, enlightening all men in this world; and on the other hand, mankind imposing upon us, by articulate speech, the outward forms of reason, and giving us, in general, a practical example of its use; and hence theologians and philosophers agree in recognizing that reason naturally leads us to what is true.

"Human reason," says Perrone,[1] "although limited, not only by its nature tends to truth, but may also attain to it with certainty. This common-sense recognizes, and this, in all ages, has been professed by those who have philosophized soundly. Christian and catholic religion admits and teaches this, concerning the value of human reason." "When," adds Perrone, "Luther denied free-will, in the sixteenth century, he at the same time maintained that the intelligence, wholly obscured, was incapable of knowing any truth without the light of revealed faith; mocking at the Scholastic doctors (notably Saint Thomas Aquinas), insulting all philosophy as hostile to Christianity, asserting that all the virtues of philosophers are vices, and all their discoveries errors. Luther was condemned by the Church on this point, as on all others. The Jansenists, taking up this doctrine in part, were condemned in their turn, and Lamennais, although he mitigated it somewhat, was also condemned."[2]

Whence it follows that, according to Catholic teaching, as in the eyes of good sense, we are born gifted with more or less sound reason, feeble though it be, yet capable of development and certainty. We are born into the human race as into a sort of natural church, where the word of our fathers, an authority worthy of respect, stimulates, regulates, and develops the germs of reason.

[1] Perrone, vol. ii. p. 1261.   [2] Perrone, *loc. cit.*

VI.

But we have not said everything on the subject of sound reason. It still remains for us to consider the noble words of Fénelon which have already been quoted: "I count on grace alone to guide reason, even in the narrow limits of reason. . . . Men have not sufficient strength to follow their reason to the end. . . . That natural philosophy which could advance without prejudice, without impatience, without pride, to the end of purely human reason, is a philosophic romance."

We believe that it is strictly true to say that man cannot, of himself, without grace, advance to the end of purely human reason. This we shall show later.

But here, let us first note, with Thomassin, that, in natural sound reason, there is, besides reason itself, — whose light is a ray from the face of God shining into the soul, says Saint Thomas, — there is, moreover, a constant aid from God, which incites, moves, urges to action and development the germ of reason.[1] Not only does this light come from God and belong to God, but also God actually continues to diffuse it, to incite and direct its radiance. As when a star shines in heaven, and besides its ordinary lustre and its peaceful light it sends out flashes and scintillations to provoke attention, and to show that what the spectator sees is not a dead luminary, but a luminary which lives and acts: so, too, in the light of the human soul, besides the gift itself of reason which man possesses once for all, there are flashes, movements, and renewals which come from God, and which are aids, benefits, and stimulants from God in the natural order.

There is more yet. As an actual fact, historically, no man is given over to natural reason alone, and to the natural aids alone of God. When we are told that the Word is the light

[1] De Gratia, tract. iii. cap. iii.

that enlightens every man coming into this world, this refers to both supernatural and natural light. God, desiring to raise all men to the supernatural order, calls them all thither by his grace, by his supernatural stimulations. "God," says Saint Thomas Aquinas, "as incessantly effects the justification of man (the appeal to supernatural justice) as the sun incessantly effects the illumination of the air."[1] Again, elsewhere, Saint Thomas utters these important words: "God desires to raise man to the supernatural state; and the effect of that desire is *the order itself of nature, so disposed as to lead to eternal life;* it is the supernatural and natural stimulations, ever offered to all, which lead to that end."[2] The reason, like the will, is therefore perpetually, and in all ways, assisted by God, who unceasingly urges every soul to its double natural and supernatural perfection.

When Fenelon says, "I count on grace alone to guide reason," he at once adds, —

"But I believe, with Saint Augustine, that God gives to every man a first germ of intimate and secret grace, which is imperceptibly blended with reason, and which prepares man to pass gradually from reason to faith. This is what Saint Augustine calls the germ of faith, like a germ conceived in the breast of a mother (*inchoationes fidei, conceptionibus similes*). It is a very remote beginning of a nearer and nearer approach to faith, as a very formless germ is the beginning of the child to be born long after. God blends the beginning of the supernatural gift with the remnants of our depraved nature so that the man who possesses them united together in his own heart cannot part them, and bears within him a mystery of grace of which he is profoundly ignorant. This is what Saint Augustine means by these kindly words: 'Little by little, Lord, with thy gentle and merciful hand, thou dost caress and reform my heart.' Man already possesses the sublimest wisdom, but it is still milk to feed babes (*ut infantiæ nostræ lactesceret sapientia tua*). The germ of faith must begin to bloom before it can be distinguished from reason.

[1] Contra Gentes, book iii. cap. clix.   [2] Sent., book i. dist. 46, q. i. art. i.

" This secret and shapeless germ is the beginning of the new man (*conceptionibus similes*); it is not reason alone, or nature left to herself, it is nascent grace hiding beneath nature to correct it gradually."

Admirable words! Yet we must beware of these comparisons. Yes, God mingles a secret germ of grace with the natural sound reason, but it is a germ not yet fertilized, not permanent in the soul; these are impulses of actual grace, but not of habitual grace, for that would be faith itself, — it would be intelligence raised above itself into a supernatural state.

But, in this sense, all theologians agree that, historically, sound reason is always sustained by generous aid from God, natural and supernatural.

What sound reason is, and what it can do unaided, is therefore, in theology, a purely theoretical question. All theologians, even those who grant the most to the natural powers of reason, — such, for instance, as Perrone, — admit that in fact and in history, reason, of itself alone, has not only never discovered the sum total of truths of the natural order, but it has not even found that portion of natural truth which, logically, it was possible for it to discover; that, for instance, philosophers such as Plato and Aristotle received supernatural aid from God for the discovery of various great natural truths; moreover, that they evidently made use of the data of tradition, deposited in language, where many traces of primitive lights may be found, given by God to the first man.

Thus, in short, sound natural reason is always sustained by God, who desires to elevate it (*ipse ordo naturæ in finem salutis*). God sustains it, stimulates and guides it by his supernatural and natural aid ; that is to say, God not only co-operates in every movement of thought, as in every other movement of his creatures, but he also co-operates in those movements by upholding and directing them, as Fénelon so admirably explains when he speaks of the two reasons within us, — one which is prone to err, and the other which corrects the first.   Moreover, God, desiring to raise all men to the supernatural order, unites the germ of grace with the natural germ of reason, and strives to fertilize that germ by his incitements; and we may say of natural reason what Saint Thomas says of the whole order of nature, — that that order, by God's desire to save all men, moves towards the supernatural goal, and that every intelligence unceasingly receives both natural and supernatural impulses which urge it towards this end.[1]

[1] We find, in a lecture by Lacordaire, thoughts exactly agreeing with our own in regard to natural faith and the relation of the two orders of the divine intelligible.   " Even in axioms," says the eloquent and learned Dominican, "I have made clear to you an obscure element, and consequently an element of faith ; not that axioms are not final evidence, but that evidence does not prevent us from seeking something beyond them, — the *substantial axiom* instead of the *logical axiom*, eternal light instead of communicated light, intrinsic truth instead of truth descended on a mind which may lose it. . . . Which leads you to see that the natural world is joined to a higher world, to the divine world ; natural knowledge to divine knowledge, natural faith to divine faith." — 1836, Lecture xii.

CHAPTER IV.

FROM what precedes, we have learned what sound reason is. It is reason such as it is when it is maintained in its natural relations; it is reason not artificially mutilated, not sophistically separated from the will first, and then from its true root in the centre of the soul, which is the divine sense, natural faith in God; it is reason not in revolt against the common reason of mankind, not insensible of the generous aids which God gives to every soul. "We must," says a refined thinker, " avoid, in our intellectual operations, all that parts the mind from the soul." Nothing could be better expressed. We must not set the mind apart. We must leave to thought its life in the entire soul and in the nourishment which the soul receives from God and from humanity. Whoever proceeds otherwise, maims and mutilates himself, forces his mind to retreat, loses his reason, and descends to sophistry, — even to the formal negation of the essential principles of reason, even to the negation of evidence and axioms. In short, sound reason, as an actual fact, is always sustained by the grace of God, which mingles with it to lead man to the supernatural order.

This established, we shall necessarily agree when we come to investigate what reason may and may not do; and nothing, I believe, should any longer prevent our recognition of what must be called the highest power and the highest achievement of reason.

This final achievement of reason is expressed by Perrone in the proposition: " Individual reason may by itself with certainty recognize and demonstrate the possibility, utility, and necessity of divine revelation." [1]

This theological theorem seems to us to be of prime importance and beauty. If we succeed in fully establishing its truth, it will be of immense consequence; the bond between Religion and Philosophy will then be found.

The question, it seems to us, may be reduced to knowing whether Descartes and Saint Augustine were right in uttering these great and fundamental words: " I am, and I feel that I am, an imperfect thing, incomplete, dependent on another, unceasingly tending and aspiring towards something better and greater than myself."

It is enough, I say, to prove this theological theorem, if we know whether human reason is or is not an imperfect thing, incomplete and dependent, incessantly tending and aspiring towards something better and greater than itself.

If it be true, as Scripture tells us, that the light which is in us is only darkness, that is, that our reason, compared to the supernatural light, is but the shadow of the light of God; if we may say of reason what the poet says of the sun, —

" Sun, shadow of his light ! "

if this be that which Plato perceived when, in the lower degree of the intelligible, he saw nought but " divine phantasms and shadows of that which is;" if Aristotle understood the same thing when he distinguished between knowledge coming from above, and that which comes from below, between that which is borrowed from visible things, and that which is pure intellect, and when he showed us above our reason another light which is, which lives, which is self-thinking, which is eternal, immutable, which is not ours, which is not essential

[1] Perrone, ii. 1638.

to the soul, from which the soul may be separated without impairing the reason; if the certain and actual objects perceived by reason, according to Saint Augustine, are clearly not God, but demonstrate him; if, as Saint Bernard says (in which he is followed by Saint Thomas and Thomassin), natural light be a reflection of God in the mirror of the soul, so that the soul sees merely the reflection of God, not God himself, and only sees that reflection in that it sees itself, which Descartes also says; if it be true that hence this knowledge of God, such as it is, as Saint Thomas everywhere declares, in which he is confirmed by the Roman Catechism and all theology, is always a thing apart from the creature, never direct and immediate, for that would be to see God, a thing impossible naturally, — if all this be true, if such be the nature of reason, do you believe that reason knows nought of it?

How did Aristotle and Plato and so many others know it, if reason is incapable of knowing it? Are Descartes' lucid words false? Is not the reason of every man, as well as his will, conscious of its own imperfection and incompleteness? Is it not conscious of its dependence on a higher being? Does it not incessantly tend and aspire to something better and greater than itself?

Yes, reason, every one may recognize for himself, as we see in history, seeks a light, not only brighter than its present light, but also a very different light, both of a different nature and better and greater than itself.

Men far advanced in the works of the mind know this: we need a better light; that which we have neither nourishes nor gives life. Shadows, phantasms, axioms, reflections, and abstractions do not satisfy our desire for knowledge, admiration, and love.

What soul is there, still living beneath the weight of years and of the most vast and dearly bought human knowledge, which does not sometimes compare these views of abstract thought with the living reality, with the vision of the earth, fertile, blooming, radiant in sunshine, with the penetrating and mysterious odors of nature, the savor of plants and their generous products, with the vigor of the vital air and the stimulating fluids which penetrate, revive, and electrify us, with the sight of men who seek and hope, with the spectacle of whatever remains to us of nobility and human beauty, with the commerce of souls, with love! What soul is there, I say, yet living, who, when this contrast is made clear, does not feel it and say: "My head is filled with shadows, genuine shadows, undoubted shadows, but still shadows! I have spent my life in discovering the world, in studying its motive springs; I have not solved the enigma; I have succeeded in grasping only certain portions, and the little that I retain is but a dead copy of life."

Read again Goethe's inexhaustible sarcasms in regard to what he calls "a foolish fellow who speculates!"[1] Above all, re-read the grander and more sublime cry which disgust for worldly wisdom wrings from Solomon: —

"Vanity of vanities! all is vanity! I gave my heart to seek and search out by wisdom all things that are done under the sun; and behold, all is vanity and vexation of spirit. I said in mine heart, Go to, now, I will prove thee with mirth. There is nothing better for a man than that he should eat and drink, and that he should make his soul enjoy good in his labor. There is no good, but for a man to rejoice in his life."

What does this prove? That our senses show us realities, and our reason, in so far as it dwells in the natural light alone, phantasms. Do not misunderstand me; I say divine, certain, axiomatic, absolute, eternal, evident phantasms, but still phantasms.

Well! shall I therefore relapse from reason into the senses,

---

[1] Ein Kerl der speculiert. — *Faust.*

like Goethe's hero, like Solomon himself? Or rather, quite
the contrary, shall I not do better to say : " Let us rise higher.
Let us see if that reflection does not proclaim a Sun, and if
there be not a Being, a life corresponding to those ideas of
eternity, immensity, perfection, and infinity, which are perhaps in my mind the cold, dry copy of eternal life? May
we, by some wondrous revelation, behold the Being to whom
these traits answer? May we touch, feel and love him?
May we, by some great and holy initiation, hold commerce
with him and live his life, as we live in nature and humanity ?"

That such a Being exists, says reason, I know. It is God.
Everything proves it. Now, what motive have I to deny
that I can see him, and that this great revelation is possible?
I indeed see material bodies and the earth, which are unlike
myself; I see myself and am conscious of myself; I see the
mind and soul of other men in their words and looks; I see
immutable truths, as empty as they are assured, which only
stimulate my glance to seek fuller light : then why should
I not see God? Cannot God, in whose light I see and know
everything, make himself known and seen, as a mind makes
itself known to my mind, as my soul is revealed to itself?

I defy all the knowledge in the world to find any trace
whatsoever of impossibility here ; or rather, I affirm this possibility simply because I conceive this new relation of the
soul to God, and seek for him.

I assert the possibility of this revelation, because I see that
it is useful and necessary.

It is necessary :[1] for if there be no living intelligible object
which I can see as I see the outward world, if all intelligibility be abstract, as atheists say, is intelligibility worth one
hour's toil? Intelligibility then ceases to be a future, a hope,

---

[1] Necessary in the sense in which the Treatises on the True Religion have
proved the necessity of revelation, and not in the sense that Baïus maintained,
that the supernatural light is due to nature.

a felicity. The intelligible is no longer heaven, or rather it is the pagan heaven, the kingdom of shades, wherein the loftiest souls must needs exclaim, with Achilles: "Why am I not again upon the earth!   Why am I not the slave of the poorest laborer!   Better that than to reign over all these shadows." No one indeed cares to reign over shadows.   Better be the living slave of a real and living being.

If there be not, beyond the cold light of my reason, the holy light, the purifying light, the vivifying light, the loving light, — a flood of ecstatic delights as well as a flood of radiance, — then my reason has deceived me. I should have done better to till the ground and rest satisfied with its gifts. I should do better even now to give up the vain labor of thought, to return to living reality, and descend from that chill height which it was idle to climb.

And indeed, this temptation assails, at the pinnacle of life, most minds which have sought light by the labor of thought. When man has passed his highest point, and begins to go down into the valley of old age, he hesitates. Then comes a critical period, when the soul returns to earth, when the senses revive and put forth all their most dangerous refinements. Medical science recognizes and teaches this.[1]

This is a lesson which nature gives us. When man has risen to his highest point, has attained his natural eminence, and has climbed as far as human strength can go, he should mount higher yet, — he should rise to the divine; if not, he will sink to the animal.

Yes, if the man who has gained the summit of life, after spending so much time in the ascent, does not desire to descend rapidly into the valley of his tomb; if, while he is yet full of unrealized hopes, unemployed powers, and possible progress, both conceived and hoped for, if he do not desire to see all his powers, all his perfections, his clear

[1] Burdach, Physiology, v. 127.

judgment, his penetration, his enthusiasm, his courage, his nobility, his very heart, decay with inconceivable rapidity; if he do not desire to return to matter, to return to earth, and to degenerate into all the indolence, the grossness, and blindness of the flesh; if he do not desire to see that flesh, at the same time that it loses its beauty, resume its tyranny over the soul, to restore it more quickly to the dust, — if man desire not this sad end, he must accept and traverse from above, and by an heroic effort, the great crisis of middle life. He must repeat the prayer of the prophet: "Lord, I am thy work! In the midst of my days, give me fresh life; in the midst of my life, show me thy light!" He must at last decide to cease being a son of earth, and become a child of heaven; to pass, still living, by the sacrifice and rupture of all earthly ties, into the higher sphere of existence; to enter wholly into supernatural reality. He must pass from nature to God, leave self behind, and enter the infinity of God, — ascend to heaven, in a word, like Elijah in the chariot of fire.

If he dare not do this; if he cannot give up earth and all its vanities; if his search after wisdom was mixed with stratagems and sensuality; if he shrink from indispensable and entire sacrifice, — he relapses into animalism; and the life of insight will soon seem to him more empty and idle than the games of childhood and the illusions of youth.

Now, it is impossible that a vain effort, followed by a fall and a return to the senses, should be the whole destiny of reason; it is impossible that the effort, be it what it may, after wisdom and truth, should be mere vanity. Therefore we must believe in the chariot of fire and in the other light.

Therefore there is, or there may be, says reason, some divine revelation which gives perfect wisdom; and that revelation I must await and seek.

For if, in this belief, a man take up the Gospel and read

these words : " Whosoever believeth in him shall have eternal life;" and these: "Blessed are the pure in heart, for they shall see God;" if he remember that all Christianity lies in offering to mankind means for attaining to the vision of very God, and his possession; that the great news which he bears is the existence of another light, greater, better, than that of reason, — a light which vivifies and beautifies; if we hear Saint Paul call faith the beginning of that light, and define it as the substance of Good to come; if we understand Saint Thomas Aquinas when he declares that this light " is called substantial because it differs from ordinary knowledge, which sees its object from without only, in that divine Faith imparts to the soul the very substance and peculiar beginning of the good things for which we hope," — then reason no longer understands merely the possibility and utility of revelation, but, as another theoretical axiom expresses it, " Man's reason may attain the certainty of the existence of divine revelation," and reason may say, "The revelation which I knew to be possible, useful, and necessary, exists; I behold it, — it is the Gospel."

II.

But this point of the question is one of such radical importance that we must needs dwell upon it, and, if possible, attain exact results in regard to our subject. Now, it seems to me that there are, indeed, at the heart of the question, results so precise that I may venture to call them geometrical.

The point at issue is the necessity, for every man, of the supernatural gift in order to attain his full perfection.

Saint Thomas Aquinas is here again our point of support and our theological authority. Let us quote him first, then we shall see how this point may be like a question in geometry. He says, —

" Throughout the hierarchy of subordinate natures we find that, for the perfection of every lower term, two things are needed, — the one depending on its individual life, the other adding to it the life of the higher term. Now, the created rational nature alone has for its higher and immediate term God himself; the other creatures do not touch the universal.

" The rational nature alone is immediately subordinated to the First Principle, to the Universal Being.

" Thus the perfection of rational nature consists, not only in that which constitutes its individual nature, but also in some supplement which is added to it by a *certain supernatural participation* in the goodness of God. And it is for this very reason that we have already said that the final beatitude of man consists of the supernatural vision of God." [1]

To our thinking, there is a sort of geometrical precision in the theological formulas of Saint Thomas Aquinas. " Harmony," says Leibnitz, " geometry, metaphysics, and morals are everywhere existent." This, I say, seems to hold good of the theology and metaphysics of Saint Thomas, which, moreover, is only Christian science in all its sublimity and precision.

This, then, is what strikes us as geometrical in the proposition that intelligent being, alone immediately subordinated to the universal and the infinite, attains final perfection only by a supernatural participation in the life of God himself.

Man is not and cannot be, of himself, absolutely perfect in anything. Neither in his being, his knowledge, his will, nor his love can he be, by himself, complete, entire, and finished. God alone is a unit, total, perfect in his nature. Man is necessarily partial, mutable, finite, and incomplete in all, for the very reason that he is created, and lives within the limits of time.

This is true of man, as of every creature. But there is

[1] 2ª, 2ªᵉ, q. ii. art. 3.

this difference between man and all the other inhabitants of our earth, that man alone, says Saint Thomas Aquinas, is immediately subordinated to the universal or the infinite.

This means, if I do not err, that, every created being having its number, its weight, and its measure, — a fixed number and determinate measure, — man alone, here below, has, for his number and measure, an indefinite number, an increasing measure, with no other higher limit but the infinite itself.

He alone, in so far as a rational and free soul, in that which constitutes human nature, is indefinitely perfectible. He alone can develop more and more, without fixed limit, the idea of God to which he corresponds. He increases in intelligence, in love; and there is no finite, fixed limit to this growth. But can he ever develop all? No, for then he would cease to be a man or a created being; he would be all act, like God. God alone is all actual. Man by his very nature is always partly potential and partly actual. If there were but one finite development to be enacted, he would enact it; but he would then be mere matter, he would be irrational, and hence he would not be immediately subordinated to the infinite. But as he possesses a possible development which is endless, he cannot complete it, since he cannot become God. God alone is all actual at the same time that he is infinite.

Let us clearly understand how the rational, free, and loving soul, having its relation to the universal, can never develop everything, and always remains indefinitely developable.

What, then, is the rational and loving being? How do we acquire love and reason? By direct illumination from him who is the Light of men. What is reason? It is a light derived from the Word, — that is, from an infinite source. So, too, with our love. Thus man, both in his reason and in his love, in that which constitutes his individual nature, is capable of indefinite development; but he will never attain the limit of development.

It is here that man and his entire rational and volitional life, both in his growth and in his effort to reach his limit and his perfection, are comparable to those marvellous geometrical quantities known as convergent series developed regularly.

Do not be alarmed by this comparison; any one can understand it.

Is it not true that the following series of terms, —

$$\tfrac{1}{2} + \tfrac{1}{4} + \tfrac{1}{8} + \tfrac{1}{16} + \tfrac{1}{32}, \text{ etc.,}$$

that is, *one half* plus *one quarter*, plus *one eighth*, plus *one sixteenth*, plus *one thirty-second*, and so on indefinitely, — is it not true that all these terms, each of which is always a half of that which precedes it, form, if added together, an increasing quantity which tends to become *equal to one?* This is self-evident.

Is it not true that if you add to the series one term more, still the half of the preceding one, — that is, the essential law of the series, — you will approach nearer and nearer to unity? This is clear.

For instance, the terms written above, taken together, form a sum equal to unity minus *one thirty-second.* But add the next term, which would be *one sixty-fourth,* the sum total will then equal unity minus *one sixty-fourth.* Thus you see that you steadily approach unity in proportion as you develop your series.

But do you not also see that, for some reason, you will never attain unity itself? Is it not possible to go on forever, endlessly, adding one term more? Undoubtedly, since to add a term we have only to take half of the preceding term; and that preceding term, small as it may be, being something, the half of something is necessarily something, never zero. You can thus always add one term more.

However far you may develop your series, there will always remain a genuinely infinite series of possible terms to be developed, while you will have obtained nothing but a finite number of terms.

The perfect image of free and rational being which is developed in time, under an increasing number and a growing measure, which always remains actually finite, — that is the necessary nature of created things; but which is always capable of potential increase, — that is the peculiar nature of man. The perfect image, we say, of a being which can never carry all its potentiality into act, since it would then be limited like matter, or infinite like God; which tends and converges constantly towards that limit, towards that universal and that infinite, to which it is directly relative, but yet which it can never attain, whatever be the duration and rapidity of its development.

But there is another point of view. How do geometricians say, and how can they say with all truth, that the series just quoted, taken *with all its possible terms*, — is mathematically, precisely, equal to one? How can they posit as true, with the utmost precision, this equation, —

$$\tfrac{1}{2} + \tfrac{1}{4} + \tfrac{1}{8} + \tfrac{1}{16}, \text{ etc., } = 1,$$

that is to say, *one half* plus *one quarter*, plus *one eighth*, plus *one sixteenth*, plus *all the rest, equals* ONE?

It is because they suppose, as we said, that the series is taken *with·all its possible terms*, — not only with all the terms actually developed, but with all its possible developable terms and all its terms in potentiality. But there is an infinite number of these possible terms, as we have seen. There is an infinite number, in the exact sense of the word, since we can never, absolutely never, reach the last. We can never develop more than a finite number of them, and there always remains an infinite number of possible ones to be developed. The number of possible terms, therefore, is really infinite.

Here, then, the infinite intervenes ; and we must indeed suppose that the infinite has actually entered into the series, and has completed the terms developed by its developable infinity, in order for it to become a unit. The infinite must intervene before this increasing quantity can have its integrity, attain its plenitude, its perfection, its absolute totality. This is plain.

Well, what does theology teach us ? It tells us that, by his own unaided nature alone, man cannot attain the perfection of his life, of his knowledge, of his will, of his wisdom, of his love, or of his beatitude. All is always necessarily partial and incomplete in man; nothing absolutely one, perfect, total, integral, belongs to him by nature. But God, who is the Infinite, may, by superadding to the created being a new gift, which is himself, give that integrity and perfection to the rational creature.

Here, then, we have a very precise comparison, on this point, of geometry and theology; and we see that our reason cannot acquire its final perfection until God himself shall descend into it.

And all this is further elucidated by theological formulas, and also aids us to understand them.

For instance, nothing could seem stranger, at first sight, than the condemnation of this proposition of Baïus : " The integrity of first creation is not a gratuitous final touch of perfection superadded to human nature, it is its natural condition." [1] The condemned proposition, for those who do not know the language of theology, at first seems evident in its terms. How can the integrity of nature be a gratuitous gift superadded to nature ? How can the integrity of nature be other than natural ? Could God create a maimed and mutilated being, a ruin like the actual humanity ?

[1] 26 Baii.

From our point of view, we understand the condemnation; we see the proposition of Baïus to be utterly false. Man, by his individual nature, no more possesses his integrity and perfection, even natural, than the series in process of development can attain its unity and totality without the hypothesis of the infinite,—a hypothesis so perfectly outside of the law of the development of the series that, by that law, it is, on the contrary, apparent that the limits and unity cannot be attained.

From this point of view also we understand this other theological theorem already quoted: "The grace of God is requisite to fallen man, for a knowledge of all the truths of the natural order."

I am well aware that, far from any intention to allude here to absolute necessity, there is no question, in the sense in which this proposition was framed, of any but a moral necessity. That is to say that, strictly speaking, man, even fallen, if he made perfect use of all the natural aids from God, all his time, all his life, might, perhaps, without special grace, know the sum total of those truths.

But what truths? The principal moral truths, the preambles of faith, the dogmas of natural religion essential to man, and not all the truths of the natural order; and he would not know them with that entire knowledge, carried to its end, such as the first man possessed. Doubtless again, as Saint Thomas Aquinas says, in the primitive state, nature attained, without supernatural grace from God, to all that knowledge; but how did man attain that state of perfect nature? In consequence of a supernatural gift from God. Therefore, strictly speaking, and in no case, have human intelligence, human love, or anything human, their full perfection, even natural, as Saint Thomas teaches, without a supernatural gift from the goodness and infinite power of God.

And our geometrical formula remains visible under the transparent veil of these dogmas.

We understand that the integrity of human nature is not the natural condition of man, but a perfecting of nature by the infinite power of God. We understand furthermore that, by this gift, man obtained the perfection of his nature ; but it did not necessarily follow from that perfection, given within the limits of nature by a supernatural principle, that man was to be raised to participation in the divine nature.

And we see that we cannot say, with Baïus, "That the elevation of human nature to participation in the divine nature was due to the integrity of the first creation, and should be called natural, and not supernatural." [1]

The gift of God might stop there, and give man only complete natural knowledge, complete empire over his passions, and immortality in his body. Only, as Saint Thomas demonstrates, man would not then have been raised to his final perfection; that is, to his supernatural end, which consists in seeing the essence of God and possessing it ; and integral nature, even more than fallen nature, would have retained the natural desire to see the essence of God and to possess it.

Man would then have been merely in that state which may be called supernatural as to its origin, and not in that which must be called supernatural as to its sanctifying effects. [2]

The supernatural gift in its origin would have as its only and complete end, natural perfection, and not that communication from the divine nature known as sanctification.

But this is only a purely hypothetical state, as is the state

---

[1] 21 Baii.

[2] There is the supernatural as to its origin (*entative*, κατ' οὐσίαν), the supernatural as to its sanctifying effects (καθ' ἁγιασμόν, or καθ' ἁγιαστικὴν δύναμιν), as Father Passaglia so ably treats them in his note-books.

of pure nature. These two states never existed. The first man was created in a state of justice and supernatural sanctity, at the same time as in that state of complete natural perfection which excludes ignorance, lust, sorrow, and death, and which implies a supernatural gift.

However this may be, what we desire to assert is that, in any case, the perfection of man is possible only by a supernatural gift from the bounty and infinite power of God.

It would then remain for us to understand how man may, through God, do what he cannot do of himself; how, in the intellectual order, man may know, through God, every truth of the natural order, all the first region of the intelligible, and enter the second, which is, in itself, supernatural. This is the mystery of divine love, the mystery of union.

We see, indeed, in the material world, the wonders of grafting, — that is, a root which bears, by a superadded germ, fruits not its own, and of a nature superior to its own.

We see, as Leibnitz observes, in speaking of that which revelation adds to knowledge, we see the human eye, the instrument of vision, acquire, by the power which other instruments superadd to it, a vision many thousand times stronger than its natural vision.

In geometry we see that convergent series by which we can prove that it cannot, by development, attain its integrity; and yet, if the hypothesis of the infinite be introduced into it, that which was impossible becomes possible.

To attain to the highest degree of the divine intelligible, let us note in passing, to the supernatural degree, is, as theology teaches, to share in the knowledge of God himself. This knowledge, by its nature, transcends all created intelligence, and belongs only to God. But God, who possesses it, enables us to attain it through him. How? By union with him, by love. We can say no more. "What we can do through those we love," says Saint Thomas Aquinas on this head, "we can, in a certain sense, do of ourselves." What I can do through my well-beloved, says love, I can do by myself. I know because you know, and I see because you see. These enthusiasms, these ecstasies of passion, are realized and made true by omnipotent God, for the souls which are united to him.

But this is not properly the question here. What we wish to demonstrate, is the geometrical precision of this proposition of Saint Thomas Aquinas: that the perfection of a rational creature depends not alone upon that which his individual nature implies, but also on a certain supernatural participation in the bounty of God.

III.

We think that we have now proved this assertion, but without as yet making clear its whole range.

Saint Thomas Aquinas not only affirms that the perfection of the rational creature depends upon a *supernatural* gift (κατ᾽ οὐσίαν), which gives it the perfection of its peculiar nature; he also affirms and proves that the rational creature attains its final perfection only through that other *supernatural* gift (καθ᾽ ἁγιασμόν), which raises human nature above itself to participate in the divine nature, by the vision of God's essence. We quote his wonderful words: [1] —

"The final and perfect beatitude of man consists in the vision of the very essence of God. This is made clear by two considerations. In the first place, man is never perfectly happy while there yet remains anything for him to desire and to seek. In the second place, the perfection of each of our powers depends upon its relation to its object.

"Now, the object of the intelligence is that which is, *it is the very essence of things*, says Aristotle. Whence it follows that in-

[1] 1ª 2ᵃᵉ, q. iii. art. 8.

tellectual progress consists in seeing the essence of things. If, therefore, the mind know the essence of any effect which does not reveal to it its essence, but only the existence of its cause, we cannot say that that mind has attained this cause, although it knows that it exists; therefore, when man is acquainted with an effect and knows that it has a cause, his natural desire is to know also what this cause is; and this desire, mixed with admiration, urges him on in his search, and this search ceases only at the sight of the essence. If, therefore, the human mind knows the essence of any created effect, and knows nothing of God, save that he is, we cannot say that the mind has grasped the First Cause, *but it still has the natural desire to seek it,* and it has as yet neither its perfection nor its beatitude. Therefore, for man's perfect beatitude, his intellect must attain the very essence of the First Cause, and that intellect can only have its perfection in a union with God, its supreme object, and the supreme beatitude of man."

Saint Thomas everywhere insists upon this point;[1] in the *Philosophic Sum* he devotes long chapters to establishing[2] —

"That the natural knowledge of God does not satisfy the natural desire of men's souls, but that, on the contrary, this knowledge incites them to desire a sight of God's substance. To know thoroughly, says Saint Thomas, is to know of a thing that which it is. Our natural desire to know is therefore not satisfied when we only know that God is. In vain we know that he is, our desire does not stop there, but we also wish to know God through his essence. Every intelligence naturally desires the vision of the divine substance. Now, it is impossible that this natural desire should be an idle one. Therefore every created intelligence may attain to the sight of the essence itself. Only no created being can, through his natural powers, attain to this vision of God."

Which is to say that man sees with his eyes, directly before him, the world, creation. He desires to see, in the same manner, God himself, God's being, God's essence. Now he knows that God is; he knows it with certainty; but he

---

[1] Notably 1ª q. xii. cap. i.; 3ª q. ix. cap. ii. et ad 3ᵐ.
[2] Title of chap. l., chap. lvii. Title of chap. lii.

wishes to see him whose existence he knows. To know that God is because the world is, is the first degree of intelligible light, it is the sight of natural light reflected by creation. When man shall see the source itself of that light, God himself, that will be the second degree, that of supernatural vision.

This is what man desires and seeks. For without this he cannot be supremely happy. Thus, according to Saint Thomas Aquinas, natural reason is a power which, through regret and privation, seeks the supernatural light, although it cannot conceive of it. The first degree of the divine intelligible leads to the other. Reason, by natural light, proves that it requires another and a different light: reason leads to revelation; intelligence seeks faith.

I am well aware that elsewhere Saint Thomas seems to say quite the contrary. In his Treatise on Truth he expresses himself thus: —

"Man's supreme good, that good which moves his will as the final goal, is double. There is the good which is proportioned to human nature, and which the forces of nature suffice to obtain. This is the felicity, whether contemplative or active, which lies in the exercise of human wisdom and the practice of the moral virtues described by the philosophers. But there is, for man, another good which transcends all the proportions of human nature, and which the natural powers do not suffice to obtain, or even to conceive or desire. And this good is eternal life." [1]

Thus in the *Theological Sum* and in the *Philosophical Sum*, Saint Thomas speaks of man's natural desire (*naturale desiderium*) to see the essence of God, which is man's supreme good; and, in this Opuscule, he denies that the soul, by its natural powers, can conceive and desire the supreme good.

But the contradiction is only seeming, and these two points of view of Saint Thomas explain the theological discussion

[1] Verit. xiv. art. 21.

which has arisen upon this subject, and which the Bull *Auctorem fidei* decides. This double point of view answers to this clear distinction which Saint Thomas continually repeats: Natural reason may know of God *that he is, not what he is.*

Natural reason may say: I know that *he is*, without knowing *what he is.* I do not know his essence. I do not see it. I lack that vision. I conceive that it may be obtained. I would that I might obtain it. Here we have that *natural desire* to which Saint Thomas refers in the Sum, — a desire which is not only inefficacious, as Billuard has observed, but which we also declare to be indirect, negative, and without substantial relation to its object. As for the other kind of desire, which conceives the object, which is created in the soul by the real attraction of the desirable and the supernatural intelligible, this desire clearly transcends the powers of nature. Between these two kinds of desire, of which one is desire through privation, and the other desire through a beginning of possession, there is all the difference that there is between reality and shadow, between fulness and emptiness, between positive and negative.

Between these two degrees of desire there are the differences expressed by the Psalmist in these words: "I have desired the true desire of justice (*concupivit anima mea desiderare justificationes tuas*)": it is nature desiring with natural desire, the supernatural desire of grace, as Saint Ambrose says.[1]

This distinction seems to us clearly established by the Bull *Auctorem fidei.* The Jansenist Council at Pistoia had established that man, given over to his own light (*relictus propriis luminibus*), might be capable of moving and rising so far as to desire light (*moveret se ad desiderandum*

---

[1] Ps. cxviii. v. 20 : Concupiscimus desiderare, quod non sit potestatis nostræ desiderium, sed gratiæ Dei.

auxilium superioris luminis). The Bull decides that this doctrine, *understood in the sense of a desire which should tend to eternal salvation* (*intellecta de desiderio adjutorii superioris luminis in ordine ad salutem promissam per Christum*), is suspicious, and favorable to semi-Pelagian heresy. Nothing can be plainer. Desire tending to eternal salvation — that is to say, salutary, efficacious, supernatural desire for eternal life — is out of all proportion to all natural lights and powers. It is in this sense, which is that of the Council of Pistoia, that the Bull condemns the statement; but it formally declares that the doctrine is condemned only in this sense (*intellecta de . . .*). It thus reserves another sense; and that sense can only be that of Saint Thomas Aquinas in his two Sums, which assuredly were not condemned on any point by the Bull *Auctorem fidei*.

Whence it results that if it be certain, if it be taught by faith, that the vision of God is purely supernatural, and that we can neither attain to it, nor desire it aright, efficaciously, save by a supernatural gift, we may yet maintain, with the Angelic Doctor, that the rational creature, created for the vision of God, has a natural desire for it, such as we have defined. Yes, the intelligence of man longs to see God, not only as in a glass, but face to face and directly; our nature desires the two degrees of the divine intelligible, and we may say of sound reason that it is a power which seeks faith.

CHAPTER V.

I.

WE have seen what sound reason is, and what it can do.

It can find and prove the existence of God. Then it can show the possibility, the necessity, of a revealed light, — that is, the necessity for seeing God, God's essence, — in order to attain final perfection, supreme beatitude.

But how does the soul pass from one to the other? How does the intellect, established in sound reason and in natural light, acquire faith, acquire the supernatural light?

We explained this in part when we quoted the admirable passage in which Fénelon speaks of the means of passing gradually from reason to faith. But we must now develop it still further.

When Fénelon tells us, "God mingles the beginning of the supernatural gift with the remains of kindly nature," and this germ is developed gradually, if our spirit respond faithfully to the help which it receives, — in these words there is an image, borrowed, it is true, from the Gospel, which compares the kingdom of God to the leaven mixed with the whole lump; but this image requires to be translated here into philosophical language.

Saint Thomas and Saint Augustine combined seem to give us this translation. Saint Thomas calls the light of reason "a light inwardly given by God, in which God speaks to us ;"[1] and Saint Augustine says, "That eternal wisdom, the primary cause of the rational creature, never ceases in any sort to speak with him, to the end that it may convert him."[2] A comparison of these two texts will explain Fénelon's entire thought.

The two doctors, taken together, affirm that God never ceases to address the rational creature, as well by the natural as by the supernatural light; and they show what results from this continual appeal of the Word to the soul.

God never ceases to address the rational creature: this is the source of reason. But why does God speak ? To the end that the rational creature may be converted to him who is. This intention to bring back his creature to him is grace, which tries to incite the conversion of the soul, — that is, its passage from natural life to eternal, supernatural life.

While reason speaks, and the natural light properly so called is made manifest, grace speaks at the same time, the supernatural light is already there, like God himself, with God himself, who offers it. This is the double speech, natural and supernatural, which the Eternal Wisdom never ceases to address to the rational creature. The Word of God is always speaking, to give the one and the other light. The one is necessarily received so soon as we are rational, but the other is freely received when the soul ceases to oppose any obstacle. Suarez says, —

" We have proved that the stimulating grace necessary to salvation is by a general law promised to all, offered to all, by Jesus Christ, not absolutely, but upon one condition, which depends upon man. This condition is neither a merit on our part, nor a tendency in any way proportioned to the gift of supernatural grace. It can therefore only be the single condition of offering no obstacle ; we cannot conceive of any other. For if, ordinarily,

---

[1] Verit., q. ii. art. 1.   [2] Ibid., iii. 106, c.

the moral act be necessary, that moral act, having no proportion
to grace, could only be necessary to remove the obstacle of sin ;
it is useful to destroy the vicious tastes which make man more
incapable of receiving grace. We readily understand this doctrine. Imagine .an adult man absolutely lacking in this inward
stimulating grace ; this lack cannot come originally from God,
who desires supremely to give grace to all. The cause, therefore,
is in the man. But what is it ? Is it that the man does not
merit grace, or has not prepared the way for it by works ? No,
since there are no preparatory merits or acts proportionate to
grace, save after a first grace. There is thus but one possible
cause for the lack of all grace, and that is, that man opposes some
obstacle to the grace which is given. The condition of God's
grace, therefore, is this, — not to oppose any obstacle to it." [2]

Thus grace is present like God, who is present to all, and
who desires supremely to give his grace to all. *God never
ceases to address the rational creature :* this is the natural
gift always received. He addresses him, *to the end that he
may be converted ;* this is the supernatural divine intention,
— it is the grace which is offered. Is it received ? Is it in
us ? Is it not ? It is received, it is in us so soon as we remove the obstacle. What is the obstacle ? It is vice ; it is
that depravity which, understanding the natural speech of
the Word in conscience and reason, does not obey it in practice and life. God would pour into the soul the supernatural gift which is always offered, if the soul would obey him
and heed it in the natural order.

The single and perfect God, the absolute, supreme Good,
is present. He speaks continually to the soul, which gives
it life in the natural order, and would give it life in the
supernatural order, if the soul would become converted. This
conversion is continually suggested by God, who never ceases
to speak through nature and grace. The same perfect God,
who is the life of the soul in the natural order, becomes its

[1] Tract. de divin. Grat., pars ii. lib. iv. cap. xv.

supernatural life so soon as it ceases to oppose an obstacle to the constant inspiration which labors to convert it.

The soul, in its natural state, beholds itself, and sees the light of God in the mirror which is itself, and that light is its reason. If it turns, beneath the watchful grace of God, if it turns from itself to God, these same rays which it saw reflected and oblique in the mirror, it sees in the direction whence they came, and its gaze follows them to their source; and that gaze is the vision of God, when the eye is capable of seeing, which can only be after our earthly journey is over; it is faith, as obscure as you like, while the eye of the soul is not yet fashioned to the supernatural light and thinks itself blinded by it.

This does not mean that God sheds his light and his gifts continuously and uniformly, like the sun, and that every man does with them simply what he will. The comparison would be unworthy of God. If God were only an impassive sun, he would be merely an element, and not the free and omnipotent Master of all creatures, the Father of men, full of wisdom and full of love.

The eternal sun of justice is not an impassive sun. Have we not said above, regarding this comparison, that even the star scintillates, and the sidereal light has its motions and its pulses? Now, the wisdom of God, his goodness, his love, have infinitely more elements, more approximations towards the soul to save it and elevate it, than the starry sky has to provoke and lift our glance. The light of God, which we perceive directly or indirectly, as it is supernatural or natural, is continually scintillating, veiling itself, revealing itself, increasing, vanishing, again increasing, and this in accord with the infinite calculations of an infinite love and infinite wisdom, diversely applied to each soul and to each moment of each soul, to save all.

God shows his natural light in the mirror of the soul only

to engage the soul to turn and behold himself, who is supernatural; and this intention itself is grace. This is the
meaning of Saint Augustine's words, which I cannot too
often repeat: " The eternal Wisdom incessantly addresses
the rational creature, to the end that it may be converted
to him who is."

II.

Saint Augustine elsewhere develops wonderfully the difference between the two lights, as well as the relation and
the passage of one to the other, when he speaks of the
double gaze which man fixes on himself or on God; when
he compares to the twilight of evening the gaze which man
fixes on himself, and to morning that other gaze which
he fixes directly on God. "After the darkness," he says,
" comes the morning; after the view which man has taken
of his own nature, which is not God, he goes on to praise
the light which is God, contemplation of whom reveals it." [1]
When the book of Genesis tells us of the evening and
the morning which follow after each other, the evening is
the knowledge which man gains of self, and through which
he sees that he is not God; but the morning, which succeeds
that evening, and which begins the ensuing day, is the conversion in which man refers his creation to the Creator's
power. Twilight returns when the mind beholds the creation, no longer as before in the Word, but actually in the
creation itself; then the morning, when the mind again
turns to praising God, and to seeking fresh knowledge in the
Word itself. " Yes," continues Saint Augustine, "there is
an essential difference between the knowledge of a being in
the Word of God, and the knowledge of that being in its own
nature; the first is truly day, and the other twilight. Compared to that bright light which we may see in the Word

[1] De Genesi ad litteram, lib. iv. cap. xxii. et xxiii.

itself, all knowledge by which we see a creature alone,
may really be called night; although that night itself, compared to the darkness and utter ignorance of those who
know not even the creature, may, in its turn, be called light.
It is thus that the life of the soul with faith, although still
in the world and the flesh, compared to the life without
faith and without piety, may justly be called light and day;
in the words of the Apostle: You were darkness at first, and
now you are light in God."

And here Saint Augustine displays the depths of his
genius, when he shows that in the everlasting home both
lights will endure.[1] To see immutably the eternal reasons
of men in the immutable light of the Word, and men in
themselves; then to refer to the glory of God this knowledge
of the creation, — is not this morning, evening, broad day?
In this sense, who would venture to say that the celestial city
either does not contemplate the eternity of the Creator, or
else is ignorant of this mutable creation, knows not how to
praise the Creator in this secondary knowledge? Day, twilight, morning, all exist there simultaneously. Yes, in that
land of spirits there is always and at the same time the light
of day, endless day, in the contemplation of immutable truth;
the light of evening in the sight of the creation itself; and
the light of morning, and a perpetual morning, in the return
of that inferior knowledge to God to praise him.

Here, then, we have the whole theory of light, or, if you
prefer, of the two lights and of their relation. The mind, if
it behold itself or creation, only sees the light mixed with
shadows, the evening light, the light of reason, purely natural.
If it behold God in himself, it is the perfect day; and if on
beholding the creation it raise its eye at once to God to thank
him for his work, it is the morning which begins the day;
it is reason seeking another and better light than itself; it is

---

[1] De Genesi ad litteram, lib. iv. cap. xxix. et xxx.

reason receiving, through God's grace, faith, the initial attempt
of vision to attain full vision.

I cannot conceive that an attentive mind, face to face with
these data of the highest reason and of the great and holy
Catholic tradition, a mind familiar with the history of the
struggles, the mistakes, or the glories, the strange and continued movements of human thought, and acquainted above
all with its 'own individual history and those of its very
variable, very uncertain thoughts, which faint and fall,
which rise again, which never cease to seek the perfect day,
which often think that they have reached the dawn, but
merely possess a waning, paling light, soon vanishing into
night, — I cannot conceive, I say, that such a mind, meditating on these data, as philosophic as they are Christian,
should fail at last to discover therein its law, its rule, and the
true theory of light as Christ has made it known to us.

Will men never observe their souls, and will they never
understand the practical conditions of light? Will they
never see in themselves that struggle between darkness and
light of which they are really the umpires? Will they
never see why these beginnings of morning light do not attain to the full light of day, but soon turn to evening, and
why the evening shades so soon change to darkness? Why
these long slumbers of the soul during 'which there is no
longer any suspicion of daylight? Why, at long intervals,
these attempts and allurements of lights which penetrate us
without our aid? Is it so hard to conclude from these facts
that there is a light which is not we, and that if it appear to
us veiled, mutable, intermittent in regard to us, it is because
we are ourselves variable, mutable, and veiled in its presence:
as we now know that it is not the sun which revolves,
but the earth which moves and passes, is veiled and turns
away, while the sun remains always motionless and radiant?

Let no one consider these as empty phrases, but rather as

very practical conclusions. And may the healthy soul which reads these pages find therein, as it meditates on the holy doctors whom we quote, efficacious lights and assured principles to guide its advance in one or the other of these two ways, or successively in both: intelligence seeking faith, faith seeking intelligence!

Let us repeat what has just been said, in order to withdraw into ourselves, to descend into the soul in presence of these truths, to the end that we may judge of our intellectual life and regulate its course for the future.

I am not the source of the light which is within me: that source is he who is luminous of himself; but the cause of vicissitudes, intermittences, diminutions, and obscurities, is myself.

There is therefore an obstacle in me; there is therefore a struggle to be made: for I am made for the light, I must reach it, and I desire to do so.

But the first obstacle, clearly, is that I do not desire it with sufficient ardor. I do indeed feel some attraction towards it; but this is its constant attraction, which proceeds from it, and not from me. I myself seek that attraction but little; I do not add all my powers to it, and it is, as it were, inactive on my side.

Such is the inevitable confession of every sincere soul.

Well, active response to the attraction, that is, prayer to him who attracts us, this is the starting-point for a more luminous life. The possibility of prayer, the grace of prayer, is always offered to us; and this attracting grace is as continuous as physical attraction among the stars.

To unite our strength to this divine attraction is the first endeavor after wisdom.

But why is all light, in the habitual state of my soul, as in the state of most souls, even when I have prayed, evening light, that is to say, fading and turning to night?

Because you look, as Saint Augustine says, only into creatures, or into yourself; inclination towards self, inclination towards inferior creatures, keeps your gaze downward. Every luminous datum of the ray, *which returns at intervals*, as the mystics express it, being applied by you only to creatures and yourself, soon becomes exhausted there, and is changed to darkness.

Do you know what that luminous datum would be if we could succeed in seeing it without this tendency of limited love for created beings and self? It would be matinal and increasing.

Thus the obstacle to be overcome is the tendency towards created beings. It must be conquered, so that God shall no longer be prevented from turning you towards him, — him who never ceases to address you to effect this divine return.

Aided by God, who forewarns us by the inspirations of conscience, and moreover by the increase which his bounty occasionally lends to the light of reason to rouse us; urged on moreover by the perpetual offer of grace, which is the presence of God himself striving to convert us; borne along by so many forces, — we needs must act, needs must destroy the obstacle. God will then convert us, and we shall move from natural to supernatural light.

When a soul, by the grace of God, reaches this point, it indeed turns to God. A deep horror of the past, a birth-pang, a great hope in the divine future, take possession of the heart; the supernatural love of God fills it, and the transformation is effected. A new series of works, of sacrifices, of labors, and of endeavors which lead to God, raise the soul from radiance to radiance in increasing light. Then the luminous data, the increments of the divine ray, become morning light, and change to day.

But I have not made myself clear. I must find other words and newer semblances for these ancient data of wisdom; I must invent forms to captivate the attention which glides over all familiar words and purposes.

Do you believe in the mutual penetration of minds ? Do you believe that, independent of word and voice, independent of distance, from one end of the world to the other, minds can influence and penetrate one another ?[1] Do you believe, as Fénelon says, that in God all men meet? Do you believe that a thought, a movement, a love, an impulse, can reach you by the secret influence of the heart and mind of another ? Or rather do you not know that every soul continually lives by the movement of other souls, resists, yields to, agrees perpetually with them ? Do you not know that a soul can feel within it another soul which touches it ? If you do not know this, you do not know the every-day things of earth ; how then can you comprehend the things of heaven ? If you do know it, if you believe in this communication of influences between souls and between created minds, so much the more should you believe in God within you. Yes, there is near you, within you, deeper far than any created mind can reach, or than you yourself can reach, God, his influence and his presence, pervading your soul to its very root, and lower yet, to the very bottom of all its powers, and farther yet. And it is not only a divine and immense force, in the bosom of which you are plunged, it is a mind which enlightens your mind, a heart which bears up your heart.

Yes, there is within you some one besides yourself. You are not alone. Is it he, or is it I that speaks within me ? said Saint Augustine. There is, I say, some one within you, at this moment, who looks upon you and loves you. You are scarcely conscious of it, scarcely credit it, because your soul is elsewhere, absorbed and carried away by other joys, other thoughts, other avidities, other affections. Silence

---

[1] Catech. Trident., pars ii⁰, de Pœnitent., xi.

these, and you will soon feel the presence and attraction of
him who has long addressed you, looked upon you, and
loved you. You will then feel and see clearly within you
the two directions of life, and you can choose between them ;
you can turn your whole soul towards him who was first to
love you, and whose infinite power can produce the marvel
of a change of soul, and make of a soul a new soul, by giving
it the divine power to be born again in the likeness of the
Well-Beloved who penetrates and inspires it.

Understand, therefore, in what sense Jesus Christ said, "I
am the beginning of all things, I who speak in you ;" and
Saint John the Baptist said, "He stands in the midst of you,
him whom you know not." And understand that admirable
commentary by Thomassin which shows us the transition
from one of the two lights to the other, and from reason to
faith, by him who is the primary cause of reason and faith :

"'He is in the midst of you, him whom you know not,' says
the Gospel. Thus no soul is born without Jesus Christ. Thus
Christ is revealed within us, rather within us than to us, since it
is he whose germ nature deposits within us when she sows in our
soul the seeds of the eternal law. It is thus that he occupies
the middle and'centre of every soul, to the end that he may enlighten all. So that even those whom the Gospel and preachers
can only touch externally, are stimulated and solicited by Christ
inwardly, by Christ, — that is to say, by reason' itself, the eternal
law, the innate germ of virtue. Let those, therefore, cultivate
that germ, let them conquer vice and all its guilty loves, and
Christ, growing ever more and more within their breast, shall
reveal himself there in all the fulness of religion and faith."[1]

Do you understand now the transition from reason to
faith ?

[1] De Incarnat., l. i. cap. ix. This admirable passage, with those which
follow, requires to be thoroughly understood, not to be interpreted in a different
sense from that which Thomassin certainly attached to it. To say that "*nature begins to bring forth Christ within us,*" is an expression which, taken literally, would be false. It is not nature which brings forth Christ within us,

Thomassin constantly recurs to these capital truths. He says, —

"Christ is Virtue itself humanly developed. No man is born without Christ, because no man is born without the germ of virtues. Thus the knowledge of Jesus Christ is as it were inoculated into all men, because nature labors to make every mind know and love good and the eternal law. To believe in Christ we must not go outside of self, but withdraw into self, to seek God and find Christ already present in our heart and in the very breath of our life. Whoever, therefore, practises a virtue as being virtue, the divine spark, an emanation from the eternal law, and not as a vain flower of human glory, — that man practises Christ, that man is a Christian.[1]

"Hence, to become a Christian we need not travel afar, but retire into our own self: the kingdom of God is within us, says Jesus Christ; and when any man *finds his reason*, submits it to the eternal reason, and submits his body to both, that man becomes a participant in Christ. This is why Saint Paul says that it is not needful to seek Christ afar off, to bring him down from above, since he is in the heart, in the soul, and in the mouth of every man. It is not needful to traverse the earth, or to traverse the seas, to find Jesus Christ, who is in the centre of every soul; for he is only the perfect and Sovereign reason descended into humanity."[2]

III.

After such words, so profound and so inspired, it only remains for us to hear, upon this great subject, Jesus himself revealing to us, from his visible mouth and in

but grace. But if it be certain that God mingles the germ of grace, the beginning of the supernatural gift, with the remants of kindly nature, as Fénelon puts it; if it be true, on the other hand, that the same Word is at once the principle of both natural and supernatural light; and if it incessantly offer both to the soul, — we understand that nature, forewarned and aided by grace, prepares the soul for the birth of the new man; or rather that the Word itself, the principle of nature and of grace, prepares its ways in the soul by grace and by nature, and is developed there when the soul opposes no obstacles.

[1] De Incarnat., lib. i. cap. ix.   [2] Ibid.

articulate words, the laws of eternal life and the genesis of light.

A learned man sought Jesus Christ by night. This man had reached that degree of human wisdom which seeks and longs for the wisdom of God and desires to see God. He questioned the Saviour, who replied: " *Verily, verily, I say unto thee, Except a man be born again, he cannot see the kingdom of God.*"[1]

Such is the truth. Man must be born again, to enter into the second degree of the intelligible, and to see the actual light of God.

But, said the wise man, "*How can a man be born when he is old? Can he enter the second time into the womb of his mother, and be born? Jesus answered, Marvel not that I said unto thee, Ye must be born again. . . . Art thou a master of Israel, and knowest not these things?*"[2] The Saviour is amazed that the doctors, whose duty it is to lead men to God, do not know that a man must be born again to see God. And he at once explains his reproach by words which reveal the innermost depths of the history of the human mind: "*If I have told you earthly things, and ye believe not, how shall ye believe if I tell you heavenly things?*"[3]

In other words: If I, who am a light to all men coming into this world, cannot convince you when I speak to you through reason, — if you do not heed your reason, the light which should guide you on earth, — how will you heed me and understand me when, in the very light of God, I strive to show you heaven?

How could the human mind attain total wisdom and the last degree of the divine intelligible, which is the sight of heaven, wherein it does not dwell, in the light of God, which it does not possess, if it cannot even see correctly the earth wherein it dwells, in human light which is its proper light?

[1] John iii. 3.   [2] Ibid., 4, 7, 10.   [3] Ibid., 12.

But, as Christ teaches, it is not by our own powers that we are asked to rise towards this faith in higher things and towards the sight of heaven. "*No man hath ascended up to heaven but he who came down from heaven, even the Son of man who is in heaven.*"[1] This text includes all Christianity. Man cannot ascend to heaven by his own unaided powers; reason, by its unaided powers, cannot attain the celestial degree of the divine light. Man, of himself, cannot make himself divine, or enter into participation of the divine nature, any more than the finite can rise to the infinite. We do not become infinite. For that we must have already been in heaven; we must have come down from heaven to ascend up into it. The Son of man who ascends up into heaven is he who, being one with God himself, is already in heaven,— this Son of man, who by a whole lifetime of suffering, sorrow, and sacrifice, and by his cross, shall raise himself to the throne of God for the salvation of all; for, he adds, "*As Moses lifted up the serpent of bronze in the wilderness* [to heal the people], *even so must the Son of man be lifted up from the earth: that whosoever believeth in him should not perish, but have eternal life.*"[2] And elsewhere he says: "And I, if I be lifted up from the earth, will *draw all men unto me.*"[3]

So, to pass from earthly things to heavenly things we must be born again. To pass from the lower degree of the divine intelligible to the higher, — that is to say, to see God, — we must have a new life. We must have the life of faith, of that faith which believes the eternal Wisdom when it tells us of heavenly things, — as in order to be in reason, in the first degree of the divine intelligible, we must have faith in Wisdom when it tells us of earthly things, and teaches us that the earth should bear witness to God and show reflections from heaven. To possess total wisdom, we must believe in the Word of God, according to

[1] John iii. 13. [2] Ibid., 14, 15. [3] Ibid., xii. 32.

these two lights, natural and supernatural, which he sheds within us.

But how can we be born again ? How can we pass from the first region of light into the second, where the inaccessible majesty of God dwells ? How can we rise from earth to heaven ? This is the business of God himself ; it is the work of the incarnate Word, of him who came down from heaven to our own nature, to the end that he might raise us up with him. Put your whole faith in him, and he will lift you up to see God.

But how are we to believe ? And how are we to cling to him ? Thus. Hear the Saviour uttering the simplest and the grandest words ever uttered in this world in regard to the search after wisdom and the obstacle to wisdom. It is the history of free choice between darkness and light. It is the practical genesis of light : " *He that believeth on the Son of God is not condemned : but he that believeth not, is condemned already. This is the condemnation. Light is come into the world, and men loved darkness rather than light, because their deeds were evil. For every one that doeth evil hateth the light, neither cometh to the light, lest his deeds should be revealed. But he that* DOETH TRUTH *cometh to the light, that his deeds may be made manifest, that they are wrought in God.*" [1]

The divine simplicity of these words of the Master admits of no commentary, and their supernatural power seems fitted to seize and lead captive every soul which ever loved truth but for a single day.

Is there, or is there not, a manifest and direct certitude that these words are the infallible truth ?

Can you hope to make any advance whatsoever towards wisdom and light, without a corresponding moral effort ?

Do you understand that there is no other salutary philoso-

[1] John iii. 18–21.

phy save that which is an effort towards total wisdom, — a pursuit of light in both degrees of the divine intelligible?

Do you understand that if you seek the truth without seeking virtue, the primary practical wisdom, you are not really seeking for truth, you are only feigning to do so, and you are but a pharisee, a scribe, like those who rejected Christ? And if, by some amazing preoccupation, you are content with such light as mere reason can give you, without the grace of God, without divine faith, you are already judged, — you dwell in the region of shadows, and in that degree of light which the Gospel calls Darkness.

CHAPTER VI.

I.

TO sum up.

There is God. There is the soul. God, the eternal wisdom, never ceases to address the rational creature, to the end that it may be converted unto him. God never ceases to solicit the soul by his twofold assistance, by his twofold natural and supernatural light.

God alone is light. God alone is the Father of all light, both natural and supernatural.

Natural light is the light of God reflected in our soul or in the mirror of created beings; and supernatural light is the light of God seen in its source, directly and immediately.

Natural light constitutes human reason properly so called, and is its source. "*The light of reason,*" says Saint Thomas Aquinas, "*is the image of the uncreated truth reflected in our soul.*" These are the most important and profound words ever uttered in regard to the nature of reason.

Supernatural light is the source of divine faith. Faith is the attempt at, the faint and feeble beginning of, the vision of God himself, in his essence and in the source of his light.

There are two degrees of the divine intelligible, — that which reason may attain, and that which can be attained only by faith and revelation. Reason has its own sphere and its relative perfection, in the first degree of the intelligible. But it cannot find there, of its own unaided powers, its entire natural development. It only reaches its final perfection, in the second degree of the intelligible, when aided and raised above itself by the supernatural light.

Sound reason is that which is not parted from its source in the soul and in God. The source of reason is the light itself which God gives. The origin in the soul of this gift is variously called *divine sense, natural faith, the attraction of the desirable and the intelligible, the hidden spring.* The actual moment, or, if you prefer, the point, at which the natural light of God touches and solicits the soul, — that point, that moment, that root, that gift, as you may choose to call it, is the source of reason. Sound reason is that which is not parted from this source in the centre of the soul, and which finds in this *faith* its orientation, in *this hidden spring* its impulse towards truth, and in *this divine sense* or *contact* its assurance.

Perverted reason is that which breaks, in so far as it may, with this source, with this heart, as Pascal says, with this divine sense, with this faith, with the attraction of the desirable and the intelligible. But as absolute rupture with God. is impossible for any being or any power, perverted reason is that which unceasingly labors to cut itself off from its source, its pursuing source. Whence follows one thing only, — an advance in a direction contrary to that of correct reason, and, as history proves, an advance towards the nothingness of thought, instead of an advance towards the vision of being ; a logical advance backwards, which, instead of displaying the consequences of first principles, actually denies first principles themselves, both speculative and practical. It is in some sort reprobate reason, which God urges to absurdity, — that is, to an indirect demonstration of the truth.

Between these two contrary courses, between these two mental states, of which one elevates and the other degrades, between sound reason and perverse reason, there is the sluggish reason, which does not advance, which does not ascend, but which does not yet decidedly descend; which does not gravitate towards Being, but which does not, as yet, rush towards nothingness; which does not deny the first principles, but yet is unable to derive anything from them, — which, according to Plato, fluctuates towards the middle region, without ever rising to the highest.

Let me represent these different mental states by a comparison.

The rational soul was created to see God, — very God, in his essence, — as the eagle, we are told, to look the sun in the face.

Imagine an eagle on the shore of a lake in which the image of the sun shines: the eagle may be content with looking at the image, without lifting his gaze to the object itself.

It may, — but eagles never do; then why should men? — it may take its flight towards the image, and fling itself into the lake, where it at once ceases to see, and at the same time loses both the image and the object.

Again, it may, excited by the image, lift its gaze, unfold its wings, and direct its course straight towards the sun itself, as if attracted by the rays which its eyes drink in. This is what eagles do; and it is this sublime action, this flight towards the source of light, which charms mankind, and has gained the king of air the glory of being the poetic symbol of the sublimities of the mind.

Thus with the gaze of the soul.

Our soul is both eagle and lake.

Sometimes we gaze stupidly at the lake, without distinguishing the water itself from the rays of light which it reflects, without distinguishing the mobile surface from the fixed image whose spherical form rests beneath the ripples. This is the sluggish reason and the sterile philosophy of the learned men who have not wisdom.

Sometimes these contrasts warn us, and we begin to understand that the light is not ourselves, that there is only an image there, a reflected light, the source of which is not within us, and that this passive water is of itself cold and dark. We understand that there is outside us an object whence the light comes to us and which the image presupposes. Sound reason advances thus towards the truth.

But instinct spares the eagle, and a diviner instinct, if we had not first stifled it in our soul, would also spare us, the vertigo with which we are sometimes seized, — the strange vertigo of a being who has wings and uses them to hurl himself into an abyss that he may seek the Sun there! Yes, we hurl ourselves into the abyss, where we cease to see, where we lose both image and object. This catastrophe is that of perverse reason, and history shows that many minds have chosen and yielded to it, seeking the source itself of light in their own innermost depths, digging out the image below the image, — below the surface of the lake, — to discover its luminous and burning roots in the water. It is thus that some have sought, in reason itself, the objective and first principle of reason, and that thought has plunged to the bottom of the shadowy abyss which exists in the soul, below the luminous point which God lights up from above.

Lastly, the soul, stimulated by the splendor of the reflection, and by the contrast between the dark, moving lake, and the glittering and motionless image, may conclude that the lake is not the object, but the mirror; it may seek the object, it may raise its eyes and seize the direct ray instead of the reflected ray; and, as it has wings far more powerful than those of the eagle, it may take its flight, soar towards the divine Sun, not in sport like the eagle, but with a genuine impulse which ends in and is united with the principle of life. "For the eagle," says Saint Francis de Sales, "has greater powers of vision than of flight;"

but the soul, aided by God, has equal power of flight and
of vision.

Let us carry this comparison a little farther, to show what
reason is capable of doing by its own movements alone, and
what it is incapable of doing unaided by the supernatural
light.

The eye is the reason, the reflected ray is the natural light,
and the direct ray is the supernatural light.

What can the eye do by the aid of each light ?

The eye by the reflected ray alone sees the image of the
sun, not the sun: that is absolutely impossible; it would be
a contradiction in terms.   When we see the sun itself, it is
necessarily by its direct rays.

The eye, by contrasting the mutability of the mirror and
the immutability of the image, distinguishes between the two,
and concludes that the image comes from some object other
than the mirror.   The eye refers the traces of the image to
a real being which it does not see.   Such is the knowledge
of God and his attributes, separated from created beings and
viewed in the necessary and immutable ideas which the soul
finds in itself.

But does the eye know the entire image as it is?   No,
certainly not; for instance, it sees it as a disk, when it is
really a sphere.

Again, it errs in referring the image to the under part of the
mirror, instead of referring it to the surface; and it imagines
that it sees direct rays, while it really sees reflected rays.
Thus it will never know the image completely until it
knows the object, its true situation, its relation to the surface, and the mystery of reflected rays and direct rays.
Nevertheless, so soon as the eye recognizes that the image is
not the sun, the eye may be strained to see the sun, to regret
that it does not see it, and to seek to see it; but evidently
it will not see anything unless the direct rays strike it.

Leaving these comparisons, we will now say that reason may, of itself (*ipsa per se*), by natural light alone, know various truths which constitute the first degree of the divine intelligible, and which have been called preambles of faith.

Reason cannot, without the aid of supernatural light, know all the truth of this first degree.

This insufficiency of reason, even in the natural order, — that is, in the first degree of the divine intelligible, — reason may and does recognize, and it proves the necessity of divine revelation, even in this order of truths.

Reason may, moreover, — and this is its highest effort, — recognize that it is not itself its own absolute or first principle, that its natural light is only the image of that principle, and as it were the shadow of its light; that this image corresponds to an object which does not exist in the image, which it does not see, and which it must be possible to see directly; it comprehends that we must see the source of light, the essence of that divine object, and that this sight is necessary to its supreme felicity and its final perfection.

It is of course understood that this natural desire for supreme felicity, that is, this natural desire to see the essence of God, is radically different from that other positive desire which is a beginning of the conception and possession of the supernatural light. But it is equally, of course, understood that these two sorts of desire for the sovereign Good, in fact and in the actual life of the soul, are perpetually blended, and perhaps, by the watchful goodness of God, succeed and correspond each to the other, like the two motions of the heart.

But this scientific analysis, by which we strive to distinguish exactly between the two orders of the divine intelligible, the natural and the supernatural, this analysis, which is essential in metaphysics, has little value in practice ; for no soul is surrendered to itself without supernatural aid from

God. God blends, says Fénelon, the beginning of the supernatural gift with the remains of kindly nature, and man
bears within him a mystery of grace of which he is profoundly ignorant. There are germs of faith in the soul, and
no soul is deprived of Christ, says Saint Jerome, whose words
are repeated and commented on by Thomassin. In fact,
natural reason is developed, is sound, advances towards its
goal under the influence of God's grace and the natural and
supernatural incitements of God. I reckon upon grace alone,
says Fénelon, to guide my reason within the limits of reason ;
and Perrone, the most decided defender of the rights of
reason, recognizes that, in our present state, the germ of reason is developed by the influence of grace.

So much for practice. But for the theory all the analytic
labor which precedes was necessary, and God grant that
it has been given us to maintain precision ; for this question
is assuredly the pivot of the human mind, — the centre of philosophy; it is, if we may so express ourselves, the point
where the mind of man and the mind of God meet: there
we find the relation, the means of transition, from one to
the other. If we, Catholic theologians, in possession of the
truth, succeed in throwing light on this point we shall have
done philosophy the greatest service ever done it. We shall
have made a decisive effort towards the pacification of the
mind, the regeneration of knowledge, and the salvation of
man.

Why is it not given to us to teach men to discern in the
centre of their soul this point, this root of life, this hidden
spring where God touches them, this double point, this
double root, which, if I may venture to say so, is at the same
time God and ourself; this point, I say, where God touches
us, where his light comes to us, reflects itself in the soul,
and forms, *after* the reflection of the divine light, our
natural life, *before* that reflection, the supernatural life ; so

that, although there is an infinite difference between the two, in practice they are hardly to be distinguished, since one and the same point, in some sort, contains both the natural and the supernatural ray.

This point of contact and this divine touch, in so far as the soul reacts thereon, are the *divine sense,* — natural divine sense when beneath this contact the soul feels itself explicitly and God implicitly; supernatural divine sense when beneath this contact the soul is explicitly conscious of God himself, and is only implicitly conscious of self in God, — a twofold meaning, which is, perhaps, mingled, and varies in the soul, let us say, like the two beats of the heart; God, according to our dogma, being ever present to the soul, with his double natural and supernatural aid, and varying his gifts according to his free bounty, and according to the free response of the soul.

Why do we not at once see the intellect, made for the two degrees of the divine intelligible, capable, by its impulses and its freedom of choice, beneath the twofold divine gift, of rising now to the one and now to the other, according as it rests upon one or the other side of the hidden spring, upon the natural divine sense, or upon the supernatural divine sense, — rising, in the first case, to the immutable shadows of the infinite, the eternal; in the second, to the infinite, the eternal itself!

So that the life of the mind, like that of the will, like that of the soul, is everywhere twofold, — at the point of departure, which is the divine sense, either natural or supernatural; in the impulse, which varies with the point of departure; and in the goal, which depends upon the point of departure and on the nature of the impulse, and which is the twofold region of the divine intelligible.

And the better to understand this marvellous duality, comparable remotely and in a certain sense to the duality of the two natures of Christ, we should know that the natural man and the supernatural man resemble each other, that the natural man is, as it were, the rough draught of the supernatural man, and that to every trait in the one, some trait in the other corresponds.

The natural man is the image of God, and the supernatural man is man united to God, — it is God entering into his image; God himself living in his substantial reality in every feature of the image, bringing by his approach the supernatural divine sense into the natural divine sense, the supernatural divine impulse into the natural impulse of the reason towards the immutable and the infinite, and placing the infinite itself in the ideas of the infinite.

We cannot better depict all this, and better represent the mystery of this double life, than by venturing to compare God, when he animates man for eternal life, to the prophet Elisha when he restored the child to life: "The prophet," says the Holy Scripture, "went up and lay upon the child; he put his mouth upon his mouth, and his eyes upon his eyes, and his hands upon his hands; and he stretched himself upon the child; and the flesh of the child waxed warm." [1] So, too, God stoops down and overspreads man; he puts his mouth upon our mouth, his love and the breath of his Holy Spirit upon our love; he puts his eyes upon our eyes, his intelligence upon ours, and the child of God is born to new life, which is God in him and upon him; he is born to eternal life, — that is to say, to the life which God himself lives for him.

II.

Let us now sum up our thought from the theological point of view, properly so called.

The light of reason is a natural gift of God, by which man

[1] 2 Kings iv. 34.

is man. The light of faith is another gift, free, supernatural, radically distinct from the first, by which God's goodness raises man above his own nature.

In the beginning, God might have left man to his own nature, without raising him, by a higher gift, to participation in the divine nature, to intuitive vision and possession of eternal life.

But, as a fact, God chose to raise man to this supernatural state; he created man to this end; he created him to raise him to intuitive vision. From this voluntary and wholly gratuitous will of God, there results for man the necessity that he shall attain to intuitive vision, if he is to reach his final perfection, and the end for which he was created.

God, according to our dogma, desires to lead all men to this end, and gives his grace to all, in order to lead them thither. "The effects of this will," says Saint Thomas, "are the order itself of nature directed towards this end, and all the impulses, whether natural or supernatural, which incessantly urge us thither." "God," as Saint Augustine teaches, "*never ceases to address the rational creature*, to the end that it may attain this goal." And therefore Fénelon is justified in saying: "I hold, with Saint Augustine, that God gives to every creature a first germ of secret grace, which is imperceptibly blended with reason, and which prepares man to pass gradually from reason to faith." But although this germ of grace, which prepares the way for faith, if we offer no obstacle to it, may be blended with reason, it remains radically distinct, as the diamond, set in gold, remains distinct from the metal which holds it, or as a seed, sowed in the earth, is not the earth.

There is in reason a natural and continual aid from God, which is, as it were, the primary cause of reason; and there is, mingled with reason, a principle radically distinct from reason, a germ of grace, which, on the one hand, favors its

natural growth, and which, on the other, gradually prepares
it to rise, beyond itself, to faith. But the mind can no more
pass from reason to faith, by a natural growth, than the
finite, by increasing, can become infinite. There is always
the whole gulf of the infinite between finite and infinite. So,
too, there is always the infinity of God between reason and
faith. God alone can fill up this gulf by imparting his own
light, which is himself, which is the only principle and the
only formal motive of faith.

Now, God desires to fill up this gulf. He labors to do so
by his grace, by his sun which he causes to shine upon the
wicked as well as upon the good. But the depraved man
opposes an obstacle. He refuses the benefit which is offered
to him ; often even, by his own fault, far from allowing himself to be raised higher than man, in the supernatural light,
he does not even stretch his intellect to the natural truths
which it should grasp. He sometimes rejects the natural
help of God, which stimulates and sustains his reason in its
proper sphere, as he also rejects the higher help which opens
a new world to his intelligence. He rejects reason as he
rejected faith, and he applies his inverted mind to the monstrous negation of the very principles of reason.

Doubtless there is a medium between scepticism and
faith, between the supernatural life and the animal life.
And yet the minds which seek or think they seek the truth,
and which reject the supernatural truth offered by grace
and revelation, usually abandon at last the worship of all
truth, the effort towards wisdom, to plunge again in the
senses, and attach themselves to earth.

It is a deep fault in reason to reject the supernatural
light of faith. It is contrary to the duty of reason. Does
not reason, by its own natural lights, see its limitations and
its imperfection ? Is it not forced to admit that it does not
see the essence and substance of the True? Does it not

demonstrate that the substantial truth is God himself? Can it maintain that, when it conceives of the absolute truths which form its domain, it sees very God in himself, and that it has an intuitive vision of God? By what right, then, should it deny that there may be another light superior to its own light? How should it maintain that God cannot raise the created intellect to the vision of the substance and essence of the True, to the intuitive vision of God?

More yet. Created intellect has, in fact, a desire for the intuitive vision of God. So soon as a mind knows that God is, it desires to see God, as Saint Thomas constantly affirms. This desire belongs to the very nature of the rational creature, also says Saint Thomas; followed by almost all theology. Now, this desire, — this negative desire, I grant you, a desire caused by privation and regret, — however indirect, blind, and inefficacious it may be in itself, is yet sufficient to prove that our intelligence, since it has this regret, will never find its perfect rest and its full perfection save in the higher light which will give it the sight of God. But whether this desire be, in man, essentially natural, or only innate, whether it result necessarily from the peculiar nature of the rational intelligence, as almost all Scholastics maintain, or whether it be merely an impulse superadded by God; whether it be contained in the fact of creation, or be derived from God's wish to raise every intelligence to intuitive vision, and thus be what Saint Thomas calls "the natural order directed towards the supernatural end," — whether this superadded impulse should be, in its turn, called natural or supernatural, matters little. As in any case this impulse from God is mingled with the reason, it always results that reason, sound reason, can demonstrate the possibility of the supernatural light, the intuitive vision, and prove its necessity, if the mind is to attain its final perfection and reach its rest.

Lastly, in our present state, where our reason is wounded, as well as our will, our reason itself thoroughly understands and demonstrates its own weaknesses. It demonstrates its impotence to conquer its entire domain, and, weak as it is, to stretch forth and grasp the very truths which, were it stronger, it might discover. It reveals, moreover, its aberrations and its constant errors. It thus proves the necessity of a superior help, and it confirms the words of Fénelon: "I reckon upon grace alone to guide my reason within the limits of reason." It therefore requires the other light, not only to be raised to its highest perfection, but even to be healed and attain its proper and natural perfection.

And this necessity for supernatural light to give the rational creature his final or his relative perfection, comes not only from the wounds and weaknesses of reason in our present state, it also comes from the nature of created reason. The finite mind naturally sees only in part; the sum total escapes it; it knows the whole of nothing; it could no more attain to the whole of its intelligibles, or to the absolute totality of a single idea, than a convergent mathematical series can, by development, attain its limit. Before such a series can be complete, we must add the infinite to it by hypothesis. So, too, before the finite mind can attain to all the truth of its degree, it must be united to the infinite mind.

But let us go back from theology to philosophy.

III.

Either philosophy demonstrates nothing, or else all that precedes proves that there are, for man, two regions in the world of intelligibility, as Plato expresses it; that there are for our intelligence two degrees of the divine intelligible, as Saint Thomas Aquinas says.

All philosophers of the first order teach this; all Catholic theology professes it; all Christian dogma presupposes it; all men feel it and can see it in themselves; the whole history of the human mind explains it, and rests upon that basis.

This, I say, is proved, because all those familiar with the human mind have seen it, and because you see it yourself, if you have understood what goes before.

There are two degrees of total wisdom. Plato calls them the two regions of the intelligible world, one of which is that of divine phantasms, shadows of that which is; the other is the intelligible itself in its divine essence, — the Sun, whence shadows and images come, and which is the supreme Good viewed in itself.

Plato speaks of it again when he speaks of those truths, the most important of all, — which it is impossible or very difficult to know in this life, yet which it is possible to know if some one teaches them, but which none can teach unless he be sent by God himself.

Aristotle distinguishes these two degrees when he says that there is in man, besides the life of feeling, the rational life; and besides the rational life, the contemplative life of pure intellect, which is like another soul superadded to the soul; which is not essential to the soul, which may be separated from it, which comes to us from without, which is supernatural rather than human, — divine, which is very God. Aristole's marvellous texts on this head may be recalled.

Saint Augustine declares that there is between rational, certain, and absolute truths, and the intelligible majesty of God, the same distance that there is between heaven and earth, between darkness and light. He repeats the very words of Plato, but develops and deepens their meaning. Of the two lights, the two forms of vision, he calls one outward (*extraria*), the other inward (*intraria*); of the two knowledges, he calls one evening light (*vespertina*), and the other morning light (*matutina*). All vision possessed by created beings, the vision which our soul has of itself, beneath the light of God, is this light akin to shadow; and only the vision of God himself is the light of day.

Saint Thomas Aquinas names them THE TWO ORDERS OF THE DIVINE INTELLIGIBLE (*duplici veritate divinorum intelligibilium*), and his two Sums, or Summaries, are these two orders of the divine intelligible treated separately.

He asserts that reason has two terms and two spheres of action, — one which displays to it the natural light, and the other which opens to it the gift of supernatural light. He also calls the lower region the region of shadows (*natura intellectualis adumbrata*); the one is, he says, a specular vision (*specularis*), the other is direct vision of the essence (*visio per essentiam*).

There are therefore these two degrees of the intelligible, corresponding to what Christian theology calls the natural order and the supernatural order, — the order of reason and the order of faith.

Now, is it certain, from the experience of each of us, as well as from the whole history of the human mind, that the first of these two degrees seeks, regrets, and desires the other, and that, the higher a mind rises in this first region, develops its reason and lifts its vision, the better it understands that its vision is partial, and that what it sees is only the shadow, but not the essence and the substance of truth? Is it certain that the natural light of reason, in proportion as it grows, produces a more and more ardent thirst? But thirst for what, if not for the truth itself, essential and total, substantial and living, whose likeness, ever more distinct, whose rays, ever more numerous in the mirror of the soul, kindle there a desire for the reality, the totality?

This is the legitimate conclusion of sound reason, of increasing reason, the source of true philosophy. Sluggish, arrested reason knows it not, and gives birth to that languishing, sterile, and changeable philosophy which revolves upon its own axis without advancing. Depraved reason denies it and utterly rejects it; but instantly reverses itself, turns against itself, denies and destroys itself; and its name is sophistry, the suicide of reason.

Are these, or are they not, the fundamental features of the history of the human mind, and of the classes into which minds may be divided?

This settled, Christians are those who believe that the second region of the intelligible world will be given, and that it is indeed given even now, in principle, by faith in Christ, divine faith which implants within us, as Saint Thomas Aquinas says, following Saint Paul, the essence and substance of the truth, in its supernatural germ, developable in eternity.[1]

As for true philosophers who are not Christians,—I do not refer to the sophists, nor to the learned who devote themselves to idle philosophy,—theirs are necessarily minds which wait, seek, desire, and regret; which suspect and conjecture the Sun whose shadows they see, the images and abstract lineaments of whose essence they perceive.

For if it be so, this is what we feel it our duty to offer all those, Christians or not, who have within them the philosophic germ,—I mean by this the effort towards total wisdom.

We would offer them, above all, in the practical order, as the daily law of their life, these words of Christ: "Every one that doeth evil hateth the light; he that doeth truth, cometh to the light;" and these others: "Pray without ceasing, and weary not in so doing;" that is to say, we

[1] 2ª 2ᵃᵉ, q. iv. 1.

should always unite our free force and an active co-operation to the permanent attraction of the desirable and the intelligible.

It is most evident that this continued inward effort and this persevering prayer, combined with a struggle against all evil and an attempt at all good, is the practical method to attain the truth.

But, moreover, in the speculative order, we would give this counsel : it is a new way to study the formulas of Christian faith.

Usually men study them controversially, from without, and from the circumference, in certain details, never as a whole; and attention is fixed far less on the dogma itself and its simple statement, than on certain human and very imperfect and incomplete considerations of it given by some preacher or writer.

Is this the way to acquire, I do not say faith, but merely a knowledge of faith and an understanding of its authentic statements ?

Behold, now, the inverse process, from which we believe we may expect much fruit for many souls.

Take the formulas of the faith as they are presented by the Church.   Add certain of the words of Christ upon which these formulas rest.

If you are a Christian, you believe that these are principles of divine truth, capable of development in the divine light.

If you are not a Christian, you may doubt this, but you have no reason to deny it.

Now, what would you do if, holding in my hand a few grains of dust, I said to you: " Here are germs. They imply plants and contain fruits."

If you doubted it, there would clearly be no way to get at the truth but to intrust those germs to the earth, and to summon that dust to germinate, and to show to all eyes that which previously they could not see.

Do the same. Root these little grains, these formulas of faith, firmly, immovably in your memory. "Do not despise memory, it is the treasury of gifts," says Bossuet; it is a soil which not only preserves, but which develops. Root, I say, all these germs in the depths of your mind; then dwell with them. Let the changes of life, its seasons, its droughts, its trials, its griefs, its weaknesses, its hopes, its joys, and its sun, act upon those seeds. Keep that attempt at a harvest alive by the ferment of your mind, by the vital fluid which nourishes it, by the light in which it unfolds. Compare all these affirmations with its wants, its regrets, its doubts, its questions, its expectations, and its conjectures.

Let these germs be cherished by those hidden forces which make everything grow which lives in man, and which are born, like a sort of electricity, of the free movement of the soul towards the universal attraction of God; in other words, pray without ceasing, and weary not in so doing.

Let not heart and will become paralyzed, but act faithfully under the influence of this holy and infallible law: "Every one that doeth evil, hateth the light; he that doeth truth, cometh to the light."

Do this, and you yourself shall see the germs swell, and whether Jesus was wrong in saying: "The word of God is a seed; if it falls into good ground, it bringeth forth some an hundred-fold, some sixty, some thirty."

Whether you be a Christian or not, this experiment should be made. If you are not a Christian, you will have a chance to find that other sphere of intelligence, that heaven of truth, which your mind longs for and pursues, and that total philosophy which you know that you do not possess.

If you are a Christian, you believe that these are germs of eternal light, and the highest principles of real philosophy and complete wisdom.

Try it, therefore.

This experiment, made under the requisite conditions, may, by God's grace, give philosophy to souls which have only faith ; faith to those who have only philosophy.

It is the first labor to be undertaken by the faith which seeks understanding, and by the understanding which seeks faith.

Let the minds which, having reached the term of human light, find it pale, partial, expiring, greatly blended with shadows; who recognize that the flying object of their pursuit is but the light of evening, which grows dim and vanishes, and the substance of which is only darkness, — let these, I say, add to their mind the principles of what Saint Augustine calls morning light.

I am well aware that at first these principles will strike them as even more obscure than that very daylight which is insufficient for them, and that, accustomed to what Descartes, I think, somewhere calls the rude evidence of geometry, they will see nought but thick night in these germs of celestial light. But let them fully understand this, and meditate on this comparison.

We, too, call the absence of our sun night. But what does the sun show us? It shows us the earth and itself. When it has vanished, what do we see? At first we no longer see earth, or sun, or anything. But patience; let night advance, and behold! The stars appear one by one; the entire vault is peopled; the sky is filled with rays, movements, and scintillations, as it were with eyes waking and imploring our gaze. We see the heaven which the sun concealed. So that, to any one who wished to see the whole heaven, it was well that the sun went away.

But, I confess, all these stars still seem to you mere drops of lustre upon the night. All together do not equal one sunbeam. And yet what have we before our eyes? We have before us the immense universe of suns, in which our own sun is but a point, — a point in which the earth is but a fraction. Every imperceptible point of that luminous dust is a sun like ours, surrounded by a hundred living earths, as great or greater than our own. Day, therefore, showed us a point; night shows us immensity.

May I venture to say that this is one of the divine reasons for the setting of the sun? If the sun reigns and then disappears by turns, it is because God desires that besides the earth, man should also see the heaven.

It is precisely the same with the obscurities of faith, relatively to the daylight of reason.

This is why our dogma teaches that reason, like the sun, should rule and should surrender by turns: should rule over all the earth, and surrender in the sight of heaven. Its reign gives it a world; its surrender gives it immensity, in which the world is but a point.

Let no one therefore be alarmed at the obscurities of faith or the surrenders of the mind.

As for Christians, they must allow me, after the example of Saint Augustine, to exhort them eagerly to seek light and love understanding.[1]

Learn to see in the light of intelligibility what you possess firmly through faith.[2] In this time of great decay and languor of reason and faith, you who have the assured principles of universal light, why do you bury them, and not display, by culture and effort, by constant labor of intellect and soul, its rays, its colors, its perfumes, its beauties, and its fruits? You who believe beforehand that every one of those drops of light is a sun, an animating principle of worlds; you who bear within you that starry heaven of faith; you are a heaven greater than the visible heaven, — why do you not seek to become more distinctly luminous, for the glory of God and the salvation of your brothers?

---

[1] Ut fidem tuam ad amorem intelligentiæ cohorter.

[2] Ut quod fidei firmitate jam tenes, etiam rationis luce conspicias.

What can excuse you and dispense you from an effort to attain perfect day and increasing light? Is it age or sex? Hear Saint Augustine, addressing his mother, when, leaning by her side from that window which we may still see at Ostia, gazing at the immense ocean and the starry heaven, and comparing them to the heaven of the soul, he said to that beloved mother: "Mother, I implore you, do not be terrified, or arrested in your task, by the wilderness of knowledges which seem requisite. One may choose, from all these, the true points, few but fruitful; difficult, doubtless, to many minds, — but to you, mother, whose mind seems new to me every day, and whose soul, whether from the advance of years, or whether from its wondrous temperance, wholly freed from the deceptions of the world and from the hard servitude of the senses, has power to grow and rise mightily within itself, — to you, beloved mother, these things will be as easy as they would be hard to the sluggish understanding of all those souls who live so miserably."

It was therefore to the weakness of sex and the decline of life that the great doctor addressed this testimony and this exhortation.

We venture, therefore, to transmit to the readers of these pages, be they who they may, that same exhortation.

But where now among us are the Christian souls whose converse is thus in heaven, that is, in the search after wisdom and truth? Where are the souls whose pleasures, wholly intellectual and cordial in their nature, lie in pursuing and gathering up the traces of God, as Saint Augustine did, in the inner history of the soul, in that of the world and of empires, in the spectacle of nature, in the history of the human mind, in the confessions of his life, in music and in letters, in numbers and in astronomy, to the end that he might refer all these things to the eternal model, and confront every thought with the word of God, with the definite dogma borne in his memory, with God carried in his heart and his faith? Where are the stern abstinences of Saint Monica in regard to the sorceries of the earth? Who suspects the ecstasies of which our intemperances deprive us? Where are the souls ever new, and growing, through their search after wisdom, from childhood unto death? And who suspects the floods of light and true love which would burst forth from Christian souls for the salvation and happiness of mankind, at the cost of a little effort?

THE END.